Great Ormond Street Hospital
Children's Charity

CHILDREN'S
MEDICAL
GUIDE

Great Ormond Street Hospital
Children's Charity

CHILDREN'S
MEDICAL
GUIDE

CONSULTANT EDITOR DR JANE COLLINS

DK

DK

LONDON, NEW YORK, MUNICH, MELBOURNE, DELHI

For Kate and Tom Evans
and all the people I have seen professionally over the years
Dr Jane Collins

Senior editor Julia North
Art editor Nicola Rodway
Project editors Jinny Johnson,
Kathy Fahey, Pip Morgan
Designers Ted Kinsey, Briony Chappell
DTP designer Karen Constanti
Production controller Shwe Zin Win
Managing editor Anna Davidson
Managing art editor Emma Forge
Art direction Sally Smallwood
Photography Ruth Jenkinson
Jacket designer Neal Cobourne
Art director Carole Ash
Category publisher Corinne Roberts

First published in Great Britain in 2003
by Dorling Kindersley Limited
80 Strand, London WC2R 0RL
A Penguin Company

Copyright © 2003, 2006 Dorling Kindersley Limited
Text for Introduction and pp.94–99, 122–167
copyright © 2003, 2006 Dr Jane Collins
All other text copyright © 2003, 2006 Dorling Kindersley Limited
Previously published in hardback as *Baby & Child Health*

2 4 6 8 10 9 7 5 3 1

ISBN-13: 978-1-4053-1965-2
ISBN-10: 1-4053-1965-8

Reproduced in Spain by AGT
Printed and bound in China by Hung Hing

Discover more at
www.dk.com

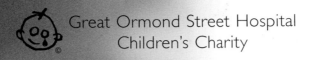
Great Ormond Street Hospital
Children's Charity

FOREWORD

For over 150 years, Great Ormond Street Hospital (GOSH)
has provided world-class specialist paediatric care, research,
training and education, and a commitment to sick children
worldwide. It is simultaneously a hospital serving its local
community, a national resource and an international centre
for specialist paediatric care, training and education.

Every year, 90,000 children from around the country
are cared for by the hospital's specialist doctors and nurses.
GOSH offers the widest range of paediatric specialities under
one roof in the UK. The hospital is the largest UK centre for
heart and brain operations in children, and sees one child in
ten diagnosed with cancer. Research undertaken at the Institute
of Child Health has benefited children with conditions as
varied as heart defects, arthritis, epilepsy or HIV.

Children's emotional health is also a key issue for the staff
of GOSH. As well as encouraging parents to be involved in their
child's care, the hospital offers an extensive range of services
to address a family's emotional, spiritual and social needs.

Great Ormond Street Hospital Children's Charity is
delighted to endorse this book, which will enable parents to
care confidently for both the emotional and physical health
of their child. The Charity will receive a royalty from each
copy of the book that is sold.

CONTENTS

INTRODUCTION

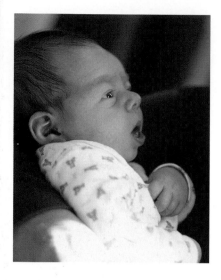

Becoming a parent is one of the most profound experiences many of us are fortunate to have. Whatever any well-meaning friends may tell you, life is never the same again! Bringing up children is both exciting and rewarding, but at times it can also be challenging and worrying. We all wonder about our children's health and safety at some stage during their development, particularly during the early years. We may ask ourselves whether an illness is serious or even life-threatening or consider whether we would know what to do in an emergency. We may also wonder about our children's development, however much we know we shouldn't we compare our children with others, either within or outside the family.

All children suffer from minor illnesses or accidents at some stage. Very young children are not able to tell you how they feel, which can be very frightening for parents. Also, during the early years in particular, the same symptoms and signs can mean different things. Vomiting is a good example of this. Babies and children vomit very easily for a whole host of reasons, some minor and others serious. So, as a parent, how do you know that a particular episode of vomiting might be serious when another episode probably is not? The age of your baby or child and any associated symptoms are important in helping you assess whether an illness is something you can manage at home or is something that requires professional help. But, equally or even more importantly, you need to take into account your own knowledge of your baby or child when assessing the severity of an illness. Your instinct is likely to be right. As a paediatrician, I had to work to develop this instinct

"...children in the developed world are healthier than they have ever been, and many infections that were once fatal can now be prevented or treated"

with children other than my own. Fortunately, with our own children we develop this instinct naturally within weeks or, at the most, months.

Children in the developed world are healthier than they have ever been, and many infections that were once fatal can now be prevented or treated. As a consequence, most people have no experience of a baby born with a serious problem or a child with a life-threatening or life-shortening condition.

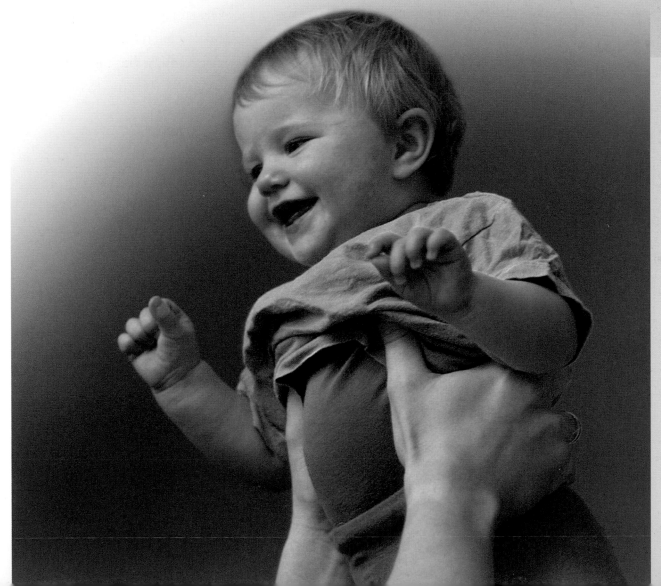

> "...Most children learn good behaviour easily if we consistently demonstrate it to them ourselves"

If your baby or child does have a serious condition, you can feel isolated, confused and unsure where to turn, and your family and friends may feel powerless to help. While this book can't describe every possible developmental problem or illness, it does cover the more common ones and gives advice about where to look for further help, particularly around the practical issues of caring for a child with a disability or illness.

For most of us these days, a major focus of concern with our children is not just on their health but also on helping them fulfil their potential and learn to behave appropriately in different social situations. As a result, children's lives have never been so filled with developmental opportunities. Rather unfashionably perhaps, I think learning to deal with boredom is also a useful skill to develop.

What we expect from our children's behaviour will vary from family to family, but learning right from wrong and how to share with and value other people are important universal characteristics of good behaviour that children can learn from an early age. The main way children learn good behaviour is by observing our behaviour and that of other influential adults in their lives. Most children learn good behaviour fairly easily if we consistently demonstrate it to them ourselves and make clear to them what we expect from them. Similarly, children learn good eating habits and the fun and importance of exercise if we make family meals and activities a regular part of family life.

Overall, we probably rely rather less on our own parents for advice nowadays, often because families are more geographically separated than in the past. Grandparents

"...We have access to more information than any other generation on how to bring up our children to become healthy, well-balanced, independent young people"

may feel anxiety about being seen as interfering, and new parents may assume that childrearing practices have changed over the years and that their own parents' way of doing things is no longer appropriate for the 21st century. We have access to more information than any other generation on how to bring up our children to become healthy, well-balanced, independent young people. This book aims to give you the information you need about your child's growth, development and health to enable you to develop, and have confidence in, your own instincts as a parent. Caring for your children and seeing them thrive is one of the most rewarding tasks you will ever undertake.

Jane Colli

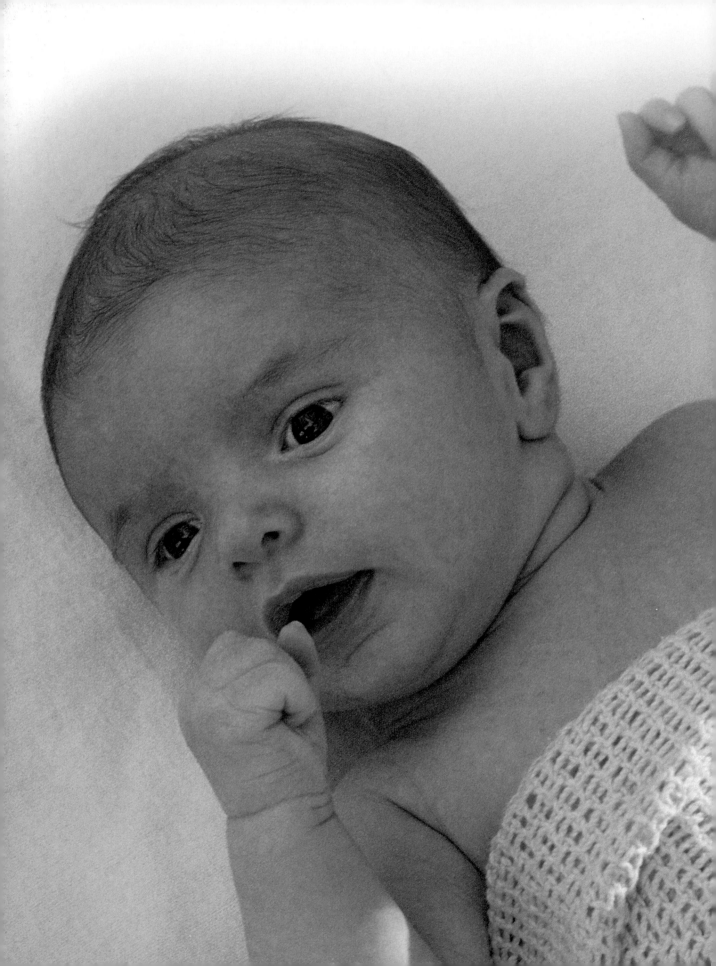

YOUR
NEW BABY

Caring for your newborn baby may seem daunting at first, and you may be unsure about health matters that concern him. This chapter has been written to help guide you through the first weeks and months with your new baby. It provides down-to-earth advice and reassurance on subjects such as feeding, sleep and general development.

FIRST DAYS

MOST BABIES ARE BORN PERFECTLY HEALTHY and adapt immediately to the outside world. But any minor setbacks in your baby's health can be distressing, especially in the first few days after the birth when you are still adjusting to becoming parents. Be reassured that most of these resolve by themselves, or with minimal medical help, within a very short space of time.

Characteristics

Your new baby might not look exactly as you had expected at first. The things listed below are often characteristic of newborns but disappear on their own in the first few weeks.

Misshapen head, caused by the descent through the birth canal.

Puffy face and puffy, sticky eyes, sometimes with a squint.

Milia, small white spots caused by blocked sebaceous glands, usually around the nose, cheeks and forehead.

Swollen genitals and breasts, in girls as well as boys, due to maternal hormones. The breasts may briefly secrete a small amount of fluid.

Red, blotchy skin. Extremities may look bluish until circulation is established. Skin may be stained yellow if the baby passed meconium (bowel contents) in the womb.

Vernix, a thick white coating, and/or lanugo, fine downy hair, may be present on pre-term babies. Babies born post-term may have dry, flaky skin and long finger- and toenails.

HOW YOUR NEWBORN LOOKS

Newborn babies often have wrinkly skin and look rather hunched up. They do not get that appealing, pink chubby look until a few weeks later. Babies have many characteristics at birth that worry parents but are normal and soon disappear. The most common are listed on the left.

Occasionally a baby may be born with a minor physical abnormality that either needs no treatment or can be corrected with minor surgery. These include extra digits, skin tags, webbing between two toes and tongue tie, when the fold of skin under the tongue is a bit tight.

After a hospital birth, your baby will be examined by a paediatrician. His hearing may be screened and he may be immunized against tuberculosis. Between days 6 and 8, a few drops of blood are taken from your baby's heel to test for phenylketonuria (PKU) and congenital hypothyroidism, rare but serious medical conditions.

BIRTHMARKS

A baby may also be born with birthmarks, of which there are four main sorts. Stork marks or salmon patches are small, pink patches that usually disappear in the first year. Strawberry birthmarks start as red spots and grow into small raised red areas with white marks. Most disappear by age 5. Port wine stains are dark red, irregular patches that are usually found on the face and do not fade with time. Mongolian blue spots are blue-black pigmented areas common in dark-skinned babies. They usually fade in the first year.

FIRST STOOLS

For the first 24–48 hours after birth, your baby will pass meconium, a sticky greeny-black mixture of bile and mucus. Once your baby starts to feed, his stools will change. Breastfed babies have loose, mustardy-coloured stools that do not really smell. Bottlefed babies have firmer, brown stools that may have an odour. Most babies produce stools after every feed. You should discuss any changes in stools with a midwife, GP or health visitor.

WHAT YOUR NEW BABY CAN DO

Babies have certain reflexes at birth, which slowly disappear within the first three months.
• Your baby sucks on anything placed in his mouth (the sucking reflex).
• He turns in the direction of something brushed against his cheek (the rooting reflex).
• Your baby grasps a finger placed in his hand (the grasping reflex).
• When held upright with his feet

on a flat surface, he makes walking movements with his legs (walking reflex), although it will be many months before he can actually walk.

• When startled, your baby throws his arms and legs out wide, then slowly curls them up towards his body (the Moro reflex).

Your baby also blinks in bright light and can focus on objects up to 20–25 cm (8–10 in) away. He quickly learns your voice and smell.

BONDING

The bond between mother and child is no weaker if the two are separated at birth for a period. Fathers need to bond too, and should concentrate on developing their own relationship with their baby.

THE APGAR SCORE

Your baby is carefully checked at birth and soon after by a midwife or paediatrician (children's doctor). The Apgar score (named after Dr Virginia Apgar, who first devised it) is done 1 minute and again 5 minutes after your baby's birth. It is used to assess five key elements of a newborn baby's health.

FEATURE	SCORE
Heartbeat	
Over 100 beats a minute	2
Under 100 beats a minute	1
Absent	0
Breathing	
Regular	2
Irregular, weak	1
Absent	0
Movement	
Active	2
Some	1
Limp	0
Reflexes (response to stimuli)	
Crying or sneezing	2
Grimacing	1
Absent	0
Skin colour	
Pink	2
Blue extremities	1
Blue	0

Babies with scores of 7 and over are healthy.

Babies scoring 5–7 may require minor treatment or a little time to settle.

Babies scoring 4 and below require immediate treatment.

BREAST OR BOTTLE

THE HEALTH BENEFITS TO MOTHER AND BABY of breastfeeding are overwhelming, but many women are surprised to find that it can be much harder initially than they expect it to be. The decision whether to breast- or bottlefeed your baby is a personal one. Bottlefeeding does have practical advantages, and mothers should be supported whichever method they choose.

Choices

Breast- and bottlefeeding both have advantages and disadvantages.

Advantages of breastfeeding
- Provides babies with essential nutrients and antibodies
- May reduce risk of breast cancer for the mother
- Unique closeness with baby
- Practical, convenient and cheap

Disadvantages of breastfeeding
- Can take several weeks to establish
- Requires patience, help and support
- Can be restricting and tiring at first
- Only the mother can feed

Advantages of bottlefeeding
- Longer intervals between feeds
- Easier to plan days and nights
- Other adults can share the experience of feeding
- Feeding in public is easy

Disadvantages of bottlefeeding
- None of the health advantages of breastfeeding
- Hygiene requires particularly close attention
- Financial outlay can be substantial
- Babies may be overfed and windier

ESTABLISHING FEEDING

Two-thirds of women in the UK start breastfeeding their baby, but many give up within the first week and, by the time their baby is six weeks old, more than 50 per cent have stopped. Most of these women say they would like to have continued longer.

There are many reasons why women switch from breast to bottle. Often, they discover that, although breastfeeding is natural, it is not always easy, particularly at the beginning. Breastfeeding requires patience, perseverance and support from others. Problems such as engorgement, sore or cracked nipples and mastitis can occur in the first few weeks. Babies often need to learn how to suck, or "latch on", properly and this too can take time and can involve tears on the part of both mother and baby as they gradually learn what to do. Until breastfeeding is fully established, which can take up to six weeks, its physical demands can be draining and limiting. In the meantime, partners or parents may advise the mother to switch to the bottle to avoid further distress and exhaustion, and health visitors or midwives may suggest giving extra bottlefeeds to ensure the baby receives enough milk.

Yet, if you persevere with breastfeeding despite any difficulties and seek help when you need it from those around you, including support groups such as the National Childbirth Trust and the La Leche League, there is no reason why you cannot successfully breastfeed for as long as you wish.

BREASTFEEDING

Babies who are breastfed gain clear health benefits compared to those who are bottlefed. Due to the essential nutrients and antibodies they receive from breast milk, breastfed babies suffer less often and less severely from common infections such as coughs and colds and are less likely to be admitted to hospital during their first year with gastroenteritis, urinary tract infections and ear or chest infections. Breastfed babies are also less likely to suffer from food allergies, eczema or asthma. Additionally, breast milk contains important growth factors that promote the development of the nervous system and gut. The Department of Health recommends exclusive breastfeeding for a baby's first six months.

The disadvantages to breast-feeding are mainly two-fold. First, until you get feeding established, a feed can take up to two hours. You may spend many hours – including several during the night – feeding your baby. This period may seem endless, exhausting and dispiriting at the time.

The second disadvantage is that, unless you express milk, only you can feed your baby. Fathers may feel they miss out on an opportunity to be close to their child. You may also feel restricted in the early weeks by the frequent, lengthy feeds.

BOTTLEFEEDING

It is important that a woman who decides to bottlefeed her baby does not feel she has failed as a mother, especially during the early weeks when she is likely to be feeling emotionally vulnerable.

Formula milk is made from cow's milk but is specially formulated to replicate maternal milk as closely as possible. Formula-fed babies need fewer feeds per 24 hours, because cow's milk has a higher protein content than human milk.

When you bottlefeed you know if your baby has had the right amount of milk. You will be giving five to six feeds per day (depending on the age of your baby) for the first six months, so the intervals between each bottle are more evenly spaced and longer. Bottlefeeding also avoids breastfeeding in public, which many women are uncomfortable doing.

WINDING

If your baby swallows air during a feed, it may cause discomfort later, so winding her helps to avoid this problem. Breastfed babies often take in less air than bottlefed babies because their mouths form an airtight seal around the nipple.

You can wind your baby by sitting her on your lap, supporting her head under her chin so that the windpipe stays straight; or you can lay her against your shoulder. Stroke her back firmly and rhythmically. Place a cloth under your baby's chin to protect your clothing from any milk coming back up (known as possetting). You will get to know whether to expect any burps and, if so, how long they take to come up.

TIMING FEEDS

Feeding on demand and feeding on a schedule both have advantages.

Feeding on demand means responding to your baby's needs by feeding him whenever he seems to be hungry. In the early days after the birth, this may mean feeding your baby every two hours and giving as many as ten feeds per 24-hour period. Many childcare experts advocate feeding on demand because babies tend to take in more milk this way and often gain weight faster than babies fed on a schedule.

Feeding on a schedule usually involves giving feeds at specific intervals, often every three or four hours or so. New parents may find feeding on a schedule easier to cope with than feeding on demand, since they know when the next feed is due and can plan around it. However, a feeding schedule should be based on the times a baby is hungry and not strictly on the clock.

BREASTFEEDING

BY BREASTFEEDING YOU CAN BE SURE THAT YOU ARE giving your baby the best possible start in life. But although breastfeeding is natural, it is not always instinctive and, for many mothers and babies, it can take time and effort to learn what to do. Once that has been achieved, however, breastfeeding is extremely rewarding.

Positions

Whichever position you use, make sure your baby is correctly latched on.

Place a pillow behind your back and under your baby so that your back is supported and you do not get shoulder and neck ache during feeds.

Avoid slouching and bring the baby up to you, rather than bending over.

Your baby's entire body should be lying facing you, not just his head.

His head should be higher than his body.

Until you get the hang of breastfeeding, it is easier to see what you are doing if you wear a top that unbuttons down the front.

When you are more confident, you can feed your baby more discreetly by simply lifting your top a little and feeding him underneath it.

To feed your baby when you are lying down, turn slightly onto one side and place your baby alongside you so that he suckles the lower breast.

HOW BREASTFEEDING WORKS

The breast is made up of about 20 lobes that together resemble bunches of grapes. Each of these lobes is drained by a milk duct that leads to the nipple. When your baby sucks on your nipple (including the area around the nipple itself, known as the areola), the pituitary gland is stimulated in two ways. First, it produces the hormone prolactin, which in turn sets off milk production. Second, it releases the hormone oxytocin, which causes the individual alveoli that make up the lobes to contract, sending milk down the ducts to the nipples. This contraction of the alveoli, known as the let-down reflex, can occur not just with the stimulation of your baby sucking but simply when you hear him, or even another baby, cry.

FIRST FEEDS

When your baby is first born, your breasts will produce a substance known as colostrum, rather than milk. This clearish secretion contains a highly concentrated form of all the essential nutrients and antibodies that your baby needs in the first few days immediately after the birth. You will only produce 10–20 ml (2–4 teaspoonfuls) of colostrum per day but this, together with the reserves of his own that nature has ensured he is born with, will keep him satisfied until your milk comes in, generally between the third and fifth day.

Put your baby to the breast as soon as you can after the birth. Even a brief attempt at suckling will help stimulate milk production and give your baby an opportunity to learn how to suck correctly, or "latch on". The more practice he gets before your milk comes in, the better.

HOW TO FEED

The key is for your baby to be latched on not just to the nipple, but to the whole areola. If he is not, he will not stimulate your nipples correctly and milk production will be hindered. You will also quickly develop painful, sore nipples.

In order for your baby to open his mouth, stroke the cheek nearer to you to stimulate the rooting reflex. Squeeze your breast so that the nipple area is tilted slightly upwards, then place the whole areola in your baby's mouth. If in doubt, put in more than you think, as your baby will make the necessary adjustment.

The whole process is not very delicate and will need to be repeated until you are satisfied that he is latched on correctly. You can tell if he is if you feel a suction effect over the nipple area. In addition, his mouth will be wide open with the top lip turned upwards, and his ears and jaw will be moving rhythmically.

ENDING A FEED

To take your baby off the breast, gently insert a finger between his mouth and your nipple. This will break the strong suction and avoid your baby pulling on your nipple, which can cause irritation.

It is best to empty one breast per feed, so that your baby will get both the thinner, thirst-quenching foremilk that comes from the breast first and the thicker, more nutritious hindmilk that follows after. If you empty one breast and continue with the other, start the next feed on that second side, which will be fuller.

YOUR MILK SUPPLY

You should eat an extra 500 calories a day (1,000 with twins) if you are to produce enough milk. Never diet while breastfeeding; this will adversely affect your milk supply.

You should drink an extra litre (about 2 pints) of water a day in order to help milk production.

Try to rest as much as possible to allow your body to recover between feeds. An afternoon nap is good (if you can manage one) to prevent excessive tiredness in the evening.

Milk is produced on a supply-and-demand basis, so the more you feed, the more you produce. Feeding on demand will therefore not diminish your milk supply, but will increase it.

Babies like to comfort suck, even on an empty breast. You may think that your baby is still hungry because he cries when he is removed from the breast, when actually he is only comfort sucking.

Avoid introducing a bottle – with either expressed milk or formula – until breastfeeding is fully established. Sucking from a teat requires a different technique and your baby will be slower at learning how to breastfeed.

Once established, breastfeeding on demand will result in shorter, more frequent feeds than feeds at regular intervals. As long as your baby is gaining the appropriate amount of weight, he is receiving enough milk, whichever approach you take.

Be prepared for problems and seek help as soon as you need it.

EXPRESSING MILK

Expressing milk can be a very effective way of combining the advantages of giving breast milk with the freedom of giving a bottle. If you and your baby are separated (because he is in hospital, for example), expressing allows you to continue breastfeeding your baby.

You can express by hand (your midwife will show you how to do this), but it rarely proves to be a very satisfactory method. You can buy or borrow small pumps that are either hand or battery operated,

with the latter usually proving more useful. Or you can hire the sort of powerful electric breast pumps that are used in hospitals. These are speedy and highly effective as well as being relatively inexpensive to hire (*see* Useful Addresses, *p.344*, for supplier information).

Milk production works on a demand and supply basis, so, providing that you do not express milk just before a feed, expressing will not deplete your store of milk. Having said that, it is nonetheless best if you express milk in the

morning, when your breasts are often fuller than they are in the afternoon or evening.

STORING EXPRESSED MILK

Freeze any unwanted milk in sterile freezer bags (these are available from good pharmacies or babycare departments), as it can keep for up to six months. You do not have to express a full feed's worth, simply as much as you are comfortable with. Breast milk will keep for up to 24 hours if stored in the fridge.

If breastfeeding is not yet fully established, freeze your expressed milk for later rather than introduce your baby to a bottle at this stage.

ENGORGEMENT

If you develop engorged breasts or mastitis, do express milk (freeze it, if necessary), since it is essential to drain the milk from your breasts. Expressing milk will actually help cure the problem rather than making it worse.

FEEDING ROUTINES

It is unlikely that your baby will be in any sort of routine before he is at least 6 weeks old. During the first few weeks, you will gradually learn how to breastfeed and how to recognize when your baby is hungry, full or just sucking on your breast for comfort. Until you do this, be prepared for feeds to be stop-start affairs that can take a longer time than you might expect.

If you are eager to establish a feeding routine, keeping a note of feed times and lengths can help to identify any emerging pattern.

Until you are able to feed easily, it is best to try to do so in a quiet environment, rather than when you are surrounded by family or friends, or, worse, in a public place.

Otherwise, you may feel nervous, making it difficult for you to concentrate. Your baby may pick up on your anxiety and end up getting fretful, which may in turn dent your confidence.

FEEDING TWINS
You will need to increase your calorie intake by 1,000 calories per day in order to cover your nutritional needs. When you are feeding twins it is also doubly important for you to drink plenty of fluids throughout the day and get plenty of rest.

There are various ways to manage the practical demands made by breastfeeding twins, and only you will be able to decide which method suits you best. You can feed your babies together, with one on each breast. You can feed one after the other, though you may find that this can lead to you spending half of any 24-hour period feeding.

Making sure each baby gets enough milk
You will need to keep a note of which baby started feeding first and on which breast, because the second baby often starts his feed on a breast (the second) that is not totally full. Do write it down; you'll be surprised at how quickly you forget which baby started first and where!

You can also alternate breast and bottle for each baby by establishing a routine in which one baby has a breastfeed and the other baby has a bottlefeed, and the babies swap over at the next feed. This gives you more of a respite and allows each baby his own exclusive feed with you.

Bear in mind that your babies will not have identical feeding patterns, so it may be difficult to plan feeds or stick to any one method throughout.

BREASTFEEDING QUESTIONS & ANSWERS

How do I prevent/cure engorgement?
When your milk comes in, it can do so very quickly. If your baby is not yet feeding very successfully, this may lead to painful, swollen (engorged) breasts. Engorgement can lead to mastitis (a breast infection), which may develop into a breast abscess if untreated, so it's important to treat engorgement promptly. Keep draining the breast, either by feeding your baby and/or by expressing milk. Try expressing a little milk before the start of each feed if your nipples are too distended to enable your baby to latch on. You do not have to empty the breast each time – feeding a little and often is better until the problem is resolved.

How do I prevent/cure sore or cracked nipples?
To prevent them, make sure your baby is correctly latched on and does not pull on the nipple as you remove him from the breast. To cure them, expose your breasts to the air as much as possible and change breastpads after every feed. Smearing a little breast milk or saliva on the nipple and letting it dry can also help and is probably as effective as using the various nipple creams on the market. You must keep feeding on that breast; otherwise, it may become engorged. If necessary, express milk from the affected breast if it is too painful to have your baby feed on that side. A nipple shield can also help, although your baby may not like using one.

How do I cure blocked ducts?
A blocked milk duct causes a tender, red patch to develop on the breast. It is vital to drain the breast as much and as often as possible to clear the blockage; otherwise, milk will seep into the breast tissue and this could lead to mastitis (a breast infection). Keep feeding your baby on the affected side and start each feed

with the affected breast. You can feed your baby on all fours so that the breast hangs down over him and gravity helps it drain. Express milk, especially if your baby is not feeding very effectively. To relieve pain, place a warm flannel on the patch, or a cold cabbage leaf (a time-honoured remedy).

How do I know if my baby is full?
Your baby will start to suck much less strongly, will stop repeatedly and may start to doze off. As a rule of thumb, once breastfeeding is properly established, a baby will receive most of the milk within the first 10 minutes of a feed, so 20 minutes per feed is usually sufficient. However, only experience can teach you when you think your baby is full, and until you reach that stage, trial and error are your main guides.

Do I really have enough milk?
Many mothers ask this because their baby cries soon after a feed and appears to be constantly hungry. In reality, it is rare not to have enough milk, and the more often you feed, the more milk you will produce. "Topping up" with a formula feed will satiate your baby, but he will suck less strongly, feed less often and cause you to produce less milk. If your baby is putting on the correct amount of weight on breast milk alone, then he is receiving enough milk.

My baby is unwell or premature. Can I still breastfeed?
If you are separated from your baby after the birth, you will be encouraged to express milk, since your baby will gain enormous health benefits. Once you are home, if your baby has to stay in hospital, you should hire a powerful electric breast pump (see above) to maximize the amount of milk you can produce. You can then bring it in to hospital to be fed to your baby.

BOTTLEFEEDING

The MAJORITY OF BABIES WILL BE BOTTLEFED WITH formula milk at some stage in their development. The key to successful bottlefeeding is organization and hygiene, so that it is both a practical and safe method of feeding. Bottlefeeding has the advantage that it enables other adults to feed a baby, so it is less restrictive and tiring in the early days for the mother than breastfeeding.

Equipment

If you're bottlefeeding, you'll need to get the following basic equipment.

Bottles: ideally, at least six are required to avoid constantly having to make up feeds.

Teats: start with slow-flow teats for newborns. As your baby gets older, she will progress on to faster-flow teats. If the teat flows too fast for her, she will swallow air and develop wind. Buying variable-flow teats avoids having to buy a new set of teats.

Bottle and teat brushes: using separate, specially designed brushes will ensure thorough cleaning and avoid the risk of cross-contamination.

Sterilizing equipment: steam or microwave sterilizers are the most popular. Sterilizing tablets or fluid can also be used and are particularly helpful if you are travelling.

Formula milk: formula milks are all fairly similar in content and are specially formulated to replicate breast milk as closely as possible. Ask family, friends and your health visitor which brand they would recommend and why.

HYGIENE

Hygiene is crucially important during the first few months. Poor hygiene can lead to your baby developing an infection such as gastroenteritis that may require hospitalization.

Wash the bottles and teats with special bottle brushes; then, importantly, rinse them under running water before sterilizing them. Any equipment, such as cutlery, that is used to make up the feeds must also be washed, rinsed and sterilized. Sterilizing must be done for the first six months.

Before you make up the feeds or give a bottle, wash your hands. You can keep a freshly made bottle for up to 24 hours in the fridge, but never reheat any used milk.

MAKING UP BOTTLES

You will soon get the hang of making up your baby's bottles. You can make up 24 hours' worth of bottles in one batch, then store them in the fridge. Follow the manufacturer's instructions precisely for making up the feeds. Never dilute or condense the formula, as this will lead to under- or over-feeding your baby. If you warm the bottle in the microwave, shake it to disperse the heat evenly. Test the temperature of the milk on the inside of your wrist.

Use cooled, boiled water to make up the feeds or use bottled water with a very low mineral content. Filtered water is all right as long as it is boiled and cooled after filtering.

Formula milk is less thirst-quenching than breast milk, so if you are giving the former, give your baby regular sips of cool, boiled water or bottled water to prevent her becoming dehydrated. Many babies do not like water at first because it lacks the taste of formula milk, but persist by offering frequent little sips. It is much healthier for your baby to drink water than juice, and getting her used to water early on means she'll drink it more willingly when she gets older.

Occasionally, babies are allergic to cow's milk, so an alternative, such as a soya-based formula, can be used. However, you must not switch until your GP or a paediatrician has confirmed that your baby needs to.

SWITCHING FROM BREAST TO BOTTLE

If, like many mothers, you switch at some stage from breast to bottle, you should aim to do this over a period of a couple of weeks at least, so that your milk supply decreases gradually. During that time, your baby can get used to the feel of a teat and the taste of formula milk. Breastfed babies may be very

resistant at first to bottles. This can be upsetting, particularly if the mother is going back to work soon. Try asking another adult to feed the baby so that she does not smell her mother's breast milk.

Start by giving one bottle a day when your baby is not too tired. In a few days, introduce another bottle at another time of day. Eventually, alternate bottle and breast, then limit breastfeeds to last thing at night and first thing in the morning before cutting them out altogether.

FEEDING YOUR BABY WITH A BOTTLE

Make sure your back is properly supported. Cradle your baby securely, with her head higher than her body. Make a lot of eye contact and talk to her if you want. Angle the bottle so that milk fills the teat without air and feed at the rhythm that your baby demands.

If your baby stops, stroke her cheek to start her feeding again. Slide a finger between the teat and the corner of her mouth to release it.

SAFE FEEDING

Hygiene and organization are of the greatest importance when bottlefeeding.

Wash, rinse and sterilize (the latter for the first six months) all equipment, including any cutlery you use when making up feeds. Use hot, soapy water when washing and make sure that you rinse everything thoroughly.

Wash your hands before making up and giving the bottles.

Formula milk keeps for a maximum of 24 hours in the fridge, which means that you can make bottles up in advance (*see below*), but leftovers must never be reheated. Bacteria in leftover formula can multiply rapidly and make your baby ill.

Make up batches of bottles for convenience and store them in the fridge for a maximum of 24 hours.

Never dilute or condense the feeds. Doing so could make your baby ill.

Shake the warmed bottle to disperse the heat and test the temperature on the inside of your wrist. It should feel slightly warm on your skin, and neither hot nor cold.

Offer your baby sips of boiled, cooled water between feeds to prevent her from becoming dehydrated and get her accustomed to the taste of plain water.

Allow at least two weeks to switch from breastfeeding to bottlefeeding. If you are returning to work, give yourself and your baby plenty of time to adjust.

Do not switch from cow's milk to other formula types without seeking medical advice.

CRYING & COMFORTING

BABIES CRY BECAUSE THEY NEED TO COMMUNICATE THAT something is not right and most parents, especially mothers, find it distressing to see or hear an unhappy baby. Although in time you will learn to recognize the various causes of your baby's cries, you may find it harder to know why your baby is crying at first, particularly if you are first-time parents.

Interpreting cries

Your baby will inevitably cry, and you may find this less upsetting once you understand what his cries mean.

There are many reasons why babies cry and there is little doubt that some babies are more content and cry less than others.

Although mothers are told that they can instinctively distinguish their baby's cry from other babies', many mothers report that it takes a few weeks to be able to do this.

It may also take you time to learn to recognize the different sorts of cries your baby makes and what they may mean.

Eventually, you will discover that your baby usually cries for one or more of a variety of common reasons. For example, he may be hungry or tired and need food or comfort. His nappy may need changing. He may be uncomfortable because he has wind, or he may have colic (*see opposite*). He may be too hot or too cold, or he may be unwell.

HOW TO CALM YOUR BABY

Most parents will instinctively pick up and cuddle their crying baby and often that is all that is required. Babies like attention; they like familiar voices, particularly those of their parents, and feel secure when they are in their parents' arms.

However, if cuddling fails to settle your baby, it may be that he is hungry or thirsty, in which case giving him a bit of milk or water will help. Giving your baby something to suck on, such as your finger or a dummy, can also be very soothing. When he gets older, he may start to suck his thumb and this too can help your baby to stop crying.

Newborns, in particular, cannot yet regulate their temperature very well, so you should feel the nape of your baby's neck to assess whether he feels hot or cold. As a rule of thumb, he should wear one more layer than you are, although on hot days this may not be suitable.

It may be that he is suffering from wind, in which case you can try laying him over your lap or forearm and rubbing his back. If he has recently been fed, you can also try burping him.

Crying with no apparent reason

If your baby is regularly crying inconsolably during the early evening and is aged between 3 and 14 weeks, he may be suffering from colic (*see opposite*). During a bout of colic it will be difficult to calm your baby. Although there are various remedies that are said to help, some traditional, some alternative, none is a proven cure.

Your baby will cry when he is tired, so you can try swaddling him in a sheet or cot blanket, which will make him feel very secure and, as a result, may help him not only to stop crying but to fall asleep as well. Shushing him in a calm, rhythmical way or rocking him, particularly when he is lying on his stomach over your forearm, can also help to calm a crying baby.

As a last resort, many parents find that a drive round the block – or

two – with the baby in his car seat usually works wonders for a screaming baby. Less drastically, putting your baby in the pram for a quick trip in the fresh air often has a similarly calming effect.

If your baby is crying persistently in an unusually ferocious manner, nothing you do seems to have any effect and you do not think he is suffering from colic, he may be in pain and unwell. Trust your instincts and contact your doctor if you are concerned. It may be that there is nothing wrong, but most doctors are understanding and do not mind allaying the fears of new parents.

CRYING IN THE EARLY DAYS

Just as some adults are naturally more cheerful than others, some babies are more content than others. During the first few weeks of your baby's life, you will get to know his personality, whether he is easy-going or more demanding, and how best to calm him. You should always remember that babies cry for a reason and that, until they are older, their only effective method of communicating their needs and emotions is through tears.

CAN I SPOIL MY BABY?

When your baby is very young, you will not be spoiling him by picking him up as soon as he cries. As your baby gets older, however, you may not feel the need to do this quite so quickly, particularly if you know that there is nothing fundamentally wrong with him – he is not hungry or thirsty, his nappy is clean and he is not unwell. How quickly you pick your baby up to calm him will depend very much on you and on the situation. You must do what feels right for you and your baby.

EVENING CRYING

Between 3 and 14 weeks, some babies develop habitual evening crying that is known as colic. If your baby has colic, he will cry loudly and continuously for anything up to several hours and will often curl up, as if his tummy is in pain.

Colic is hard to define and diagnose. Some theories say that it is caused either by trapped wind or by the gut having spasms as it adjusts to digestion in the weeks following the birth.

Sometimes hunger, rather than colic, may be a cause of continual evening crying, particularly if your baby is breastfed, because the milk that you produce at that time of day can be less rich and filling. Try to rest in the afternoon if possible, which will help replenish your milk supply.

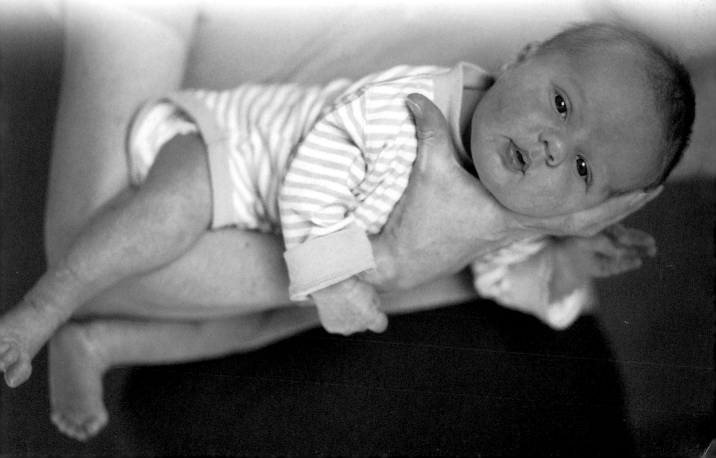

Do not let yourself lose confidence in your ability to parent because you are being swayed by the opinions of friends or family or even by so-called childcare experts. Always remember that no one knows your baby better than you do.

TIREDNESS AND CRYING

After about three months, babies' body clocks start to distinguish between night and day, so they often get tired in the early evening and this can lead to crying (a different type of sound from colicky crying). If this is the case with your baby, it may be that he is ready to go to bed. Bear in mind that babies have to learn how to fall asleep on their own and that crying is part of that learning process (*see p.31*).

CRYING AND OLDER BABIES

Older babies (over the age of 6 months or so) are also creatures of habit and if their routine is disrupted, they can become very unhappy and unsettled. They are also very determined, so if, for example, their bottle is late, they might cry until it finally arrives. Equally, they might cry during mealtimes because of a clash with you about a particular food or drink. In short, even though they cannot yet talk, babies are remarkably communicative through their crying.

SHOULD I LET MY OLDER BABY CRY?

Simply because your older baby is crying does not mean that you have to give in to his every wish and, again, only you can decide what your approach will be to any particular circumstance. Despite parents' desire not to upset their children, sometimes it may prove necessary to do so.

Clearly there are times when it is inappropriate not to soothe your child, but there will also be occasions when you will have to stand firm and let your older baby cry. For example, he may want something that is dangerous for him. If you always accommodate your baby, he may become inflexible and used to having his own way in everything. Remember that you will not be a bad parent if you follow this path; you will simply be following your own instincts about how you wish to raise your child.

DUMMIES & THUMB-SUCKING

Opinions on dummies and thumb-sucking vary and it will be up to you to decide what your attitude is towards them. If one of these methods works, many parents are simply relieved, since hearing their baby cry is highly distressing and their only wish is for the tears to stop.

Thumb-sucking has the advantage that your baby can remove his thumb from his mouth himself if he wants to babble, put something else in his

mouth or simply start crying again. The disadvantage is that a thumb is always readily available and can become a difficult habit to break. Thumb-sucking may also lead to dental problems later on.

With a dummy, the parent can decide when to dispense with it, although this may be easier said than done. Dummies are considered less harmful to dental development than they used to be, as many are orthodontically moulded. However, research shows they may impede linguistic and general development, because sucking a dummy restricts a baby's ability to babble and makes him less alert. Dummies also prevent babies from putting things in their mouths, which is an important way in which they explore their world.

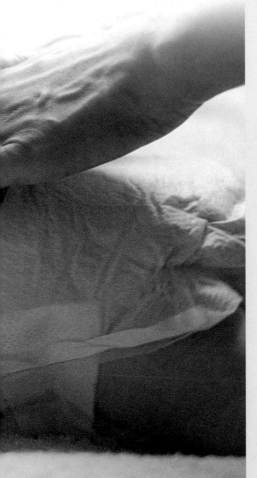

My baby seems to cry all the time. Are there any alternative therapies that can help?

If your baby cries a lot and for no obvious reason, you may consider complementary therapies (*see p.318*). Remember that most of these are not regulated by any governmental or medical authority and that there is a lack of clinical evidence of efficacy. This does not mean that they do not work, simply that it is hard to know how much they can help any given problem.

Could osteopathy help my baby sleep through the night?

Osteopathy, through the General Osteopathic Council, is one of the few regulated alternative therapies and all practising osteopaths should be registered (*see* Useful Addresses, *p.344*). Ideally, a specialist paediatric osteopath should be consulted.

A paediatric osteopath will work on calming down the baby's nervous system and, to the untrained eye, it may appear that the practitioner is barely touching the baby. The osteopathic approach claims to rebalance the body through gentle manual techniques. Because a baby's bones are so soft, practitioners say that even the gentlest touch can have a powerful response, which may enable the nervous, immune and circulatory systems to work more effectively. As a result, a baby may become calmer and more content.

What is cranial osteopathy?

Cranial osteopathy is a specialized form of osteopathy that concentrates on realigning the bones in the skull. Like osteopathy, it is regulated by the General Osteopathic Council (*see above*).

During birth, the skull bones are able to move to some degree to accommodate the passage of the head through the birth canal. The seams between the bones, known as sutures, and the soft gaps between the bones, known as the fontanelles, do not close and fuse completely until a child is around 2 years old. Cranial osteopathy aims to realign these skull bones gently. The practitioner may seem barely to be touching the child, since babies' skulls are so sensitive that even the gentlest touch can be very powerful.

Could homeopathy help my baby be calmer?

Homeopathy is used for a wide range of ailments. In homeopathy, the principal idea is that the body's immune system can be stimulated to overcome illness by very small doses of a substance that would provoke symptoms of the illness if given in larger quantities.

What will the homeopath do?

Homeopathy also works by treating the whole person, rather than just the ailment. The homeopath will first of all talk to you at length about your baby to try to establish a picture of his personality and behaviour. He or she may also want to know about your personality and how you interact with your baby. On that basis, he or she will prescribe a remedy that may reduce or cure the problem.

What if there is no immediate improvement in my baby's condition?

Sometimes it takes a few attempts to find the right remedy. If there is not a marked improvement after the first round of treatment, another remedy will be tried, and so on until the homeopath finds the precise remedy for the problem. It can therefore take time before any significant improvement is seen – and of course, there is no guarantee that this will ever be the case. However, problems with crying and sleep are among those that homeopathy claims to be able to address most successfully.

SLEEP

Wʜᴇɴ sʜᴇ ɪs ꜰɪʀsᴛ ʙᴏʀɴ, your baby has no notion of night and day and you should be prepared for it to take several weeks, if not months, before she sleeps through the night. Although this does not affect your baby's health, you may find that your own health is affected because your sleep will inevitably be disrupted during this time.

Beds and bedding

There is a wide range of beds and bedding for babies.

Crib Suitable from birth to 3 months.

Moses basket/carrycot Suitable from birth to 3 months.

Cot Suitable from birth to 2 years old. Babies often sleep better once in a proper cot.

Pillows, duvets, quilts Not suitable for babies under 12 months. Babies can shuffle under them and overheat.

Blankets Cotton cellular blankets are best because they are warm yet breathable. Wool can irritate a baby's delicate skin.

Sheets Cotton sheets are best. Avoid synthetic fabrics, which can trap heat.

Grobags/Baby sleeping bags Not recommended, since babies cannot wriggle out of them if they get too hot. Never use extra bedding on top.

Cot bumpers Unsuitable for babies under 12 months.

WHO SLEEPS WHERE?

It is up to you where your baby sleeps, and there are advantages and disadvantages to all the options. Your baby can sleep either in your bedroom or in her own, in your bed or in hers. (Be aware that she must not sleep with you if either parent is very tired or has been smoking or drinking alcohol.) She may start off doing one thing, then move on to another when she is a little older.

Many parents like their baby to be in the same bedroom with them for the first few weeks, especially if the mother is breastfeeding, because the baby can then be fed in bed during the night with minimal disruption to all concerned. Later, if the baby will take a bottle, some parents take turns sleeping in another room so that at least one parent gets a night of uninterrupted sleep. Once a baby is having longer intervals between feeds, she can be put in her own bedroom, which may have a baby listening device for added reassurance.

The disadvantage of having your baby in the same room as you is that newborns can be very noisy sleepers, shuffling and grunting so much that they keep you awake. Even if she is in her own cot, your baby will soon realize that, when she wakes, you are in the same room and this makes it impossible to ignore her cries for very long. It is difficult to decide at what point to put your baby in her own room, but you could plan to do so once she is feeding every four hours and see how it goes.

Should our baby sleep with us?

The matter of whose bed your baby sleeps in is a highly individual one. Again, many parents, for the sake of sanity, take their newborn into bed with them for some or all of the night during the first few weeks, particularly if the mother is

breastfeeding. They find that the baby sleeps better and consequently so do they. At that stage, they are just grateful to have a couple of hours of unbroken sleep. A baby can also suckle while the mother dozes, allowing her precious resting time.

However, if you decide to have your baby in bed with you beyond the first few weeks, you should be prepared to share your bed with her for several years. Once your baby has learned to recognize the parental bed as the place she sleeps in – and this will probably happen within the first three months – it will be very difficult to persuade her to sleep anywhere else. The longer you leave her in bed with you, the harder it will be to get your baby used to her own bed. It can put stress on your relationship, not to mention your sex life, if you and your partner are not in agreement with the idea of being three in a bed. One of you may end up sleeping badly or be

worried that you might roll over and smother your baby or that she might overheat. These things need to be considered before deciding how long to keep your baby in bed with you.

HOW TO GET YOUR BABY TO GO TO SLEEP

Parents tend to fall into two categories: they either fit their baby into their own lives, or they fit their own lives around their baby's. Their attitude towards their baby's sleep is very much influenced by which of these categories they fall into. However, if parents resign themselves in advance to having broken nights for months on end, if not years, then this can become a self-fulfilling prophecy.

There are two basic questions to think about when considering babies' sleep. The first is how to get a baby to fall asleep on her own, and the second is how long she is able to sleep at night. While there is much

SLEEP PATTERNS

The following is a typical pattern of sleep for a baby in the first year of life.

First 6 weeks
Until an infant is approximately 6 weeks old, she will be awake for only 6–8 hours per day. She will sleep randomly during the day and the night, as her brain does not yet have the maturity to have developed a cycle of day and night.

6 weeks to 3 months
Your baby will sleep less and less during the day and may start to sleep for longer stretches at night. Her body clock is slowly establishing itself.

3–6 months
Day and night are now established in most babies. Stretches of four hours between feeds – the core night – are achievable for most babies.

6 months onwards
Your baby should be able to do 6-hour stretches, if not more. From 6 months old, babies no longer need night-time feeding. If your older baby wakes in the night wanting a feed, try giving only a few sips of water (or formula or breast milk that has been diluted with water), and encourage her to go straight back to sleep.

You'll find that establishing a good bedtime routine for your baby (*see p.30*) during her first year will help her establish good sleep habits that will last into childhood. A routine can also make bedtimes easier, because your baby learns the cues that mean it's time for her to go to sleep.

SIDS (COT DEATH)

Sudden Infant Death Syndrome (SIDS) occurs very rarely and usually only to babies aged between 2 months and 6 months. Over the last few years, research has shown that parents can take certain measures to minimize the risk of it happening.

Put your baby to sleep on her back in preference to her side, and never on her front.

Do not over-dress your baby. Grobags and baby sleeping bags are difficult for babies to wriggle out of if they get too hot. They should not be used with additional bedding.

Do not over-heat your baby's room and keep it well ventilated, particularly in summer. 18–20° C (66–68° F) is fine.

Use cotton bedding, which is both breathable and warm. Do not use duvets, quilts or sheepskins, or pillows or cot bumpers.

Never smoke in the room in which your baby sleeps or when you are with her. Better still, give up altogether (research shows that if mothers smoke during pregnancy, their baby is 15 times more likely to die of cot death).

If you smoke, drink or are very tired, do not sleep in the same bed as your baby. Ideally, do not share a bed with your baby at all, especially in the first four months.

Place your baby's feet at the bottom of the cot ("feet to foot") to prevent her from wriggling down under the covers.

that can be done to teach a baby to fall asleep – since it is a skill that has to be learned – there is less that can be done to help a baby to sleep through the night. In addition, during the first three months, a baby's sleep pattern will depend to some extent on whether she is breast- or bottlefed (*see pp.16–17*), because a breastfed baby will wake more often to be fed. The box on page 29 is a rough guide to what sort of sleep patterns you can expect from your baby during her first year.

Learning how to fall asleep on their own is something that comes more easily to some babies than to others. Babies get into habits – both good and bad – extremely fast, but these habits can be changed. The main thing is to be consistent and persistent about your baby's sleeping and to remember that the longer you leave things, the harder it will be to change them. Your baby may need to cry a lot at first before falling asleep on her own, but that is part of the learning process.

The importance of bedtime routines

Most sleep experts agree that, for a baby to learn to fall asleep, it helps to establish a bedtime routine. This

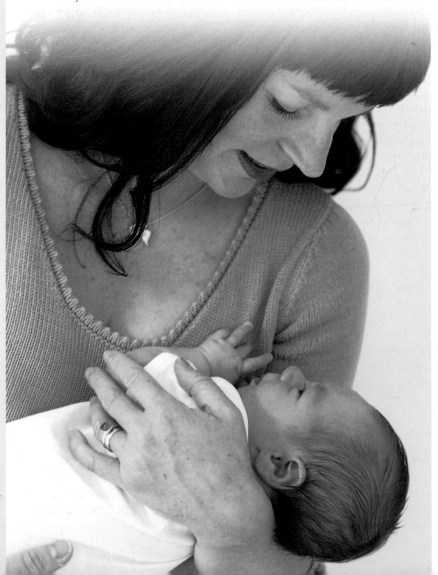

enables your baby to recognize the cues that will tell her it is time to sleep, whether for a daytime nap or at night-time. It is never too early to introduce a bedtime routine, even if the results of your efforts are only seen once your baby is around 3 months old.

The aim of an evening routine, aside from giving your baby cues for going to sleep, is to calm her and help her wind down. Try giving your baby a bath, and dress her in different clothes from the ones she was wearing during the day. Feed her in the room in which she sleeps (which should be dimly lit), give her a big cuddle, then put her to bed. Do not linger. The whole process should take you no longer than 45 minutes from bath to bed.

Bedtime comforts

After the bath, some parents like to massage their baby with essential oils, such as lavender oil, as an additional part of the routine. Many find that their baby is comforted by the familiar smell of a soft cloth – often a muslin cloth that is used during feeds – or by a particular toy. Others find that dummies are useful in helping their baby learn to fall asleep on her own. What you need to avoid is stimulating your baby through play at the end of the day.

The final part of the routine is that your baby should be awake when she is put in her bed so that she can learn to recognize this essential cue for falling asleep. A baby who has previously fallen asleep elsewhere may feel panicky if she wakes because she will not immediately know where she is. So, while it is fine to let your baby fall asleep outside her bed in the first few weeks, you should avoid this becoming a habit as she grows older.

SLEEP QUESTIONS & ANSWERS

When can I expect my baby to sleep through the night?

Some bottlefed babies start sleeping six-hour stretches – what could be called sleeping through the night – from as early as 4–6 weeks old, but most babies, both breast- and bottlefed ones, will not be doing such long stretches regularly until they are around 3 months old. Establishing a bedtime routine in the early weeks will eventually help your baby to recognize cues for going to sleep.

Why does my 6-month-old baby still feed during the night?

Make sure she is eating enough during the day and that her last meal and bottle are not too early and no more than two hours apart. The bottle should not be taking the place of supper, but should rather be a way of topping it up and settling your baby.

If your baby is waking for a feed, it may be more out of habit than genuine hunger. Try diluting her milk gradually with water or, if you are breastfeeding, simply give water or expressed milk diluted with water. It may be that your partner has to do this so that your baby knows she will not be getting your breast to suckle.

Why can't I settle my 6-month-old baby when she wakes at night?

If your baby needs an increasingly long cuddle or to be taken into your bed in order to settle, try just talking to her and stroking her to reassure her. Avoid picking her up and make sure you stimulate her as little as possible (keep the light off, or very dim, in her room).

You may have to let your baby do some controlled crying (see below); otherwise she will soon realize that if she cries when she wakes, she gets a long cuddle with her mother or father and perhaps even a chance to lie in their bed. If this continues, it will become a

habit before you know it. The older your baby is, the longer it will take to get her out of the habit of waking and crying.

What is "controlled crying"?

This is a technique that is used to settle babies when they are in their cots and should only be attempted with babies over 6 months old.

With controlled crying, you leave your baby to cry, initially for five minutes, then go in to reassure her by talking to her and stroking her briefly, but never picking her up. You repeat the process but gradually space out the intervals to 10, 15, 20 minutes and so on, until your baby falls asleep on her own.

Controlled crying can be a distressing method, and the older the baby is, the longer it can take to be effective. However, if you are determined and always consistent, controlled crying does work in the end and your baby will have learned once and for all to fall asleep on her own.

Why does my baby sleep badly during the day?

Babies like routine and, if you establish a pattern to your day, your baby can develop cues for falling asleep. She may also have to do some controlled crying (see above) before naps.

Try to ensure that at least one of your baby's daytime sleeps is always in the same bed and at a similar time. If your baby only falls asleep at random times while you are out and about and only in her buggy or in the car, she will not develop the cues to learn how to sleep in her bed during the day.

In addition, if your baby does not sleep enough during the day, it can make it harder for her to sleep at night, although this may sound contradictory. If she becomes whingy and upset in the evening from being overtired during the day, it can make it hard for you to settle her into her cot and get her to sleep.

CARING FOR YOUR BABY

As A NEW PARENT, YOUR BABY'S WELLBEING IS YOUR FIRST CONCERN. However, many new parents have no previous experience of looking after a baby: they have never dressed or fed a baby before, changed a nappy or given a baby a bath. Learning to do these things correctly comes easily to most parents and ensures that your baby stays as healthy as possible.

Keeping healthy

Wash your hands before and after every nappy change.

Use cotton wool and cooled, boiled water to clean the nappy area and allow your baby's skin to air as much as possible.

Meticulously clean and dry the stump of the umbilical cord every day.

When bathing your newborn, hold him at all times. Do not use soap or bubblebath – a hypoallergenic bath oil is best.

Use separate pieces of cotton wool when washing your baby's eyes.

Clean his teeth as soon as the first one appears.

A young baby should wear one more layer than you do. Cotton is best for clothes and bedding – avoid wool or synthetic fabrics.

Heat rooms to 18–20°C (66–68°F). It's better to add a cotton blanket than another layer of clothing; avoid turning up the heating in the room.

CHANGING A NAPPY

Your hospital or midwife will show you how to change your baby's nappy. It is up to you what sort of nappy you choose to use; some families prefer to use disposable nappies while others prefer to use terry. Whatever you decide, hygiene is very important both for you and your baby. Always wash your hands before and after each nappy change.

Cleaning the nappy area

Use cotton wool and cooled, boiled water to clean your baby's nappy area for the first few weeks and for as long as possible thereafter. Your baby's skin is so sensitive that even the mildest hypoallergenic wipes may irritate it. (If you are using terry nappies, make sure that they are thoroughly rinsed of all washing powder before they are dried, since washing powder residue can also irritate your baby's delicate skin.) Keep the wipes for when you are out and about or travelling, or use aqueous cream and cotton wool, which are less irritant than wipes.

Some people recommend using barrier cream after every nappy change, while others use nothing at all and prefer to let their baby's skin breathe as much as possible. Whatever you decide, you should change your baby's nappy after every feed and before and after every sleep.

The less he sits in a soiled or wet nappy, the less he risks developing nappy rash, which is caused when the ammonia in the urine burns the skin. If your baby does develop nappy rash, you should treat it promptly (*see p.56*); it may become infected otherwise.

Boys and girls

For boys, never pull back the foreskin and, for girls, simply wipe the labia and vaginal area. Always wipe towards the anus, never away from it, since this can spread bacteria towards the baby's penis or vagina. Remember to clean inside any skin creases, and make sure the skin is

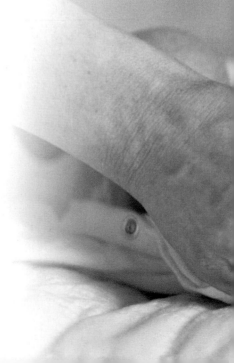

properly dry before putting on a clean nappy. Ideally, leave your baby's skin to air as much as possible, as this will let it breathe and help prevent nappy rash. One note of caution: if the room is too cold, boys, in particular, will tend to urinate when their nappy is left off.

TOPPING & TAILING

Newborn babies are not yet mobile and so they do not get dirty quickly, unlike older babies. It is not essential to bath your newborn on a daily basis. Instead, you can simply wash your baby's face and bottom, as well as any other part, such as his hands or under his arms, that you would like to clean up a little. This is called topping and tailing.

How to top and tail

You will need a bowl of boiled water that has been allowed to cool to body temperature, some cotton wool and a soft towel. Remember to wash your hands before you begin. Start by wiping your baby's eyes. Dip a piece of cotton wool in the water, squeeze it out, then gently wipe one of your baby's eyes, from the nose outwards. Repeat with a fresh piece of cotton wool for the other eye to avoid transferring an infection from one eye to the other. Then wipe the rest of your baby's face and neck using a third piece of cotton wool, remembering to lift your baby's chin up to clean any folds of skin underneath it. Pat the skin dry with the towel. Clean your baby's hands and under his arms with further pieces of cotton wool and clean his nappy area likewise.

If your baby dislikes washing

If your baby finds it upsetting the first few times you wash him, try talking to him in a soothing voice or singing as you do it. He will soon come to regard being washed as part of his everyday routine.

UMBILICAL STUMP

You should be aware that the stump from your baby's umbilical cord will remain attached to his tummy for around the first ten days after the birth. It gradually dries up and then eventually detaches by itself, leaving your baby's belly button.

Keep the stump clean and dry while it dries up. This is vitally important to prevent it from becoming infected, so you should wash and dry the umbilical stump area thoroughly every day.

If you want, you can use special antiseptic wipes and powders to help dry up the umbilical stump. These may be supplied either by your hospital or community midwife, or you can buy them yourself from a pharmacy (your doctor, health visitor or pharmacist will advise you on what product to buy).

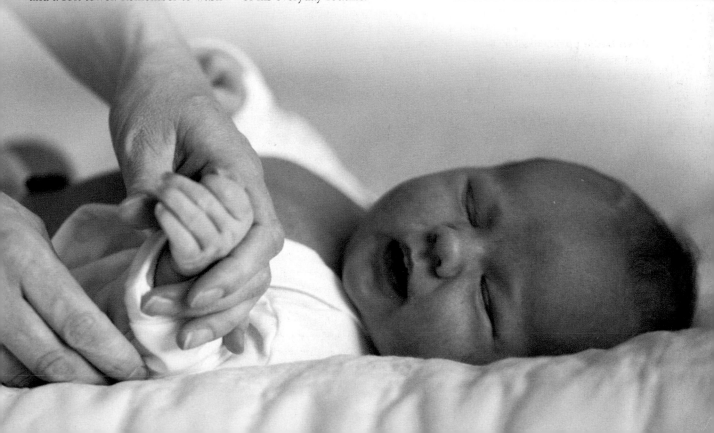

WASHING YOUR BABY'S HAIR

Even if you bath your baby every day, you do not need to wash his hair more than once a week. To do so, wrap your baby in a towel and hold him along your forearm, so that your hand supports his head. Hold him over the bath and gently wash his hair with the bath water. Baby shampoos are not necessary until your baby is a little older and has more hair. When you have finished, pat his head dry with a soft towel.

LOOKING AFTER YOUR BABY'S TEETH & NAILS

Your baby will not start teething until he is around 6 months old, although it is not unusual for babies to remain toothless during the whole of their first year. As soon as the first tooth does appear, you must begin your baby's dental care. Clean his teeth with a dampened piece of gauze or a baby toothbrush, using a tiny spot of children's fluoride toothpaste on them. Keep his finger and toe nails short using nail clippers or small scissors.

CLOTHING & BEDCLOTHES

Babies cannot regulate their body temperature very well for the first few weeks, so it is particularly important that they do not become too hot or too cold. At this stage, your baby should wear one more layer than you are, unless it is very warm weather. A vest, stretch suit and cardigan should be sufficient indoors, although you may want to wrap a cotton, cellular blanket or shawl around him as well depending on the temperature of the room. He should never wear a bonnet indoors.

Gradually, your baby will gain greater control of his body temperature, so dressing him in one more layer than you will become unnecessary. Outdoors, in cold weather, make sure his head, hands and feet are well covered, as a vast amount of body heat is lost through the head, in particular.

Cotton clothes are best because they offer warmth and breathability. Wool clothes, such as cardigans and bonnets, may prove too scratchy for an infant because his skin is so sensitive. Clothes made from synthetic fabrics, such as fleeces, are less breathable, so they may make your baby sweat in hot weather and, in cold weather, will retain the heat less well.

The ambient room temperature, particularly of your baby's bedroom, should be 18–20°C (66–68°F) and you should never put your baby to sleep near a fire or source of heat. Rather than duvets, use sheets and blankets, since these prevent overheating (see pp.28–29).

As with clothes, the best fabric for bedding is cotton because it is breathable yet warm, and you will probably find that a sheet, plus two or three cellular blankets, are sufficient for keeping your baby warm at night. If you are not sure whether he is too hot or too cold, feel the nape of his neck, which provides a good indication of his general temperature.

If you think your baby may be a little cold, it's best to put another cotton blanket on him rather than another item of clothing, and avoid turning up the heating in the room.

BATHTIME

Whether you had your baby in hospital or at home, you should have been shown how to bath him. Despite this, you will probably be all fingers and thumbs the first few times. Fathers are notoriously terrified of dropping or injuring their newborn, yet it is crucial that they get used to bathing him from the outset. Otherwise, they will have no confidence and will soon devolve this task to the mother. This is a shame, especially if the mother is breastfeeding, as bathing a baby can be a very pleasurable experience – as well as being of great help to the mother.

Handling your baby in the bath

Babies like firm handling and are a lot tougher than you think. Hold your baby securely under his far armpit by reaching around behind his back, thereby allowing his shoulders, neck and head to rest along your forearm. This frees up your other hand to wash him or grab anything you need, such as a towel.

It is very important to hold your baby at all times while he is in the bath, at least until he is able to sit up. Even then, you should never leave your baby unattended, even for a split second.

Babies feel quite slippery when they are wet, so baby baths can be useful because they are compact and there is less room for your baby to move around in. Using a baby bath also places less strain on your back, because you are not reaching down into a large, adult bath when you wash your baby.

Bathing your baby

When you are bathing your baby, don't put any bubblebath or soap in the bath water, because these will have a drying effect on your baby's already sensitive skin. Using an emollient bath oil or a very mild hypoallergenic baby bath oil is all that is required.

Bathtime should be a fun time, even if your baby seems anxious or nervous about it at first, so remember to talk and smile a lot throughout. Some babies will be more at ease at first than others, but all will get used to having a bath, however much they protest at the beginning. When he's old enough, give your baby toys to play with. It also helps if you allow plenty of time for the bath and don't rush.

As your baby gets older, you can get him used to having water on his face or head or having water splashed around him. Don't try this until your baby is confident in the bath, though, or it may frighten him. Many parents like to share a bath with their baby. This is a wonderful experience, which babies usually love and which is safe from birth. Wash his face and hair beforehand. Use your baby's bath product and make sure that the temperature of the water is right for your baby, which may be a little cool for you.

Having fun

Bath toys can make bathtimes much more fun and appealing for babies. Look out for brightly coloured boats and bath books; anything that provides a distraction can help.

When your baby is slightly older and is able to hold things, include plastic beakers that he can use to pour water from one to the other or on himself.

Whatever games you are playing, remember to always hold your baby securely when he is in the bath. Never leave your baby or young child unattended in the bath.

TIPS FOR HAPPY BATHTIMES

When you bath your baby, keep the bathroom and the room in which you will dress and undress him nice and warm. Newborns get cold very easily and that, together with their frequent dislike of being undressed, often means they cry a lot during bathtime in the early days.

Wear clothes you don't mind getting wet when bathing your baby – you may get wet too.

You should wash your baby's face using cotton wool before he is in the bath (*see* Topping and Tailing, *p.33*). Similarly, you should wash your baby's hair beforehand (*see* Washing Your Baby's Hair, *opposite*). Remember that you don't need to wash your baby's hair more than once a week.

Before you put your baby in the bath, gather anything that you will need around you, such as a towel and any toys you may want to include, so that they are within easy reach.

Test the temperature of the water with your elbow, as it is more sensitive than your hand. The bath water should feel warm rather than hot. Never add hot water to a bath while your baby is in it.

If your baby cries whenever you give him a bath, be reassured that most babies outgrow their dislike of baths quite quickly. He will soon come to see bathtime as an enjoyable occasion he shares with his parents.

FIRST WEEKS

THE FIRST WEEKS WITH A NEW BABY ARE USUALLY HECTIC, exhausting and intensive. You are slowly getting to know your baby and adjusting to the enormous changes that she has brought to your life. For the first few weeks, there is often no pattern to your days or nights, but during that time your baby is developing from being a sleepy newborn into an alert infant.

What to expect

Your baby can respond to the world around her as soon as she is born.

After the first few weeks, some of the reflexes your baby was born with, such as the Moro (startle) and walking reflexes, will have almost or totally disappeared.

She will still be able to focus only a short distance away but will be able to follow you around with her eyes. She will close her eyes in response to bright light or seek out a darker area to look at. It is very rare for babies to be significantly visually impaired, but if by about 6 weeks old there is little sign that your baby is doing the above things, mention it to the doctor at the 6-week check (*see opposite*).

Your baby will be startled by loud noises and will also be soothed by the familiar sound of her parents' voices. She may turn her head if she hears them. If your baby seems surprised to see you because she has not heard you approach, or if she is not reacting to loud noises or voices, mention it at the 6-week check, even if she had her hearing screened at birth.

ADOPTING A ROUTINE

Whatever anyone tells you, it is unusual for a baby to be in any sort of routine before she is 6 weeks old. Bottlefed babies may be feeding more regularly and sleeping for longer stretches than their breastfed peers, but it will still be difficult to predict how long those stretches will be and when the next bottle is due. So if your baby still feeds or sleeps very erratically by this stage, do not despair. This is very common and things will gradually settle down, especially if you want them to.

When should I start?

Although 6 weeks is often the time when people start talking about establishing routines, it must be emphasized that this is only an approximate guide and is not cast in stone. It merely coincides with the time when your baby will have her first full check-up, during which her general development will be assessed by a doctor.

After the first few weeks, you can start to adopt a daytime and evening routine, although there is no precise ideal time to start. The best time is simply when you feel able to. If you are breastfeeding, you are probably feeding on demand, although hopefully by now your baby is feeding efficiently and not taking more than about 20 minutes per feed. If you are bottlefeeding, your baby should be having six bottles a day and is probably drinking reasonably speedily at this stage.

She should also not be taking too long to settle after each feed, so that she can either have a sleep or, if she does not seem tired, a little play. Even young babies like company and lying on their own in a bed or pram can get lonely and boring. You can lay your baby out on the floor on a playmat, so that she can enjoy moving her arms and legs about in an unhindered way.

By about 6 weeks, your baby will also be considerably more alert. You can sit her slightly propped up in a reclining baby seat so that she can see and react to what is going on around her. Don't let her sit up this way for more than about 15 minutes and never put the seat on a raised surface – she could bounce off.

NAPTIMES

You should be aiming for your baby to have a morning and an afternoon sleep, even though this is a pattern that may not establish itself until she is a little older. Don't worry that, by sleeping twice during the day, your baby will not be tired at night. The reverse is often the case: a baby who is deprived of sleep during the day becomes overtired and finds it hard to settle at night.

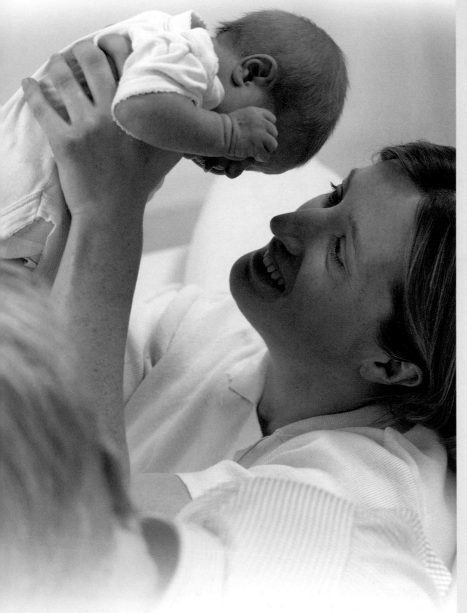

6-WEEK CHECK

When a baby is about 6 weeks old, she will receive her first check-up since birth. This is usually separate from the 6-week check that the mother receives. Your baby's check-up will usually be done by your GP but may be done by a paediatrician.

Your baby will be examined and a number of things relating to her general development will be assessed. These include her size, weight and head circumference. The doctor will also check her sight and hearing, her reflexes, her heartbeat and her hip alignment.

Her hip alignment is checked because some babies are born with congenital hip dislocation, which means that the hip joint is unstable and the hips can become dislocated. It is usually treatable if detected in infancy, but if left untreated the child will limp in later life. Girls are more prone to having congenital hip dislocation than boys.

If your baby is a boy, the doctor will check to make sure that his testicles have both descended completely into the scrotum. If they have not descended by the 6-week check, you may be advised to wait another few months, because undescended testicles often descend on their own during this time.

If your baby was born prematurely, this will be taken into account when the doctor assesses her development.

The 6-week check also gives you the chance to discuss with the doctor any concerns you might have about your baby's growth or her general progress.

BEDTIME

You can also start to introduce an evening routine (*see p.30*), which will eventually help your baby recognize that it is time to go to bed. Evening baths have the benefit that they tire a baby out as well as help develop bedtime cues, making her more ready to sleep.

To help you establish a routine, both day and night, you could try keeping a note of feed and sleep times. This will identify any emerging patterns – both good and bad – and will show you clearly when you are progressing in the right direction.

Although you should accept that no routine can always be applied rigidly – parents who fail to realize this soon become very tense and frustrated – it is also true that babies like routines. Babies with little pattern to their daytime or night-time sleeps often become poor sleepers. If you are happy with this, it's fine, but otherwise establishing a routine can benefit all concerned.

WEANING

WEANING YOUR BABY IS AN IMPORTANT STEP in his healthy development and involves introducing him to foods other than breast or formula milk. This is usually done when he is around 6 months old, and, although it is often a messy business, it can also be a fun time for parents and represents another milestone reached.

Finger foods

Once your baby is old enough to start feeding himself (usually around 8 months, when babies begin to explore things with their mouths), you can try giving him the following finger foods:

Small pieces of steamed vegetables, such as carrots. Don't give small round vegetables such as peas or sweetcorn, as these could cause choking.

Small pieces of soft fruit, such as bananas or ripe pears. Don't give whole grapes or any fruit with pits or pips, since these are choking hazards.

Raisins, but limit the amount because these have a laxative effect if eaten in quantity.

Breadsticks and rice cakes, which are also good for dipping.

Rusks, but make sure they do not contain sugar.

Small pieces of toast, which can be spread with any number of foods, including puréed vegetables. Toast can also be used for dipping.

WHEN TO START

The Department of Health recommends that babies shouldn't be weaned before the age of 6 months. Until he is 6 months old, your baby can receive all the nutrients he needs from milk (ideally breast milk) and only after that time will he need additional food. Certainly before 4 months his digestive system is immature and not able to cope with certain foods, so feeding him solids is more likely to trigger an allergic reaction or lead to the development of eczema, asthma or hay fever, which are allergic conditions.

You will know when you should start to wean your baby because he will still be hungry after a full feed, he will be increasingly hungry between feeds, or he will wake up hungry in the night.

Solids should not take the place of milk, as your baby still needs to drink at least 600 ml (1 pint) of breast milk or formula a day until he is 1 year old. So you must make sure that any food he eats allows him to drink his bottle or breastfeed sufficiently to maintain this intake.

Ideally, homemade food is better for your baby than anything you buy ready prepared. Ready-prepared food, even if it is the best quality, has a less distinct taste than homemade and is smoother. Your baby will get used to this and may

in turn become a picky eater who does not like chewing on what could be called "real" food.

INTRODUCING SOLIDS

Start by introducing solids once a day at a particular meal and continue with this pattern for a few days until your baby seems to have got the hang of eating. Once he is eating well at this meal, you can

introduce solids at another meal, until your baby is having the equivalent of three meals a day, plus his usual quantity of milk.

Many parents start by giving baby rice as the first food. This is bland and can be mixed with a little breast or formula milk to be as liquid as you wish. You will need only a tablespoonful at first.

Once your baby is ready to move on from baby rice, you should introduce him to a variety of fruit and vegetables (*see* First Foods, *right*) that you have cooked by boiling, steaming or microwaving and then puréed. Do not add fat or salt; your baby doesn't need them. Freeze the food in ice cube trays and then put the cubes in labelled freezer bags. You will soon find that you are able to cook a week or so of meals in about an hour.

HELPING HIM FEED HIMSELF

From about 8 months, your baby can hold his own bottle and start to drink from a cup with a spout, although many babies still like a bedtime bottle or breast feed for some time, since it calms them.

At about 8 months old, babies also start putting all sorts of things into their mouths, edible or not, and become keen to start feeding themselves. This may involve using a spoon or their fingers. Both methods are messy at first, but babies who are allowed to feed themselves often become less fussy eaters when they are older.

To encourage your baby to feed himself, eat with him whenever possible and give him finger foods (*see box, opposite*) or foods he can eat with a spoon.

FIRST FOODS

The following represents the sorts of food you can safely give your baby around the age of 6 months.

Around 6 months Potatoes, courgettes, sweet potatoes, carrots, cauliflower, broccoli, green beans, leeks, apples, pears, bananas (ripe, uncooked).

If you are in doubt about any other foods, you should speak to your health visitor.

After 6 months, your baby's digestive system will be more settled, so you can slowly start to introduce a wider range of foods.

From 6 months Mashed peas and other pulses, dairy products such as full-fat yoghurt (do not give cow's milk as a drink yet), chicken, red meat including liver (introduce between 6 and 9 months), wheat-based foods such as bread or pasta.

From 9 months Tomatoes, red fruit, citrus fruit, grapes, fruit that has kernels such as plums and peaches, fish (but no shellfish).

From 12 months Eggs, cow's milk (as a drink).

Some of these new foods, such as kiwi fruit, will be raw, so offer only tiny amounts the first few times; they may upset your baby's digestion a little. Give small amounts of all new foods and wait 24 hours to see if there is any physical reaction.

FOODS TO AVOID

Certain foods are to be avoided during your baby's first year (and, indeed, beyond) because they are nutritionally poor or positively unhealthy. Others should be avoided because they are known to cause allergies in susceptible babies, particularly if you, your partner or close relatives suffer from allergies.

Nutritionally poor or unhealthy foods

Foods with a high salt content, such as crisps and ready-prepared adult foods, should not be given because they could be harmful to your baby's kidneys. Sugary foods, such as cakes and biscuits, have little nutritional value and only serve to give your baby a sweet tooth.

Conversely, low-fat foods should be avoided as well. Children need fat in their diet because it provides instant energy and allows them to metabolize certain essential vitamins. As long as your baby has a steady weight gain, you should not concern yourself with cutting down on fat. For this reason, children should drink only full-fat milk until they are 5 years old.

Special diets

If you are raising your child on a vegetarian or vegan diet, you need to be particularly vigilant that he is getting all the vitamins and minerals required for the correct development of his bones, muscles, nervous system and brain. People following vegan diets are particularly at risk of vitamin deficiencies. Since calcium and vitamin B12 (both of which are essential for proper growth) are only found in animal products, you should consult your doctor or a state-registered dietitian to ensure that your baby is following a balanced diet.

Allergenic foods

At birth, your baby's immune system is not fully developed. If you or your family have a history of allergic tendencies (such as asthma or eczema, for example), your baby may react adversely to certain foods if they are given too early.

An allergic reaction occurs when the immune system feels under attack and produces antibodies to counteract the foreign substance. The most common allergenic foods are eggs, nuts, sesame seeds, soya, wheat, fish, shellfish and cow's milk.

Eggs should be avoided during the first year. After that, start with a quarter of a well-cooked egg, then proceed to a half and then a whole egg. Do not give scrambled or whole eggs at first.

Nuts and sesame seeds are an increasing problem for many children. Ideally, wait until your child is at least 3 years old before

introducing any nuts or seeds, slowly, to his diet. Before this, or if your child has a known allergy to nuts, read food labels carefully, since nuts, seeds and their oils are ingredients in many prepared foods.

Fish should not be given until your baby is around 9 months old – when you do introduce fish make very sure that there are no bones in it. Shellfish should be avoided until he is at least 2 years old.

When is it safe to give milk?

Cow's milk should not be given as a drink before your child is 1 year old, since it is the most common cause of food allergy in infancy. However, giving your baby yoghurts, small amounts of cheese and other such dairy products in small quantities is acceptable. Do not switch to soya milk without the approval of your GP, because your child could also be allergic to soya.

If you suspect that your child has an intolerance or allergy (the latter causes an immediate, severe reaction), consult your GP right away. He or she will arrange for tests.

WEANING QUESTIONS & ANSWERS

How much food should I give my baby?

At first, one tablespoonful (one ice cube of food) will be enough. Your baby will soon progress to eating 2–3 tablespoonfuls of food per meal. After that, your baby's appetite will be your best guide. You should try to give him mostly non-sweet foods because his taste buds will naturally prefer sweet foods and he will not need much encouragement or practice to get used to them.

How do I space out milk and solids during the day?

Most parents find that it works best if they alternate solids with milk. Typically, at about 6 months, their baby's meal patterns will be as follows:

Early morning:	milk
Breakfast:	baby rice or cereals
Mid-morning:	milk
Lunch:	solids
Mid-afternoon:	milk
Supper:	solids
Bedtime:	milk

Gradually, your baby will drop one of his milk feeds, usually the mid-morning or mid-afternoon one (this often coincides with dropping one of his daytime naps). However you choose to space out milk and solid feeds, do ensure that, for the first year, your baby continues to drink 600 ml (1 pint) of breast milk or formula a day.

When should I introduce lumpy food?

After 6 months, your baby is able to eat lumpier food, even if he has no teeth. You will be amazed at how efficient his gums are at chewing on bits of food. However, never leave your baby unattended when he is eating lumpy food because he can easily choke on a small piece, especially once he is old enough to feed himself with finger food.

To introduce lumps, instead of puréeing the food, mash it up with a fork and, later, chop it up into small pieces. Homemade food will feel lumpier than ready-prepared lumpy food and will train your baby to chew more effectively.

What should my baby drink?

Water is the best drink (use cooled, boiled water for the first 6 months), because it is thirst-quenching and not harmful to teeth. Many babies do not take to the taste of water after drinking milk exclusively, which is slightly sweet. So do persist by giving your baby regular little sips. Eventually, most babies get used to the taste of water.

What if my baby refuses to drink plain water?

If your baby really does not like water and starts to become dehydrated (he will become constipated), you can dilute some fresh fruit juice half-and-half with water. You should avoid giving commercial baby juices because these are sweetened and bad for your baby's teeth. Filtered water can be used if it has been boiled and cooled after filtering. Bottled water with a low mineral content is also fine.

Is it all right to give my older baby snacks between meals, or should I insist that he eat only "three square meals" a day?

Older babies and small children burn up a lot of energy, but they are usually unable to eat a large amount of food at a single sitting. Snacks can be useful for keeping a small child's energy levels up and preventing the fussiness that can come from being hungry. Having said this, don't expect your child to eat up his dinner with gusto if he's just had a snack an hour or two beforehand! Good snack foods include pieces of soft fruit, breadsticks, rice cakes and cubes of cheese.

GETTING OUT & ABOUT

ONCE YOU HAVE SETTLED INTO A RHYTHM WITH YOUR BABY, you will begin to want to go out. You don't need to rush into doing so but you can start, at your own pace, to go for walks, meet with friends and maybe join clubs and playgroups where you can meet other parents with young babies. This social contact will help you as well as your baby.

Equipment

There are many different ways to take your baby out and about with you.

Slings

These are good for young babies. They leave your hands free, so they are good when shopping. Babies feel secure and often sleep in slings, but their heads do need to be supported. On the other hand, slings can be bad for a parent's back. Around 3–4 months, a baby can put strain on the mother's back, in particular.

Back carriers

These are good for slightly older babies, once they can hold their heads upright. Back carriers are useful in places where pushchairs won't go, and leave the parent's hands free. However, back carriers can be bad for a parent's back once children are 2–3 years old.

Pushchairs and buggies

There are many different models of pushchairs and buggies. All-terrain large-wheeled versions and "travel systems" incorporating a car seat are now available. Traditional pushchairs are often cheaper and offer more flexible seating arrangements.

BENEFITS FOR YOUR BABY

Even young babies like variety and can easily become bored. If they never see anything other than the four walls of their home and the same old toys and faces, they can become restless, whingy and unstimulated.

Simply taking your baby for a daily walk will be of benefit to her. Unless it is really very cold, you can take her out in almost any weather. Make sure she is wrapped up well against the cold, put a rain cover over her pushchair if it is raining (or snowing!) or, if it is hot and sunny, protect her with a sunshade, hat and total sunblock. Fresh air will stimulate her (and then tire her out) and seeing the world around her will interest her as soon as she is a few weeks old.

As well as taking regular walks, you can meet friends and family in places other than your own home. This gets your baby used to mixing with other people and used to different environments, which in turn helps her to become more sociable and adaptable, something you will appreciate as she gets older.

Enquire about what sorts of clubs, activities and playgroups you might join with your new baby. Your local library is usually a fund of information for this. Many swimming pools run parent and baby swimming groups, which are hugely popular (don't take your baby swimming before her first immunizations, however – she must have her polio vaccine before she swims). Accident-proof swimming nappies now take away the worry of mishaps. Playgroups and activities are a wonderful, safe way for babies to explore different ways of playing and interacting with other children of their age. They can develop their social and motor skills while having access to a whole range of different toys and activities that they would not necessarily have at home.

BENEFITS FOR YOU

Babies become grumpy if they are bored and so do many adults. Many women who had been working full-time before having their baby are quite shocked at how lonely, isolated and bored they can become when they are at home for weeks on end with a tiny infant.

In addition, new parents often realize that they know very few people in their area because they had been working and had not developed a network of local friends.

However much you may have thought that you would hate gatherings such as playgroups and coffee mornings, you will soon find that the parents who attend them are a lot like you and that having a baby

is a great ice-breaker. With a little effort, you will make friends with many other parents. These new-found friends can provide you with emotional and practical support and can give useful information and advice (but beware of competitive parents who boast about their baby – unfortunately there are always some of these!)

CAR TRAVEL

The law requires that your baby is strapped into a child seat when she travels by car. Only use a second-hand seat if you know it has not been in an accident.

The first size of car seat covers babies from birth to 13 kg (29 lbs) and is good for the first nine months or so. These seats are rear-facing and usually have a handle so you can take the seat out of the car and carry the baby with you without unstrapping her.

The second size covers babies from 9 kg (20 lbs) upwards and lasts until a child is at least age 2. These seats are front-facing and designed to stay in the car; fit one in the back seat for greatest safety. Never fit a car seat in a seat with an airbag.

YOUR WELLBEING

Postnatal depression affects at least 10 per cent of mothers, and around 50–80 per cent suffer from the milder baby blues. To help prevent either of these conditions from developing, it is essential for a new mother to avoid becoming isolated and lonely at a time when she might be feeling vulnerable in her new life.

Try to go for a walk on a regular, if not daily, basis. You can take your baby out with you in a pram or pushchair, or strapped into a baby sling or carrier. Fresh air and exercise will make you feel better and will lift your spirits, and will be good for your baby too.

You should also aim to have at least some form of adult contact during the day, either by seeing friends or by taking part in some sort of activity at a playgroup, club or swimming pool.

Whichever parent takes on the role of primary carer, making sure that you have sufficient adult company and variety to your day can help your mood enormously. This social contact and change to your routine will have the added benefit that you will rely less heavily on your partner for your emotional and psychological wellbeing, something that can otherwise be a cause of strain between you.

If a low mood, weepiness and feelings of inadequacy are severe or last longer than the first few months after having a new baby, consult your GP. Much can be done to treat postnatal depression, and the earlier treatment is started the less likely the condition is to become chronic.

MOVEMENT

DURING THE FIRST TWELVE MONTHS OF HIS LIFE, you will see your baby develop from a tiny infant who cannot move by himself and can barely lift his head to a child who is crawling or even walking. These first twelve months represent the period of most rapid physical and mental development in childhood and they are a fascinating time for all parents.

Childproofing

So that your baby can move around freely and gradually develop his motor skills, you need to ensure that your house is childproofed to minimize the risk of him injuring himself (see p.165).

Find a comfortable playmat that he can enjoy moving around on unhindered.

When he is on the verge of being able to sit up, do not place him in a baby bouncing chair, because he is in danger of tipping forwards out of it.

Put up stairgates at the top and bottom of stairs just before he starts to crawl.

Remove unstable pieces of furniture that he may bring down as he attempts to haul himself up on to his feet.

Bouncing chairs must never be placed on raised surfaces; only put them on floors.

Anticipate each new stage in mobility, think how it affects your home and, above all, never leave your baby unattended.

PHYSICAL DEVELOPMENT

When your baby is born, his movements consist largely of involuntary or reflex actions. He will curl and uncurl his fingers, for example when he is feeding or sleeping (the grasp reflex); he will throw his arms and legs out when he is startled (the Moro reflex); and he may curl up or kick his legs out if he is crying or in pain.

In order for his motor skills to evolve from involuntary to voluntary, his nervous system needs to develop. This "wiring" takes place from the head downwards and from the trunk outwards to the fingers and toes. The first parts of the body to develop more deliberate movements are the head and neck. The gross motor skills of the trunk and limbs develop before the fine motor skills of the fingers and toes.

Early development

By the time your baby is 3 months old he can lift his head and, if you place him on his front, he will try to raise his head by supporting himself on his arms. This position also helps your baby exercise his neck and back muscles and is a good way of encouraging him to develop new movements (but remember never to leave him unattended outside his cot or playpen).

The beginnings of movement

Your newborn infant will not be able to roll over, but he will learn to do so at any time between 2–5 months old. Since you never know when he will start, you must never leave him on his own on any sort of raised surface, whether it is a bed, changing mat or sofa.

When he is approximately 3 months old, your baby will be able to support his own weight when standing, if he is held. He will flatten his feet out and his legs will be firm. Between 3 and 6 months, he then learns to bounce up and down while standing when held.

His back gradually straightens in the first few months of his life and, when he is 6–9 months old, he learns to sit up unaided. At first, he may still topple sideways or backwards, so you will want to surround him with cushions to

ADDRESSING YOUR CONCERNS

At what stage should I be worried if my baby is still not crawling or walking?
It may be difficult to know whether there is a physical problem with your baby during his first year. It may be that he was late to sit up or that you or your partner were late walkers. If the rest of his physical development and motor skills appear to be progressing normally, there is probably no need for concern but, if his development seems generally slow, seek medical advice.

soften any fall. Soon, however, he will be sitting up confidently and gaining a whole new and exciting perspective on the world.

CRAWLING

The next stage, for most babies, is crawling. Some miss out on this stage altogether, but the vast majority will find a way of getting around that involves either crawling about on their hands and knees or shuffling forwards on their bottoms. Crawling of whatever sort usually begins between 6–10 months. (Remember that, as with all stages of child development, the figures given are simply a guide.)

Once your baby learns to move around independently, there is usually no stopping him. He soon learns to crawl frighteningly quickly and, if you turn your back for a second, he may be in a totally different place the next time you look. As a result, this stage is one of the most exhausting because you need to watch your baby constantly.

WALKING

Generally, babies need to go through one stage before moving on to the next, but there are exceptions. Some babies bypass crawling and stay sitting for months on end before getting up, virtually from one day

to the next, and starting to walk. However, most babies get the urge to haul themselves up on their feet soon after learning to crawl. So, at around 6–10 months old, babies usually start pulling themselves up on any stable – or not-so-stable – object, such as their cot bars or a chair.

"Cruising" and walking

After this, it is a small step between standing and walking, so, at around 9–15 months, most babies start to "cruise" by holding on to furniture or an adult's hands. Your baby will enjoy walking sideways around a low table or walking with you while holding both of your hands. Then, one day, he will let go and take his first few tentative steps alone. This can happen at any time between 10–20 months, the average age being around 15 months.

No amount of practising will speed up the development of your baby's motor skills. If parents were late walkers, it is likely their children will be too. A baby who walks early is no more likely to be a gifted athlete than one who doesn't. It all depends on nervous system development, and that is out of parental control.

HAND SKILLS

At birth, your baby will not be able to use her hands in any conscious way but, gradually, she will become aware that they belong to her and that they are very useful in performing a whole range of actions. These hand skills will continue to develop, not only over the first year but over the next few years as well as she develops her fine motor skills.

Safety

Babies start to put everything into their mouths from about 8 months old. This means that they have to be watched very closely because they can choke on small objects.

Keep loose change and small objects out of the way. Babies are at greater risk from things such as these than they are from picking up odd pieces of household dirt.

Buy special safety plugs for electrical sockets. A curious baby may poke something into one.

Special covers can be bought to prevent your baby from "posting" things into your video recorder.

Make sure floor-level cupboards do not contain sharp or dangerous objects. If they do, either buy child-locks or transfer the contents of the cupboard to a safer place. You could allow her access to one floor-level cupboard that contains objects she can play with. This allows you to get on with household tasks in the kitchen while your baby enjoys herself in safety.

HAND RECOGNITION
By the time she is 3 months old, your baby will have realized that she has hands. This requires her cognitive skills to develop at the same time as her motor skills – her understanding enables her to use her motor skills. By realizing that these hands belong to her, she will start to move them together.

Between the ages of 3–6 months, your baby becomes conscious that there is a cause and effect relationship between reaching out her hand and being able to hold an object such as a rattle. You can encourage her to make this connection by putting toys just out of her reach and letting her practise grabbing them. Your baby also knows how to wave her hands when she wants something, for example her bottle or a toy. Since she has now recognized her hands and is gaining control over where she puts them, she is also able to suck her thumb at will.

DROPPING THINGS
The next stage, which occurs at around 6–9 months, is when your baby learns to pass objects from one hand to another. This leads to her noticing that when she is holding something and she opens her hand, it drops. By the end of this stage, dropping things becomes a game that your baby enjoys playing repeatedly: drop the object and watch it being picked up by a cooperative adult. As a result, objects such as bottles or spoons are often used to play the dropping game, particularly if your baby is not especially hungry.

THE PINCER GRIP
Up until now, your baby has been developing the ability to hold larger objects. The gross motor skills that this requires need to be in place before the fine motor skills can progress. Between 7–10 months, however, you will notice your baby's increasing ability to use her thumb and index finger to pick up small, fiddly objects. The development of this "pincer grip" means that

everything from raisins and other finger foods to pieces of dirt, coins and beads start to go into your baby's mouth.

The development of fine motor skills coincides with the stage in your baby's cognitive development when she puts unknown things in her mouth in an effort to identify them and explore the world around her. Some babies put things in their mouths more than others, but all will go through this essential phase in their development to some degree. It should not be discouraged, unless your baby is trying to put something that is dangerous into her mouth.

If your baby uses a dummy, this can sometimes discourage her from putting things into her mouth, since she will already have the dummy in her mouth much of the time. Although this might seem like a

desirable state of affairs, "mouthing" is an important stage in your baby's development as she uses her hands and mouth to explore her world and should not be hindered. You might try making sure she has her dummy only when she really needs comfort to give her the opportunity to put other things in her mouth instead.

CLAPPING & THROWING

At 9 months, your baby can clap, and by 12 months she can throw things, which comes in useful when, out of anger or frustration, she feels like throwing her toys, spoons, plates and other objects! This is a messy period, as your baby develops both greater physical autonomy and her own independent personality.

TALKING

A BABY'S ACQUISITION OF LANGUAGE IS, for many parents, the most exciting and fascinating development of all. It seems completely extraordinary that, without any formal teaching, he learns to understand what his parents and other people are saying, sort out the complexities of a sentence and, usually by the end of his first year, utter his first few words.

Communicating

Tiny babies like adults to talk up close to them, since their eyes cannot focus very far. Older babies benefit from seeing their parents talk to them and watching their mouths move.

Babies like the speaker's face to show expression, and the smilier it is, the better.

Babies seem to prefer higher-pitched, deliberate talking; this "baby talk" or "parentese", as it is often known, is something that many people seem to do instinctively when they talk directly to a little baby.

Once your baby starts to utter sounds, you can copy them and see if he will do them back to you. This enables your baby to practise sound-making and shows him how conversations work.

Talking out loud to your baby about what you are doing is also an excellent way of teaching him about language. From about 9 months, he will also enjoy looking at simple books while you talk about the pictures.

EARLY COMPREHENSION

In many ways, the most remarkable period of your baby's language acquisition is during his first six months, when research has shown that he is able to distinguish between all the different sounds not only of his mother tongue, but also of other languages with which he has no connection. Sadly, he will lose this ability from the age of 6 months, as his mother tongue establishes itself as the system of sounds with which he is most familiar. He will then listen out for the sounds that are specific to that language and gradually start to make sense of what is being said. This is why babies who are introduced to two mother tongues from birth do not confuse them but simply sort them into separate-sounding codes.

EARLY COMMUNICATION

At birth, your baby very soon learns to recognize the familiar voices of his parents and will be calmed by the sound of them; he may be familiar with them from the time that he was in the womb. By the age of 3 months, he will be squealing and gurgling, usually with pleasure, as an early means of communication. Many babies also love to blow endless raspberries at this age, which helps exercise their facial muscles for speaking.

PREPARING TO TALK

Between 4 and 6 months old, your baby will start to babble, which involves making a repetitive consonant-vowel sound, often "goo" and "ga" (irrespective of which language he will then go on to speak). It was once thought that babbling was simply a meaningless succession of random sounds, but it is now believed that babbling represents a baby's first attempts to practise his speech.

After 6 months, your baby begins to show the first signs that he is understanding what you are saying to him. However, it is important to remember that there is considerable variation from one child to another.

First-born children may develop language skills slightly faster than younger siblings, simply because they generally have greater undivided attention from their parents. Older siblings also may ask for things that their younger siblings want or say things that they mean, saving them the trouble of having to say it for themselves. In any case, between the ages of 6–9 months your baby will start to understand when you name a familiar person, such as Daddy, or an object, such as "bottle". He may also start to understand his own name. Around this time, your baby may also start to make some single-syllable sounds, although these will not yet be recognizable words.

FIRST WORDS

By the time your baby is between 9 and 12 months old, he understands certain simple commands and questions, such as "No", "Give me" and "Where is….?". He increasingly responds to words, music and the world around him.

At this stage, your baby may often say "dada" and "mama" as part of his more expressive babbling, which can sound quite melodious, as if he is talking to himself. Babbling can also convey, with surprising effectiveness, whether your baby is happy or angry.

The first few recognizable words your baby utters can occur at any time from 9 months to when he is over a year old. Sometimes your baby creates his own first word by amalgamating two words or mispronouncing a word (someone's name, for example). The word may not be recognizably English to other people, but if he consistently uses it and you understand it, then it counts as a word as far as you and your baby are concerned.

ADDRESSING YOUR CONCERNS

My 12-month-old baby has still not shown signs of saying his first words.
First of all, get his hearing checked thoroughly. Children who are slow to speak may have an underlying hearing problem.

If he appears to understand what you are saying and is successfully communicating by other means such as pointing and babbling, then there is probably no cause for concern. It is simply taking him a little longer to sort out his language (this is especially the case with bilingual children and second or subsequent children). Some children bypass the first words stage altogether and, some months later, launch straight into uttering two-word mini-sentences.

Only if your baby seems to be slow in other areas of his physical or mental development or is not successfully babbling should you seek medical advice at this stage. You will probably have a gut feeling about whether seeking professional advice is necessary or not, although you should bear in mind that it is usually too early to diagnose any major learning difficulties when your baby is under the age of 1 year.

My 2-year-old's pronunciation of certain sounds is much less clear than her older sister's was at the same age. Does this mean there's a problem?
Again, it may be worth getting her hearing tested just to rule out any possible hearing problems. However, speech development varies from child to child, even within the same family. Most children at the age of 2 mispronounce many sounds, especially "r"s and "y"s, which are often the last sounds a child learns to pronounce correctly. At such an early age there is unlikely to be a problem, but consult your GP if you are concerned.

SOCIAL SKILLS

YOUR BABY WILL GAIN INCREASING AWARENESS of the world around her during her first year. She will learn about her own separate identity and will learn to interact with people with whom she comes into contact. Although there is not much that you can do to speed up the development of her motor and language skills, you can have a greater influence in the way that her social skills evolve.

Milestones

6 weeks Your baby may give you his first smile. Many parents believe that their baby smiles earlier than this, and recent research indicates that babies may in fact produce real smiles earlier than 6 weeks.

3–6 months Your baby will be increasingly responsive to you and your partner and will watch you with interest.

6–12 months Your baby may begin to show separation anxiety (crying and clinging) when you leave her (see opposite).

9–12 months Your baby becomes increasingly responsive to people other than her parents.

12–18 months Your baby will play alongside other babies, sometimes imitating their actions.

15 months Your baby's separation anxiety may begin to lessen, although in some babies it persists into early childhood (see p.129).

SOCIAL DEVELOPMENT
As early as 6 weeks, if not earlier, your baby will be producing her first smiles – one of the first signs that she is reacting to the world outside. By the time she is 3 months old, she will be looking at her parents with particular interest, following them with her eyes and turning her head towards them as she hears them entering the room.

Between 3 and 6 months old, she is able to play more because she is holding toys and waving her arms about. She now responds more to her parents than to other people, even those she sees regularly.

From 6 months onwards, your baby's sense of humour begins to emerge and she will start to laugh and delight in games such as tickling and peekaboo. However, between 6 and 12 months, she may also start to show what is called separation anxiety (see opposite), where she starts to cry and even cling to you if you leave her. This is normal and arises because she now has a sense of people's separate identities and of things existing outside her field of vision (that is, beyond the confines of the room).

RESPONSE TO OTHERS
By the time your baby is 9 months old, she will react warmly to people she knows and may be a little wary of those she does not. She responds to simple questions and can point and babble, so she is increasingly able to interact with other people.

Babies are usually very sociable, and the more they can spend time with other children of roughly the same age, the more they will develop their social skills. This means that, as well as learning to play with another child, rather than simply alongside, they learn the notion of sharing and exchanging toys. This is a concept that can be introduced some time during their second year.

Possessiveness
It is important for children to learn that not everything belongs to them, but don't try to introduce the idea of sharing to your child before she is ready. Also, be prepared for your child to take some time to get used to sharing. Like many other things, sharing comes more easily to some children than others.

SETTING BOUNDARIES

Babies adore cuddles, kisses and positive words of encouragement and praise. But at some stage before the end of the first year, you will also have to start saying no to her and to set boundaries on her behaviour. Children are born with no pre-set notions of boundaries, but be assured that they thrive on knowing where the limits of acceptable behaviour lie. Only you can decide what the boundaries are for your child, but by being firm and consistent in your approach whatever they are, you will give your child greater confidence and security when she ventures out beyond the immediate family group.

Loving your child means providing her with enough social awareness that she will be able to fit in with the world at large, as well as giving her the more usual marks of affection, such as cuddles and kisses, and telling her you love her.

SEPARATION ANXIETY

Separation anxiety, when your child cries and clings if you leave her, is normal but is still distressing for most parents. To overcome the hurdle of leaving a crying baby, don't make too much of the situation. Stay calm, provide a distraction such as a toy, then say goodbye quickly, without lingering – lengthy hugs give out alarming signals to your baby. She will invariably cease crying within minutes of you leaving.

Knowing you always come back, your baby will realize that she is not being abandoned. This will make her more confident and independent than a child who is never left with anyone other than her parents.

Why doesn't my 6-month-old make eye contact with me?
By this age, she should be keen to look at the world around her and to watch her parents in particular. Failure either to follow you around the room or to notice when you enter her field of vision could indicate a visual impairment. Lack of interest in making actual eye contact when you are near her and talking to her could indicate autistic tendencies (*see p.299 for other symptoms*) or some form of learning difficulty (*see p.147*). Talk to your doctor or health visitor if you are worried.

My 6-month-old baby doesn't always respond to noises around her. Is this normal?
Many babies do not always react when they hear even quite loud noises around them – it may depend on their mood. If in doubt, get her hearing checked, even if she was screened as a newborn – it may be that she can hear certain sounds but not others. Profound deafness is rare, but hearing difficulties, many of which are treatable, are relatively common. It's important to detect these early so that speech development isn't delayed.

My 12-month-old baby isn't interested in playing with other babies – is something wrong?
Babies don't learn to play with their peers until they are much older, usually between the ages of 18 months and 2 years. Up until then, babies tend to play alongside one another, often looking to see what others are doing and sometimes copying them. When the time comes, encourage your baby to interact with other children, but not before she's ready.

PLAY

CHILDREN ARE NATURALLY CURIOUS AND WILL EXPLORE the world they live in through play, particularly during their early years. One of the most rewarding aspects of having a baby is being able to play with him. This gives you the opportunity to see how his games and imagination develop over months and years and to share unforgettable memories and experiences with him.

Toys and activities

Toys are important for a baby's development, because they stimulate him both mentally and physically. Below are some toys and activities that are appropriate at different stages:

0–3 months
- Mobiles
- Baby gyms
- Musical or squeaky toys

Bold, contrasting colours and shapes are best for all of the above.

3–6 months
- Rattles and toys he can hold easily
- Squeezy, squeaky toys
- Pop-up toys
- Activity mats

6–9 months
- Bells, maracas
- Activity toys that rattle, spin, reflect
- Soft toys
- Easy-stacking toys

9–12 months
- Baby walkers to push
- Stacking and sorting and push-along toys
- Books (picture/pop-up/activity)
- Songs (with actions, especially)

LEARNING THROUGH PLAY

Play will entertain your baby, and, by broadening his knowledge of the world, will have a crucial role in developing his intelligence. There are many ways of having fun with your baby: some involve toys, some consist of physical, musical or verbal games and some simply make use of everyday household objects. Children, especially very young ones, are like sponges and they will absorb new experiences and learn from them.

A good playmat is invaluable, even if you have carpeted floors. Once your baby is 6 weeks old, buy or borrow a bouncing chair so your baby can be propped up to play on the floor (stop using it when he is on the verge of sitting up alone).

All children get tired of constantly playing with the same toys, so consider having a rota: put some toys away for a week or so while your baby plays with others, then swap these over with the ones that were put away.

Resist the temptation to give your baby toys that are too advanced for his age in a misguided attempt to make him more "intelligent". Giving him toys that are too advanced will have the reverse effect, because he will get frustrated that he cannot play with them properly and will have lost all interest in them by the time he is actually old enough to play with them.

Refrain too from finishing off a game for your baby that he is finding difficult (such as a stacking game). Unless he is getting truly annoyed, let him persevere, because this will develop his concentration and determination. Remember to praise his efforts!

WHICH TOYS ARE BEST?

From 0–3 months, your baby can't discriminate among colours but can distinguish between red and yellow more than blue and green. He prefers things that move (such as mobiles), have a high degree of contrast, and have interesting or complex contours (such as black and white patterns). He also prefers symmetrical designs and circular outlines rather than square ones.

Between 4 and 6 months, your baby will enjoy holding rattles and

other easy-to-hold toys. In particular, he will like any that he can wave around, hit or squeeze to create a sound. Place toys just out of his reach to encourage him to reach out and pick them up.

Once he is between 6 and 9 months old, your baby will probably be sitting up and crawling, and this opens up vast possibilities for play. This is the sensory motor stage and

he loves toys that rattle, spin and pop up, as well as jingly bells and maracas that he can shake. Babies also adore mirrors at this age, because they are fascinated by their own reflection. All toys will go into his mouth, as it has more nerve endings than any other part of his body and is the best way of exploring things.

When he is 9–12 months old, his added mobility and understanding of the world will mean that baby walkers that he can push, particularly those in which he can store other toys or objects, become very popular. Stacking and sorting toys, easy-to-hold building bricks and toys that can be pushed are also good.

ADDRESSING YOUR CONCERNS

My baby does not seem interested in people or playing.
You should have his hearing checked, because he may have impaired hearing that prevents him from connecting with the outside world.

Although rare, your child may have suffered some sort of damage at birth or have one of the many forms of learning difficulties. He may suffer from autism, especially if he does not seem to enjoy physical contact with you, makes poor eye contact and has slow language development.

It is difficult to form any firm judgement during the first year but, if in doubt, consult your doctor for further assessments to be arranged, although it may not be possible to provide a conclusive diagnosis at this early age. Make sure your concerns are taken seriously. If there is a problem, the earlier it is identified, the more help can be given to your child.

I don't really know how to play with my baby. What is the best way to begin?
Playing with your baby can be fun for you both, and play is essential for developing his imagination and intelligence. You don't need expensive toys to have a happy playtime.

- Play repetitive games with him and, eventually, he will mimic you.
- Play peekaboo and hiding games.
- Use ordinary objects as toys (keys, big wooden spoons, saucepans and lids are favourites, though, as ever, supervise).
- Accept that untidiness is necessary once you have a baby. Enjoy knocking down that pile of bricks!
- Going to a park is always fun and your child will meet other children too. Swings, slides and climbing frames will help develop his coordination and self-confidence.

GOING BACK TO WORK

I F YOU ARE PLANNING TO GO BACK TO WORK, you will need to weigh up all sorts of issues and do a good deal of advance preparation before deciding which working and childcare arrangement suits you best. Although, ultimately, the decision should be a personal one, outside factors such as financial considerations and social pressures can also play a major part.

Childcare

Decide what type of childcare suits your situation, whether it involves a nanny, a childminder, a nursery or a relative who can help you out. Whichever you choose, arrange it well before your return to work.

Before your baby starts with his carer, make sure he is used to taking milk from a bottle. Ideally, try to get him used to drinking from a bottle at least two weeks before you return to work.

Remember that your carer will not do things the same way that you do them, nor should you expect her to. If you do not trust your carer completely, your return to work may not go well.

Be prepared for some upset, from both you and your baby, when you first leave him, but be reassured that he will soon settle down and that you too will get used to leaving him.

Don't go in for long, tearful goodbyes or emotional reunions with your baby, which will only serve to upset you both.

PREPARING FOR THE TRANSITION

If you are organized on a practical level for returning to work, you will feel a lot calmer and the transition between being at home and returning to work will be easier.

If this is your first baby, do your research early concerning the various childcare options. If you want a nanny, start looking for one at least two months before your planned date of return. This allows time to find someone, time for her to hand in her notice to her employers and time for a handover period. For childminders and nurseries, it is never too early to start making enquiries.

If this is not your first baby, plan with your existing childcarer how she will manage the new baby along with your existing children. Routines may have to be adapted.

You should start getting your baby used to drinking from a bottle at least two weeks but preferably one month before your start date. You can still breastfeed if you are working. Either express sufficiently to cover his needs during the day (some women express at work but this is not always possible) or breastfeed mornings and evenings and give formula during the day.

HANDING OVER TO A CARER

Start noting down your baby's routine a few weeks before going back, so that the carer can have a written diary of your baby's typical day. You should also allow at least one week's "handover time" between you and any nanny you employ. This allows her to get to know you, your baby and your home. You can also show her around any local parks or playgroups and introduce her to local friends and other nannies.

PREPARING MENTALLY

Unless you are mentally ready to hand your baby over to someone else, your return to work could prove very stressful. Depending on the length of your maternity leave, you may also be apprehensive about your ability to do your job.

If possible, go in to work for a couple of hours before actually starting back. This will give you a chance to reconnect with your workplace and will make the first true day back much less daunting.

It also helps if you accept that the person who will care for your baby will not do things as you do. This does not mean that things are worse, simply that they are different. You must trust your carer implicitly. If you do not, the relationship will soon break down.

PARENTAL RIGHTS QUESTIONS & ANSWERS

How much leave can I take?
All pregnant employees in the UK can take 26 weeks Ordinary Maternity Leave, regardless of how long they have worked for their employer or how many hours they work.

You are entitled to 26 weeks Adoption Leave if you adopt a child.

If you have worked for your employer for 26 weeks by the 15th week before your baby is due, you are entitled to a further 26 weeks Additional Maternity Leave, which is unpaid.

What am I entitled to financially?
Statutory Maternity Pay (SMP) is paid for 26 weeks at 90 per cent of your average weekly earnings for the first 6 weeks, then at £100 per week thereafter. To qualify for SMP, you need to have worked for your employer for 26 weeks by the 15th week before your baby is due.

If you do not qualify for SMP, your Citizens Advice Bureau (CAB) or benefits agency can inform you about what benefits you are entitled to.

You do not have to repay SMP, even if you decide not to return to work.

When can I start my maternity leave?
The earliest date you can start your maternity leave is the 29th week of your pregnancy. You can work as late as you like into your pregnancy; there is no date by which you must start your maternity leave.

What notice must I give once I start my maternity leave?
From 15 weeks after the start of your leave, your employer can write to you asking you to confirm that you are going back to work. You must reply in writing within 21 days, stating that you intend to return to work. You can change your mind later. Writing back protects you from unfair dismissal.

Can I have time off work to attend my antenatal appointments?
You are entitled to time off work with full pay for attending antenatal appointments and hospital clinics.

I work with chemicals in my job. Am I allowed to do different work while I am pregnant?
If your job is physically demanding or dangerous, or involves working with hazardous substances, your employer must give you alternative work during your pregnancy.

Do fathers get any time off?
Two weeks' paternity leave can be taken from the date of the birth up to the eighth week after. To qualify for Statutory Paternity Pay (£100 per week), the father must have worked for his employer for 26 weeks by the 15th week before the baby is due. He must give his employer notice of the date he wants to start the leave in the 15th week before the baby is due.

Both parents can take up to 13 weeks unpaid Parental Leave per parent per child if you have worked for your employer for one year by the date you wish to take it. Leave can be taken at any time up to the child's fifth birthday.

What about further rights?
On return from maternity leave, employers are legally obliged to give you back your old job or one of a very similar level and salary.

You have the right to ask to work flexible hours or part-time. Employers can only refuse if there is a good business reason to do so.

It is illegal for your employer to dismiss you or select you for redundancy for any reason connected with having a baby.

For information on your rights, contact your local CAB or the Maternity Alliance (*see* Useful Addresses, *p.344*).

EVERYDAY CONCERNS

At some stage during his first year, your baby's health will almost certainly give you cause for concern. In most instances, the problem will be minor and can be solved by you alone. In others, you may need to consult a doctor. You will soon learn to distinguish between the different situations but, if in doubt, you should always contact a doctor – it is better to be reassured than to worry about your baby's health.

Other problems

The following conditions are also common in babies up to 1 year old and are covered in the Diseases & Disorders chapter:

Bronchiolitis, an infection of the smaller airways (see p.228)

Common cold, a minor viral infection frequent in babies (see p.221)

Conjunctivitis, an infection of the membrane covering the eye (see p.244)

Croup, a form of laryngitis that affects babies and children (see p.224)

Febrile convulsions, seizures that may occur during a fever (see p.292)

Gastroenteritis, an infection of the gastrointestinal tract (see p.254)

Gingivostomatitis, inflammation of the mouth and stomach lining (see p.247)

Hernia, protrusion of an organ through a weakness in the abdominal muscle (see p.260)

Impetigo, a bacterial infection of the skin (see p.235)

Oral thrush, a yeast infection of the mouth (see p.248)

Roseola infantum, a mild infection that causes a rash (see p.267)

Seborrhoeic dermatitis, a skin condition (see p.230)

NAPPY RASH

Nappy rash causes the skin on your baby's bottom, and sometimes in his crotch and inner legs, to become red and sore. Occasionally the skin can become blistery and infected, in which case your doctor may prescribe a mild corticosteroid cream to reduce the inflammation and perhaps an anti-infective ointment for the infection.

Babies' skin is very sensitive, particularly during the first 6 months. Ammonia, which is naturally present in the urine, as well as illness and diarrhoea, can all act as a trigger for nappy rash. Some babies are more prone to it than others, but the majority of babies will have nappy rash at some stage. Happily, babies' skin heals very quickly, so, with proper treatment, nappy rash should disappear within a few days or a week at most.

If your baby develops nappy rash, use only cotton wool and

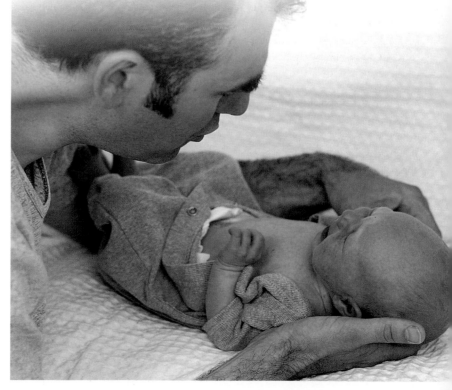

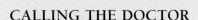

warm water to clean the area. Do not use any wipes or baby creams, even hypoallergenic ones, and pat your baby's bottom dry with a soft towel or, better still, leave it to dry naturally. Leave his bottom uncovered as much as possible. Change his nappy very frequently and immediately after every bowel motion. Consult your doctor if there is no improvement after 3–4 days.

To help prevent nappy rash, you can apply a barrier cream or petroleum jelly after each nappy change, although if you use cotton wool and water and change the nappy frequently, you may not need to do this. It is best to limit the use of baby wipes until your baby is around 6 months old.

GASTROESOPHAGEAL REFLUX

Gastroesophageal reflux (GOR) is a common problem for babies during the first year of life because the muscle at the entrance to their stomach is weak, which can cause some or all of the stomach contents to be regurgitated. The condition most often develops in the first few weeks after birth but, in most cases, babies outgrow the problem by the time they are 1 year old.

The main symptoms of GOR are persistent vomiting, regurgitation of feeds (they may dribble continuously from the mouth), crying, irritability and failure to thrive (if the problem persists). If vomit is bloodstained, see your doctor at once.

If you think your baby has GOR, consult a doctor. He or she will perform tests for a definitive diagnosis and may also prescribe drugs to help reduce the vomiting.

If your baby has GOR, place him on his side when he sleeps and raise the end of the cot so that his head is slightly higher than his stomach. During the day, put your baby in a reclining chair (or a high chair if he can sit up). Thicken his feeds with a little cornflour if the problem is persistent and severe. Give food that is more solid where possible, but do not introduce solids until your baby is old enough (*see p.38*) and make sure he does not become constipated from lack of fluids.

EARACHES

Earaches are very common in children and inflammation of the middle ear, or otitis media, is the most common cause (*see p.240*). If your baby has an earache, he may cry and try to pull or rub his ear. He may also have a fever (over 38°C/ 100° F) and may wake at night. Consult your doctor. Give your baby paracetamol to relieve the pain and lay him on his side with the infected ear down to help drain any fluid.

TEETHING

Your baby will probably cut his first tooth when he is between 6 months and 1 year old (perhaps slightly older). His final milk, or primary, teeth will emerge when he is aged around 3. Although the eruption of the milk teeth at the front of the mouth (the incisors) often causes no pain, the eruption of the canines and molars may be more painful.

When teething, your baby may develop red cheeks and sore gums and may dribble a lot. He may become irritable, cry more and sleep badly. To alleviate pain, try rubbing a teething gel on the gum, letting him chew on something hard and preferably cool (such as a special teething ring, but never place one in the freezer) and giving him liquid paracetamol. Fever and diarrhoea are never symptoms of teething.

CALLING THE DOCTOR

As a rule of thumb, trust your gut instinct: if you think there is something wrong and you are worried, call your doctor. If the surgery is shut, go to your nearest accident and emergency department, where the staff will quickly assess whether your baby needs treatment.

You should call the doctor when your baby:

- Has a fever higher than 38°C/100.4° F (invest if possible in a thermometer that takes swift accurate readings via the ear). Babies' temperatures can rise and fall very quickly and are a good gauge of whether something, however minor, is wrong.
- Cries more than usual and cannot be calmed.
- Cannot sleep, or sleeps only fitfully.
- Is unusually lethargic or drowsy.
- Has a rash.
- Is not feeding well.
- Vomits more than once during a 24-hour period.
- Is unable to keep down any foods or even water.
- Has diarrhoea or any blood in his stools or urine.
- Has sunken or, conversely, swollen fontanelles (see a doctor at once).
- Is not breathing easily (he may be wheezing or breathing unusually quickly).
- Develops a cough.
- Appears to be in pain or to have developed an infection.

Remember that babies can quickly become dehydrated, so it is important that you see a doctor very soon if your baby is persistently not taking in fluids and/or vomits repeatedly or develops diarrhoea.

FEVER IN BABIES

FEVER DEVELOPS WHEN THE BODY'S TEMPERATURE rises significantly above normal. This usually happens when the body is fighting an infection. If your baby is hot or appears listless or irritable, take his temperature (*p.328*): normal is between 36°C (97°F) and 37°C (99°F); a fever is 38°C (100°F) or above.

SYMPTOM	POSSIBLE CAUSE
Is your child under 6 months? If your child is 6 months or older and has a rash, see RASH WITH FEVER (*p.186*).	Fever in babies younger than 6 months is unusual; it may be a sign of a serious illness.
Does your baby cry and pull at one ear or wake up screaming?	Inflammation of the middle ear (*p.240*).
If your baby's breathing rate is normal, does he have a cough or a runny nose?	A common cold (*p.221*), or possibly influenza (*p.225*) or measles (*p.264*).
Is your baby's breathing rate faster than normal?	Pneumonia (*p.227*) or bronchiolitis (*p.228*).
Does your baby suffer from vomiting without diarrhoea, abnormal drowsiness, or unusual irritability?	Roseola infantum (*p.267*) or meningitis (*p.294*).
Is your baby vomiting with diarrhoea?	Gastroenteritis (*p.254*).
Is your baby wearing a lot of clothing or is the room very warm?	Your baby may have become over-heated.
Is your baby reluctant to eat solid food?	A throat infection, such as tonsillitis (*p.223*) or a mouth infection, such as gingivostomatitis (*p.247*).

DANGER SIGNS

Call your doctor at once if your baby is showing one or more of the following symptoms:

- Abnormally rapid breathing
- Noisy breathing
- Difficulty with breathing
- Abnormal drowsiness
- Irritability that is unusual for your baby

- Refusing to drink any fluids
- Vomiting that lasts for 6 hours or more, with or without diarrhoea
- A temperature that reaches above 39°C (102°F).

ACTION NEEDED

Urgent! Call your doctor at once!
Self-help Bringing down a temperature (*right*).

Get medical advice within 24 hours.
Self-help Bringing down a temperature (*right*) and Relieving earache (*p.205*).

If your child makes no improvement within 48 hours, or if he develops breathing problems or a rash appears, call your doctor.

Urgent! Call your doctor at once!
Self-help Bringing down a temperature (*right*).

Urgent! Call your doctor at once!

Get medical advice within 24 hours.

If you think over-heating might be the problem, remove some of your baby's clothing and reduce the room temperature. If your baby's temperature is not normal within one hour, or if your baby shows any of the danger signs (*above*), consult your doctor.

If no improvement in 48 hours, call your doctor.
Self-help Relieving a sore throat (*p.198*) and Bringing down a temperature (*right*).

SELF-HELP

Bringing down a temperature

When you bring down your child's high temperature, he starts to feel less irritable and more comfortable. If your child is between 3 months and 5 years of age, you are also reducing the chances of febrile convulsions (*p.292*). The following measures are for a child of any age:

- Remove almost all of your child's clothing. If he is lying in bed, take away any sheets and blankets.

- Cool your child down either with a sponge dipped in lukewarm water or in a lukewarm bath. Avoid cold water as this can raise the infant's core temperature.

- Give liquid paracetamol. Keep within the recommended dose for his age group. Ibuprofen can also be used for a child over 6 months of age.

- Keep your child's room at approximately 15°C (60°F).

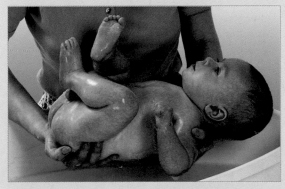

COOLING RELIEF *Give your child a bath of lukewarm water to help reduce his temperature and bring him relief from his fever.*

VOMITING IN BABIES

Y OUNG BABIES WHO VOMIT may be suffering from an illness or harmlessly regurgitating small amounts of milk. Contact your doctor at once if the vomiting continues for six hours or if the vomiting is accompanied by small amounts of dark urine, abnormal drowsiness, sunken eyes or loose skin.

SYMPTOM	POSSIBLE CAUSE	ACTION NEEDED
Does your baby seem well and feed normally but brings up a large amount of milk effortlessly?	Gastroesophageal reflux (p.57).	Get medical advice within 24 hours.
Does your baby bring up a small amount of milk effortlessly?	Regurgitation is the most likely cause. It is usually due to wind and is seldom serious.	**Self-help** Dealing with wind (p.65). Check you are not overfeeding your baby.
If your baby is under 2 months, does she vomit after every feed?	Pyloric stenosis (p.260).	Get medical advice within 24 hours.
Does your baby vomit unpredictably, have a fever, or is she either abnormally drowsy or refusing to eat or drink?	Roseola infantum (p.267) or meningitis (p.294).	**Urgent!** Call your doctor at once!
Does your baby vomit unpredictably and have diarrhoea?	Gastroenteritis (p.254).	**Urgent!** Call your doctor at once! **Self-help** Preventing dehydration (p.63).
Does your baby vomit unpredictably and have a cough?	Bronchiolitis (p.228) or whooping cough (p.269).	Get medical advice within 24 hours. **Self-help** Bringing down a temperature (p.59) and Relieving a cough (p.197).
Does your baby vomit unpredictably and produce a greenish-yellow vomit?	Intestinal obstruction (p.256).	**Emergency!** Call an ambulance! While waiting, do not give your baby anything to eat or drink.

FEEDING PROBLEMS

Parents and babies can both suffer if difficulties with feeding develop. The first few weeks after birth in particular can be difficult while breastfeeding is established. If your baby is well and gains weight normally, you need have no cause for concern.

SYMPTOM	POSSIBLE CAUSE	ACTION NEEDED
Is your baby failing to gain weight normally?	Failure to thrive.	Consult your doctor.
Is your baby gaining weight normally yet you are worried you are not producing sufficient milk?	Mothers commonly feel they are not producing sufficient milk if their baby cries a lot and seems difficult to satisfy.	If your baby continues to cry and you are concerned, consult your health visitor/doctor. See also EXCESSIVE CRYING (*pp.64–65*).
Is your baby refusing to feed when usually he is eager?	Suddenly refusing to feed may be a sign of a cold (*p.221*), but it could be more serious.	**Urgent!** Call your doctor at once!
Is your baby usually unwilling to feed but is gaining weight normally?	Some babies need to be coaxed to feed and may even fall asleep while feeding. If the baby seems well, there's no need to worry.	If other symptoms develop, consult your health visitor/doctor.
Does your baby feed more often than other babies?	Frequent feeding, as often as once every 2 hours, is normal in breastfed babies, particularly in the first few weeks of life (*see* Breastfeeding, *pp.18–21*).	**Self-help** Frequent feeds may be making you tired. Express breast milk for your partner to feed to your baby at night. If you are depressed or irritable, consult your health visitor/doctor.
Does your baby often cry at the beginning of a feed?	The breasts may not release milk immediately, or the flow may be too forceful.	**Self-help** If your milk isn't released at once, try to relax. If the flow is too forceful, express some milk before your baby starts to feed.
Does your baby often reject certain solid foods you offer?	Unfamiliar foods and textures may be rejected and even foods that were accepted initially may later be refused.	**Self-help** Keep offering a varied diet to give your baby the best chance of receiving sufficient healthy nutrients (*see* Weaning, *pp.38–41*).

DIARRHOEA IN BABIES

I F YOUR BABY PASSES RUNNY STOOLS twice or more in a row, or intermittently in 24 hours, she probably has diarrhoea. Remember, though, that the semi-fluid faeces that breastfed babies often pass is not the same as diarrhoea. Babies with diarrhoea are prone to dehydration unless you give them plenty of fluids.

SYMPTOM	POSSIBLE CAUSE
Does your baby have a fever – a temperature of 38°C (100°F) or above?	Gastroenteritis (*p.254*).
If there is no fever, has the diarrhoea lasted for 2 weeks or more, even if it has been intermittent?	A viral infection is the most likely cause. Other possible but much less common causes are allergies to food (*p.252*), giardiasis (*p.262*), coeliac disease (*p.256*) and cystic fibrosis (*p.315*).
If your baby has had diarrhoea for less than 2 weeks, has she suffered from vomiting, poor feeding or lethargy in the past few days?	Gastroenteritis (*p.254*).
Have you been giving your baby prescribed medicine for any other disorder?	Your baby's diarrhoea could be a side effect of the medicine that she is taking.
Is your baby drinking more juice than usual?	In large quantities, the sugar in fruit juice can lead to diarrhoea.
Has your baby's diarrhoea appeared within 24 hours of new food being introduced?	New foods may cause diarrhoea.
Has your baby not yet been weaned or have you introduced a new food into your baby's diet more than 24 hours ago?	Reactions to food (*p.252*) or mild gastroenteritis (*p.254*).

DANGER SIGNS

Phone your doctor immediately if your baby is showing any of the following symptoms:

- Abnormal drowsiness or irritability
- Refuses feeds for 6 hours or more
- Vomiting for 6 hours or more
- Sunken eyes
- Passing small amounts of urine.

ACTION NEEDED

Get medical advice within 24 hours.
Self-help Preventing dehydration (*right*) and Bringing down a temperature (*p.59*).

Consult your doctor within 24 hours.
Self-help Give small, frequent feeds of your baby's usual milk. If weaning, stop giving solids until your baby has seen the doctor.

Get medical advice within 24 hours.
Self-help Preventing dehydration (*right*) and Bringing down a temperature (*p.59*).

Ask your pharmacist or doctor to find out whether the medicine may be causing your baby's symptoms and whether you should stop giving it.

Always mix fruit juice with an equal quantity of cooled, boiled water. Try giving your baby cooled, boiled water instead of fruit juice. Avoid giving your baby squash.

Such episodes are usually short-lived. If it is not, or if it seems to be associated with particular foods, consult your health visitor/doctor.
Self-help Preventing dehydration (*right*). If you know which food is causing the diarrhoea, stop giving it until you see the health visitor/doctor.

Get medical advice within 24 hours.
Self-help Stop solid food until you see the health visitor/doctor. Preventing dehydration (*right*).

SELF-HELP

Preventing dehydration

Water is a vital fluid which must always be replaced after it leaves the body. When a baby loses more water than she is taking in, then there is a danger of her becoming dehydrated. Dehydration is extremely serious and may result from conditions such as persistent diarrhoea, a fever, or from vomiting for 6 hours or more. In each case, it is important to give extra fluids. Consult your doctor if you are in any doubt about which rehydrating solution is best to use.

- The best way to give your baby the extra fluids she needs is as an oral electrolyte rehydrating solution, such as Dioralyte or Rehidrat. You can buy these over the counter without a prescription.

- You can prepare your own rehydrating solution at home: dissolve 2 level teaspoons of sugar in 200 ml (7 fl.oz) of water which you have first boiled and then left to cool. Use this temporarily until you can buy the oral rehydrating solution.

- Every baby needs to drink between 500 ml (18 fl.oz) and 1500 ml (53 fl.oz) of fluids each day. Exactly how much fluid depends on the baby's weight – see the table below to find out how much fluid to give your baby every day.

- Be sure to give your baby small amounts of the rehydrating solution every 1–2 hours for as long as she shows symptoms of diarrhoea.

- If your baby's diarrhoea is accompanied by vomiting, give her even smaller amounts of rehydrating solution every hour – anything more may be regurgitated.

THE FLUIDS YOUR BABY NEEDS

BABY'S WEIGHT		DAILY FLUID INTAKE	
kg	lb	ml	fl.oz
under 4	under 9	500	18
4	9	600	21
6	13	900	32
7	15	1050	37
8	18	1200	42
9	20	1350	48
over 10	over 22	1500	53

EXCESSIVE CRYING

CRYING IS THE WAY THAT BABIES COMMUNICATE THEIR NEEDS. If they are hungry, thirsty or irritable they simply cry. You soon grow accustomed to what your baby is trying to tell you. However, if the crying persists despite your efforts, or if it sounds unusual, consult your doctor.

SYMPTOM	POSSIBLE CAUSE
Does feeding your baby stop the crying?	Hunger is one of the most common causes of crying in a young baby.
If your baby's crying is unusual, was he reluctant to take the last feed?	Your baby may be in pain as a result of a disorder, such as inflammation of the middle ear (*p.240*).
Has there been a change in household routine or increased tension at home?	Your baby may be unsettled because of the change in routine or increased tension.
Is your baby comforted by a drink of cooled, boiled water?	Thirst may be causing your baby to cry excessively, especially if he is bottlefed or if the weather is particularly hot.
When you burp your baby, does he stop crying?	Wind (*p.17*).
If your baby is under 3 months, does he cry in late afternoon or early evening?	Evening colic (*p.25*).
If your baby is 3 months or older, does he stop crying when you pick him up and give him your full attention?	Your baby may need more comforting and parental reassurance than other babies of the same age.

CRY BABY *Crying is the most effective way your baby can attract your attention. You soon learn to recognize whether the cry is urgent or not.*

ACTION NEEDED

Self-help If your baby stops crying after a feed, you may need to reduce the intervals between feeds to keep up with the demand.

Urgent! Call your doctor at once!

Self-help During a period of domestic upheaval, give your baby extra attention. If your own tension could be upsetting your baby, try to eliminate the cause. Having more time to yourself, using relaxation techniques, or talking over problems with friends or relatives may be helpful. If you are feeling angry or resentful at your baby's crying, consult your doctor.

Self-help Give your baby extra drinks of cooled, boiled water from a sterilized bottle or spoon.

Self-help Dealing with wind (*right*).

Self-help Feed your baby first. You can then try to calm him by rocking, by patting his back, or by massaging his abdomen.

Self-help Cuddle your baby as often as he wants; there is no risk of "spoiling" your child at such a young age.

Dealing with wind

If your baby cries just before a feed, or if he feeds greedily, he may take in air which will irritate him when it is trapped in the intestine. The following tips may either prevent wind or help to release it:

- If you are bottlefeeding, make sure the hole in the teat in the bottle is unblocked and the right size.

- Let your baby lie in a semi-upright position when he feeds so the milk falls to the bottom of his stomach.

- Burp your baby after every feed to release any trapped air. Either hold him against your shoulder or sit or lie him face down on your lap. Calm him by rubbing him or patting his back.

WINDING YOUR BABY *After every feed, move your baby to a different position, such as upright against your shoulder, so that any wind can be released.*

Calming your baby

Hands-on techniques
Some therapies that use gentle manipulation can relieve problems that may be making your child cry excessively. See osteopathy (*p.323*), chiropractic (*p.323*) and craniosacral therapy (*p.324*).

Homeopathy
Colicky babies may respond to homeopathic remedies (*p.321*). If your baby's symptoms are relieved by firm pressure on the stomach, then try Colocynth 30C. If your baby is impossible to please but improves when carried try Chamomilla 30C.

Sound
A recording of a rhythmic sound, such as your heartbeat (or even the vacuum cleaner) may settle your baby.

SKIN PROBLEMS

YOUR BABY'S SKIN IS SO SENSITIVE it can easily become inflamed or irritated. If the inflammation or irritation does not fade naturally, or if it is accompanied by any other symptoms, consult your doctor. If your baby seems unwell with a fever, see RASH WITH FEVER (*p.186*). If there's no fever, see SPOTS AND RASHES (*p.184*).

SYMPTOM	POSSIBLE CAUSE	ACTION NEEDED
If your baby is under 3 months, does she have an inflamed, scaly rash in two or more of: neck, face, groin, behind the ears or armpits?	Seborrhoeic dermatitis (*p.230*).	If the rash does not clear up within a few weeks or if it is extensive or weeping, consult your doctor.
Does your baby have a scaly, itchy rash on the face, insides of the elbows or behind the knees?	Atopic eczema (*p.234*).	If the rash is extensive, weeping, very itchy or upsetting, consult your doctor.
Does your baby have crusty yellow patches on the scalp?	Cradle cap (*see* Seborrhoeic dermatitis, *p.230*).	If the crusts are extensive or if other symptoms develop, consult your health visitor/doctor.
Does your baby have inflamed spots on the genitals or anus?	Nappy rash (*p.56*).	If the rash lasts for over 10 days or if the skin breaks or ulcerates, consult your health visitor/doctor.
Does your baby have spots or blotches anywhere on the body yet is well and feeding normally?	A minor skin irritation.	If the rash lasts for over a day or if your baby becomes unwell, consult your doctor.

SELF-HELP

Relieving itchiness

If your child scratches her itchy spot, an infection may develop. The following tips may help discourage her:

• Herbal creams, gels or ointments – for example, calendula, chamomile and aloe vera – are very effective on dry, itchy skin, while liquids and lotions are better for oozing lesions.

• When bathing your child, use a non-irritating substance, such as a water-based (aqueous) cream, a baby soap or a special oil. Make sure that the water is not too hot.

• Dry skin may mean itchiness is more severe. Moisturize the skin several times a day with an emollient, such as a water-based cream.

• Clothe your baby in natural, not synthetic, fabrics.

SLOW WEIGHT GAIN

I F YOU AND YOUR CHILD ATTEND A BABY CLINIC on a regular basis, you will be able to keep a close eye on how well your baby is putting on weight. The clinic may have standard growth charts which can help you if you are worried about your baby's failure to put on weight as expected.

SYMPTOM	POSSIBLE CAUSE	ACTION NEEDED
Does your baby seem unwell?	An underlying disorder may be responsible for your baby's failure to thrive and gain weight normally.	Consult your doctor.
Has your baby started on solid foods?	You may not be giving enough solids to meet all your baby's nutritional needs.	See your health visitor/doctor, who may recommend that you make changes to your baby's diet. *See also* Weaning, *pp.38–41.*
Do you mainly breastfeed whenever your baby cries?	You may not be producing enough milk to provide all the nutrients your baby needs. At 6 months your baby should start on solids.	See your health visitor/doctor, who may recommend that you offer your baby supplementary bottles or start him on solids (*see* Weaning, *pp.38–41*).
Do you mainly breastfeed or bottlefeed your baby according to a routine?	Insufficient milk may be responsible for your baby's failure to gain weight normally.	If there is no normal weight gain within 2 weeks, see your health visitor/doctor. **Self-help** Offer a feed when your baby cries, not in a strict routine.
Could you be adding too much water or too little milk formula to the bottle?	If feeds are too diluted, your baby may not be receiving enough nutrients.	If there is no normal weight gain within 2 weeks, see your health visitor/doctor. **Self-help** Always follow the instructions for making up feeds.
Does your baby always finish the entire contents of the bottle?	Your baby may need more food than the amount you have been offering him.	If there is no normal weight gain within 2 weeks, see your health visitor/doctor. **Self-help** Allow your baby to have as much milk as he wants. At 6 months your baby should start on solids.

RAISING A HEALTHY CHILD

As your child grows from babyhood into childhood, you'll be able to interact with her on an increasingly equal basis. You'll also find that new questions arise concerning her physical, emotional and social development. This chapter is designed to help you find your own answers to these questions.

GROWING UP

ALTHOUGH A CHILD'S RATE OF GROWTH IS VERY RAPID during the first year of life, it slows down considerably in the second year. Children's rates of development in other areas vary from child to child within a range of what is considered normal. Your child's general development will be checked at certain ages to make sure that all is well.

> "...a rough rule of thumb is that a child is likely to be about half his or her adult height at age 2"

GROWTH

A child's final height tends to be a reflection of her parents' heights, regardless of whether she was large or small at birth. Tall parents tend to have tall children, and shorter parents, shorter children. A very rough rule of thumb is that a child is likely to be about half his or her adult height at the age of 2.

But height isn't the only growth change that occurs after the first year. Your child's head, which at birth was only about one-third of the size of an adult's, is almost full size by the age of 2. Muscles are stronger, bones have become less flexible, and the heart strengthens and becomes more proficient at pumping blood so that the heart rate decreases and blood pressure increases. Digestion of food is more efficient and the immune system, which is persistently challenged over the first year of life, is now stronger.

Studies over the years show that children have been getting taller – better nutrition, smaller families and improved living conditions having played their part. Today, 5-year-olds are, on average, 7–8 cm (3–3½ in) taller than 100 years ago. A child's growth isn't consistent either – it tends to happen in spurts, with children growing more rapidly in spring and summer than in autumn and winter. One study among 7- to 10-year-olds in the UK showed that between the months of March and July they grew three times more quickly than during their three months of slowest growth.

In between periods of growth, the body seems to rest, hardly growing at all. Children also tend to grow more at night, because higher levels of growth hormone are secreted during sleep. The rate of growth can sometimes be as much as 1.5 cm (½ in) in one night. For some children, growth at night can lead to periods of restless sleep. You should ensure that your child gets adequate sleep throughout childhood.

Rates of growth

Apart from the rapid growth in the first year, and a growth spurt around mid-childhood, both boys and girls grow at a steady rate of around 7–8 cm (3–3½ in) a year. Just before puberty, this slows to around 5 cm (2 in) a year, with boys typically being a little taller than girls. (For girls, puberty usually begins at around 11 years of age and for boys at around 12 years.) During the growth spurt that takes place in puberty, both boys and girls grow about 30–45 cm (12–18 in), generally reaching mature height by age 16 in girls and age 18 in boys. Not only do girls begin puberty earlier than boys, they tend to grow fastest at the beginning, while boys grow fastest in the last third of puberty. This means that for around two years, girls are often taller than boys of their own age.

Pre-puberty growth

In the years leading up to puberty, many girls carry a little extra weight, often referred to as "puppy fat". With the rapid growth that occurs at puberty, this extra weight soon disappears. For boys, rapid growth may make them appear underweight for a while, before they fill out. In both cases, this temporary ungainliness may give rise to the typical self-consciousness teenagers feel about their bodies. Many teenagers need extra sleep during this period. While boys tend to develop enormous appetites during puberty, girls may have a tendency to become weight-conscious and picky about food. For healthy growth, both boys and girls need regular, nutritious meals, without too

IS MY CHILD'S SIZE NORMAL?

There is a great variation in what is "normal" in terms of a child's height, and although most children follow the normal pattern of growth, there can be individual variations within this. Height is largely an inherited characteristic, and if both parents are tall or short, you can expect their children to be similar heights as adults. However, if you have a tall mother and a short father, for example, initially the baby's birth size will probably reflect the mother's size. During the first two years, the child's true genetic height, inherited from both parents, will emerge.

After the first year, a child's height is of more importance than his weight when it comes to detecting growth problems. A child may lose some weight during illness and growth in height may halt briefly, but after health returns there is usually catch-up growth.

If your child seems consistently small for his age as compared to his peers, or appears shorter than you might expect for your family, it's worth monitoring him for a short period and then consulting your doctor. Measure your child accurately several times over a six-month period, and record it on a growth chart (you can ask for one at your doctor's surgery, or contact the Child Growth Foundation; see Useful Addresses, p.344). The height of a child with growth delay may not appear low on the chart, but the growth curve won't run parallel to the one on the chart. Monitoring your child's height will give an accurate summary of your concerns when you visit the doctor, which will help to ensure that your concerns are taken seriously.

many snack foods and fizzy drinks that contain empty calories. In particular, adolescent boys and girls need an adequate intake of calcium from milk, yoghurts and cheese to promote healthy bone growth. This is especially important for girls to help reduce the risk of developing osteoporosis (brittle bones) later in life.

Growth delay

Around 3 per cent of children are up to two years behind the average for their age in terms of growth, with boys being affected by this ten times more frequently than girls. In addition, children with asthma or eczema seem more likely to show a pattern of growth delay. Although this delay in growth may occur in early childhood, it also may not happen until the time at which puberty is expected. Growth delay may be a family trait, with a parent or other family member having had a similar problem at puberty. For the majority of children with delayed

growth there is no reason other than being a late developer, and they will catch up in time.

However, there can be a number of other reasons why a child's growth may be delayed, including a range of hormonal deficiencies that need treatment. These problems can't be identified without referral to an appropriate specialist doctor for specific tests, which may include X-rays of the bones of the wrist to assess the child's bone age and blood tests to check hormone levels.

Some children may have a dietary deficiency, such as anaemia, or a problem absorbing food, such as coeliac disease. These children will have other symptoms as well, including listlessness and feeling generally unwell. Rarely, psychological distress can affect the production of growth hormone and so affect growth, but levels of distress have to be quite severe for this to happen. In these cases, normal growth resumes once the distress has been alleviated.

TOILET TRAINING

"Toilet training" is a bit of a misnomer, because you can't "train" any child to use a potty or the toilet until she is physically ready. Toilet training is only possible when your child is physically able to control the muscles of her bottom and bladder, which mature between roughly 18 and 30 months of age. For this reason, it is only after the age of 2 at the earliest that you should begin to consider toilet training. It's also worth noting that girls tend to be earlier than boys in their readiness for toilet training.

When should I start?

When your child's bladder is large enough to hold a reasonable quantity of urine and she is aware that she has been passing urine or having a bowel movement, then toilet training should be straightforward. It's also important that she is willing to learn. It's a good idea to have a potty around and available in the bathroom for some months before your child is likely to be ready, since this allows your child to get used to sitting on it. She may even occasionally manage to use it successfully, which is a good basis from which to start.

In addition to being able to control her bowel and bladder muscles, there are other skills your child has probably been developing that will come in useful during toilet training. Can she remove her tights or trousers and pants without help? Is she able to sit down on the potty and get up again easily? Is she able to tell you she needs the potty? All these things will make it easier to be successful when the time comes.

Studies have shown that many children who begin toilet training before the age of 18 months aren't

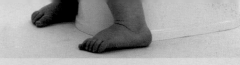

completely trained until after the age of 4, whereas those who started at around 2 years old were completely trained before their third birthday.

Once you have taken the first step of replacing nappies with pants, you may want to use training pants for a while. However, these can still feel rather nappy-like, so you may find that you have more success moving straight to ordinary pants.

You will also need to give your child regular reminders that she might like to use the potty. Having asked, don't sit her on the potty unless she says yes; otherwise, she won't make the connection for herself. Sometimes she may say no, and two minutes later realize she

does feel the urge to go. Although this may be stressful for you both, it's actually better, because in spite of your reminder your child is feeling the urge and then deciding for herself.

Some accidents are inevitable, but if your child is ready to manage without a nappy, these should be few. If they do occur, gently remind her what the potty is for, change her, and make no fuss. Reacting negatively may make your child resentful and less inclined to try. Work on the principle of praising her efforts and successes and ignoring accidents as far as possible. If, after a week's effort, you find that no progress has been made, go back

HOW TO START TOILET TRAINING

Start looking for signs that your child is ready to manage without a nappy.

- Has she seen you or other family members use the toilet?
- Is she aware of passing urine or having a bowel movement, even when wearing a nappy, and does she tell you?
- Does she sit on and try to use a potty, perhaps before her bath in the evening?

When you feel your child is ready to start learning to use the toilet, the following tips may help.

- Avoid times when your child is coping with changes in her life: a house move, a new baby, or some other change to her life. It will be easier in the end for both of you without additional stresses.
- Make sure you have a potty that is easy and comfortable to sit on. For boys, it's helpful to have one that has a higher splashguard at the front.
- For a boy, you will also have to help him understand that his penis needs to point inside the potty to be successful. It's very easy for a boy to sit down quickly without checking and find he is weeing outside the potty, which is very dispiriting!
- Explain to your child that without nappies she will need to use the potty. Modern nappies are designed to prevent the child from feeling wet, so it may not be until your child is nappy-free that she can really make the connection between wanting to pass urine and what it feels like. Be aware that you may have to tolerate several "accidents" before this becomes clear to your child. If your child is not making progress after a week or so, try going back to nappies for a short time and try again later.

"...being handled
and touched is
important to babies
and children. It gives
them a sense of their
physical existence"

to nappies for a few weeks. It may
be that she isn't yet developmentally
ready. It's less frustrating for you
both if you take a break and try
again in a few weeks. Remember
that around 15 per cent of children
aren't trained by age 3, and 4 per
cent are still not trained by age 4.

Even when your child is happily
out of nappies during the day, she
may still need a nappy for naps or
night-times, but you can introduce
the idea of doing without by getting
her to use the potty before going
to sleep. She may well have a dry
nappy as a consequence, especially
when she wakes from her daytime
nap, and you can praise her. If she
is waking in the morning regularly
with a dry nappy, then you can
probably try going without at night.
Make sure you have a protective
waterproof cover for the mattress,
and that there is enough light at
night for her to be able to manage
to use the potty or toilet alone.

SENSORY DEVELOPMENT

Although your child was born with
all her senses – sight, hearing, taste,
touch and smell – it is only through
their use after birth that they
continue to develop and mature
fully. Sensory development depends
on stimulation, which creates the
necessary neurological pathways
to enable their further development.

Touch

Although the sense of touch is by
no means fully developed at birth,
it is more advanced than your child's
sense of sight, hearing or even taste.
Being handled and touched is very
important to babies and children. It
gives them a sense of their physical
existence and also helps the
development of the nervous system.

A fully developed sense of touch
is dependent on nerve endings that
can differentiate between, for example,
touch and pressure or acceptable
temperature and pain. Touch also

helps a baby understand the physical world and develop tactile sensitivity and motor skills. As every parent will notice, the mouth is very touch-sensitive in a young child, which is why it is used to explore physical objects. Even at 5 years old, a child's face is still more touch-sensitive than her hands, although using the hands to explore will have become second nature by this age. By her first birthday a child can process information from touch four times faster than she could at birth, and by age 6 her ability is almost on a par with that of an adult.

Touch is also an extremely important form of non-verbal communication that can comfort a toddler in a tantrum, an 8-year-old with a bruised knee, and a disappointed teenager. The experience of being cuddled and cherished physically helps promote a child's emotional development as well as general health and growth.

Smell

After touch, smell is the most developed sense at birth and is important for a baby who can hardly focus beyond about 16 cm (8 in). Smell is a useful ability for early recognition and bonding between parent and offspring. It has also been shown that young children prefer the smell of their siblings to that of other children, which helps create a special sibling bond. Familiar smells add to a child's sense of security, and this can partly explain the attraction of a favourite soft toy or blanket.

Taste

Even quite young children will show definite and sophisticated tastes for different foods if given the opportunity to try them. Babies show a natural preference for the sweetness of breast milk, which is nutritiously advantageous. It also allows the possibility of other flavours to filter through from the family foods eaten by a breastfeeding mother. Taste helps stimulate salivation, swallowing and tongue movements, which are all important for learning to eat solid food later. Distinguishing between the four different tastes – sweet, sour, salty and bitter – occurs over time as your child experiences different foods. However, there remains in most of us a natural inclination to sweet and high-fat foods which, like breast milk for babies, have calming properties.

Hearing

Hearing is quite advanced at birth, because your child has had about 12 weeks' actual listening experience in the womb. The mother's voice is the most familiar and reassuring sound to a baby after birth.

The development of hearing has a number of different aspects. One of the first to mature is sensitivity to higher and lower frequencies of sound, followed by being able to locate where a sound is coming from. Younger children find it difficult to distinguish specific sounds against a noisy background. In fact, this is something to bear in mind when your child is learning to talk – if she doesn't get enough one-to-one conversation, with no background noise, her language development can suffer. Make sure you have quiet times when you talk to your child without the television or radio on in the background. Hearing improves until puberty.

Sight

Sight is probably the sense that is least developed at birth, because the eyes need to see things in order to develop and for the brain's ability to interpret images to mature. The eyes' muscles also need to strengthen.

ENCOURAGING CONCENTRATION

Your child's ability to concentrate will take a long time to mature fully, although there is much that can be done to encourage it.

- Alternate busy, more boisterous activities with quieter times, whatever the age of your child.
- Choose a time when your child is contented and more likely to focus on a one-to-one activity.
- Turn off background noise, such as the television or radio, to reduce distractions.
- Select one toy and put the rest away so your child isn't distracted.
- Choose an activity suitable to the attention span your child seems currently capable of achieving and try to complete it.
- Engage your child's attention by asking questions and talking about what you are doing.
- Listen to what your child says and respond appropriately so she knows you have heard her.
- Choose activities relevant to the age of your child, which may include looking at or reading a book together; doing a jigsaw puzzle; playing "I Spy"; doing dot-to-dot puzzles; building with a construction toy; painting a picture.
- Avoid the temptation to over-assist your child, allow her time to try to work things out for herself.
- Encourage her to complete an activity, and praise her efforts.

Some children are by nature more active than others, and this is normal. But there are a number of children whose continued poor concentration needs specific help. If you think your child has a problem concentrating, first check that there is no health problem such as overtiredness or hunger. Keep a diary noting specific behaviours and then consult your doctor for advice.

One of the first aspects of the eyes to develop is their ability to work together. The ability to see detail takes longer to develop. We refer to normal adult vision as being 20/20 vision. The bottom figure means that someone with perfect vision can see detail at 20 feet; the top figure means that the person tested can see that amount of detail at 20 feet as well. Babies are born with 20/600 vision and so are very short-sighted, with some development needed before the eyes reach maturity. Colour vision takes time to develop too. But by the end of the third year, colour vision has matured and the development of visual nerves is complete, although many children continue to show a slight degree of short-sightedness until around 10 years of age.

DEVELOPMENTAL CHECKS

Sight and hearing require particular checks because of their impact on other aspects of physical and intellectual development.

Sight checks

Your child's eyes will be checked at each health review, carried out at 6–8 weeks, 6–9 months, 18–24 months, and before she starts school, at around 4 years of age.

Although babies sometimes seem to have a squint (strabismus), as they develop the ability to use the eyes together it should disappear. However, it's important that a squint doesn't linger or develop in a baby or an older child. A squint must always be treated; although it won't damage the eye itself, it will affect the development of the brain's visual centre and can affect a child's vision permanently if left untreated.

Unless there is a family history of sight problems at an early age, regular vision checks probably aren't essential until your child is school-age. However, have your child's sight checked regularly once she starts school, in case she needs glasses for school work. Wearing glasses as a child will not weaken her vision as she grows up.

Hearing checks

Some babies have their hearing checked at birth before they leave hospital. All babies have their hearing carefully assessed at each health review, but particularly at 6–9 months. This is because being able to hear clearly is essential to the development of speech. And given that during early childhood it's difficult for children to distinguish specific sounds against a noisy background, hearing problems need to be identified.

Slight deafness may be caused by something as temporary as a blocked ear due to a cold. Repeated ear infections and the condition known as glue ear, in which a persistently blocked ear impairs hearing (see p.241), need prompt treatment.

If you have any concerns about your child's hearing, you should discuss them with your GP or health visitor as soon as possible. Even if there is nothing wrong, it is better to be reassured.

DEVELOPMENT OF CONCENTRATION

The development of concentration comes more easily to some children than to others, but it's worth encouraging early because it is essential for learning.

The attention span of a young child is naturally short and is easily affected by tiredness, hunger, thirst or being unsettled in some way. Young children also have a lot of energy and may find it difficult to settle, but it's worth encouraging even quite young children to focus on a particular activity briefly.

Parents will notice short periods of focused behaviour in their baby, encouraged by talking and playing one-to-one. But it's not until towards the end of the first year that the area of the brain responsible for concentration, the frontal lobe, is sufficiently developed to make a difference to a child's attention span. At the same time, her ability to ignore things is developing too.

Some children, when they are school age, may show continued poor concentration and need help to gain the skills they need to concentrate for longer periods. It's important to address any problems early because concentration is essential to learning and schoolwork.

ATTENTION DEFICIT HYPERACTIVITY DISORDER (ADHD)

Below is a list of symptoms that may be associated with ADHD (see p.299). Bear in mind that many pre-school children who do not have ADHD exhibit these behaviours and later outgrow them as they mature; ADHD is not normally diagnosed until a child is school-age or older.

- Clumsiness
- Irritability and deliberate disruptiveness
- Impulsiveness
- Poor sleep pattern
- Fidgety, aimless activity
- Inability to sustain concentration for any length of time
- Difficulty with doing things in sequence, like dressing
- Aggressiveness and social ineptitude
- Poor self-esteem

If you think your child may have ADHD, consult your GP, who can arrange the appropriate investigations.

PHYSICAL SKILLS

Bᴠ ᴛʜᴇ ᴇɴᴅ ᴏꜰ ᴛʜᴇ ꜰɪʀꜱᴛ ʏᴇᴀʀ, ᴍᴏꜱᴛ ʙᴀʙɪᴇꜱ ʜᴀᴠᴇ the physical strength and motivation to move to the next stage of developing their "gross motor skills", learning to walk and then to run, jump and hop. As a child grows older, developing a range of physical skills through imaginative and active play and dressing herself will help her develop self-confidence and independence.

ABOUT MOVEMENT MILESTONES

We use milestones as a marker for developmental stages, but all children are individual, so while one child might walk at 10 months, another might not be ready until 14 months or later. Both are within the normal range. What is true about milestones, however, is that all children follow the same sequence of development even if they reach their milestones at slightly different stages. Quite literally, you can't run before you can walk!

It's also worth remembering that some children are, by nature, much more physically active than others, which in turn influences their rate of physical development. The quieter, more contemplative child may simply have less motivation to charge about and so have less inclination to get on with walking. So encouraging a balance of activities, alternating more active games with quieter ones, is important for all children.

Try not to be too anxious as your child moves towards greater mobility. She will need to feel your confidence in her ability to be able to manage new activities in order to feel confidence in herself. Encourage her competence and offer assistance only when it is needed, rather than imposing it on her.

"...progress is individual, but all children show the same sequence of development...you can't run before you can walk"

Walking
Before walking, your child has probably practised standing upright, holding on to you or the furniture. Supported by you, she has probably taken practice steps, all of which help strengthen the leg muscles in preparation for independent walking. These practice steps, often taken by side-stepping from one piece of furniture to another (sometimes referred to as "cruising"), are useful preliminaries to independent walking.

The next stage in walking is to balance unsupported. Your child is likely to be a bit wobbly at first while she adjusts to the new sensation of standing upright alone. If standing upright feels too insecure, she will probably sit down suddenly to avoid toppling over. Eventually, with feet planted wide apart, toes pointing outwards and arms raised to the sides to aid balance, she will take the first few steps unaided. These are inevitably a bit cautious and the whole attempt may end with your child suddenly sitting down or toppling into your arms, but progress from here is usually fast.

Running
Early walking has a certain lurching momentum, which isn't quite the same as deliberate running. Initially

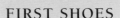

the "go" mechanism in the brain is more effective than the "stop" mechanism, so toddlers tend to launch themselves into walking at speed, then sit down to stop. With practice, as she finds her centre of gravity towards the end of the second year and her legs are less widely spaced, walking becomes easier to control. Prior to running effectively, your child also has to learn to stop, start and change direction. Once her leg muscles strengthen and her coordination improves, running becomes more natural. You'll probably find that your child will be running by the end of her second year.

Jumping

At 2 years of age, your child may try to jump, but somehow her feet don't quite leave the floor! You may find that jumping on a springy surface, such as a small trampoline while holding onto the rail, is easily done. Jumping off a low object, holding your hand, may also be manageable. By 3 years, with practice and as muscles strengthen, your child can master jumping easily. At first your child will tend to raise her feet high when she jumps, bending her knees to take the impact when she lands.

Hopping

Like jumping, hopping requires muscle strength before it is manageable, but also requires greater balance. Even standing on one leg requires adjustment for balancing in a more lop-sided way and takes practice. Start by encouraging your child to hop from leg to leg, which isn't too far removed from jumping, and then to try hopping on one leg

FIRST SHOES

While your baby is learning to walk, it is easier for her to have bare feet. Close contact with the surface on which she is walking provides a greater sense of stability, which is lost when feet are in shoes. Allow her lots of opportunities for safe, barefoot exploration; if you must put her in shoes, choose the softest ones and make sure they have non-slip soles.

Proper shoes only become necessary once your child begins walking outside, and then her feet need to be accurately measured and shoes properly fitted. If your child is walking confidently before shoes are fitted, the adjustment to wearing shoes is easier. Avoid first shoes that have hard, unyielding soles.

before swapping sides. Your child will probably be able to hop before she can stand still on one leg.

Standing on tiptoe

Standing and walking on tiptoe is another way to challenge and assist the development of balance and coordination. You will probably find that your child naturally stands on tiptoe in order to reach or see something more easily. She may not even realize she is doing it. Towards their third birthday, most children can stand and then walk on tiptoe.

Kicking a ball

At first your child's balance isn't good enough to give a ball a hefty kick, and it's more a case of pushing the ball a distance with the foot. By 3 years of age, if given regular opportunity, most children can kick a ball some distance and will generally favour one foot for kicking over the other. This is normal. Just as we are right- or left-handed, we also tend to be right- or left-footed.

Throwing and catching a ball

Throwing a ball isn't possible until babies have learned to let go of an object deliberately, which usually happens towards the end of the first year. You may not want to encourage your child to throw things until she is old enough to understand that some things can be thrown but others can't! Catching a ball is harder than throwing one because it relies on hand-eye coordination. You will probably notice that when your child first practises catching a ball, she will hold out both hands but keep her eyes on your face, in anticipation of what will happen rather than watching the ball. Again, these are skills that require practice, and some children are more naturally skilled and coordinated at these activities than others. But by 3 years old, most children can catch a ball from a short distance, as long as it is a reasonably large size.

Climbing stairs

At 2 years old your toddler can probably manage the stairs, placing two feet on each step and supported by the banister or wall. The big difference at 3 years is that she can probably walk upstairs using alternate feet, although coming down she may continue using two feet on each step, supported by the wall or banister. It's worth encouraging your child to manage stairs safely to avoid accidents, but you should discourage her from carrying anything on the stairs while she is learning to cope with them.

DEVELOPMENT OF FINE MOTOR SKILLS

Fine motor skills refer to those that develop in the hands and arms. What began with your 2-month-old swatting at a toy has progressed considerably by the end of the first year, but there's a still a great deal more development to come.

For example, whereas to start with your baby would tightly grasp a toy in her fist until she dropped it accidentally, releasing the toy becomes deliberate. Around her first birthday, she can use her hand to pick something up, move it from hand to hand or to another place, and let it go. Simple though this seems, it is an important new skill, giving her more control over her environment. This grasping of objects now begins to refine into the ability to use the fingers and the thumb to pick up an object, and then the ability to use just the thumb and forefinger, known as the pincer grip. You will probably notice your child's development of the pincer grip in the increased efficiency with which she can manage finger foods, although eating with a spoon may still be difficult (and messy!).

At birth babies have developed very few bones in the wrist, restricting movement. As these bones grow it becomes easier to

make a twisting movement with the hand, so at around 15 months your child will have greater dexterity in her hand movements. By 18 months she will also be able to hold objects between the thumb and fingers and let go voluntarily. This means she can place objects such as building bricks one on top of the other and manage simple tray puzzles. Developing hand-eye coordination also contributes to success in activities such as these.

More sophisticated hand movements, such as poking, squeezing, rolling and twisting, are being practised as your child plays, especially with something like play dough. At 2 years old, being able to hold a crayon or marker pen means that scribbling on paper, the forerunner to drawing and writing, is an exciting new activity. It is also

at this stage that hand preference (the hand your child consistently uses for things such as throwing, scribbling and using a spoon) becomes evident. Handedness is genetically determined, and although small children will continue to swap hands for some activities, the use of the dominant hand soon becomes consistent.

At 3 years old a child should be able to manage to eat with a spoon and fork, dress herself (with help with buttons and laces), play with construction toys designed for her age group, thread large beads on a string, and copy simple line patterns, such as a cross, with a crayon on paper. All these activities both demonstrate and encourage manual dexterity, on which greater skills, such as doing up buttons and using scissors, will be built.

"...your child's increasing mobility coincides with a greater desire for independence...you should work towards instilling a sense of caution in your child"

SAFETY

With your child's increasing mobility and instinct to explore the world, safety issues emerge that need consideration. It can be an exhausting time for parents while a child's intellectual ability catches up with her physical ability and she can understand some of the safety measures you need to enforce. Your child's increasing mobility also coincides with a growing desire for independence, leading to a battle of wills which, when it comes to safety, you need to win!

While it's essential to take standard precautions to avoid hazards, you should also work towards instilling a sense of caution in your child, on which she can build her own instinct for self-preservation. This includes allowing your child to try things, with your guidance, to help her understand why some things are unsafe.

It's also important to establish those rules that are non-negotiable. At first it's simplest to say to your child that she must simply follow the rules, for example about car safety, which apply to everyone. As your child grows, you can explain more fully why we take the precautions to keep safe, reinforcing the message at every opportunity.

You will need to repeat information again and again, as young children's memories and lack of experience mean they won't necessarily take it on board the first, or even the second or third, time.

Toys and safety

As your child becomes increasingly coordinated and mobile, she will begin to do things such as riding a bike (with stabilizers at first), a scooter or a skateboard. These are all lots of fun and learning to use them correctly will increase your child's confidence as well. However, it's vital that your child always wears appropriate safety equipment, especially a helmet, when participating in these activities. Make it a non-negotiable rule that your child must wear the right safety equipment before riding her bike, scooter or skateboard.

"Stranger danger"

The unfortunate truth is that children are more at risk from people they know than from strangers. Introducing the idea of a "stranger" can be unnecessarily scary and ineffectual and may also reduce your child's confidence, so it's better to establish some straightforward rules that apply to every situation.

• Teach your child from an early age that she must never go anywhere with anyone, even a friend, without checking that it's all right with her parent or carer.

• Tell your child that only good secrets should be kept, like birthday surprises. Anything that feels wrong should be shared with you and you will never be cross with her for telling you something.

• As your child grows, discuss what behaviour in another person might make her feel uncomfortable so she can learn to trust her instincts.

• As soon as she is old enough (about age 5), teach your child your home phone number and address. Check periodically that she can still remember them.

KEEPING YOUR CHILD SAFE

Road safety

Accidents to child pedestrians tend to occur when they are crossing the road. A young child cannot judge distance or speed effectively and can neither see nor be seen above or around a parked car, all of which make roads extremely hazardous. So from the earliest opportunity, even when your child is still being pushed in a buggy, start explaining about road safety. With luck, by the time she is around 8 years old and ready to start crossing roads alone, it will be second nature. Here are some important road safety rules to teach your child.

• Always use a zebra or pedestrian crossing to cross when available.

• Even at a zebra or pedestrian crossing, wait to be sure the cars stop. Otherwise you can't be certain that the driver has seen you.

• For children too young to cross on their own, always stop when you reach the kerb and only cross holding a grown-up's hand.

• Stop, look and listen before crossing. When teaching your child about road safety, ask her to tell you if she thinks it's safe to cross, which helps her learn to concentrate.

• Avoid crossing roads in between parked cars, which obscure vision.

• Wear light-reflecting strips on your coat in winter.

Safety in the car

If your child is correctly restrained in the car, she is 90 per cent less likely to be killed in an accident, so use of a child seat or seat belts is a must even on the shortest journeys. Holding a child on your lap is never a safe option.

• As soon as your child is old enough, encourage her to take responsibility for her own seat belt. However, you should always check that it's secure, and praise her efforts to be safe.

• Child locks come as an option on most cars now, so make sure that yours are on.

• Make it clear that buttons and handles in cars are not for play.

Safety in the garden

While the garden can be an enjoyable place to play, make sure it's safe. Any access to a road should be securely gated, with a lock if necessary. Any pond, no matter how small, must be fenced or covered, and children in paddling pools should always be supervised. Any garden utensils, including garden chemicals, must be stored securely out of reach of children.

• Make it clear to your child that she must never eat any garden flowers, leaves or berries, as many common garden plants (such as laburnum and yew) are poisonous.

• Encourage your child to wash her hands after playing in the garden, and especially before eating.

Safety in the kitchen

A kitchen can be hazardous, but it's also where a child is likely to spend time. So it is necessary to teach important safety rules and take steps to keep the kitchen as safe as possible (see p.166).

• Demonstrate what's hot so your child understands why it's important not to touch. Don't rely on her to remember this, though, and keep all hot dishes, kettles and appliances well out of her reach. The same applies to sharp implements.

• No running in the kitchen should always be the rule.

Water safety

Small children should never be left unattended around water, no matter how shallow. Never leave a child alone in the bath, even for a few seconds. Fit garden ponds with a mesh grid or fill them in, and supervise children in paddling pools.

THINKING
& UNDERSTANDING

CHILDREN ARE PROGRAMMED TO LEARN. They learn through trial and error, exploration, interaction, quiet times and making mistakes. Young children learn primarily through play, and they learn best when they are relaxed and having fun. Older children should be encouraged to do their homework on their own as far as possible, and to take responsibility for getting it done.

> "...bear in mind that a balance between physical activity and quieter activity is important"

HOW CHILDREN LEARN

Providing learning opportunities for your child doesn't mean that you need a large number of educational toys, or that you must do structured activities. Understanding roughly the stage of development your child has reached, and meeting her need for activities that engage her and enable her to practice new skills, demands a certain amount of commitment and input. In the long run, though, this commitment pays dividends when your child becomes happily absorbed in an activity after you have shown her how. There is no point having an excess of colourful plastic building bricks if you don't show your child what she can do with them. Bear in mind, too, that some children need more input than others to stay focused, and that achieving a good balance between physical activity and quieter activities is important.

Your child doesn't need a huge number of toys, but what she does need are play materials. These include materials that allow her opportunities to express herself, develop her fine motor skills, and extend her imagination: crayons and paper to scribble on, old clothes for dressing up, modelling clay and building blocks, all of which will allow her the chance for exploration and discovery.

Children also learn by imitation. Long before they can understand the meaning of what they do, children imitate the behaviour of others. They then apply meaning later. Imitation also allows the beginnings of imaginative play, which is an important component of learning because it aids creativity, problem-solving, and role-play and enables a child to imagine how other people feel in different situations. All of these things contribute to a child's emotional development as well as to her learning.

Learning social skills

Playing with other children will help your child learn about social interaction with her own peer group. Unlike adults, children make few allowances for another child's behaviour, so it's an opportunity to learn how to negotiate and compromise, how to be assertive and handle rejection, and how to make friends and have fun. These important social skills can only be learned by spending time with other children. Some children find it more difficult to learn these things than

Apart from enjoying books, there are other activities that contribute towards the development of the skills your child needs in order to read. Remember that these are games and should always be fun for your child, when she is old enough to enjoy them. If your child grows tired of the game and doesn't want to play it any more, stop and do something else.

Listening Talking one-to-one, playing Chinese whispers.

Memory Action rhymes, nursery rhymes, memory pairs.

Shape recognition Jigsaw puzzles, simple games such as picture lotto and other games that involve matching shapes.

Sequencing Games that depend on putting a series of items in the correct order, such as putting a pack of playing cards in order. These games are better for an older child.

Sound recognition Playing "I Spy" using letter sounds for objects.

others, and in any case your child will probably need some help from you at first to develop ways to deal with social situations. Showing your belief that she can manage and enjoy friendships will help your child feel confident that she can do this.

Regular one-to-one interaction with you is important, especially for language development in a younger child. Although you may feel as if you are with your child 24 hours a day, there may be a lot of routine activity going on where you are not particularly "tuned in" to your child. Children need some time every day

when they are given undivided attention. Complete attention all the time would be too intense and intrusive, but for at least half an hour every day you should try to make your child the focus of your attention. During this time you could share an activity, look at a book together, talk about the day in a relaxed way, or discuss feelings or events, all of which allow your child to feel cherished. Making sure your child gets some one-to-one attention every day has the additional advantage of reducing her need for attention-seeking behaviour.

Learning and language

Language development is essential to a young child's learning. Through language your child can ask questions, name objects and express ideas and feelings, all of which contribute to her learning. And if you listen to her attentively, taking turns in conversation, then she will learn how to do that too. Try not to correct early language mistakes overtly; just repeat back what has been said, speaking correctly and clearly. Hearing words pronounced correctly will also help her later in identifying written words.

Quiet times are also important to young children. They need periods of reflection to make sense of what they learn; they are not sponges that merely absorb information. Intelligence is the ability to use what you know and to build on it, and that requires the evolution of a thinking process that only periods of time for reflection can supply. It is even important for children to be bored sometimes, because it's through the experience of occasional boredom that they can develop the resourcefulness and imagination to overcome it. Constantly providing activities and structured things for your child to do can actually deprive her of this opportunity to develop independence and imagination!

The ability to learn through experience also relies on the development of memory. One reason that young children like repetition of enjoyable experiences – of games, stories or activities, for example – is that it reinforces what has happened before and starts creating memories.

Learning in the classroom

Once your child starts school, she will begin to learn in a more formal way. Much early learning takes place in groups, so it's important for your child to know how to get along with other children. For this reason, attending a playgroup or pre-school is important. It's also important for your child to know how to listen and take turns.

LEARNING DIFFICULTIES

The term "learning difficulties" covers the full range of anything that makes learning difficult for a child. A learning difficulty may be something specific, such as dyslexia or autism, or something more general, such as developmental delay. If there's no obvious problem at birth, parents are often the first

to notice a problem in their child's development. A learning difficulty might also be identified by a health visitor or doctor during a routine check-up, or later by a teacher when a child starts school.

One of the benefits of the routine checks carried out in the first few years of life is that they monitor each milestone and when your child reaches it, which can give an early indication of any emerging problem. The earlier any learning difficulty is picked up, the better, because early intervention means a child's particular needs can be met more adequately. Sight and hearing tests are also part of these checks and are similarly important in identifying problems early.

ENCOURAGING CONFIDENCE

Confident children find the world a much easier place to negotiate, and their confidence comes primarily from feeling unconditionally loved and accepted for who they are. Confident children have an expectation that they will be able to manage, or that there will be someone to help them overcome a difficulty. Some children are more naturally confident than others, depending on their personality, but there is much that you can do to encourage confidence in your child from babyhood to teens.

Children need to know that they matter, their feelings are respected, their needs will be met and their opinions listened to, even if you may not agree with them. They need to feel your confidence in them, and to feel that they can meet your realistic expectations – a child needs to feel loved for who she is and not just for her achievements. Your child will want to please you, and will take pleasure in your pleasure, giving her the confidence to keep trying.

- Praise your child's efforts as well as her achievements.
- When she misbehaves, make it clear that it's her behaviour you disapprove of, not her.
- Never humiliate a child if she can't manage a task or activity, saying she is clumsy or stupid – she will resist trying again.
- Don't over-assist when she is trying to do something; otherwise she will feel she can't manage alone. Ask if she needs some help rather than imposing it on her.
- When accidents happen, avoid over-reacting or making it personal, and instead show her how to clear it up.
- Find an activity your child enjoys, and encourage her – succeeding at something makes her feel confident about trying other things.

- Encourage your child to speak for herself rather than always answering for her.
- Encourage basic skills, such as swimming or riding a bike, which give a child a sense of achievement and mean she can participate in activities with other children.
- When giving your child instructions, promote the positive rather than the negative. Instead of saying, "Be careful you don't spill it" say, "Use both hands and you'll be fine".
- Don't make comparisons between your child and her siblings or other children.
- Don't dismiss your child's negative feelings about something, or over-praise something she is dissatisfied with. Instead, you can offer alternatives, or suggest taking a break before the frustration becomes overwhelming.
- Try to avoid expressing your anxieties about her ability to manage alone, especially when she is facing a new situation, such as starting school or taking an exam.
- Emphasize to your child that making a mistake is an opportunity to learn how to handle a situation and not the end of the world.

What also gives a child confidence is the ability to cope with new situations. For example, being able to put on her own shoes or use a pair of scissors before starting school can help your child feel that she is competent, which will in turn give her greater confidence in trying new activities. For this reason, it's important to encourage children to manage age-appropriate tasks on their own, rather than always doing things for them. Be careful not to give more difficult tasks before they are ready.

The seriousness of learning difficulties varies widely; they are usually described as ranging from mild to moderate to severe. When a learning difficulty is suspected, accurate assessment by a specially trained doctor or psychologist is needed to clarify the type and extent of the difficulty, so that appropriate learning support can be provided. This support allows a child to reach her own potential, in spite of any limitations. Early support and help for a child with a learning difficulty can also prevent the frustrations that may arise from it, which often cause additional problems with behaviour. Around 20 per cent of children in the UK are identified as having some sort of special educational need and require extra help to manage in a mainstream school. Other children, whose needs are greater, may need to attend a special school.

READING

Encouraging your child's interest and pleasure in books from an early age is an essential precursor to reading. From the first time you sit your baby on your knee and look at a board book together, you are beginning the journey that leads to independent reading. At this stage you aren't teaching your baby to read but are simply introducing the idea that books provide a source of entertainment and information. Sharing books also provides relaxed, one-to-one time with your child, talking together, which aids language development.

An important stage before reading is being able to recognize word sounds and to differentiate between letter sounds. These abilities develop from talking with your child and not correcting her language mistakes, but repeating what she has said correctly. For example, if she points to a picture of a dog in a book and says "woof", you can say "Yes, that's a dog. And dogs go 'woof'". You could then use this as an opportunity to ask, "What colour is the dog?" which develops the conversation. Make sure there is no background noise when you are talking to your child in this way, so that she can hear your words clearly.

Your child's first books should also include a selection of rhymes, because repetition and rhyming helps develop an idea of how language – written and spoken – works. Other books include action rhymes, stories or songs. Actions help develop memory in young children who don't yet have much language – and they are also fun! You will probably find that your child enjoys the same book read over and over again, and this is fine.

It's worth visiting your local library, which will have a children's section and librarian who can help you choose books suitable for your child. Many libraries run special story times for young children.

Learning the alphabet

In due course, learning the alphabet should include learning not only the letter names, but also the letter sounds. And check the letter sounds are correct – "s" should be for sun, not snake! Although individual word recognition forms part of the way in which children learn to read, they also need to understand how the building blocks of words – the letters – work together. Use lower case letters when showing your child words, not capitals. Capital letters are too uniform in shape, while lower case letters give a word a more distinctive shape, making it easier for your child to recognize them.

"...from the first time you look at a book with your child, you are beginning the journey that leads to independent reading"

PUSHY PARENTS

While all parents want what's best for their child, it's sometimes hard to get the balance right between doing what you feel is right and following your child's inclinations. With the best will in the world, many parents know what their child needs to do to succeed but overlook what she enjoys doing. It can be very tempting to impose your own interests on your child, but if you take it too far you may end up by causing only resentment and resistance. If you always wanted to play the piano, take lessons yourself!

Homework, after-school activities and private coaching are all becoming more prevalent as children start school. For an 8-year-old to spend six hours at school, followed by additional activities afterwards and an hour's homework every night with perhaps an instrument to practise as well, is just too much. Children need freedom to relax and the personal space to develop their own ideas and interests. Encouraging your child's own interests is important, so try as much as possible to take your lead from your child.

DON'T OVERDO IT

It's worth bearing in mind how pushing a child too far can backfire.

If children's time is over-structured, they never learn to be self-motivated, which is essential to future successful learning.

Over-emphasizing the importance of meeting expectations can breed resentment and resistance, even if your child does as you ask.

A continuous emphasis on the next achievement for achievement's sake reduces the sense children have of taking pleasure in a task. Whatever they do, it isn't good enough when the emphasis is always on the next thing.

Stress isn't good for a child's health, and it shows up in physical ways such as stomach aches, poor sleep and behavioural problems.

Try not to reward children with money or material goods for success. Success should always be its own reward.

LANGUAGE
& COMMUNICATION

MOST OF US TAKE OUR CHILDREN'S SPEECH AND LANGUAGE development for granted because it seems to happen so naturally. It is a fascinating process, both because of the speed with which it takes place and because children almost seem to teach themselves. A child's early utterances are often the subject of pride and amusement as parents begin to see their young child as a person in his own right.

> "...language is essential for school 'readiness', enabling communication in both the classroom and the playground"

LANGUAGE IN THE PRE-SCHOOL PERIOD

After the acquisition of early speech and a small repertoire of single words, toddlers gradually start using two- or three-word sentences and we soon forget their early faltering steps into language. Instead we start to respond to our children as conversational partners. Of course, children in these early stages are focused on what they see or feel and cannot engage in conversations as such. But it is not long before they start to be able to comment on what others are doing, and by 4 years of age children are able to sense what other people are thinking and respond appropriately. By this age children are also using complex sentences, many of which resemble adult sentences. They continue to make errors, for example in the way they use irregular verbs (saying "go-ed" for "went" or "see-ed" for "saw"), and they often make minor errors with their speech (continuing to confuse "s" and "ch"), but these are perfectly normal steps on the road to fluency.

Language and communication are essential for school "readiness". It is often assumed that most speech and language development occurs before children start primary school (at about age 5 in the UK), and indeed for many children this is true.

By the time they enter school, children need to have developed listening and attention skills to allow them to cope in the classroom. They also need the verbal comprehension and expressive language skills to understand what their teacher is saying, to respond when asked questions and to create stories about their experiences. Children's language skills also allow them to communicate with their peers in the playground and to form the strong social bonds that are essential for a child to be happy in school. Finally, children need to develop the early literacy and numeracy skills that will allow them to go on to tackle new subjects in class, which form the foundation of the broader curriculum on which their later education will be based.

LANGUAGE & OTHER DEVELOPMENT

Sometimes people think that language and communication are separate from other things that a child does. In fact, speech and language development is closely related to your child's sensory abilities – for example, it is much

There are a few key things parents can do to help the early stages of their child's language development:

Actively engaging in the earliest communication with your baby gives the message that communication is important and makes her want to try to get her meaning across.

Helping your child listen carefully can be invaluable to early language development. High levels of background noise can make it difficult for a child to "tune in" effectively.

Limiting exposure to television and recorded music may help, since they probably don't help develop the process of listening.

Engaging in early verbal interaction with your young child and responding to what interests them, rather than talking at them, helps them focus on the meaning of words and pick out consistent patterns of sounds and words.

Once your child has started to speak, interacting with her and repeating back what she has said helps her see that what she has to say is interesting to those around her. Don't forget that young children love familiar rituals and they often want to go on repeating things that they like saying long after the adult has lost interest – so be patient.

Reading books to your child can be a useful way to help her concentrate on language. Children love to listen to an adult talking about the pictures that they are looking at. However, it is important that parents don't quiz their child on what she sees before she is ready for it.

easier to learn to speak if your child can hear and see effectively. This is not to say that children who cannot see or hear will not learn to speak, just that they will find it more difficult. Language and communication skills are also closely related to the ability to walk, manipulate objects with the fingers, play with toys and other objects, remember things and listen and pay attention. Language is related to a child's overall development, and while there can be differences in the route that children take through the process, on the whole children who are managing well in one area of development tend to do well in other areas as well.

WHERE LANGUAGE CAN GO WRONG

There are some children who struggle with the whole process of acquiring speech and language. They may not understand as well as their peers or pick words up so quickly; they may not be able to get their words out fluently and start to stammer; they may not produce the sounds at all or may mix them up and be unintelligible to everyone except their closest family members. These problems, and how to separate them from what is "normal" development, are outlined in the box, opposite. Parents may need to talk through their concerns with a speech and language professional

before assuming that there is something wrong. Having said that, early speech and language difficulties often lead to problems in school and so they need to be taken seriously.

HOW CAN I PROMOTE MY CHILD'S LANGUAGE DEVELOPMENT?

Parents may be uncertain as to whether they should "teach" speech and language to their child or whether they should just leave their child to get on with it, assuming that there is little that can be done to help. We now recognize that children are to an extent "wired" to acquire language, much as a

flower is wired to grow given water or a child is wired to reach puberty given the necessary nutrition. In the main, children do develop language and communication skills without much deliberate teaching from their parents. Of course, it is a different situation when we are talking about things such as teaching children the meaning of specific words, speaking grammatically and the use of what we consider polite expressions. Aspects of written language are also deliberately taught, for example punctuation.

Although there may be relatively little to teach about language, children always benefit from being listened to, so that they come to believe that what they have to say is important. Listening to your child will give her confidence and make her want to contribute to conversations at home and at school. It is this confidence in her own ideas and her ability to communicate them effectively that will carry her forward to being a competent communicator as an adult.

OUTLINE OF NORMAL LANGUAGE DEVELOPMENT IN THE PRE-SCHOOL YEARS

2–3 YEARS
- Good range of sounds, though may have difficulties with the sounds /f//sh//s//th/.
- Two- and three-word utterances.
- Language used for a variety of purposes – possession/assertion/refusal/attribution and so forth.
- Able to find two or three objects on request.

Seek advice if these are features:
- Single sounds only, e.g. /d/.
- Poor control of facial muscles.
- People outside the family do not understand much of what is said.
- No word combinations by age 2.
- Very restricted vocabulary.
- Unable to find two items on request by age 2.

3–4 YEARS
- Most speech sounds correct. May have difficulties with /ch/ or /j/.
- Intelligibility may decline when excited.
- Talks increasingly fluently.
- Able to refer to past and future events. Marks past tense with -ed, but may be some confusion with irregular verbs, e.g. "I go-ed to the park".
- Able to understand concepts such as colour, size etc.
- Will understand most of what a parent is saying.

Seek advice if these are features:
- Very limited repertoire of sounds – much of what is said is unintelligible.
- Non-fluency that is common in younger children persists.
- Little feeling of interaction in conversation, either because the child says very little or because the child continues to echo what is said to her.
- Restricted use of verbs/attributes.
- Comprehension outside everyday context very limited. May still not be aware of the function of objects.

4–5 YEARS
- Completely intelligible except for occasional errors.
- Grammatical errors may persist but rarely affect the meaning of what is said.
- 4–6 word sentences used consistently.
- Question forms, such as "why?", now common.
- Able to construct own stories.
- Can now understand abstract words, e.g. "always".
- Understands and can reconstruct a story sequence from a book.

Seek advice if these are features:
- Much of what is said is still unintelligible.
- Pattern of stammering may be emerging – especially if beginning to "block" on certain words or sounds.
- Increasing awareness of problems and frustration with language.
- Child avoiding situations where she must talk, e.g. nursery.
- Continues to respond in single words or uses very simple grammatical structures.
- Little idea of tense.
- Cannot retell a story.
- May be able to understand enough to cope with familiar routines but cannot cope if structure changes.
- Child often isolated because cannot deal with the verbal level of peers.

General points to look out for:
- Family history of speech or language difficulties.
- Any history of hearing difficulties.
- Concerns about parent/child interaction.
- Associated difficulties with behaviour or attention.

If you are in any doubt about your child's speech and language development, ask your GP to refer her to a speech and language therapist.

LIVING AS A FAMILY

THERE ARE MANY DIFFERENT SORTS OF FAMILIES. Children whose parents are married, children whose parents are cohabiting, single-parent households, foster families and stepfamilies are only a few of them. Each family has different characteristics and problems, and what works for one family doesn't necessarily work for another. You need to find your own "style" as a family that suits you.

"...the challenge is to arrange a way of living that suits you and your children"

FAMILIES TODAY

Being a parent has never been easy and it isn't any easier today. Combining work with bringing up children, for instance, can often be a complicated juggling act. Children face many different sorts of pressures too, including sitting more school tests than ever before.

One thing you probably aren't short of is advice, from relatives, friends, health professionals, books and magazines. The challenge is to arrange a way of living as a family that suits you and your children and gives them the healthiest possible start in life.

There are various approaches that may help. Accepting that stress is an inevitable part of modern life, and planning how to deal with it, is a good start. For instance, if your toddler always has tantrums in the morning when your older child

needs to get to school, try getting up a little earlier to allow extra time. That way you may make it a little easier to get everyone out of the house in time.

GETTING ALONG WITH YOUR PARTNER

It can often be difficult to agree with a partner on childcare issues, but your child will benefit if you are both consistent, even over small things. For instance, your child will be confused if your partner insists she eats up all her vegetables and you don't. She will soon learn to play you off against each other. Agree a line with your partner and stick to it. If you find it difficult to agree, try to avoid arguing in front of your child and do it behind closed doors instead. If you can't come to an agreement on a matter of your child's health or safety, get another opinion from someone qualified to advise you.

If sharing household tasks is an issue for you and your partner, outside help with cleaning or laundry will make a big difference if you can afford it. Or you could organize a babysitting arrangement with your partner, a relative or friend to give you time to get on with chores yourself. Make an effort to get to know other families. Many parents say they benefit tremendously from friendships with other parents in terms of discussing problems and supporting each other.

Remember, too, to make time for yourself, even if it's only half an hour in the evening to take a bath or read a book. It can be easy to forget your own needs when children are around. Plan in time alone with your partner as well. It's a good idea to arrange a regular babysitter so you can share time together.

RELATIONSHIPS BETWEEN SIBLINGS

The arrival of a new baby is the starting point of a relationship that will greatly affect your child's life. As they grow together, your children will go from being the best of friends to arch enemies, often in the space of half an hour. You will see them attacking each other physically and verbally and also ganging up on you to defend each other. Sibling rivalry is normal, healthy and positively beneficial! Children feel a sense of freedom and security with their siblings that they don't with other children. This lets them try out all sorts of emotions that they wouldn't dare show anyone else. Sibling rivalry is usually at its peak in the early years, but be prepared for your children to be competing against each other into their teens and sometimes even into adulthood.

How you can help

Parents can do a lot to help smoothe the relationships between their children. Preparing your older

HANDLING DISAGREEMENTS

As children grow up they are bound to fight. It's best to try to let them sort out their own disputes as far as you can, because this will help them develop problem-solving and negotiating skills. However, if they are not resolving their own argument or if there is a chance that someone might get hurt, you do need to step in.

Try to act as an arbitrator and avoid blaming one child or the other as far as possible. Ask what's going on – getting a straight answer may not be easy. Ask them to apologize to each other and if they won't, try walking away and saying "I'm not happy about that". The chances are that they will make up later on. You could try talking about the incident with your children later when things have settled, suggesting what they could have done instead.

Sly behaviour is more difficult to deal with. For instance, one child might hide something that's precious to the other. If you confront the suspected perpetrator, you'll probably get a denial. If you can be sure that the child did commit the deed, tell him you know he did it and that it's hurtful to you and his brother.

Comparison and competition are natural between siblings. Regardless of who wins, always praise your children simply for joining in. It is important to avoid comparing things outside your child's control, for example appearance or academic achievement.

When your children are playing well together, be positive. Simply saying "you played very nicely together this afternoon" will give them the message that you appreciate it when they get along well.

GRANDPARENTS

Many people find that becoming a parent puts their own relationship with their parents into a different perspective. Seeing things from a parent's point of view may give you a new empathy with your parents. You may also think about your own childhood, what you enjoyed and valued, and perhaps about any mistakes that you would like to avoid with your own children.

The part that grandparents play in your child's life depends very much on how near they live, what sort of people they are, and how physically able they are. If they live nearby, they can help out in practical ways, for instance by babysitting. But even if they live far away, grandparents can still be a source of support and often develop special relationships with their grandchildren, which are rewarding on both sides.

There are bound to be some differences in the way you and people from an older generation approach childcare. For example, your mother may have strong views about early toilet training with which you don't agree. Try to discuss differences in opinion openly with your child's grandparents on both sides of the family. You could explain that your child will benefit from consistency and that you would like them to follow the same basic rules as you do at home.

Many grandparents say that one of the joys of having grandchildren is that they can indulge them for a short time, then hand them back to their parents. Be careful not to ask grandparents for more help than they feel they would like, or are able, to give.

child for a new arrival is a good starting point. Initiate a discussion when the bump becomes fairly obvious. There are lots of good books that can help. If your child is under age 4, though, he won't really understand pictures of the baby in the womb. It might be better to read him a story about another child or an animal who becomes a big brother or sister.

Once the baby is born, the way you introduce her is important. It might help if your baby is in a cot, or being held by someone else, when your older child meets his sibling for the first time. Having your arms free to hug your older child, and spending your first few minutes giving him your full attention, is particularly important. Having a present ready for your older child from the baby is a useful trick. These things make your older child feel special and also introduces the idea of give and take.

Some studies have demonstrated that the way a mother interacts with the new baby affects the future relationship between the siblings. It is very natural to feel protective, but if you are overly protective of

your new baby an older child is more likely to feel resentful and show aggression as a result.

Try to spend time with your older child alone. You don't have to plan anything special; just being together, reading a book or watching a favourite video, will help. However, it can be difficult to find the time for this and you will find that you don't have as much time to rest as you might have done with your first child. Be sure to ask for help from family and friends when you need it. Organizing someone to take your older child out for special treats so you have time on your own with your new baby, or to rest, is also a good idea if you can manage it.

RELATIONSHIPS WITH OLDER CHILDREN

Your child's character might seem to change overnight as he approaches puberty. One moment he will be striving for more independence, making him appear difficult, pushing boundaries and creating arguments. The next, he may seem childish again. This behaviour can be tiring and frustrating for parents.

Your child will probably want to start spending less time doing family activities and more time with friends as he enters puberty. This is an important step for him in gaining a sense of his own identity as distinct from his family. These friendships are not just about learning to get along with other people but are about identifying with a peer group as well.

Real disagreements can begin to emerge as your child starts to develop views of his own that are not necessarily shared by you. Even if you do seem to have frequent disagreements, your child is still likely to hold you in high regard

(although he probably won't let you know this). The rejections and conflicts you may experience often have little to do with your personality but happen simply because you are his parent, from whom your child must increasingly separate himself if he is to have his own life.

Rules and negotiation

It will help you if you can keep one step ahead. Your first job should be to provide a secure base for your child. As when your child was younger, the key here is for parents to agree between themselves and support each other. One parent allying himself with a child against the other is always a recipe for disaster.

Set rules and limits, outlining what you and your partner consider acceptable behaviour and what you don't. However quickly your child

seems to be growing up, you are still his provider and it is reasonable that you should decide on the ground rules. These should be clear, so that everybody knows where they stand, and they should be applied consistently. However, ground rules should be reasonable and become less restrictive as older children become more responsible.

You will need to sort out what you and your partner consider important and what you don't, so that there aren't too many rules. While some issues will not be negotiable, there should be room for bargaining on others. Sanctions such as grounding, when a child loses the privilege of going out with his friends, or loss of pocket money, will work better if they are established in advance. Sanctions should never be threatened if they are not going to be carried out if

"...as they grow together, your children will go from being best friends to arch enemies, often in the space of half an hour"

"...your child needs rules to rebel against...rebellion and the questioning of authority is a normal part of growing up"

rules are broken. If you do this, sanctions soon lose all meaning.

It may be comforting to know that rules actually help your child feel safe during this transitional phase. Paradoxically, your child also needs rules to rebel against, and rebellion and questioning of authority is a normal part of growing up. Rules also help your child as he learns to think things through and starts to develop his own set of values and morals.

Listening to your child
If your child seems bored doing things with the family, ask him what he'd like to do instead. He may

suggest something you could do together, but don't worry if he doesn't. Take opportunities to talk to him whenever you can. Travelling time in the car is often a good time to talk. Parents often complain about ferrying their children around, but in fact these trips can provide good opportunities to listen to your child's views and to discuss things. He may also appreciate spending time alone with you now and then, perhaps going for a walk together, seeing a film, or going to a football match.

The most important thing is to listen to your child. You will only be able to offer advice and comfort to your child if he knows that you are a sympathetic listener and won't immediately jump down his throat with a judgement or criticism.

WHEN PARENTS SEPARATE

Parents are more likely to separate than ever before. As many as 1 in 4 children born to married parents will experience their parents breaking up before they are 16 years old. The figure is higher for children of cohabiting couples. When parents separate, a child's life is turned upside down, but research shows that if the break-up is handled carefully and sensitively harm can be minimized.

The break-up of his parents can be a very confusing time for a child. He might feel a bewildering range of emotions, from anger and rejection to being worried about whether there is anything he has done to cause the split. A child can feel a tremendous sense of loss, which may be like a bereavement in some ways.

How children are affected

Emotional and behavioural problems are common in children when their parents separate. If parents have been fighting for some time, these problems can emerge in children long before the actual separation takes place. When it does, a child may feel that his loyalties are being pulled in two directions. As a consequence of this, he may suddenly have trouble concentrating at school when he did not before. Boys often fare worse than girls during a separation because, in general, they tend to find it more difficult to express their feelings.

When parents split up, it is usually the father who is expected to leave the family home and it's subsequently more likely to be the relationship between fathers and children that suffers. Research shows the importance of a father's involvement to a child's wellbeing and performance at school. Children need to know that both parents still love them and will continue to be involved in their lives and that they can still love both their parents.

Preparing for the separation

A good starting point for helping your child through this difficult time would be for both parents to write a plan together, setting out how they will continue to share responsibility for co-parenting their children. The plan should be flexible, reflecting both the temperaments and changing needs of each child, along with specifying how each parent will try to meet these needs.

It is a good idea to give a concrete, practical role to the parent who has left home; for example, picking the children up after sports practice once a week. Keeping a consistent approach between parents to issues such as discipline and treats is still important.

It is also worth discussing maintaining contact with grandparents. Not only are they likely to be important in your child's life and want to remain involved, they may also be able to give support and help to the parent who is the main carer of the children.

What to do if communication breaks down

If parents find it difficult to talk to each other, outside mediation can help. However, taking legal action should be a last resort. It's costly, time-consuming and upsetting, and ultimately it may not even help to resolve matters.

Even if you find it hard to talk to each other, talking to your children throughout the separation process is vital in helping them understand and come to terms with the

STEPFAMILIES – HOW CHILDREN COPE

The National Stepfamily Association estimates that 1 in 8 British children now lives in a stepfamily. Their research shows that some young people find being in a stepfamily a positive thing, while others feel powerless and excluded. Above all, young people in stepfamilies say they need to feel that someone is listening to them.

There is an expectation that if you and your new partner love each other, you will love each other's children and they will love you. However, it does not often start that way. For a child who has already gone through the experience of being bereaved of a parent or of parents divorcing and remarrying, joining a stepfamily is a huge transition. Each parent may bring different parenting styles to the family, which children in the new stepfamily may find difficult and confusing.

There is much to work out and work through in building a stepfamily. It usually takes about four years (but may take up to 10) for a stepfamily to stabilize.

situation. Parents tend to want to protect their children from distress, but they will know what is going on. It is important to give children a coherent story without blaming either parent.

It's also important to allow children the space and time to show their feelings of loss and upset. Older children might find it useful to talk to a third party, such as a grandparent, other relative or counsellor, especially if they need to discuss issues concerning loyalty and feelings of blame.

PLAY

WHEN WE THINK OF CHILDREN, we invariably think of them playing. Playing is what being a child is all about, for older as well as younger children. Play isn't just an activity that keeps your child happy and busy – it is in fact vital for her mental, physical and social development. Yet many parents see play as an activity that has little importance, if not as an actual waste of time.

"...play is children's own unique and natural way of learning"

WHY PLAY IS IMPORTANT
According to child play expert Dorothy Einon, many parents take the view that play is a waste of time because "adults play when they have nothing better to do".

Children are different. The phrase "play is children's work" has a lot of truth in it. For children, play isn't motivated by the need for relaxation, although it can be relaxing. Instead, play is children's own unique and

natural way of learning. A child needs to learn in order to survive. That may sound dramatic, but from the earliest months, play is the only means by which your child can acquire the skills she needs to learn and grow physically, mentally and socially.

You don't, for example, teach your child to talk using books and tapes the way you would teach a second language to an adult. Instead

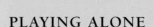

ENCOURAGING PLAY – WHAT YOU CAN DO

Children love to play. And while it helps for parents to appreciate the purpose and meaning of play, it's important not to lose sight of the fact that play is also all about having fun.

With that in mind, there's a lot you can do to facilitate your child's play. From the earliest age your child will enjoy toys. They don't need to be expensive or numerous, but they should be appropriate for your child's age. You can get great value out of toys that will grow with your child. For example, simple building or construction kits, which you can add to over the years, will be played with again and again.

Children also need opportunities to play. Toys are no good if your child never has the time to play with them. For many parents, childcare needs and the desire to give our children a "head start" can tempt us to overfill our children's lives with extra-curricular classes and activities. Giving your child uninterrupted time to play at turning her bedroom into a shop, for example, can be of more value than buying the latest game or dragging her off to a new activity.

Stimulation

New environments can provide fresh and exciting stimulation. While your 4-year-old may still enjoy building dens out of blankets and chairs, your 8-year-old will be looking for new challenges. Going for a picnic in the forest, for example, may inspire your older child to attempt to create a whole new kind of den using leaves, stones and sticks.

Offering stimulating play opportunities can become increasingly hard as your child

you sing nursery rhymes to her and look at picture books together, and slowly she starts to understand the basis of language. Instead of signing your child up for a crash course in physics, you buy her a rattle – when she shakes it and discovers it makes a sound she realizes that she can make things happen. It's an early lesson in cause and effect.

Different types of play have different roles. Physical play, for example, is essential for developing your child's strength, balance and coordination. Messy play – exploring water, mud and sand – helps your child find out about the physical world around her.

Playing with other children teaches your child vital social skills, such as cooperation and empathy. Playing also enables your child to develop problem-solving and communication skills. There's only one ball, both children want it, what's the best solution and how is it best conveyed?

In these ways, play is always a constructive activity as well as being essential for the development of a happy, healthy child.

PLAYING ALONE

The child used to having a playmate – whether it's a parent, sibling or friend – may find it hard to amuse herself when she is on her own. On a practical level, parents need their child to be able to occupy herself occasionally so they can get on with the day-to-day business of life. But playing alone is also a skill worth encouraging because it helps a child develop her own ideas. The following suggestions may help your child learn how to amuse herself.

Stock up on supplies for activities that your child enjoys and can be done alone – building a model, drawing and colouring, painting by numbers.

Negotiate by telling your child that if she can amuse herself for half an hour while you finish cooking supper, you'll play with her afterwards.

Praise your child for playing on her own, especially when she has occupied herself without you asking.

Don't expect too much too soon – young children have a very short attention span and even a new toy will only occupy them for minutes.

While most school-age children will be content to be in a room by themselves for stretches of time, younger children will still depend on your reassuring presence.

gets older. Outdoor play is especially important in offering children the chance to build their confidence, make decisions and develop their own skills in terms of risk assessment. Yet research has shown that many children think British parks and playgrounds are boring. Also, many parents prefer their children not to ride bikes or skateboards, nor climb trees or climbing frames because of the risk of injury. We are also wary of offering them the freedom of their environment that we experienced as children because of the increase in traffic on the roads and our natural fear of "stranger danger".

How far you are prepared to go to give your child a sense of freedom and adventure is an individual matter. To a certain extent it will depend on where you live and the age and maturity of your child. For many families, holidays and weekend breaks – renting a cottage with a field next door or staying in a campsite close to the beach – give their children the chance they need to spread their wings safely.

FANTASY PLAY

Watching your child play make-believe is one of the real pleasures of parenthood. Your toddler pretends to sip from a plastic cup. Your pre-school child turns the bunk bed into a castle, a broomstick into a horse, and insists you call him "Sir Knight" when you call him for tea. By the time he's in junior school your child is still enjoying fantasy play, only now he is more likely to be the director of the story, turning his action men into a mountain rescue team and manipulating all the characters to help his story come to life. Some children prefer to share their fantasy play, so siblings and friends become part of the cast. Others become absorbed in their own private imaginary world. It's not uncommon for young children to invent imaginary playmates.

Fantasy play is good for your child. It stimulates his imagination, creativity and problem-solving skills. Sigmund Freud believed that a child can confront and overcome his fears through pretend play. Children often imagine that they are being threatened by a monster or a baddie. By playing at being the conquering hero they gain a sense of both power and control.

PLAYING WITH YOUR CHILD

From day one you are your child's preferred playmate and, like it or not, your child will spend many hours badgering you to join in with her favourite activities. For some parents, play comes naturally. For others, dressing up as a pirate and spending the afternoon in a makeshift ship isn't very enticing, especially when chores are piling up.

Play, however, is one of the primary ways parents and children bond. And while ignoring the chores can be hard, if you want to nurture a good relationship with your child it may be worth postponing the housework for a couple of hours.

Playing together is also a social activity. It is one of the main ways in which a child learns how to relate to other people. Think of the hours you and your baby spent passing a rattle backwards and forwards. This kind of give and take is your child's first experience of turn-taking, a skill which in later years will be the foundation of good relationships.

Making compromises

At certain periods of your child's development you may feel more in tune with her needs. Some parents, for example, are very baby-orientated and love cuddling and tickling games. You may be bored silly by playing "pretend" games but be happy to sit down for half an hour doing colouring. If this is the case, there's little point in feeling guilty or forcing yourself to do an activity you hate. Your child will sense your resentment. Instead,

it's better to look for activities that you both enjoy. If you are actually having fun yourself instead of just pretending to (which children often sense and resent), your child will be much more likely to see the activity as being worthwhile.

TV, COMPUTERS, VIDEO GAMES – GOOD OR BAD?

Lots of parents grumble that their children watch too much TV or spend too much time on the computer. But how much is too much? And is it all bad? It's unlikely, for example, that snuggling up with your older child on the sofa a couple of evenings a week to watch a favourite programme will adversely affect her. Television is also a valuable source of information. Watched carefully, it can broaden your child's outlook on the world.

Computers, too, are an important learning tool and part of everyday life, and information technology is part of the National Curriculum. But if you leave your child to her own devices she may spend many hours mesmerized in front of the screen.

The obvious worry is that your child may be viewing unsuitable material. Many computer games have aggressive themes, and violence appears regularly on our TV screens. Of equal concern is that a child who is sitting indoors in front of a screen all day is inactive and solitary.

If you are worried that the TV or computer is taking over your child's life, set limits. Allow your child a reasonable period of time each day, or a certain number of hours a week, for watching programmes or playing on the computer. With computer games, an egg timer will prevent arguments when time's up. Keep TVs and computers in a communal area so you can monitor your child.

> "...allow your child a reasonable period of time each day, or a certain number of hours each week, for watching television or playing computer games"

EXERCISE

K EEPING CHILDREN FIT IS ESSENTIAL FOR THEIR HEALTH. Whether your child is naturally sporty or not, and whether or not you are interested in sports yourself, there are lots of fun ways to help keep her active. Encouraging activity from an early age will get your child into good habits that will help her stay healthy into adolescence and adulthood.

WHY EXERCISE IS IMPORTANT

At a brief glance, it may appear that we are a nation addicted to fitness. Pick up a programme from your local leisure centre and you will see a vast range of activities from which to choose. Magazines and newspapers are crammed with advice on diet and exercise. But sadly, it seems that children today are getting fatter, not fitter.

Making sure your child is fit and healthy is vital for her health and wellbeing. Getting off the couch and into action helps build a healthy heart, develop strong muscles and bones and reduce body fat. It also has a positive impact on your child's wellbeing. During exercise, for example, chemicals called endorphins are released by the brain, causing the body to feel more relaxed. Doing well at a chosen activity also helps boost a child's self-esteem. Joining in with sports and activities also has social benefits. It gives children a chance to mix with others, make friends and learn about the "give and take" needed to keep play fun and fair.

Encouraging children to exercise also helps them stay fit in later life. Research has shown that physically active children are more likely to remain active in later life. Fit adults have less chance of developing

serious diseases including heart disease, diabetes and osteoporosis.

HOW MUCH EXERCISE IS RIGHT FOR MY CHILD?

How do you know whether or not your child is getting all the physical activity she needs? Research has shown that to maintain necessary

"...getting off the couch and into action helps build healthy hearts, muscles and bones"

levels of fitness, children of all ages need to have at least one hour of activity at what is described as "moderate intensity" every day. Examples of moderate-intensity activities include brisk walking, swimming, dancing, active play, cycling and most sports.

The type of exercise your child enjoys is also important. Health experts recommend that children take part in activities that are beneficial for developing and maintaining muscular strength and flexibility and bone health at least twice a week. Activities such as climbing, skipping, jumping and gymnastics are good for this.

One hour a day may sound challenging, but children prefer, and are more suited to, short bursts rather than sustained periods of activity. For example, a child who walks briskly to and from school, plays outside most days, does a regular activity such as football or dancing and joins in with family activities at weekends is probably averaging the recommended level of exercise over the week.

FAMILY ACTIVITIES

At primary school age, children find almost any activity more attractive if their parents are prepared to be involved too. Putting the emphasis on fun and family participation rather than physical activity per se can inspire even the most sedentary child. If your child sees the value

IS YOUR CHILD ACTIVE ENOUGH?

Use this simple question-and-answer guide to find out whether your child is getting enough exercise.

Does your child watch less than 3 hours of television each day?
Yes/No

Does your child walk or cycle to school regularly?
Yes/No

Does your child play outside most days (not including school break times)?
Yes/No

Does your child take part regularly in extra-curricular organized physical activities?
Yes/No

Does your family do physical activities together, such as walking, swimming and active games?
Yes/No

Here's how to interpret your answers:

All yes
Your child is probably getting enough exercise out of school – keep it up!

All no
Your child isn't active enough. She needs at least an hour of activity a day, but start by building up slowly.

A mix of yes and no
You are nearly there. Try incorporating an extra activity or making a few lifestyle changes to meet the required level of activity for your child.

Source: The British Heart Foundation

you attach to being out and about and on the move, they are more likely to see it as worthwhile as well.

Try, for example, planning specific physical activities for the whole family at the weekend, such as swimming, cycling, ice skating and walking. Thinking ahead will help keep it fun. No child will enjoy being marched across a hilltop just because it's good for them, but take a picnic and a kite and it will be an afternoon to remember.

Taking out a family membership at your local leisure centre or tennis club is also a good idea. In addition to the fun you can have doing activities together, there will probably also be structured activities for pre-school and school-age children included in the membership.

You don't always need to go out for the day to be active. If you have a garden, make the most of it. When you can't face another game of football, get your child to help you

with garden chores, such as digging up the weeds or sweeping the leaves. Make a big pile and then let them jump in the middle.

As summer fades and the winter sets in, it's easy to become lazy and spend more time indoors, but with the right outdoor clothes there's no excuse. Dress your children in a warm fleece, a raincoat and a pair of Wellington boots and they will have great fun splashing around in puddles outside.

On rainy days you can have active fun indoors as well, especially with younger children. Putting on a tape or CD and dancing is good for you and your child. Hopping, skipping and jumping games don't require much room either, if you are not too houseproud!

Small children are naturally active and love movement, so it won't take much effort to get them going. If you are active yourself and have healthy habits, your children will follow. Walking or cycling to the shops instead of jumping in the car can make a big difference. If being active becomes a natural part of your child's day, she is more likely to keep it up for the rest of her life.

PHYSICAL FUN FOR CHILDREN UNDER AGE 5

Toddlers and pre-schoolers don't often need much encouragement when it comes to being active. Once they are mobile, most young children seem to be permanently on the go and parents need to find constructive ways to channel this natural energy. Activities where parents participate as well are best for the under-3s, while a pre-school child may be happy to join in to an activity with you just watching. Music and movement and mini-gymnastics are popular choices. Classes like these help children learn a whole variety of skills, such as climbing and jumping, and encourage coordination, balance and agility. Your child can build her muscles while having fun too. Swimming is also a good choice.

At this age, it's especially important to balance periods when your child is expending physical energy with quieter times when she can recharge her batteries. Children don't know their own

limits and can find it difficult to wind down. Overactive children can become sleep deprived, which may in turn lead to behavioural problems. Incorporating calm, relaxing activities into your child's day to balance the more physically demanding ones will help her maintain her energy levels and her good humour.

ACTIVITIES FOR OLDER CHILDREN

Once your child is settled at school, she may enjoy taking part in an after-school activity. Your local leisure centre, community centre or library will have information on which clubs, games and activities are on offer in your area. Think in terms of health and fitness rather than organized games, and the range of activities to choose from is enormous, from football and tennis to ice skating and judo.

The more activities your child tries, the more likely she is to find something she enjoys doing. These trial periods can be frustrating for parents, as well as expensive. To a certain extent you can avoid false starts by making sure your child is really keen and knows what's involved with the activity that interests her. You may love the idea of your daughter learning how to play tennis, especially if it's something you wish you had taken up when you were younger, but will she enjoy it? Ask her first and let her go along to watch a session before signing her up. This will also give you a chance to check out how well the activity is run. Do the children look as if they are having fun, as well as developing new skills? Are the coaches friendly and encouraging? Do they take into account each child's individual needs and abilities?

IDEAS FOR FIT KIDS

Set a good example – if your child sees you enjoying active pursuits, she is more likely to join in.

At least once a week try and do an activity together as a family, such as swimming or cycling.

Take your pre-schooler along to a music and movement or mini-gymnastics class.

Encourage your older child to join an after-school activity class or club.

Help your child by teaching her basic skills such as hopping, jumping, skipping, throwing and catching.

Invite friends round to play – active games are more fun with others.

Limit the amount of time your child spends in front of the TV and computer.

Provide equipment for active fun such as a bike, skipping rope, and balls of different sizes.

Try to get your child outside for at least part of the day.

"...the more activities your child tries, the more likely she is to find something that she enjoys doing and will keep up"

CHECK IT OUT

Children are also more likely to take part in a new activity if they have a friend going with them. Speak to the parents of your child's friends and see if they might be interested in joining too. An added bonus is that you will be able to share the responsibility for supervising the children and picking them up and dropping them off.

Your child's personality may be a factor in choosing a new activity. Children who are naturally sporty may flourish in a more competitive environment. If your child finds it hard to be assertive, a game such as football where she needs to be an active participant might become dispiriting. Joining a swimming or pony-riding club where she can progress at her own speed might be a better choice.

Once your child has decided on an activity, be prepared to ease her in slowly. Some children may just

want to sit and watch during the first session. A good coach will come and have a friendly chat and make your child feel welcome, and then she will probably feel confident about joining in the following week. Don't put her under pressure. Instead, point out how much fun everyone else is having and reassure her that chances are she will have a good time.

Once your child has started, remember to give her lots of praise and encouragement, particularly if she is learning a new skill. Keep the feedback positive and avoid pushing her too hard. Remember, the emphasis should be on having fun.

READY FOR ACTION
If your child has previously done very little activity, she should build up slowly. This is also important if your child has been unwell or out of action for any other reason. Doing too much too soon could exhaust your child and she may simply get run down. Start instead by aiming for no more than half an hour's activity a day and gradually increase this over a period of time.

Your child will enjoy activities more if she is feeling energetic. Small children, especially, will flag without regular rest and food. Take snacks for after school so your child has a chance to refuel before going on to her dance class or swimming lesson. Make sure she has breakfast before leaving for school in the morning and encourage her to stoke up with a good lunch before going on a long walk or cycle ride.

Children also burn up calories very quickly, so providing nutritious snacks, such as bananas, will help keep them going. When they are

active, children also lose fluid very quickly and becoming dehydrated will make them irritable and lethargic. Offer your child plenty to drink, preferably water, during physical activities.

Growing children get tired easily, so having plenty of rest is important if they are to recharge their batteries properly. Between the ages of 5 and 11 children need at least 9 hours of sleep at night. Getting to sleep, however, may be a problem if they are overstimulated. Finish games such as dancing around the living room well before bedtime, so your child has a chance to wind down.

THE GREAT OUTDOORS

If you have a garden, make the most of it. Garden play equipment needn't take up too much space, and although it can be expensive if bought brand-new, you can often buy it secondhand. Check out the small ads in your local paper. A climbing frame, swing, or just a rope hanging from a branch will encourage your child to be active outdoors. Other toys that can get children moving outside include rubber rings, hula hoops, trampolines, bikes and roller skates.

Don't forget the local park. It's free and can offer children great entertainment value. Play equipment will encourage younger children to develop their strength and coordination. For older children, it can provide the space for them to kick a ball or play chase, tennis or catch. Take your child's friends with you and organize a rota with other parents for days when you can't supervise yourself.

Although lazing on the beach can be very relaxing, active holidays can

be invigorating and refreshing too. There are also lots of adventurous activity holidays and outdoor breaks available for families. A week spent learning to canoe or sail could spark off a lifelong interest for your child.

WATCH OUT FOR BURN OUT!

Encourage your child to try a range of different activities rather than specializing in just one at a young age. Many sports experts recognize that children who play one sport obsessively can become bored and burnt out. Playing a variety of sports also helps develop different skills.

WALKING TO SCHOOL

If you can walk to school you'll not only boost your child's fitness but also help cut down on road congestion and pollution. Some schools have a "walking bus" scheme, led by volunteers. The "bus" operates along a route, picking up "passengers" before delivering them safely to school.

"...growing children get tired easily, so having plenty of rest is important for them to recharge their batteries...they need to wind down well before bedtime"

SLEEP

SLEEP IS ESSENTIAL FOR CHILDREN. IT STIMULATES GROWTH, plays a crucial role in brain development and affects how well your child manages everyday life. We all know that children need their sleep, and not just because bedtime allows parents some well-deserved time to themselves! Sleep is vital because it gives children the energy they need to enjoy life.

> "...sleep is crucial for brain development, allowing your child to process new information"

WHY SLEEP IS IMPORTANT

Most parents will recognize that, without regular sleep, children become bad tempered and difficult and find it hard to concentrate. Their appetites are affected, their immune systems are weakened, and they are more likely to pick up viruses and other infections.

For a child, sleep is also essential for growth. New babies seem to sleep all the time. This is because they are developing physically at a tremendous rate and it is during sleep that growth hormone is released and cells multiply fastest; as your child gets older, he will tend to grow in spurts, almost overnight sometimes, and may need extra sleep to compensate.

Sleep is crucial for your child's brain development, too. Research has shown that newborn babies need 50 per cent more rapid eye movement (REM) sleep than adults. During the REM phase of the sleep cycle, the body is relaxed but the brain is incredibly active. You may notice your baby's face twitch and eyelids flicker. It may not look like it, but your sleeping baby is actually achieving a huge

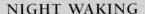

amount, processing and storing the mass of new information taken in during his waking hours.

HOW MUCH SLEEP DO CHILDREN NEED?

Children vary in the amount of sleep they need, but there are guidelines. Your newborn baby will sleep between 16 and 18 hours a day. This amount gradually decreases until, by 6 months old, he is averaging 14 hours' sleep in a 24-hour period, including a couple of one- or two-hour daytime naps. By the age of 2, most toddlers sleep between 10 and 12 hours in every 24, including a daytime nap that may vary from 20 minutes to a couple of hours. By the age of 3, sleep needs vary from 9–12 hours in every 24, and daytime naps are often only a happy memory.

As your child continues to develop, his sleep pattern will stay roughly within this range. Children starting school are often very tired for the first few weeks and will need extra sleep to compensate.

If you are unsure whether or not your child is getting enough sleep, look at how well he manages during the day. A difficult, irritable child may need to go to bed earlier. Bringing bedtime forward by half an hour can make a big difference.

BEDTIME ROUTINES

Like adults, children need a "get sleepy" ritual. Follow the same routine every night and your child will quickly learn what's expected.

You could start bedtime with a relaxing bath followed by a story, a goodnight kiss and cuddle and then lights out. The key is to help your child unwind, so boisterous bedtime games are not a good idea. Putting a child to bed while he is still awake is also important. Only by learning

how to drop off on his own at bedtime – without being cuddled or fed to sleep – can a child discover that he can go back to sleep by himself if he wakes in the night.

Even if your child is old enough to put himself to bed, he may still need help winding down. Activities such as watching TV or chatting to friends on the phone could be over-stimulating just before bedtime. Encourage him instead to read or listen to a music tape instead.

DEALING WITH SLEEPLESSNESS IN OLDER CHILDREN

Older children can be prone to the occasional sleepless night. Tossing and turning because they can't drop off only makes matters worse. It may be time to let your child stay up a little later so he can go to bed when he is properly tired. Otherwise, suggest that he reads or listens to a story tape. Letting him turn off the light when he's ready will stop him worrying and help him get to sleep.

NIGHTMARES & NIGHT TERRORS

If your child wakes in the night distressed, reassure him that it was just a dream and dreams can't hurt. Tell him everyone has dreams and when he goes back to sleep it will be gone. Stay with him until he falls back to sleep. Night terrors are an extreme form of nightmare and, as with nightmares, they are no cause for concern unless your child has them frequently. Your child will appear to be awake with his eyes open and will be very scared. It's important to stay calm yourself. Don't try to wake him. He will soon settle down without waking and in the morning he will remember nothing about it.

NIGHT WAKING

For some children night waking continues to be a problem, which can last throughout the toddler years and beyond. Breaking the habit of your child needing you in the night is emotionally and physically exhausting but helps everyone.

The process known as "controlled crying" (see p.31) can be as effective at breaking the night waking pattern in children as it is in babies, although you may find that you need to be even more persistent with an older child. You could try the following things:

When your child wakes, avoid feeding or cuddling him or chatting to him.

Check that your child is safe, say a few comforting words and then kiss him goodnight. If your child has come into your bed, take him back to his own straight away.

If your child cries out again, don't go back immediately. He needs a chance to cry, stop crying and go back to sleep by himself.

Go back if the crying sounds more desperate, and repeat the sequence above.

You may have to do this repeatedly for many hours before your child finally drops off. But it's worth persevering now and for the next few nights. After a week or so, most children learn how to drop off to sleep again alone.

HEALTHY EATING

OVER THE NEXT 10 YEARS YOUR CHILD WILL CONTINUE to grow and develop, but at different rates depending on his age. His diet will also change from being predominantly milk-based to including a wide variety of foods. The first five years particularly will involve a lot of trial and error, as your child learns to feed himself and becomes accustomed to new textures and flavours.

GOOD HABITS START EARLY

We all know that it is difficult to break habits once they are formed, and this is especially true of dietary habits. So, although adulthood may seem a long time away for your child, setting a good example now will make him more likely to eat a healthy diet throughout adolescence and adulthood. Introducing your child to a healthy diet early in life is perhaps one of the best presents you can ever give him.

A healthy diet does not simply involve eating the right balance of foods, but also takes into account the social and psychological aspects of eating. It has been shown that good eating habits, including aspects such as eating together regularly as a family, can improve children's communication skills and language development.

WHAT IS A BALANCED DIET?

A balanced diet is one in which the foods that are eaten provide all the nutrients that are essential for growth and development. Your child will achieve a balanced diet if he eats as wide a variety of foods as possible. In the UK, foods are split into five groups:
• Carbohydrates, including bread, cereals and potatoes
• Fruits and vegetables

• Dairy products, including milk and alternatives
• Protein foods, including meat, fish and alternatives
• Fatty and sugary foods (these should be kept to a minimum).

Foods from each of the first four major food groups should be chosen to ensure adequate intake of all nutrients. You should eat plenty of carbohydrates, at least five portions of fruit and vegetables, and a few servings of dairy products and protein foods each day. This model can be used by the whole family, but should be adapted for children under the age of 5 to include more carbohydrate-rich foods and fats. Energy (or calories) from these foods is essential to fuel the rapid growth and development that takes place in this age group. Although it is important to progress towards a healthy adult diet, the diet of young children should not be too high in bulky fibre-rich foods or too low in fat. Young children are unable to eat enough of these foods to meet their energy and nutrient needs. Low-fat products are also not recommended for children under the age of 2.

FEEDING YOUR PRE-SCHOOLER

To fuel the rapid growth that takes place during the pre-school years, your child will need to consume adequate calories and nutrients. Since young children have small stomachs, they cannot eat a great deal at one sitting and their diet needs to be high in both of these. For this reason, adult dietary advice to eat high-fibre, low-fat foods does not apply to young children.

However, these early years are the right time to start influencing your child's eating habits. Toddlers and pre-schoolers are wholly dependent on their parents and carers for their food and they form their eating habits by copying the adults and siblings around them.

For the first 3 years, milk will still be providing up to half of your child's calorie requirements. After this, foods given at mealtimes will gradually provide more calories than milk. Eating a variety of foods can sometimes become an issue with a child, but it is less likely to be a problem if your attention is not focused wholly on him and what he is eating. This is why bringing the whole family together for mealtimes and making them social occasions is so valuable.

National surveys have found that children in the pre-school age group often do not consume adequate quantities of vitamins A and D. The Department of Health recommends a supplement containing vitamins A, C and D for children between the ages of 1 and 5 years, unless their diets are known to be adequate.

EXERCISE IS IMPORTANT

Exercise is also important for good health. The increase in obesity in the UK is strongly associated with reduced activity levels. Children are becoming "couch potatoes" because they spend more time playing with computers and video games and watching TV and less time being physically active. Activities need

GMO & ORGANIC FOODS

Genetic modification of food has attracted both praise and disapproval. So what is genetic modification? A Genetically Modified Organism (GMO) is one in which specific genes from one organism that carry certain qualities are isolated, copied and placed in another organism. All GM foods undergo stringent assessments for safety by the EC Advisory Committee on Novel Foods and Processes (ACNFP) before they are allowed into the marketplace. Tests are carried out on animals and the information is extrapolated to humans. No long-term trials have investigated effects in humans.

All food containing 1 per cent or more of GM material must be clearly labelled as such. This means that some GMO substances can enter the food chain, as cross-contamination cannot be eliminated. *See* Useful Addresses (*p.344*) for further information.

Organic foods are produced with the minimum use of pesticides and contain significantly lower levels of pesticide residue than food grown conventionally. But there is no evidence to date to suggest that organic foods are either more nutritious or safer than non-organic foods (although they are commonly believed to be so).

Organically farmed animals are not given antibiotics routinely as preventatives against disease or as growth promoters.

The extra cost of organic farming is reflected in the higher cost of organic products. Whether you buy organic food or not is up to you. Greater demand for organically farmed food may eventually lead to lower prices for organic goods.

PROTECTING YOUR CHILD'S TEETH

Good dental health is closely linked to a good diet. Along with regular trips to the dentist, there are many ways you can protect your child's teeth from decay.

Fizzy, sugary drinks should be avoided. The acidity in these drinks combined with the sugar damages teeth faster. Sugar-free varieties of drinks raise other issues. Diet drinks are not intended for young children. If children drink large quantities of such drinks, they will have a high intake of artificial sweeteners, such as aspartame and saccharin, and it is not known whether these present a problem for growing children.

Fruit juice should always be diluted half-and-half with water. Fruit juice naturally contains both acid and sugar, which will damage teeth.

Introduce your child to a training cup as soon as he is ready and encourage him to drink from this. Bottlefeeding should be phased out from the age of 6 months.

Teach your child to brush his teeth as soon as possible. Try making this fun so it becomes a habit for life. This may take time to begin with and you will have to do most of the work, but by the age of 6 or 7 your child should be able to brush his teeth on his own under your supervision. It's a good idea to let him brush his teeth in the morning, and you brush his teeth in the evening, or vice-versa, until he is in secondary school.

Start taking your child to the dentist at about 2 years of age for regular check-ups. Children receive dental care free under the NHS, even if you go to a private dentist.

parents we have to be realistic – it is impossible to avoid all sweet foods. It is thought that we all have a tendency to like sweetness, possibly from when our ancestors used sweetness to distinguish ripe fruits from raw, decayed or poisonous fruits, which were bitter or sour. Breast milk is also naturally sweet. However, we can minimize the damage that sweet foods can cause. Studies show that it is the frequency and not the quantity of sugar consumed that does most damage to teeth, so when a sugary food is eaten, it should be with meals and not in between them.

IS MY CHILD DRINKING ENOUGH?

Fluids are essential to prevent dehydration, of which thirst is a very early sign. Children have a greater requirement for fluids than adults due to the greater fluid losses through their relatively large surface area. Fluid requirements depend on how active a child is, whether he has a fever and so forth, but the average requirements are 6–8 drinks a day. The amount taken in a drink will increase with age. An average drink for a 1- to 3-year-old is about 150 ml

(5 oz), while an average drink for a 10-year-old is about 250 ml (9 oz).

Water should always be the first choice for drinks. Small, frequent sips of water are recommended at and between mealtimes. Drinks containing caffeine or sugar are not recommended, since these can actually increase fluid requirements. A simple but useful guide to whether your child is drinking enough is the colour of his urine. The darker it is, the more dehydrated he is. Urine should be a pale yellow, almost clear, colour, except first thing in the morning, when it has been concentrated overnight and will be darker.

FUSSY EATERS

Your child may like and dislike certain foods at different times. If he refuses a new food, you can introduce it again later in a different

Illness or fever. If your child is coming down with, or recovering from, a cold or flu, he may be off his food. This is all right; his appetite will return later.

Snacking between meals, especially close to mealtimes. Snacks will fill any child up. If you want your child to eat well at mealtimes, avoid snacks or keep them low in calories.

Drinks. Children's stomachs are smaller than adults', so drinking large quantities of milk or anything else can fill them up.

Constipation. Constipation may be the result of too little fibre and/or too little fluid. Check that your child's urine is very pale yellow in colour, and if it is not, encourage more drinks (plain water is best).

Be reassured that, with good guidance, most children will eventually form healthy eating habits.

form. However, if he repeatedly shows a dislike for a specific food, try an alternative – we all have our own likes and dislikes! If your child consistently refuses a particular vegetable or fruit, try another one. If he won't eat cheese, try giving him yoghurt instead. Research shows that offering a child a variety of foods at a young age reduces the chance of him becoming fixed on refusing a type of food.

It is also not unusual for children to have erratic eating patterns at some point in their development. On some days a child may eat everything on his plate and on other days eat very little or refuse a meal altogether. Such erratic eating may reflect a child's growth spurts and/or his activity levels on that day. Studies from the US show that erratic eating patterns do not lead to poor overall food intake.

Children may also pick up on stresses around the home and may learn to use mealtimes as a battleground. As distressing as this is, it's important not to make a fuss and to avoid focusing your attention wholly on your child's refusal to eat or the small quantity that has been consumed. If your child refuses to eat a meal, just remove his plate and dispose of the food after the whole family has finished eating. Do not offer your child a complete alternative. Try to remain calm and encourage conversation among other members of the family. Your child will not starve and will eat at the next mealtime when he is hungry. If he asks for a snack before the next mealtime, offer a piece of fruit or a glass of water only. It is important that you remain consistent, so make sure you don't give in to demands for additional snacks.

If you feel your child is not growing adequately (*see p.70*), you should get professional advice from your GP, who may refer you to your local state-registered dietitian.

THE VEGETARIAN CHILD

There is absolutely no reason why a child cannot be brought up healthily on a vegetarian diet. Millions of people throughout the world are

ARE VEGAN DIETS SAFE FOR CHILDREN?

If you wish your child to follow a vegan diet, more attention to detail is required. With the increase in availability of tofu, textured vegetable protein and calcium-enriched soya drinks in local supermarkets, the choice for and quality of vegan diets is improving. But such diets do lead to a high fibre intake and care is needed when planning meals for children under the age of 5. A high-fibre diet will fill a child up quickly without providing adequate calories and nutrients, so growth may be affected. Parents wanting their child to follow a vegan diet should consult a state-registered dietitian to ensure their child receives adequate nutrition.

To make sure a vegan child's diet contains enough energy and nutrients, fat and nutrient-dense foods should be chosen. These include:

- Nut butters, such as peanut butter (best avoided until at least 3 years of age if there is a family history of asthma, eczema, hay fever or food allergies), almond butter
- Seed paste (tahini)
- Hummus, made from tahini and mashed chickpeas
- Avocados, which are also an excellent source of essential fatty acids
- Margarine or oils, which should be used liberally when cooking and preparing bean and lentil dishes

Vitamin B12, which is essential for the formation of healthy red blood cells, is another nutrient that is often low in vegan diets. Low-salt yeast spreads, fortified cereals and some fortified soya drinks are good sources of vitamin B12. Standard soya drinks are low in fat, so it may be best for your child to continue with infant soya formula until they are 2 years old. You can discuss these issues with a dietitian. Fortified soya drinks can be introduced from 2 years.

perfectly healthy and strong on a vegetarian diet. Vegetarian alternatives are now widely available in all major supermarkets as well as health food shops, and recipe ideas are plentiful. In addition, studies show that children brought up on a vegetarian diet consume more fruit and vegetables and are less likely to suffer from diseases such as obesity, bowel cancer and heart disease as adults. The most important thing for vegetarian children is to keep their diet varied and make sure the fibre content of the diet is not too high. This is especially true in children under the age of 5.

Iron and vegetarian diets

The body does not absorb iron from vegetable sources as well as iron from meat sources. Vitamin C helps the absorption of iron, so foods rich in vitamin C should be part of your child's meals. These could be in the form of diluted fruit or vegetable juice, fresh vegetables (carrots, tomatoes) and fruit.

Ensuring an adequate protein intake is often a concern for vegetarians. As long as your child's daily diet contains a mixture of vegetable sources, tofu, textured vegetable protein, beans and pulses, dairy products, calcium-enriched soya dairy alternatives, eggs, nuts and seeds, it should provide all the protein he needs.

MAKE BREAKFAST A FAMILY AFFAIR

For all of us, breakfast is the most important meal of the day. It is usually 12–14 hours since we last ate and our blood sugar levels in the morning are low. It is especially important that children start the day with a good portion of starchy carbohydrate. This helps replenish

energy stores and keeps blood sugar levels from dropping mid-morning, helping concentration in school.

It is best to avoid giving your children sugar-coated cereals. Good alternatives include porridge and other oat cereals, bran flakes, muesli (with no added sugar), cereals such as Weetabix and Shredded Wheat, and Rice Krispies. Look at the nutritional label on the packet and choose brands with less than 20 g of sugar per 100 g of cereal.

Your child may not view these healthier cereals as the most exciting breakfast options in the world. However, you can adapt them in your own way by adding in chopped fruits or a small teaspoon of cane sugar. Some parents add puréed fruit. Again, if the whole family adopts this style of breakfast, your child will accept it more readily.

SHOULD I GIVE MY CHILD SUPPLEMENTS?

Your child's vitamin and mineral requirements can all be met from food alone. However, the Department of Health recommends

a supplement of vitamins A, C and D from the ages of 1 to 5 years unless you are sure your child is getting all the nutrients he needs from food. The more varied his diet, the more likely he is to be getting a variety of vitamins and minerals. There is no reason to take supplements over and above the recommendations.

Research shows that vitamins and minerals in isolation do not benefit health as much as vitamins and minerals consumed as food. Over-consumption of one specific vitamin or mineral can prevent absorption of another, and high intakes of certain vitamins and minerals can be toxic to the body. It is important not to

introduce any vitamin or mineral supplements to your child's diet without consulting your doctor.

The action of sunlight on the skin provides the majority of our vitamin D requirement, which is necessary for healthy bone development. People with low sunlight exposure are at risk of having low vitamin D

HEALTHY BREAKFAST & SNACK IDEAS

Some breakfast ideas:
- Porridge made with milk and sliced banana with a glass of diluted fruit juice
- Scrambled egg (with optional bacon) on toast with a glass of diluted fruit juice
- Fortified breakfast cereal with chopped strawberries
- Toast with polyunsaturated margarine and yeast extract with a glass of hot milk
- English muffins with a poached egg
- Bagels with cream cheese

Some snack ideas:
- Plain biscuits, such as rich tea or garibaldi biscuits
- Currant buns, tea cakes, hot cross buns, fruit scones
- Toasted muffins or crumpets with margarine and jam
- One-slice sandwich with banana and peanut butter (for over-3s)
- Plain popcorn
- Non-sugar coated cereal with milk (full-cream for the under-2s)
- Fruit. Slicing and chilling it makes it more appealing
- Pitta bread or bread sticks and dips
- Cheese and crackers

"...introducing your child to a healthy diet early in life is perhaps one of the best presents you can ever give him"

levels. Examples include people who are in hospital for long periods of time, people who are housebound and people (especially women) from ethnic groups who don't expose much of their skin to sunlight. Adequate dietary intake of vitamin D is essential in these circumstances. The British Dietetic Association recommends that people in these groups may benefit from vitamin D supplements. Ask your doctor or dietitian if you are concerned about your child's intake of vitamin D.

OBESITY AND YOUR CHILD

Unfortunately, the UK has the highest incidence of obesity in northern and western Europe, with the exception of Germany. It is a situation that is getting out of control and one that the Government is taking seriously. Obesity increases the risk of premature death, diabetes and heart disease as well as severe back pain and other joint problems.

The pattern of obesity in the young does not bode well, with the incidence of obesity in 6-year-olds doubling since the mid-1980s. An overweight 7-year-old has a 41 per cent chance of being an obese adult.

Is it all in the genes?

There is some truth in the idea that obesity is due to genes – genetic factors do play a part. Children with parents who are both obese have an 80 per cent chance of becoming obese themselves, compared to a 20 per cent chance if both parents are lean.

However, research shows that poor lifestyle is the main cause of obesity. Obese parents are more likely to be less active and eat high-calorie, energy-dense foods, passing these bad habits on to their

children, who in turn become obese. And it is not just the type of foods children eat but also their activity levels that determine whether they will be overweight.

Obesity in childhood needs to be taken seriously and tackled. Beyond the physical problems it causes, it can also cause psychosocial problems, including depression and loss of self-esteem. Overweight children may be teased, bullied and socially excluded.

What to do if your child is overweight

Children whose weight centile is much higher than their height centile (for example, a 95th centile for weight and a 50th centile for height) are overweight and may become obese. Body mass index (BMI) is also a useful measurement to see if your child is overweight. Divide your child's weight in kilograms by his height in metres squared. For example, if your child weighs 30 kilograms and is 1.3 metres tall, the formula for his BMI would be 30/(1.3 x 1.3); the result would be 17. If your child's BMI is between 25 and 30, he is overweight. A BMI greater than 30 indicates that your child is obese.

Treating obese and overweight children is different from treating obese and overweight adults. Using a weight-loss regime intended for adults may compromise your child's growth and development. Dietary restrictions should be supervised by your GP and/or state-registered dietitian. The key to success is a change in lifestyle, and this means appropriate dietary changes together with increased exercise. Also, your child must be motivated to lose weight himself or efforts are unlikely to be successful.

If your child is overweight and not obese, the goal will be to maintain a static weight so he becomes leaner as he grows in height. If a child is obese, actual weight loss may be needed, but it is essential that you seek professional advice before attempting this. Very low-calorie diets and any diet resulting in excessive and fast weight loss in children will compromise their development and should not be used. The diets of children under 5 years old are easier to change, because you have greater control over food choices. Older children will be eating and spending more time away from home, so the child must be trusted to follow the diet. At this age, it is important that the child himself wants to do something about his weight. The whole family will need to provide support for the child and alter their eating and activity habits, too. A sensible, balanced approach towards food and weight has to be adopted, though, or an affected child could develop an eating disorder.

EATING DISORDERS

Eating disorders include problems such as anorexia, which is deliberate self-starvation, and bulimia, which is a tendency to binge on food and then purge the body through vomiting or laxatives. Although eating disorders are common in young children or children of primary school age, children in both of these age groups are becoming increasingly aware of body image and dieting.

You can help prevent your child from developing an eating disorder by emphasizing the importance of a healthy diet and exercise from an early age, and by setting a good example for your child by eating healthily and exercising yourself. If you are worried about your own weight or are dieting, do not make too much of it in front of your child, who may pick up on your anxieties and apply them to him- or herself.

Some warning signs of eating disorders include distorted ideas about body size, weight loss and irritability. Children who have perfectionist tendencies and children who perceive that they are under a great deal of pressure to succeed may be more susceptible to eating disorders. If you are concerned that your child may be developing an eating disorder, see your GP for advice as soon as possible.

GROWING INDEPENDENCE

As CHILDREN DEVELOP, THEY WANT TO DO THINGS FOR THEMSELVES. It's part of growing up and parents need to encourage a child's independence. You can do this by helping your child practise new skills, with help at first. As your child grows older, encouraging him to do things on his own, such as homework or getting ready for school, will help him develop a sense of responsibility.

> "...doing something simple, like taking the dog for a walk, helps your child feel special"

STAGES OF DEVELOPMENT
Much of what a child can do depends on his stage of mental and physical development, which in turn depends on the growth and maturation of his brain, nerves, bones and muscles. The brain, which controls the body through the peripheral nervous system, develops particularly rapidly during the first two years of life. A child gains control of his head, then his limbs and trunk, and finally achieves fine control of his fingers. This means he can carry out more delicate tasks, such as holding a pencil and writing. As his nervous system continues to mature, your child becomes able to control the nerves supplying his bladder and bowel.

Complex interconnections in the nervous system occur with rapid learning of all sorts of skills during childhood. Bones and muscles also lengthen and become stronger in this period. Later on, during puberty, sexual maturation begins.

How you can help
How can you support and help your child as he develops, encouraging his independence? In the beginning, it's important to learn to pick up on the signals your child gives you that

he is ready to do things by himself. For instance, when your baby reaches out for something, let him see if he can get it himself; don't hand it to him right away. Give him a spoon and let him try feeding himself. Give toddlers simple choices to help them feel in control. Would your child like an apple or a pear, or a red or yellow toothbrush?

As soon as he has the manual dexterity, give your child a brush to hold and show him how to brush his hair. Let him have a go at brushing his teeth, although you'll still need to help until he is 6 or 7 years of age. At age 3, he might be able to wash his face and brush his hair with a little help. At age 4, he'll probably be able to dress himself but may need help doing up buttons.

When he's learning something, like tying his shoes, give him the time he needs. Whatever he's doing, let him get on with the task himself. This will give him the message that you are confident in his abilities. Only offer help if he really needs it.

BUILDING YOUR CHILD'S SELF-ESTEEM
A sense of self-esteem is essential for a child to develop independence. Children develop self-esteem

As a child grows older, he'll want more physical independence. He might want to visit the shops, walk to a friend's house or go to the park without you. This worries today's parents more than it would have worried their own parents. Traffic has increased, making roads more dangerous, and well-publicized cases of child abduction mean that the fear of this, however rarely it happens, is very real. But children need to learn the skills to be able to look after themselves and they won't do so without practice.

I started with my own children when they were age 8, doing things in small stages. When I felt they were ready they tried a short trip up to the shop at the top of the road using the pelican crossing. By the time they were 9 or 10 years old they were walking round to the next road to visit friends, phoning when they had arrived. At 10 or 11 years they started to walk home from school on their own. We first walked the route together in advance, to see where to cross roads and agree how long the journey should take. This gave them the message that I trusted them and believed in their abilities.

Independence also means a child having time doing nothing much at home. It's very easy to pack a child's life full of activities, but it's important to get the balance right. Your child needs time alone for quiet and unstructured play. I am a great believer that being bored at times encourages resourcefulness in a child because he looks for something to do.

Allowing children some private space as they get older also helps reinforce self-respect. Not all children can have or want a room of their own, but it's helpful if they have at least one area they can think of as theirs alone.

through being loved and appreciated by their parents. They need love consistently and unconditionally in order to feel valued. Knowing that he is loved and that his opinions and thoughts matter to you will make your child feel secure and help develop his confidence.

You don't need to organize lots of special outings or buy presents to let your child know you care about him. Spending time together doing something simple, like taking the dog for a walk, talking to your child and listening to what he has to say, and letting him know you enjoy his company, will all help him feel special.

You should also tell your child you love him and explain why. For instance, you could say "I love the way you kiss your sister better when she's feeling upset". Notice things your child does without being asked and comment positively on them; for instance, "Thank you for tidying your toys away, you've done a good job". Give specific compliments rather than general praise.

Praise is just as important for older children, whether they've done well at school, have been helpful around the house, or have simply been thoughtful to someone.

Encouraging your child's interests

Working together to discover your child's strengths and areas of interest will not only boost his confidence but also help him get to know himself a little better. If he is not interested in a hobby or sport that

you are passionate about, it can be disappointing for you but it is best to follow your child's lead in this. Listening, and making it clear to him that you have taken in and understood what he is saying, is important. You don't always have to agree with him but the fact that you are taking his thoughts and feelings seriously will help him develop confidence in his opinions. You will sometimes need to give criticism, but if this is done constructively it can help improve his self-knowledge. Do pick your time carefully and don't offer criticism in front of friends or siblings or when he is hungry or tired. Try to start with a positive comment such

as "You are usually really good at practising your reading, but in the last few days…"

Developing physical skills

Having a good range of physical skills will help your child feel confident. If he can run, ride a bike, climb a tree and generally have the opportunity to be physically adventurous, he will come to trust in his own abilities. In the first five years, there is little difference between boys and girls in terms of their growth and physical shape. But girls seem better at games that involve precision and judgement, such as hopscotch and running short distances, while boys prefer

throwing and catching and may often seem stronger than girls.

If your child shows an interest in a particular activity, encourage and support him, since this will help his confidence as well as fitness. Most children find at least one physical activity they enjoy, and there are hundreds available, such as football, swimming, cycling, dancing, gymnastics and judo.

Encouraging your child's skills in other areas will also help give him a sense of worth. See what he enjoys, whether it's learning a musical instrument, drawing, making or collecting things. Give plenty of praise and let him know you think he's good at his chosen activity.

Children learn by example, and parents are their most influential role models in the early years. This means that your own self-esteem is important too. Making time for yourself is often difficult, especially when children are very young. But if you can find time for simple things, whether it's just having your hair cut or playing a game of tennis, your children will benefit.

STRIKING A BALANCE BETWEEN INDEPENDENCE & RULES

As your child grows and becomes more independent, he will need to know the rules and boundaries that you place on his behaviour. Abiding by rules is an important part of being able to live in a community. For families, rules are important so that everyone can live comfortably together under one roof. Even babies need to learn the meaning of "no" and "yes". Children actually like rules, because rules give them a clear idea of what's expected of them and, as they grow older, something to rebel against.

When children are young, rules can be very simple, outlining the behaviour you would like from them. As your children grow up, some rules can be renegotiated, but you can stick with the original principles. Involving your child in reviewing rules will help him understand what they are there for.

Within this framework of rules, your child will need to know that his opinion does count. Encouraging him to develop his views and opinions will help him understand himself better and increase his confidence. Discuss what happened at school today, what he enjoyed, what he didn't and why. As your child grows older you can widen this to include more abstract ideas, such as politics or global issues.

Also, involve your child in family decisions as much as possible. Some families find setting aside a regular time and place to talk is a good way to discuss issues together. For others this approach may be too formal, and just spending time doing an

"...growing with your child means trusting him and respecting his decisions in issues such as choosing friends"

DISAGREEING WITH AN OLDER CHILD

There will be times when you feel your child's decision is the wrong one. With older children, pick your moment and discuss your views with him. Give him the chance to explain his decision and listen carefully to his views. Set forward the reasons why his choice isn't a good idea in clear terms he will understand. Be prepared to negotiate on the outcome.

By the age of 11, a child who has been given practice in decision-making feels confident in his own abilities and has a good sense of who he is will be well prepared for the next phase of his life – the turbulent years of adolescence.

everyday activity, such as driving in the car, can be a good time to talk.

You don't always need to agree with one another; in fact arguments and disagreements are inevitable and an important part of family life. They provide a child with a safe opportunity to experiment with making his views known and standing up for his beliefs. They also help prepare him for life outside the family, where people often disagree. If you feel you need to get your children talking more, try taking the other side in an argument and playing the devil's advocate.

BEHAVIOUR & ROUTINE

Young children like routine because it makes them feel secure. From an early age, a bedtime routine can help your baby settle. A bedtime routine will help your older child sleep too.

As children grow up, families often find routines helpful in getting things done. If your children know what to do and when to do it on a daily basis it will help you get them out the door on time.

Children also need to learn how to behave. If they don't, they'll find it hard to get on with friends and to cooperate, both of which are important at school. Discipline isn't really about punishment. It's more about teaching your child how to behave so that he eventually learns how to control his own behaviour.

There are some basic principles of discipline that most people agree on. For instance, most families encourage their children to be truthful and polite, rather than rude or aggressive. The best way to achieve good discipline is to make sure that your child feels secure and loved and receives plenty of attention when he is behaving well. You must also watch your own behaviour and make sure that you are setting the right example; children learn from their parents.

> "...if children don't learn how to behave, they'll find it hard to get on with friends and cooperate with others"

Dealing with problem behaviour
Setting firm guidelines about the behaviour you expect will give your child a clear idea of what is acceptable and what isn't. Be consistent in how you apply the rules. If you ignore them one day and impose them the next, he will become confused. Be prepared to give an ultimatum then a quick, clear punishment if a rule is broken. If you find one child hitting another, you could say: "No hitting! Stop now or there's no TV today". If the hitting doesn't stop, follow through and make sure the TV stays off.

When your child behaves badly, let him know you disapprove of his behaviour but not of him personally.

For instance if he hits someone, make it clear it's not acceptable by saying that he has hurt the other child, not that he is a bad boy.

It's never a good idea to smack your child. Not only does this give a child the message that physical violence is acceptable, but there is a wealth of research to show it does nothing to help children learn to improve their behaviour. Other strategies, such as withholding treats or taking "time out", work better.

Consistency

Discipline needs to be consistent from both parents and others involved in the care of a child. If your child lives between two homes, ensure that everyone's following the same rules. Make sure your child understands what's expected of him. Less commonly, he might have a hearing problem, be hyperactive, or be upset because of family problems or trouble at school.

Difficult behaviour can make it hard for you and your child to get along. It's important to spend time having fun, so plan this into your lives, whether it's half an hour in the park after school or reading a book together before bed. If you are having trouble handling your child's behaviour, talk to your GP.

GROWING WITH YOUR CHILD

Growing with your child means recognizing his capabilities and encouraging him to test them at each different stage. This will help him improve his sense of independence and self-reliance. For young children, it could mean encouraging personal skills, such as dressing. For older children, it could mean respecting their decisions in issues such as choosing friends.

"...encouraging decision-making skills, such as choosing clothes, can help children develop self-reliance"

EMOTIONAL DEVELOPMENT

ONE OF THE MOST IMPORTANT SKILLS you can help your child develop is his ability to express his emotions in a clear, appropriate way. If you do this, it will stand him in good stead as he grows older. Learning to express his emotions clearly and without aggression will also help him get to know himself better and will help others understand why he feels as he does.

HELPING YOUR CHILD EXPRESS HIS FEELINGS

It isn't always easy for a child to express himself, and it may be something boys find harder than girls. If your child expresses himself too aggressively or loudly, he may be told off. If he's too quiet, he may be ignored. With your help, your child can learn to assert himself in an appropriate way.

The first step is to put names to different emotions. You can start by naming positive as well as negative feelings in everyday conversation.

It might be tempting to avoid talking about feelings of unhappiness or anger, but it's important for a child to recognize these feelings and learn how to deal with them. You could say "I can see you are feeling angry because Tom has taken away your book", or "You look happy today. Is that because we're going to go to grandma's house?"

As your child's vocabulary improves, encourage him to describe his own emotions. You could say: "You look unhappy. Perhaps you're cross or tired – how are you feeling?" Asking open questions such as "what do you think about?…" or "how did you feel when?…" can help this process.

You will need to give your child guidance about the best way to express his feelings. For instance, being angry is fine, but hitting someone because you're angry is not. Suggest alternative strategies, such as counting to ten before saying something when you're angry, or walking away from the situation until you feel in control again.

DEALING WITH TANTRUMS

Many children go through the "terrible twos". In fact, 1 in 5 children this age has two or more tantrums a day. Around this age, a child's intellectual and cognitive abilities are developing fast. Children start to realize they are separate beings and are becoming increasingly independent. In short, they begin to assert themselves.

A tantrum is more likely to happen if a child is hungry, tired, bored or overstimulated. He may be frustrated at his own limitations, if, for example, he can't fasten buttons on his shirt, or if he wants to tell you something but lacks the verbal skills to do so. He may be angry at

It's perfectly normal for a young child to cry when he's left with someone else or at nursery, playgroup or even school for the first time. This can be upsetting for parents but in most cases it doesn't take long for a child to be comforted and enjoy his day. Remember that being left with another trustworthy person helps your child learn to form new relationships and develop social skills. Preparation is important. If your child is starting at a nursery, visit it together beforehand and meet his carers. Talk positively about what fun he'll have. Read books together about starting nursery.

When you leave, kiss him and tell him you are going and when you'll be back in terms he understands, for instance "I'll be back before tea". Wave and walk away. Don't be tempted to go back, even if he's crying. This will only reinforce his tears. It will help if he has someone nearby to comfort him. Most children settle in a few weeks but if your child consistently cries when you leave, try standing outside for a few minutes to reassure yourself that his crying stops. Children may also cry when you collect them. This doesn't mean they haven't enjoyed their day. Until the age of 3 or 4, a child will often feel a rush of overwhelming emotion that results in tears when he sees his parents again. Check with his carer or teacher and if they say that he's been fine, believe it. Showing your child that you feel confident about leaving him will help him feel confident too.

After age 5 or 6, separation anxiety is much less common. If by age 7 your child is still reluctant to go to school, it could indicate a problem and you should talk to your child's teacher.

being thwarted in some way; for example, you may have said "no" to a biscuit before lunch.

When a tantrum does happen, the best strategy is often to ignore it completely. Make sure the environment is safe, and let him get on with it. The whole purpose of your child having a tantrum is to get what he wants. If you give in, he will learn he can get his own way by having a tantrum again.

Your reactions

There's no point in trying to reason or argue when your child has a tantrum. It's also important not to laugh, even if the reason for the tantrum seems ridiculous – the anger and frustration that triggered it are genuine. Just stop listening and remind yourself what the

tantrum is about, for instance, "This is because I said no to a biscuit". Your child will get a reassuring message that you are in control.

Occasionally, a child will hold his breath during a tantrum. This can be frightening for parents. Stay calm and don't panic or your child will panic too. If he holds his breath for long enough, he will pass out and will then start breathing again naturally. For this reason breathholding is not harmful.

Distraction and avoidance techniques

Sometimes it's possible to distract a child out of a tantrum. It might be worth offering a favourite book or toy or just talking calmly and quietly. There might be something you say that catches his attention.

The time to give your child attention again is when he calms down. There's no point in telling him off. Join him in something he enjoys and won't find frustrating, such as looking at a book together or playing a game. He will probably appreciate a cuddle to remind him of your continuing love.

Averting a tantrum is better than dealing with one and there are some tricks that may help. Give your child plenty of opportunities to let off steam by running around the garden or in the park, or even playing noisily in the house if it's raining. Make sure he has a regular routine of daytime naps, bath and bedtime. Avoid long stretches without food by carrying snacks when you go out. Don't wait until his behaviour deteriorates before you offer them. Providing simple choices, such as letting him choose what kind of sandwich he'd like at lunch, can help your child feel in control and may reduce the chance of a tantrum.

If you work, don't feel you have to provide something more exciting than your child's nursery, childminder or nanny does when you get home. Just being there, by sitting quietly looking at book or watching a video together, is likely to work best.

It may be useful to keep a record of your child's tantrums. This will help clarify when they are most likely to occur and what provokes them. You could then try to avoid these situations.

Be reassured that children eventually grow out of tantrums. See your doctor if your child has more than two temper tantrums every day, if they continue regularly after the age of 4, or if you feel you can't handle them. Extra support may be needed.

"...averting a tantrum is better than dealing with one and there are some tricks that may help...if they don't work, the best strategy is often to ignore it completely"

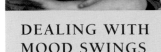

HELPING ANXIOUS CHILDREN

It's very common for babies and young children to be afraid of things. Fear of water, dogs, loud noises and new places are some of the most common fears at this stage.

These fears do make sense. Your baby is still finding out about the world, and fear is a natural protective response that prepares the body to flee or face the things you feel threatened by.

There may be ways you can help. If your child is afraid of water, he may feel safer in a baby bath placed in the bathtub. Introduce toys and encourage him to splash. At other times, for instance if there's a loud noise, there won't be much you can do but be there; giving him a hug will reassure him.

At around the age of 3 or 4, children develop powerful imaginations and very often are afraid of things that seem puzzling to adults. Tigers and lions in the garden, monsters in the wardrobe, the dark, a loud noise such as a lawnmower and even the sound of the wind can be frightening. These fears may be a way of giving shape to feelings of anxiety at a time of change in the child's life, such as starting playgroup or school, or when a new sibling arrives.

It's important not to dismiss your child's fears, which for him are very real. Reassure him that you are taking his fears seriously by gently asking why he is worried. Children often have funny ideas about things, which you could correct. If he is afraid of a particular object, gradually introduce it. For instance, if he doesn't like the vacuum cleaner, prepare him by telling him that you are going to do some vacuuming but he can stay in the next room.

It helps if there's someone else with him to give comfort; remember to praise him for being brave. If it's something more intangible that's frightening him, such as the dark, use a nightlight and leave the light on all night outside his room. Reassure him that you are close by.

Many children instinctively work through their fears through play. If your child enjoys drawing, provide plenty of crayons and paper to allow him to express his feelings in this way. Don't be worried if he doesn't seem to reveal anything you think is significant.

Very occasionally there may be a medical reason behind a child's fear. For instance, if he seems upset by loud noises or runs away if he hears anything loud, he may have a problem with his ears and it's worth a visit to your GP.

Pre-adolescent anxieties

It is very common for children to develop anxieties about specific things just before adolescence. There is some evidence to suggest that there is a genetic component to this. Anxiety can also be learned from other people around you.

Certain life events can also play a role in triggering anxious feelings

DEALING WITH MOOD SWINGS

Once past the "terrible twos", young children are rarely moody and irritable for long. If they are, there is usually a good reason for it.

Hunger, tiredness and thirst can play a part in moodiness in younger children. Making sure that your child has eaten enough and isn't overtired or thirsty can help alleviate moodiness. Keeping a few healthy snacks, such as raisins or granola bars, and a bottle of water on hand when you're on outings can help prevent any sudden deterioration in mood.

If your child suddenly becomes moody and hunger or tiredness do not seem to be the problem, explore whether there's a problem at nursery or school, or with friends. Or have there been any changes in your family or routine he feels unhappy about? For some children, depression (*see below*) can cause a range of symptoms, including mood swings.

As puberty approaches, your child will be exposed to hormonal changes that could make him feel moody. Although adolescence usually starts at around 11 for girls and 12 for boys, the hormonal changes responsible for initiating the process begin some years earlier. Your child may not understand himself why he feels as he does or be able to explain his feelings clearly. Consequently, this can be a difficult time for the whole family.

If your child seems so moody and unhappy that it is affecting his ability to get on with and enjoy his life, it may be down to more than adolescence. He may be depressed. If you think this might be the case with your child, ask your GP for advice. Help can then be arranged if it is necessary.

"...it's very common for children to be shy, but with support and encouragement most are able to overcome it"

and behaviour. Try to establish whether there is a pattern to your pre-adolescent's fears. If he is afraid of taking the bus, does he feel the same for other forms of transport? Is there any occasion when he can manage to travel? It is also worth exploring whether his fears could be masking something else. For instance, are there any problems at school or with bullying (*see p.151*)?

Most fears do pass in time and with your encouragement your child should grow out of them. If you feel he would benefit from further support, a child psychologist can offer advice. There are effective interventions available that work to help children overcome their fears.

HELPING SHY CHILDREN

It's very common for young children to be shy. With plenty of support and encouragement, most children can overcome it. The key is to build confidence and self-esteem. Choose games and puzzles you know he'll be able to do and give plenty of praise when he does them. Involve him in activities with tangible results such as cooking. Notice little things he does without being asked, such as tidying away. Explain things in advance. Every night talk through what he'll be doing the next day. If he's being cared for by someone else give him a clear idea of when you'll be back, for instance before lunch or after tea.

If your child is starting playgroup or school, ask his teacher to let you know if he's not talking to anyone at school after about a month or so. He may need extra help. It's important that he can communicate effectively to develop relationships with teachers and children as well as for learning.

BEHAVIOURAL PROBLEMS

Behavioural problems often start in early life, although they can affect children of any age. Tantrums, biting, hitting or kicking are usually a temporary part of normal development. An older child might cheat, steal or lie, refuse to follow rules, or get involved in fights.

If problems are dealt with quickly and appropriately, they can usually be resolved fairly rapidly. But sometimes these antisocial behaviours can be more serious. A child might develop a hostile attitude, be consistently disobedient and defiant, or lie or steal without any sign of remorse or guilt. Refusal to follow rules might lead to breaking the law. This is known as a conduct disorder.

There are some predisposing factors. A child who has always had a difficult temperament, is depressed, or has been bullied or abused may be more prone to developing a conduct disorder. Children who are hyperactive have problems with self-control, paying attention and following rules. A child with learning and reading difficulties who is not receiving the appropriate help can find it difficult to understand and take part in lessons, which may lead to boredom and misbehaviour.

Conversely, a bright child who is not being challenged enough by his schoolwork may also misbehave for the same reason. Parents who feel overwhelmed by problems with their child's behaviour may also feel exhausted or depressed and find it hard to cope.

What can help? Giving your child attention and praise when he is behaving well from an early age will give him a clear message about the sort of behaviour you appreciate.

Giving most of your attention when your child is behaving badly, even if it's in the form of being told-off, will give your child the message that he gets attention when he breaks rules. Being firm about rules, and fair and consistent in the way they are applied, will help him learn that rules are important.

If you are concerned about your child's behaviour at home, it's worth talking to your child's teacher. Extra help at school may be necessary. You may need advice from the school doctor or from an educational psychologist.

If serious problems continue for more than three months, it is worth asking your GP for advice. If more specialist help is needed, a referral to your local child and adolescent mental health service might be needed. Specialists can help find out what is causing the problem and suggest ways of improving behaviour.

Telling lies

Very young children rarely lie. However, at about age 3 or 4, children often can't separate fantasy

"...if behavioural problems are noticed early and are dealt with quickly and appropriately, they can usually be resolved rapidly"

"...for most children, being the winner is much more important than playing by the rules, but it's important to teach your child about playing fairly"

from reality and might genuinely believe in something they've dreamt about or made up. What seems like a lie to you might be something they think is really true. As your child grows older and becomes able to distinguish fantasy from reality, he might tell lies to protect himself after a misdemeanour, to impress other children or to please you.

Talk to your children about the importance of telling the truth. You could tell the story of the boy who cried "wolf", whose lies led others not to believe him when he finally told the truth.

Praise your child when he tells the truth. If he is recounting what is obviously a tall story, talk about what's real and what's not. If you see your child doing something wrong, such as pinching his sister, and he then denies it, let him know you saw what he did. On the other hand,

if you didn't actually see what happened and are just suspicious, check the story carefully; he might be telling the truth. It helps to set the right example for your child by not telling white lies in front of him.

Cheating

For most children, being the winner is much more important than playing by the rules. It's important to teach your child about playing fairly. If you let him get away with cheating, he will get the message that it's easy to win by devious means rather than luck or merit.

Whatever game your child is playing, make sure everyone knows the rules in advance. Explain that it's much more fun to stick to the rules, and encourage your child to think about how he would feel if someone cheated on him. If you see cheating happening, stop the game.

With young children, it might help having an adult on each side at first.

If an older child is cheating at school, talk to him and also to his teacher. He may need extra help.

Cruelty

When a toddler hurts or teases a person or an animal, it is rarely intentional; your child does not have the level of understanding to allow him to empathize with others. But sometimes this kind of behaviour can develop into a habit if a child sees it as a way of getting attention.

If your child engages in cruel behaviour, tell him "no" very clearly and sit him away from whatever or whoever he has hurt. Ignore him for a minute or two while you get on with something else. This sends a clear message that hurting others is not the best way to get attention.

When an older child acts cruelly, it's more serious, since an older child understands fully what he is doing. If you suspect that your child is being cruel by bullying another child, whether on his own or as part of a group, you need to act straight away (*see p.151*).

When older children are cruel to animals it can be a sign of emotional disturbance. Your child may need extra help; talk to your GP.

Stealing

A young child who takes something will probably not realize that it's wrong. If your child has taken something, it's best if he goes with you to return it, explaining that it was taken by accident. Tell him that taking things upsets people.

When a school-age child steals, it's important to establish the facts. Keep calm, and bear in mind that it's very common for a child to steal something at least once. Discuss how to remedy the situation, suggesting that he return the property and apologize himself.

Repeated stealing may indicate a deeper problem. Try talking to him or suggest he talks to someone else he can trust, such as a family friend.

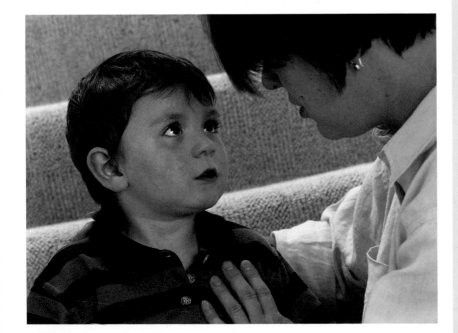

AGGRESSION

Biting, hitting, pinching and hair-pulling are fairly common among pre-school children and are rarely done with a full understanding of how much these behaviours hurt others. Children usually grow out of these behaviours, but sometimes they can develop into habits and it's best to stop them before they do.

If your child bites you, put him down if you're holding him, or sit him away from you to show that he has hurt you, and say "no, don't bite". If he has bitten another child, remove him firmly, saying "no" and giving your attention to the other child for a couple of minutes.

School-age children occasionally bite, but it's usually done with the knowledge of how much it hurts others and in the context of fighting. The same goes for hitting, pinching and hair-pulling.

When a child has outbursts of temper and hits someone, you need to intervene. It could be happening because your child needs an outlet for feelings of anger or aggression. Acknowledge his anger, but make it clear what the boundaries are for acceptable and unacceptable behaviour. Suggest alternative strategies for dealing with anger. Your child might find doing something physical helpful, such as playing football, dancing, singing or shouting into a pillow.

Alternatively, if your child is aggressive towards a sibling, suggest that he comes to talk to you whenever he feels angry rather than hitting out. If the problem persists, find out whether he's worried about anything. A problem at school or with friends may be behind his aggression.

SOCIAL DEVELOPMENT

IN THE TODDLER AND PRE-SCHOOL YEARS, you will be your child's main role model. He will pick up many of his ideas and attitudes about people and relationships from you. After your child starts school, his peer group will have an increasing influence on his thinking. Although interaction with his peers is important for your child's development, their influence may cause friction between you.

LEARNING ABOUT MORALITY

Most children have a strong sense of what is fair and what isn't. Even young children are more morally sophisticated than we used to assume. Ask any 4-year-old a question such as "which is worse, hitting someone or sticking your tongue out at them?" Most will reply that hitting is worse.

Parents can do a lot to help their child develop his own moral judgement. The way parents approach this can powerfully influence the way their child develops and the sort of person he becomes. Setting out your own family values is a good first step. Make it clear what you consider to be right and wrong in your family and discuss this openly.

The best way to teach your values is by example. How closely and how well you live by what you say will determine how your child views your values. For instance, if you impress upon your child that he should always tell the truth, make sure you do this too. It's convenient sometimes to tell white lies (such as "tell her I'm not here"), but for your child, who may overhear, this will be confusing.

As your child grows, continue to be open about your own values. It will give him the opportunity to challenge them. Some families like to have regular meeting times when they can discuss issues. These discussions could take place at a particular meal, for instance, although it may be easier to approach things a little less formally.

As your child develops, he will feel valued if he can see that what he does and how he behaves give you pleasure. It's important to make

> "...friendships are very important in a child's life and your child's peer group becomes increasingly influential as she grows up"

it very clear to your child which actions and behaviours make you pleased. This will give him a clear idea of what you expect from him.

LEARNING ABOUT TOLERANCE

Racism is not just something that happens between white people and black people. It involves people from many different racial backgrounds in countries throughout the world. As parents, irrespective of our own racial heritage, we must be vigilant about racism and challenge it so that our children can grow up in a healthier society.

Racism is not necessarily obvious. Underlying racism is a more general attitude of intolerance to people who are different for reasons other than race, for instance religion, language, gender, sexual orientation, age, physique, or even dress or hair style.

Most of us welcome variety in our lives and find sameness very tedious. We enjoy different kinds of food and drink, clothes, plants and products that are produced in countries around the world.

However, some people find difference difficult to deal with and can even find it threatening. In order to bring up our children to be confident and respectful of others, and to have inquiring minds and enjoy all of the things that our multi-ethnic, multi-cultural world can offer, preparation needs to start at home.

EMOTIONAL LITERACY

Most children need to learn to respect the feelings of others, but doing so will help your child understand the consequences of his actions.

From an early age, name emotions so that your child learns to recognize them. For instance, you could say "your sister is crying because she's feeling sad". As your child develops, start naming emotions in response to actions. You could say "you've drawn me a lovely picture and that makes me happy"; or "you've taken away your brother's toy and he's cross. Please give it back and play with something else."

As your child grows up he may still need reminding about other people's feelings. It's all right to let your 11-year-old know when he upsets someone. Helping your child take responsibility for his actions and feelings is important.

It will help both of you if your child can acknowledge his feelings in a positive way. You could start this process from an early age. For instance, if your 2-year-old trips over a step and hurts himself, it may be tempting to absolve your child of any responsibility by saying "naughty step". But don't blame it on the step. Give your child a cuddle and remind him that steps can trip people up – it's best to look where he's going.

With your older child, you may find yourself getting blamed for all kinds of things. For instance, your child may say "you make me go to school". Refuse to accept the blame. You could reply by saying something like "all children need to go to school but you don't sound very happy about it today. Is there something you are upset about?"

"...exposing your child to a range of different tastes and images from an early age can help prepare her for the diverse world in which she lives"

Exposing your children to a range of different tastes, images and musical sounds from an early age can help prepare them for the diverse world in which they live. When children start learning the names of different foods, you could start explaining which countries they're from (with the help of a children's map).

Check your child's play materials. It's a good idea to include black, brown and white dolls and action figures in a variety of roles, which will encourage a positive attitude to different skin colours at a later age.

With such a simple, positive approach, you'll be helping to lay the foundation for your child's respect for different countries and for people whose heritage is wholly or partly linked to those countries.

Another very important starting point is allowing your child to socialize and interact with people from other races and cultures or religions. This helps challenge perceptions of what is "different", since it often reveals that, essentially, we are not different! In places where there are not many children from other racial backgrounds, it would be a good idea to use various media selectively to raise your child's awareness. Nowadays many children's books and programmes in Britain include cartoon characters and children of different heritages.

Anti-racism at school
Racism needs to be addressed in school by taking responsibility for what children are learning. Racism

brought from home may surface in the classroom, in the playground and on the way to school.

Schools need to work very hard on this issue because what children learn at a young age can be retained throughout life. Your child's school should have an anti-racist policy. This should set out clearly how the school tackles any form of racism. Check to see if it could be improved and if you think it can, discuss your ideas with the school's headteacher. Ask whether the school celebrates minority festivals and whether they invite minority speakers to address the school.

Once your child has started school, there is a great deal you can do to reinforce the anti-racist message. Invite parents and children from different racial groups into your home, and make the effort to pronounce any unfamiliar names correctly. When appropriate, refer to members of different racial groups as Black British or Asian British, so your children realize how diverse Britain is. Check that your child's reading materials depict characters from all walks of life and show people in a variety of real roles rather than in one category that is linked stereotypically to a particular racial heritage.

Acknowledge the origins of universal knowledge, inventions, food and clothing and let your child know that the world as a whole has contributed to this, not just Britain. Also let him know that people from all races have contributed to Britain's wealth, health and safety. Highlight that in Britain, mixed relationships and children of dual or multiple heritage are common. Above all, monitor what your child is hearing and understanding, and be aware of your children's attitudes and those of their friends and classmates. Look out for any negative attitudes and views from your children, which you could challenge. Put older, more racist or sexist TV programmes into an historical context.

ANTISOCIAL BEHAVIOUR

No child is perfect. All children try out various forms of challenging behaviour at some point, whether it's being rude, disobedient or aggressive or spoiling or breaking something that's precious to someone else. The way you tackle challenging behaviour will have a big influence on whether or not your child chooses to repeat it. It does take time for children to learn how to behave in a socially acceptable way, but with help from parents and teachers, most do learn fairly quickly.

Most young children reserve their worst behaviour for their parents or carers. It's a way to test their boundaries in the environment where they feel most secure.

"...it takes time for children to learn how to behave in a socially acceptable way, but with help from parents and teachers, most learn fairly quickly"

YOUR CHILD'S PEER GROUP

Friendships are very important in a child's life and a child's peer group becomes increasingly influential as he grows up.

One of the reasons that the peer group is so important to children is that it provides the context in which they can begin experimenting with different behaviours in social situations. By doing this, children are learning important lessons about negotiation and cooperation and how to deal with conflict and competition without adults present to advise or intervene.

Children are usually desperate to "fit in" and be just like their friends. There are different patterns to friendships. Some children have lots of friends. Others prefer to have one or two close friendships. Girls especially tend to form a strong bond with a special friend. What matters is that your child has at least one close friend. If you feel that your child is not making friends, there are several things you can do to encourage friendships (see p.150).

Friendships sometimes hit a rocky patch, and your child's "best" friend may change on a regular basis. These things are normal and are not usually anything to worry about, unless your child seems unduly concerned or upset.

It's important that you encourage your child to start thinking about, valuing and expressing his own opinions and judgements in the years before adolescence. If you do this, it will help him go on to secondary school with an idea of who he is and the ability to express his opinions, which may help him resist being overly influenced by the crowd.

When your child starts school, the school will have behaviour codes and rules that he will be taught and will need to adhere to, or risk being reprimanded. Before your child goes to school, it will help if you introduce some simple rules for the way you expect him to behave at home. Without overburdening him, a few simple rules, such as not taking his brother's toys without permission, will help him get used to obeying rules and to the idea that rules can help make life easier for everyone.

Make sure you set a good example yourself and be consistent in your own behaviour. There's no point having a "no swearing" rule if you swear in front of your child.

It also helps if you involve your child in the rule-making process. Make sure he feels the rule is reasonable and that he understands what it involves.

Dealing with rudeness or cheekiness

If your child is rude or cheeky, ask him to stop it straight away and give him the chance to alter his behaviour with the threat of a quick, clear punishment. For instance, you could say: "if you carry on doing that, you can't play your computer game today". This strategy will work better than a long-term threat, such as saying a child won't get a certain present for birthday or Christmas, which will almost certainly be forgotten by the time the event comes around.

It is essential that you carry out your punishment if the behaviour recurs. This is not always easy, but empty threats will only undermine your authority and can actually make behaviour worse over a period of time.

It can be difficult to keep calm when your child deliberately seems to be behaving badly. Getting angry won't help, though. Respond quickly, for instance by sending him to his room for a few minutes immediately. This should help everyone feel calmer.

WHEN BEHAVIOUR BECOMES A PROBLEM

Some children might carry on behaving badly for weeks or months in a way that is more than ordinary cheekiness. Their behaviour breaks the rules of what's acceptable at home, at school and in their community and can be difficult for parents to handle. This type of behaviour is known as a conduct disorder (see p.301).

A child is more likely to develop a conduct disorder if he has a difficult temperament, has problems with reading or writing, has been abused or bullied or has some form of hyperactivity, which makes it difficult for him to concentrate and follow rules.

In some cases, children with conduct disorders grow out of them as they get older and their behaviour improves. But about half of those affected unfortunately don't. If a conduct disorder isn't tackled early, a child is at risk of getting involved in fights, developing an aggressive attitude and becoming hostile and defiant as he gets older. He might lie or steal without feeling any guilt.

Teenagers with conduct disorders can get involved in criminal behaviour and then in trouble with the police. They sometimes start taking risks with their own health and safety, for instance by joyriding or taking illegal drugs.

This sort of behaviour puts a tremendous strain on the whole family. At school, a child might find

it hard to make friends because he is rude and aggressive. Even though the child may be bright, he may cause problems in lessons and be asked to leave. A child with a conduct disorder may seem irritating and troublesome, but inside he may feel worthless and does not know how to change for the better.

How you can help

Parents can help improve the situation. Clear, fair and consistent discipline will help, as well as praise and rewards when the child behaves well or improves his behaviour. But parents don't need to struggle with their child's behaviour on their own. If you are concerned about your child's behaviour, it is worth discussing it with his teacher. Extra input may be needed. You may also benefit from advice from your GP or an educational psychologist.

If serious problems with your child's behaviour continue for more than three months, see your GP. More specialized help may be needed, and you may be referred to the child and adolescent mental health service in your area. The specialist team will try to help by identifying any causes for your child's problems, giving practical advice on how you can manage your child's difficult behaviour and suggesting strategies for how it could be improved.

"...with their peers, children begin to experiment with different behaviours in social situations"

LIVING WITH
ILLNESS & DISABILITY

WHEN YOU DISCOVER THAT YOUR CHILD HAS A CHRONIC ILLNESS or disability, you'll need time to adjust. The news will come as a shock. You may feel isolated and extremely worried about the future for both your child and yourself. You are not alone. Every day in the UK, over 75 children are born or diagnosed with a serious disability or rare condition.

INITIAL REACTIONS

Sometimes a condition can be detected in the womb, such as a heart abnormality or a genetic condition such as Down's syndrome. For other children the problem isn't diagnosed until after the birth. It's also important to remember the children who acquire their disability through injury or infection. Many parents describe feeling a sense of bereavement when their child is diagnosed with a serious condition. Numbness and disbelief can be followed by anger, a sense of despair and finally, for most parents, acceptance. They then feel more in control and can start to plan for the future. Sometimes, if a child has a problem that has been puzzling doctors for a while, a diagnosis comes as a relief because it can be the start of getting the right treatment and care. In some cases, though, a diagnosis can't be made. In other cases, a diagnosis can be made but no specific treatment is available yet. These things do not mean that you won't be able to get support and practical help for you and your child.

Some parents describe having mixed feelings towards their disabled child in the early months.

It's not uncommon to feel a fleeting sense of dislike towards him because he will need extra time and attention. This is perfectly normal and doesn't usually last long.

Most families learn to cope remarkably well. I often hear parents saying they have discovered courage and inner strength they didn't know they had. For others, it remains a struggle and they should not feel embarrassed or as if they have failed if they ask for more help.

Parents who seem to cope best often say they find it helpful to focus on one problem at a time, rather than letting themselves become overwhelmed by the situation. Be positive about small achievements, and prepare for disappointment as well as success. For instance, if you are trying out a new treatment for your child, be realistic and don't raise your hopes too soon.

Most people you meet will have no experience of a child with a disability or illness and won't know how to react. It's almost inevitable that some will say the wrong thing, which can be upsetting. Make it clear that although your child has a disability or a health condition, he is valued no less as a human being. Demonstrate that he has

the right to love and understanding and that you value his individuality. Try to be positive. Others are then more likely to follow your lead.

HELPING BROTHERS & SISTERS COPE

A recent study carried out by the charity Contact a Family focused on the siblings of children with

disabilities. The study found that siblings face many difficulties, including being teased or bullied at school; feeling jealous of the amount of attention their brother or sister receives; feeling resentful because family outings are limited and infrequent; having their sleep disturbed and feeling tired at school; finding it hard to complete homework; and being embarrassed about their brother or sister's behaviour in public, usually because of the reaction of others.

Siblings seem to cope best when parents and other adults in their lives can accept their brother or sister's special needs and value him or her as a person. Inevitably, though, siblings may feel the focus of the family is on the child with the disability and that there is not enough time for their own needs. Getting this balance right can be difficult for parents, who are often already short of time and energy.

There are ways to help. Giving siblings the chance to talk things over and express their feelings can help them deal with worries and concerns. Putting aside certain times for siblings, for instance story time before bed or a special outing once a month, may also help. Your children will be able to cope better at school if you take the time to discuss ways to explain about their brother or sister's condition and help them rehearse responses to any unpleasant remarks people make.

HEALTH IN DISABILITY

You and your child may find specific help, support and advice useful. Your GP or hospital specialist can refer you to a range of medical, nursing and other services. These may include:

A community paediatric nurse to help with practical tasks involved in nursing a child at home, such as changing dressings or giving injections.

A health visitor to suggest practical ways of caring for your child and to give you advice on common problems.

An occupational therapist to help your child manage daily tasks, such as dressing and going to the toilet. He or she can also advise on and sometimes arrange for you to be supplied with aids and adaptations to your home.

A physiotherapist to provide treatment to relieve pain and increase mobility. He or she can also advise on things like how to lift your child.

A community psychiatric nurse to give you advice if your child has mental health problems and sometimes to give a child medication.

A community dental officer if your child's disability affects his teeth.

A speech therapist to help children with language or communication disorders.

A continence adviser if your child is incontinent; you may also be eligible for nappies or incontinence aids.

A child development centre to assess your child's needs and organize therapy if necessary.

A buggy or wheelchair if your child has serious walking difficulties.

Ask for help. Friends and relatives can play an important role here, taking your other children on outings or special activities or simply spending time with them. Support groups are a good way of swapping ideas with other parents. There are support groups especially for siblings, too.

HELPING GRANDPARENTS COPE

When a child is born with a medical condition, it affects the whole extended family, not just parents and siblings. Grandparents can experience feelings of anger, grief and denial similar to those experienced by parents.

These days grandparents may be more involved in helping with childcare and support than ever before, due to pressures of work and financial constraints faced by families. The role of grandparents may be increased if a grandchild is diagnosed with special needs or a disability. However, many grandparents may not have had a great deal of contact with disabled children, since they were often cared for away from home in the past. Grandparents may be keen to help, but unsure what level of input to give.

A workshop for grandparents, organized by Contact a Family, found that many grandparents felt that they were at a time in their lives when they were able to devote time, attention and support to their family. In return, they felt that having a child with special needs in the family helped them be more understanding and learn more about disability. A common complaint was that many grandparents felt excluded from normal information networks and wanted to know more about their grandchild's condition.

Grandparents can also play an important role by giving special time to other children in the family, or by including them in activities they would otherwise miss. Help could be as simple as providing a quiet place for siblings to do their homework.

There are now a few support groups that have been set up specifically for grandparents of children with disabilities, recognizing that they too may feel isolated and need support.

GETTING THE SUPPORT YOU NEED

When you have a child with a specific condition or disability, you are likely to face many challenges. It can be difficult for both parents to go to work, and finding a babysitter

may not be easy. It's particularly difficult for single parents. Help from family, friends, health professionals and support agencies can make life more manageable.

Under recent Government acts, Social Services departments in England, Wales and Scotland have a duty to assess the needs of a child with a disability. The aim of these laws is to support you as a parent and to help you care for your child.

An assessment will be the first stage in identifying what help you need from Social Services. This will be carried out by a social worker, who will probably visit you at home. The assessment involves you, your child and anyone else who helps with caring for your child. It will take into account your child's particular health needs and any needs in relation to development, disability, education, religious and racial preferences, as well as the degree to which these needs are currently being met. The social worker will then organize help.

The kinds of services offered might include advice about benefit entitlements; practical help you are entitled to have at home; provision of recreational or educational facilities; travel assistance; home adaptations to which you are entitled; meals; holidays; and provision of a television or telephone. (*For more information, see* Useful Addresses, *p.344*.)

Your local authority may provide other services, but they are discretionary. These may include advice and guidance, laundry services and financial help in exceptional circumstances.

Respite care, where you and your child have a short break from each other, can be very helpful. Without an occasional break you could start to feel exhausted or unwell. Your child is also likely to benefit from the break from you, contact with other people and new experiences. See Useful Addresses (*p.344*) for organizations that help with holidays for children with special needs.

EDUCATION & DISABILITY

Helping your child get the most out of education may be one of your key concerns. If your child has a medical condition, discuss it with his teacher and headteacher. There may be ways to help him cope in the classroom. If your child needs medication, let his teacher and headteacher know, and then send the school instructions in writing. You will need to let the school know when he takes the medication and how. Many schools do not allow teachers to administer medication of any sort, so check the school's policy on this. If your child isn't allowed to take his medication at school, discuss with your doctor whether the times for the medication can be safely changed so that he can have it immediately after school instead.

If your child has special educational needs, he may need extra support to get the most out of the education system. For children who have special educational needs that can't be met within the early years setting or by using the school's own resources, your Local Education Authority (LEA) may carry out an assessment to help decide whether further assistance is required (the Library and Education Board is responsible for this in Northern Ireland). A document may be issued, known as a Statement of Special Educational Needs (SSEN), that sets out how your child's needs should be met (*see p.147*).

PLAY FACILITIES FOR CHILDREN WITH DISABILITIES

Play has an important role in the development of all children, whatever their abilities. It also offers a valuable way for your child to socialize with other children. For disabled children, play opportunities in the community can be limited. However, the situation is improving, and many organizations are working hard to make more opportunities for disabled children available.

If your child has a medical condition or special needs, think about the sort of activities he may be interested in. For instance, he might enjoy attending a playgroup. Schools often run holiday play schemes and are a good source of information about other activities, such as sports clubs.

To find out what play facilities and other leisure opportunities exist in your area you could try contacting the following places:

- Local authority leisure, amenity or community service departments
- Your local library (these now often run year-round activities for children)
- Specific local play and leisure facilities, such as toy libraries (sometimes there are special needs toy libraries), playgroups, adventure playgrounds, leisure centres and pools
- Voluntary organizations, such as Play Associations and the Council for Voluntary Service
- Agencies working in the area with disabled children and their families, such as Mencap, Scope, Barnardos and Contact a Family

STARTING SCHOOL

Going to school is about much more than academic achievement. It's the main way children socialize and is an important step for them in becoming more independent and well-rounded. Your child will fit into school life better if he has acquired some everyday skills and the basics of how to behave. These include going to the toilet on his own and knowing how to listen and take turns.

PREPARING YOUR CHILD FOR SCHOOL

The best way to prepare your child for school is to start early. The most important factor in determining a child's academic success lies in language acquisition. Reading regularly to your child from babyhood will increase his comprehension and vocabulary and should be fun for you both. Set aside a special time for reading to your child, perhaps half an hour before bed, which you can continue as he grows older.

Going to playgroup or nursery prepares your child for school. Make sure the one you choose focuses on play rather than on strictly academic learning. The most important lessons your child should be learning are about getting along with others, and this should be fun.

Visiting the school

Once your child has been offered a place at school, start talking to him about it. There are lots of books for children about starting school that you can read together. Most schools offer pre-school visits, which give your child the chance to look around his classroom, meet his teacher, see where the toilets are and see where his coat peg will be.

Find out about the school's routine so you can talk about what will be happening and when. The school should also give you the opportunity to ask questions or discuss any issues relating specifically to your child. If he has a problem, such as an allergy or a medical condition, let both the teacher and headteacher know and confirm it in writing. If relevant, you should also ask about the school's policy regarding medical items such as inhalers and Epipens and whether any staff are trained in their use.

First days

The night before your child's first day, get everything ready so he feels well prepared. Lay his clothes out and have his bag packed. It's a good idea to do this every night for the first few weeks so that neither of you has a last-minute panic in the morning. From then on, encourage him to prepare for the next day. For example, if he has been asked to bring something in, encourage him to choose the item the night before and put it where he won't forget it.

Your own approach to school is important. If you are positive and tell your child you know he can cope, he will feel more confident. If you're visibly upset when he goes, he may feel discouraged and believe that you don't think he'll manage.

Be sensitive to his behaviour during the first few weeks at school.

"...if you are positive about school, your child is more likely to be positive too"

The most important thing is that he's making friends. Try inviting one or two of the children he seems to like to your house after school, which should help them bond.

When you pick your child up from school, don't worry if he doesn't talk about his day right away. He might start chatting about something, or singing a particular song he's learned, later on. Even if he doesn't do this, everything is probably fine.

ACHIEVEMENT & YOUR CHILD

There may be occasions when you become concerned about your child's progress. For instance, if he's not reading fluently by age 7 or 8, you might want to discuss his progress with his teacher.

It's worth remembering that most children are of average ability and it's the exception rather than the rule to be above average. It's also worth bearing in mind that girls tend to do

CHILDREN WITH SPECIAL EDUCATIONAL NEEDS

If you feel your child is generally falling behind at school, or if he has a problem with a specific subject such as reading, you should seek professional advice. Ask your GP to check for physical problems that could be making school hard for him, such as vision or hearing difficulties. If your child's linguistic skills are behind, you may be referred to a speech and language therapist. The next step may be a full educational assessment to pinpoint areas of difficulty; a plan to help him achieve his potential may then be drawn up. See your school's headteacher to find out your next steps and arrange a meeting with your school's special needs coordinator.

There are four stages to the Special Educational Needs Code of Practice (which is a Department for Education and Skills statutory guidance document), and all will be done in consultation with you.

- Interventions tailored to your child's needs will be tried at school.
- External specialists from the Local Education Authority will advise your child's teachers.
- Your child's school can request a statutory assessment from the Local Education Authority if your child demonstrates "significant cause for concern".
- A Statement of Special Educational Needs (SSEN) may be made, with specific recommendations – for instance, that your child needs extra help with reading or assistance using the toilet. Funding should be made available to provide this help.

"...don't compare your child with others...focus on the things he can do and seems to enjoy, and give him plenty of praise and encouragement"

better than boys initially at school. They generally have better language skills and as the British education system is geared to linguistic ability, girls are getting better results right up to GCSE level (16 years). Boys seem to catch up after that.

For children of high-flying parents, life at school can be especially difficult. They may not be as academically able as their parents, and they may feel that the standards their parents have set them are too high. Children, like adults, become stressed if they are persistently asked to perform beyond their capability.

During the first few years at school, if your child is a good talker and listener and has the basics of numeracy, there should be nothing to worry about academically. Nonetheless, it will be difficult not to compare him with others. Some children will be better at drawing or writing while others will be better at class discussion or ball games. You should focus on the things your child can do and seems to enjoy, and

give him plenty of praise and encouragement. Appreciating his strengths will give him the message that you value him.

However, it's important to get the right balance between playing on your child's strengths and encouraging him in areas where he may be weak. If you feel your child is not achieving to the best of his ability, trust your instincts. As his parent, you know him best. Young children are not usually lazy at school and there is often a good reason for any problem. It may be that your child has a specific worry, which could be about something very simple. It could be that he does not relate well to his teacher, or he may have general or specific learning difficulties. Ask your child's teacher for help.

If you feel your child could do with being a little more challenged than he is at school, look at what you could do together at home. Slightly more difficult books will develop his linguistic skills. Simple board games such as Snakes and Ladders and Ludo will help his numeracy skills and also help him learn about taking turns. Card games such as Happy Families and 21 are also good for numeracy.

Bring maths into everyday life by letting your child use money in a shop and involve him in cooking and weighing ingredients. Learning in this way is much better than sitting down with workbooks.

IF YOUR CHILD REFUSES TO GO TO SCHOOL

Your child must be in full-time education in the term after he turns 5. However, it can take a young child several months to settle into school. Take it slowly and don't expect too much to start with and

your child should gain confidence. If your child seems very unhappy about going to school, speak to his teacher; there may be things that can be done to help him settle in. A buddy system, where an older child helps your child find his way around, might work. You could then invite that child to your home so they can get to know each other.

Inviting one or two children from your child's class back home will also help build his confidence and self-esteem. It shouldn't take longer than six months for a child to fully settle into school. If he has still not settled by the time he is 5 ½ to 6 years old, there is probably a reason and you should speak to your child's teacher. You may need expert help.

Older children
Sometimes, an older or more confident child will come up with an excuse for not going to school. Most children do this at least once. He might complain of a headache or of feeling sick when you think he's probably fine. If you do let him have the day off school, don't give him too much attention. If he is well, he will be glad to get back to school.

If your child has previously been happy at school and suddenly doesn't want to go, it's likely that there's something worrying him. He may not like his teacher or he may be being bullied, which is more common than we'd like to think. If your child seems unhappy at school, cries on the way and seems very reluctant to go, take it seriously. Bullying can never be ignored. Your child's school should have a policy to deal with bullying (*see p.151*).

Occasionally, if your child doesn't want to go to school, the problem can become very difficult. Talk to your child's teacher and agree a plan

to help him. Rehearse his day, discussing each lesson. Remind him about reassuring things – for instance, that he will be sitting next to a particular friend in maths. Positive statements about things he does well, such as "you're good at English", help. Taking a favourite object or toy to school may help, but check with the teacher first.

Many children feel under great pressure to do well at school, and it is worth thinking carefully about

how your expectations affect your child. You should ensure that he still has plenty of time in his day for enjoyable non-competitive activities. If you can't get your child to school at all, ask your GP for a referral to a child psychologist.

HELPING GIFTED CHILDREN
If your child excels academically, he'll need to feel challenged at school to help him make the most

of his abilities. Teachers know that bright children can easily feel bored and frustrated if the pace of work is too slow for them, which can lead to disruptive behaviour. However, it's not always appropriate for a child to go up a year. He may not be ready socially or emotionally to mix with older children. Extension work, where your child will be given work at a faster pace in his existing class setting, is usually preferred.

Children who are exceptionally good at sports, music or the creative arts could also be described as gifted. There are government initiatives aimed at promoting the talents of gifted children; your child's school should have a policy on this. You can also do things to help at home. For example, if your child is good at music, take him to concerts and look out for relevant TV programmes.

DEALING WITH EXAMS, TESTS AND ASSESSMENTS

Children face more testing than ever before during their school years, and this can be worrying for parents as well as for children and teachers.

The SATs (Standard Assessment Tasks)

In primary school, your child will do the Key Stage 1 and 2 SATs. The Key Stage 1 SATs take place in Year 2, when your child is 7, and the Key Stage 2 SATs take place in Year 6, when your child is 11. The SATs are meant to reflect the school's ability to meet government targets for children's achievement in areas such as numeracy and literacy. They are not meant to test a child's individual performance in these areas, and although the results will be passed on to your child's secondary school, they won't form part of his record.

However, the SATs can be useful individually in assessing your child's strengths and weaknesses. A limited amount of stress and pressure of extra work can also be good for helping children prepare for the examination process they'll have to go through in secondary school and if they go on to higher education.

Your child will be prepared at school for the SATs. Usually, children doing the Key Stage 1 SATs are not told that they are being prepared and may even be unaware that they are being tested, since schools do not want to subject young children to examination stress. At Key Stage 2, your child's teacher will run through sample questions and talk about what the test will be like. You can support this by giving your child practice at home if you wish. SATs workbooks are available from major bookshops.

PROBLEMS WITH FRIENDS OR TEACHERS

Most children will come across at least one teacher they feel they don't get on with during their school years, and if this happens your child will need to learn to cope with it.

Make the experience into a learning one. Talk to him about how important it is to get on with different people and suggest some strategies for coping. Ideally, do not intervene directly and let him deal with the problem himself.

Similarly, there will almost certainly be times when your child falls out with friends. If you feel your child is being bullied, you should take this seriously (*see opposite*). If it seems to be more the case that the friendship is going through a negative phase, consider strategies that might help. For instance, you could invite his friends round to your house, or get your child involved in after-school activities with friends.

IF YOUR CHILD IS BULLIED

Unfortunately, bullying at school is quite a common problem. Most people think of bullying in terms of kicking, hitting or other forms of violence. However, emotional bullying, which involves name-calling, sarcasm, spreading rumours and/or persistent teasing or ignoring, is more usual and can be more difficult to cope with and prove. Persistent bullying of either kind can result in depression, low self-esteem, shyness, poor academic performance, isolation or in extreme cases even threatened or attempted suicide.

If you are worried that your child is being bullied, you must take the matter seriously. Try to establish the facts – ask him directly what is happening. Talk with his teacher and headteacher, and with the playground supervisor. The school should have a policy for dealing with bullying. Make a diary of all incidents and write to the school so that your complaint is on record.

If your child is being physically bullied, help him practise strategies such as shouting "no!", walking with confidence and running away. If the bullying is happening on the way to or from school, meet your child or ask that the bullies be kept at school until others are home.

If your child is being emotionally bullied, teach him to avoid the children who are bothering him and encourage him to make friends with other children. Teach him to ignore name-calling or teasing, and explain that if he stops reacting to taunts, the bullies will soon lose interest.

IF YOUR CHILD IS A BULLY

If you discover that your child is bullying another child, try to stay calm. Talk to him and try to establish the facts, and talk to his teacher and headteacher. Let your child know why bullying is wrong. Reassure him that you love him, but make it clear that you don't like his behaviour. A reward system for good behaviour might help. If he can't see that his actions are wrong and won't stop bullying, he may need referral to a child psychologist.

SPOTTING THE WARNING SIGNS OF BULLYING

According to the children's charity Kidscape, signs of bullying include:

Being frightened of walking to and from school or changing their usual route

Not wanting to go on the school bus

Begging you to drive them to school

Being unwilling to go to school

Regularly feeling ill in the mornings

Truanting

Doing poorly in school work

Coming home regularly with clothes or books destroyed or possessions missing

Becoming withdrawn, starting to stammer, lacking confidence

Crying themselves to sleep, having nightmares

Asking for money or starting to steal (to pay the bully)

Continually "losing" their pocket money

Refusing to talk about what's wrong

Having unexplained bruises, cuts, scratches

Beginning to bully other children, including siblings

Becoming aggressive and unreasonable

Becoming distressed and anxious, losing appetite

SEXUAL DEVELOPMENT

Think back to your own adolescent years and it's likely that you won't remember them altogether fondly – the hormones that bring about puberty also mark the start of a turbulent journey. Your child's emotional development during this time is slower than her physical development. She won't be ready for an adult relationship for some time, which can be confusing and frustrating.

"...oestrogen and testosterone are the principal hormones that bring about the physical changes of puberty in girls and boys"

HORMONAL CHANGES

Both female and male hormones are present at low levels in children of both sexes from birth. However, the balance of these hormones changes dramatically at puberty as the levels of male sex hormones rise in boys and levels of female sex hormones rise in girls.

Up to a year before any physical changes appear, and as early as age 8 for girls and age 10 for boys, changes start taking place in the amount of certain hormones produced by the hypothalamus in the brain. These hormones cause the ovaries in a girl to develop follicles, which first produce the female sex hormone oestrogen and later on, progesterone. In a boy, these hormones cause the testicles to enlarge and begin producing the male hormone testosterone.

Oestrogen and testosterone are the principal hormones that bring about the physical changes of puberty in girls and boys, although there is a contribution from the adrenal glands in stimulating the growth of pubic and underarm hair.

PHYSICAL CHANGES IN GIRLS

Girls usually start producing sex hormones between the ages of 8 and 11 years, with the average age of beginning puberty at around 11. The first and most obvious external sign

that a girl is entering puberty is the development of breast buds. These may be asymmetrical in size at first and quite tender, which may require some reassurance.

This early breast development is usually accompanied by the adolescent growth spurt. There is often a feeling of awkwardness, since a girl's hands and feet may grow rapidly at first, with the legs and spine taking longer to catch up. There is also a change in body shape and fat distribution as girls gain fat in the area of their breasts and hips. This distribution of fat and the wider pelvis that girls have (which is needed in order to deliver a baby) account for the adult female figure being "curvier" than that of a man.

As well as the obvious external changes, a girl's internal organs also increase in size and shape. Her uterus and vagina become larger and the lining of her vagina thickens and starts to produce clear secretions.

By the end of the pubertal process (which in both boys and girls may take up to five years from the first sign until adult height is reached), a girl's height will increase by around 21 cm (9½ in), with only 6 cm (2½ in) of this growth occurring after periods start.

Pubic hair is very different from the soft vellous hair that may be present in young children. In girls

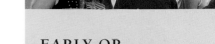

it starts as coarse dark hair along the edges of the labia, subsequently increasing in both amount and area of distribution.

Pubic hair usually starts to appear after breast budding, but not always. In particular there may be an early "switch on" of the adrenal glands, which can occur around the age of 7 and is independent of true puberty. If this happens it is termed "premature adrenarche" and is most commonly seen in children who have one or more parent of Afro-Caribbean or Mediterranean origin.

In addition to pubic hair there may be some underarm hair and even some body odour. The appearance of "androgen" hair is often accompanied by other effects of androgen secretion, such as acne on the face and back, greasiness of the skin and scalp, and body odour. Your daughter may find she needs to wash her hair more frequently and also use a deodorant. Underarm hair develops at varying times but may be relatively late.

Menstruation

The onset of periods (menarche) usually occurs towards the end of puberty. Periods usually start when the breasts are well developed but not quite "adult" in size and shape (this takes up to four years) and as the adolescent growth spurt is coming to an end. On average, menarche occurs between the ages of 12 and 13 years, but may occur as early as 10 or as late as 15 years in normal girls.

EARLY OR DELAYED PUBERTY

Early puberty in girls
You may want to visit your doctor if your daughter begins to develop breasts or pubic hair before age 8. While early puberty can run in families, it can also result from unusually early or excessive hormone production linked to a medical condition. Your daughter may need hormone measurements, which take the form of a blood test, to determine if this is the case. She may also need a pelvic ultrasound scan, similar to those for pregnant women, to assess the size of her womb and ovaries.

Delayed puberty in girls
Puberty is considered delayed if your daughter has no breast buds or pubic hair developing by the age of 14. You should also be concerned if her periods have not started within five years of the appearance of breast tissue. Again, delay can run in families. As is the case for early puberty, hormone levels may be measured with a blood test. In certain cases, puberty can be induced by giving extra hormones at the appropriate time.

Early puberty in boys
If your son has experienced an increase in the size of his testicles and/or penis, or has developed any pubic hair, before age 9, visit your doctor. He may need hormone tests.

Delayed puberty in boys
You may also like to see your doctor if your son has not had any of the signs of pubertal development by the age of 14. He may simply be a late developer, especially if this runs in the family, but he could be producing insufficient hormones for a variety of reasons and may need medical tests.

Periods during the first year often happen without the release of an egg (ovulation), and because of this they are often irregular before settling into a cycle of between 28 and 35 days. Some girls do not establish a regular cycle and may need to be investigated for this if it goes on for longer than a year or so.

There is an impression that periods are starting earlier than they did 30 or 40 years ago. The age of menarche, and probably the onset of puberty, has followed a secular trend to occur on average two to three months earlier per decade, probably reflecting improvements in socioeconomic status, especially in the industrialized world. This trend is now beginning to reach a plateau in most of western Europe and the US.

However, the trend for an earlier age of menarche may be ongoing in parts of the developing world, where nutrition and living conditions are continuing to improve. It is certainly the case that girls from different ethnic backgrounds may vary significantly in the expected timing of puberty, with girls from an Afro-Caribbean or Mediterranean background maturing earlier.

PHYSICAL CHANGES IN BOYS

Puberty in boys starts, on average, six months after it does in girls. The first sign of puberty – an enlargement of the testicles – occurs at around 12 years of age, but can happen between the ages of 10½ and 14 in normal boys. Pubic hair development and growth of the penis usually begin within six months of the initial testicular increase, but the adolescent growth spurt in boys is a relatively late event, taking place on average at age 14 or so. This means that puberty in a boy may go unnoticed at first.

The testicles continue to enlarge symmetrically as the rest of the physical changes occur, and any inequality in the size of the testicles or pain in either testicle should be reported to your doctor. Pubic hair develops as coarse dark hairs around the base of the penis at first and then gradually spreads into the adult male distribution. Hair spreading up the lower abdomen or over the chest occurs relatively late, and in some boys not at all. As hair growth is happening the penis also begins to grow, at first just in length, but later in breadth also, with development of the glans, the sensitive tip of the penis. Underarm hair and greasiness of the skin and acne are later events, and the average age for the development of facial hair is around 15 years. Voice changes, which are partly due to growth in the voice box (larynx) and change in length and thickness of the vocal cords, usually start between the ages of 13 and 15 years.

A boy going through an "average puberty" may begin to experience nocturnal ejaculation, or "wet dreams", at around 13 or 14 years of age. This may worry him unless it has been explained to him before. Nocturnal ejaculation is a reflection of semen production and should alert parents to the need for a discussion with their son about potential relationships. He will probably also start to be more interested in girls around this time, who will be more physically mature at this stage.

As with girls, skeletal growth in boys is at first disproportionate. A boy's hands and feet grow more quickly than his arms and legs, and they in turn lengthen before his torso, creating an impression of gawkiness. This temporary unevenness also affects your son's face, since his chin, nose, lips and ears grow before his head attains its full adult size.

By the time puberty is completed, your son will have gained about 28 cm (11 in) in height. He will have become leaner, with more muscle than fat, and will, to a greater or lesser extent, have developed a more "male" body shape, with relatively broad shoulders and narrow hips. By this stage his facial hair will probably be growing more fully and he may need to shave occasionally.

As with girls, the surge of hormones and body changes may cause a boy to become moody, withdrawn or aggressive. It is important to avoid too much confrontation and allow him to develop into a mature adult while at the same time preserving basic ground rules at home.

> "...as puberty begins, boys start to be more interested in girls, who will also be more physically mature at this stage"

SEX EDUCATION

TALKING TO CHILDREN ABOUT THE FACTS OF LIFE isn't something that many parents find easy. How much information do you give your child? And when do you give it? The way you approach sex will depend on both you and your child. It's not something you can cover in a single half-hour chat. It's an ongoing process. Your child will need different information at different stages.

> "...the best approach to sex education is to take the lead from your child"

WHEN IS THE RIGHT TIME TO START?

Most experts agree that the best approach is to take the lead from your child and wait until he asks you a question. "Where do babies come from?" is often the first. It's important that you be open and honest right from the start and avoid tales of storks or gooseberry bushes. They might seem easy explanations at the time, but as your child grows up and finds out what actually does happen, he will be less likely to trust you.

It's worth doing some preparation before your child is old enough to ask you questions. Think about how you might answer your child's questions when he asks them. Replies should be appropriate to his age and understanding. For instance, a child of 5 will probably be satisfied with hearing that a baby is made by a mummy and a daddy and grows in mummy's tummy. There's no need at this stage to go into a detailed biological explanation and you don't need to cover issues that he hasn't asked about. Doing so could just confuse him.

If your child asks you something that takes you by surprise and you're not sure how to reply, be honest. You could say something like: "That's an interesting question. I'm not sure what the answer is. Let me think about it and we can talk later." This gives you time to think what to say, and for your child it leaves open the idea of talking about the subject again. It's worth investing in a book with simple diagrams that helps you show your child what you are explaining. There are many available for different age groups.

SEX EDUCATION IN SCHOOL

Sex education is now part of the National Curriculum, so all children will receive some lessons in it at school. At primary school, children aged between 5 and 7 will learn that animals, including humans, grow and reproduce. Between the ages of 7 and 11, pupils will learn more about life cycles and human reproduction. It's worth talking to your child's teacher to find out how the school tackles sex education specifically, and when it will happen. You can then be ready to talk to your child about what he has learned, make sure he has understood it properly and give him the opportunity to ask any further questions. Parents have the right to withdraw their children from sex education lessons if they feel they are inappropriate.

The content and tone of sex education lessons is left to the discretion of schools, where policies on sex education are set by school governors in consultation with parents. However, there have recently been clear messages to schools from the government on how sex education should be taught. This guidance takes into account recent concern about a dramatic increase in the number of young people seeking help for sexually transmitted diseases, and according to NHS figures, some clinics are seeing children as young as 11 years old.

Is sex education in schools adequate?

A recent report by Ofsted, the school inspection service, suggested that sex education is failing to teach pupils adequately about the dangers of sexually transmitted diseases.

The team studied lessons in 140 primary, secondary and special schools and the results of the study suggested that teaching about sexual health was "poor" in as many as one lesson in five. Apart from this, there is also concern that Britain has the highest teenage pregnancy rate in western Europe.

ATTITUDES TO NUDITY

Young children don't have any sense of privacy. They are often happiest when they don't have any clothes on and will be very interested in your body. Some parents are very relaxed about this and are happy to let their children see them without clothes. Others aren't. But if you are comfortable with it, it can be helpful for young children to see that you are relaxed and confident about your body. And it can help your child begin to realize why boys and girls, men and women, are different.

Often, around the time of starting school, children tend to become more aware of their bodies and are less keen to take their clothes off. As your child's boundaries begin to emerge, be careful to respect them. Don't burst into the bathroom when your 8-year-old is in the bath, or into his room when the door is closed.

If you are concerned that your child doesn't show any inhibitions, you could gradually introduce the idea of personal privacy and boundaries. For instance, you could close the door to your bedroom or bathroom and gently explain that there are some things that people do prefer to do in private.

It's important to make clear the distinction between privacy and secrecy. For instance, a child exploring his body isn't something that's secret, but rather something that is private.

When children are young and happy to be seen naked it's easy to see anything obviously wrong. As your child grows older and becomes more inhibited, you need to tell him that he needs to be aware of his body and talk to you if anything is wrong.

ANSWERING YOUR CHILD'S QUESTIONS

Answer your child honestly when he starts asking you questions about where babies come from. You don't need to give him details he won't understand, but you can simply explain that he came out of his mummy's tummy.

When your child is older, a good book with diagrams aimed at the appropriate age level is helpful in explaining how reproduction works.

Don't rely on sex education in schools to teach your child all he needs to know – your child may not understand issues about relationships and peer pressure.

Help your child understand that only a minority of teenagers are sexually active and that it's normal not to be.

Make sure at each stage of development that your child knows it's all right to approach you with any questions or problems about sex and relationships that he may have. Let him know that, whatever the question or issue, you are always there to listen to him.

While education on sex and relationships, HIV, AIDS and other sexually transmitted diseases is provided at secondary school, the government has published guidelines telling all schools that sex education lessons should not encourage early experimentation with sex.

PUTTING SEX EDUCATION IN CONTEXT

As children grow, it is often easy to assume that they will learn everything they need to know at school and to think that they understand more about sex, sexual development and relationships than they really do.

Children are more sophisticated these days in terms of being aware of fashions and music, and are used to seeing images of sexuality in the media – usually the bare flesh variety rather than images depicting relationships.

Girls tend to be more knowledgeable about sex than boys. There are lots of magazines aimed at girls, usually containing responsible information on sexual issues. Boys tend to rely more on sex education at school. But both boys and girls can pick up an underlying, but inaccurate, message from movies, videos and music that all young people are sexually active. One study found that 80 per cent of 14-year-olds believe that most people lose their virginity before age 16. In fact the reality is that, at the most, a third of girls and fewer boys have had sexual intercourse by 16.

There is a huge amount of material on the Internet on sexual issues, and this is becoming an increasingly important source of information for young people. There can be some very helpful sites, but you may feel that some are too explicit for younger children.

Most children say they would like to continue hearing about sex and relationships from their parents as well as at school. For parents, it is useful to check that your child has accurate information and above all to give guidance. With your help, your child will develop the confidence to make the right choices at the right times.

If your daughter enjoys reading magazines, a good starting point would be to pick out some of the information they contain and discuss it together. This would give you the opportunity to listen to any messages your daughter may be picking up and to correct them if they're inaccurate. You can also give her the opportunity to ask any questions.

Boys can often be too embarrassed to talk openly about sex. Mentioning, almost casually, things that are relevant to sex education that you have read in the paper or seen on television together can give him the opportunity to ask questions or at least hear your views.

Talking to older children

Once the basic information on sex is imparted and children go through puberty, it can often become more difficult to talk about sex. Part of the reason for this may be that your child likes to appear as though he knows everything. Or, he may really think he knows all there is to know.

In reality, your child may know some facts about sex and reproduction but may not grasp their full implications. He also may not understand what the real issues are in relationships or how to resist pressure from peers or partners to be sexually active before he is ready. All of these things can be difficult for an adolescent to admit to.

As parents, it's a good idea to let your child know that it's all right for him not to understand how to cope with relationship issues or peer pressure at his age. Being open may help your child feel more able to ask for your advice and more comfortable about receiving it.

ALCOHOL, SMOKING & DRUGS

PARENTS TODAY ARE INCREASINGLY WORRIED ABOUT their children being tempted by alcohol, smoking or drugs. These all seem to be more readily available than before and it's impossible to protect children from opportunities to experiment. You might think this doesn't apply to children age 11 and under, but research shows that by age 11 a third of children will have tried smoking.

"...listen to your child's views on alcohol, smoking and drugs and use them as starting points for discussion"

WHAT YOU CAN DO AS A PARENT

While the chances are that your child will not be involved in smoking, drinking alcohol or using drugs during his primary school years, this is a crucial time for providing him with information and opportunities to develop his understanding. This will help equip him with the skills he needs in order to make informed decisions about his lifestyle when the time comes.

Schools are now required to provide drugs education, which includes alcohol and tobacco, as part of science education in the National Curriculum. While they are required to teach children about the dangers of drugs, most primary schools do not yet have a formal policy covering drug use at school.

There is a lot that parents can do to educate their children about drugs, alcohol and smoking. Listen to what your child has to say about these things and use it as a starting point for discussions. As well as talking to your child, you need to be involved in his life and get to know his friends. It might be useful to talk to other parents, friends or teachers.

Why might a child try any of these things? It could be through curiosity, for fun or to be like his friends. Most young people who experiment with drugs, alcohol or smoking do not continue or develop drug problems. It's also worth remembering that there are significantly more health and social problems relating to use of the so-called "acceptable" drugs, alcohol and tobacco, than to harder drugs.

ALCOHOL

Both parents and schools have a crucial role to play in terms of preparing children for life in a world where there is alcohol.

If you drink alcohol and intend to introduce it to your children, when is the best age? Research shows that the younger a person starts drinking, the more likely he is to run into problems. Although there is no "right" time to introduce your child to alcohol, it's probably better for young people to start drinking later rather than earlier.

Ensuring that this happens can be problematic, however. While your 11-year-old might not like the taste of wine or beer, sweet "alcopop"-type drinks are popular and appeal to young people because they cannot really taste the alcohol that these drinks contain.

Most primary school children do know something about drugs, although drug use is not commonly an issue at primary school age.

Drug use is most common among teenagers and people in their early 20s. But, according to the Department of Health, the average age of first drug use is becoming younger. Young people are most likely to try sniffing volatile solvents, such as glue or butane gas, or use cannabis.

Occasional drug use may be hard to detect, but if your child is using drugs on a regular basis, his behaviour might change. The signs to look out for include:
• Unexplained moodiness
• Behaviour that is out of character
• Loss of interest in school or friends
• Unexplained disappearance of money or clothes
• Unusual smells

If you do suspect your child of using drugs of any sort, make sure of your facts. Be gentle, helpful and reassuring and consistent in your views about drugs. Your continuing help and support will be vital.

Don't be afraid to ask for help. You could talk to your GP or practice nurse in confidence, to your child's teacher or the school nurse. There is also a wide range of voluntary counselling centres and drug and alcohol agencies that will be able to provide information and support.

Bear in mind that most children do grow out of a phase of drug experimentation.

SMOKING

Research shows that three out of four children are aware of cigarettes before they reach the age of 5, whether their parents smoke or not. By age 11, a third of children will have experimented with smoking.

Girls are more likely than boys to be regular smokers, and the proportion of those who smoke increases sharply with age. One per cent of 11-year-olds smoke regularly, compared with 22 per cent of 15-year-olds. Children are three times more likely to smoke if both their parents smoke, and parental approval or disapproval of the habit is a significant factor in influencing whether your child takes it up.

Most young smokers are also influenced by friends and older brothers or sisters who smoke. There is a significant impact on the health of a child who smokes. This includes being two to six times more susceptible to colds, increased phlegm, wheezing and shortness of breath. Children are also more susceptible than adults to the effects of passive smoking.

STAYING WELL

W E ALL WANT TO KEEP OUR CHILDREN HEALTHY and may wonder what we can do to ensure that our children stay as well as possible. As parents or carers, we are responsible for our children's wellbeing from day to day, and it is largely the things we do on a daily basis – such as providing healthy meals and making sure they get enough sleep – that help keep them healthy and strong.

"...there are lots of simple ways that you can encourage your family to live healthily"

ENCOURAGING A HEALTHY LIFESTYLE

A great deal of emphasis is now rightly placed on preventing illness and encouraging children to live as healthily as possible. For parents, this can almost be a full-time job in itself. As well as helping to keep your child in the best possible physical health by providing him with a good, balanced diet, and ensuring he gets plenty of sleep and exercise, his mental health and emotional wellbeing are important too. A child brought up in a loving, supportive family, who grows up with a sense of self-worth and his own set of values and beliefs, will also be getting a healthy start in life.

It's not always easy. You will be faced with decisions that are important for your child's health. For instance, it is generally agreed that vaccinations are extremely valuable in protecting children from a variety of diseases. But many parents have agonized over whether the MMR vaccination in particular is right for their child.

What you can do

There are some simple ways in which you can help your child live healthily that are easily forgotten. As well as immunization, there are simple steps you can take to ensure that your home is as safe as possible for your child. Thousands of children need medical help every day following accidents that happen at home. You can also keep your child safe in the sun. Above all, you can equip him with the information and confidence he needs in order to keep himself safe, and make sure that he knows what he should do in an emergency.

CAN I BOOST MY CHILD'S IMMUNE SYSTEM?

It's tempting to think that an extra dose of vitamin C in the form of a supplement will give your child a boost during the winter and help protect against coughs and colds. Unfortunately, there is no good scientific evidence that any sort of vitamin supplement will offer additional protection to that provided by a balanced diet and healthy lifestyle.

Plenty of fresh air, exercise and enough sleep are the best ways of keeping your child as healthy as possible, along with a diet that is rich in natural vitamin C – oranges and other citrus fruits, potatoes, tomatoes, red peppers and leafy green vegetables are all good sources.

IMMUNIZATION

Babies in the UK are offered three separate routine immunizations against diphtheria, tetanus, whooping cough, polio, Hib (*Haemophilus influenzae* type b) and meningitis C. These are usually given at 2, 3 and 4 months, although this can vary slightly from area to area. At around 12 months, babies are offered their first MMR (measles, mumps and rubella) immunization. At around 3½ years, children are offered a pre-school booster of diphtheria, tetanus, whooping cough and polio and a second MMR immunization.

A child with a cold can still have immunizations, although it's best to postpone them if your child has a high fever. Occasionally, a child may have a minor reaction. He could seem more irritable than usual or run a slight fever. There can also be a local reaction. It's fairly common to develop a small lump under the skin at the injection site, which may swell to the size of a ten-pence piece. Any larger swelling should be reported to your doctor.

THE MMR DEBATE

Some parents have decided against the MMR vaccine for their children. This follows adverse media publicity after a paper was published in *The Lancet*. The paper reported a study among 12 children and suggested a link between MMR and autism and bowel disease. However, the paper concluded: "We did not prove an association between MMR vaccine and the syndrome described".

Since the *Lancet* report, many studies have been conducted to look for a link between MMR vaccine and autism and bowel disease, and none has been found. In addition, all the scientific evidence has been thoroughly reviewed by independent scientific committees, including the World Health Organization, the

"...it's worth remembering what measles, mumps and rubella meant for children before MMR was introduced"

WHY MMR?

There are very good reasons why MMR is the vaccine of choice.

There is overwhelming evidence of the safety of the MMR vaccine.

Separate vaccines subject the child to six injections instead of two.

Receiving the equivalent of two injections of MMR in the form of the separate injections requires at least five years. The child is left susceptible to the diseases for an unnecessarily long period, which poses a risk to individual children, but as herd immunity also falls it poses a risk to the community too. Those who cannot be immunized, such as young babies, pregnant women and the immunosuppressed, will be at increased risk of disease.

Compliance is likely to be lower with separate vaccines, which will inevitably lead to lower uptake, and lower uptake will allow resurgence of all three diseases.

Separate measles and mumps vaccines are not licensed for use in the UK. Independent quality control by a government does not take place for these separate vaccines, as it does for licensed vaccines.

While there is now a large body of evidence showing the safety of the MMR vaccine, there is no experience of using the three separate vaccines in the manner suggested, and so the safety and efficacy of these are not supported by scientific evidence. Giving the vaccines separately is untried and untested anywhere in the world.

American Academy of Pediatrics and the British Medical Research Council. All have concluded that there is no good scientific evidence to support a link between MMR vaccine and autism or bowel disease, and that MMR is the vaccine of choice to protect children against measles, mumps and rubella. Over 100 countries around the world continue to use the combined vaccine and no country has ceased to use it because of these concerns.

It's worth remembering what measles, mumps and rubella meant for children before MMR was introduced. Before the measles vaccine was introduced in 1968, there were 85 deaths a year from measles in the UK. By age 10, 95 per cent of children had contracted it. One in 15 developed complications, including pneumonia, middle ear infections and convulsions, and 1 in 70 had to be admitted to hospital.

Mumps causes inflammation of one or both of the parotid glands under the jaw. It lasts for about 7–10 days and a child will usually have a fever, headache, abdominal pain and will be generally unwell. But some children will suffer hearing loss, which usually recovers at least partially, and 1 in 30 will have pancreatitis (inflammation of the pancreas), which causes pain, nausea and vomiting. Before the introduction of the MMR vaccine, mumps was the most important cause of viral meningitis in children. Teenage boys and men who contract mumps run a 1 in 5 risk of developing swollen, painful testicles because of the illness, which can in rare cases reduce fertility.

Rubella is usually a mild condition in children, lasting for 2–3 days, and for most means a rash with a sore throat, slight fever and headache. But if a woman contracts rubella in the early part of her pregnancy the results for her unborn child can be devastating.

To prevent outbreaks of measles and to protect children who can't be immunized, uptake of the vaccine needs to be 95 per cent nationally.

Are separate vaccines better?
Many parents have asked whether it would be better to give the three parts of the MMR vaccine separately. Giving three vaccines at once, they believe, could overload their child's immune system. However, the components of MMR work at different times. Measles takes effect after 7–10 days and the mumps and rubella parts take effect later. Furthermore, a child's immune system is used to being bombarded with hundreds of viruses and other challenges in the environment and it can easily cope with these vaccines.

When vaccine coverage falls
There are many examples of what happens when vaccine coverage falls. In Britain, there was a controversy over the whooping cough (pertussis) vaccine in the 1970s amid concerns over a possible link with brain damage. This led to a dramatic fall in uptake, followed by three whooping cough epidemics with more than 300,000 notified cases and at least 70 deaths. Subsequent research never found a link between whooping cough and permanent brain damage.

There is no evidence to suggest that the MMR vaccine is anything other than highly effective with a good safety record. The final decision to immunize does of course rest with parents. But if parents choose not to have their children immunized against measles, mumps and rubella, levels of these diseases will rise. There have already been several outbreaks of measles. Children who have not had the MMR immunization are at risk of catching these diseases. So are very young and non-immune children (there will always be some who can't be immunized for medical reasons, such as children with leukaemia).

CHILD SAFETY

Accidents happen so quickly. Every day in the UK, 6,500 children are taken to accident and emergency departments. Fortunately, most have only minor injuries, but some are far more serious.

Many accidents can be prevented. It helps to try to keep one step ahead of your child. Being aware of the different risks your child faces at each age and stage of development will help you keep your home as safe as possible. Children do learn through experience, though, and most parents say they find it difficult getting the balance right between being over-protective and giving their child too much freedom.

For children aged 5 and under, accidents at home are the most common. Babies under the age of 1 are most often hurt through falls, even in their first months. A baby can wriggle off surfaces and will soon learn to roll. Make sure your baby is never left unattended on any raised surface, even strapped into a car seat on a table. Fit safety gates at the top and bottom of your stairs before your baby crawls and fit locks and catches that will stop windows opening more than 10 cm (4 in).

It is also vital to keep your baby safe around water, even if it is shallow. Never leave a baby or small child alone in the bath, and make sure that children playing in

"...try fitting a stairgate across the kitchen door so that your child can see you but is out of harm's way"

has boiled. Keep hot drinks out of your child's reach. Use placemats rather than a tablecloth that your child could grab, and put a curly flex on the kettle. Tap water should not be hotter than 46°C (115°F).

Microwaved food and drinks can also cause burns. Stir or shake anything from the microwave before you give it to your child to even out any hot spots.

House fires are often caused by children playing with matches. Keep them out of sight and reach. Fit smoke alarms and check them regularly, and make sure any fires are always covered with a guard.

In the pre-school years, falls are the most common accidents. It's almost impossible to stop children climbing onto things at home, so look around and make sure furniture is not next to steps or glass.

Safety and older children

By the time your child starts school at about age 5, accidents outside the home become increasingly common. Make sure your child is always supervised when out. Make it a rule that your child is not allowed to cross the road without a grown-up until he is at least age 8. Although your child won't be ready to cycle on the road yet, this is a good time to get him cycling in a safe place, such as a park. He should wear a cycle helmet from the start. Your child will also be ready to learn how to swim.

For children aged 7–11, road accidents begin to feature in the statistics. Cycling accidents also feature. Ensure your child is aware of the Highway Code and takes responsibility for maintaining his bike. Find out about local cycling proficiency courses. It's also a good idea for your child to wear reflective clothing when cycling.

paddling pools are supervised at all times. Garden ponds must always be fenced or covered if small children are playing in the garden.

Choking accidents are most likely to happen during your baby's first year. Babies love putting things in their mouths and can choke easily, even on drinks. Keep small objects out of his reach and don't leave your baby alone with a feeding bottle.

Incidents of suspected poisoning peak around the age of 2. Toddlers can often open containers at remarkable speed from as early as 18 months. Keep all household cleaners, especially wash tablets that can look like large sweets, out of

your child's reach, and store all medicines, alcohol and cosmetics in a locked cabinet.

Preventing burns and scalds

Burns and scalds are also common. Each year around 41,000 children in the UK are injured by burns and scalds. Two-thirds, nearly 28,000, are under the age of 5 and over half of these incidents took place in the kitchen. If possible, keep your toddler out of the kitchen when you are cooking. Try fitting a stairgate across the door so your child can see you but is out of harm's way.

Hot water is a particular hazard. It can scald up to 30 minutes after it

SAFETY IN THE SUN

Make sure your baby or child is fully protected in the sun. A baby's skin is much thinner than an adult's and so is much more prone to sunburn. Skin turns red only after the damage has been done, so take precautions before this happens. Keep babies completely in the shade.

For toddlers and older children who are unlikely to sit still for long, applying lotion with a high sun protection factor (SPF) of 30 or above is a must. Apply it liberally 30 minutes before your child goes into the sun and again throughout the day, especially after swimming, even if it is waterproof. A sunhat with a wide brim or back flap is essential. Also make sure you avoid being out in the middle of the day and early afternoon when the sun is strongest. Remember "slip, slap, slop" – slip on a shirt, slap on a hat, slop on a high sun protection factor sun cream when spending time in the sun.

Keep a close watch for symptoms of heatstroke if your child is playing outside on a sunny day. These include headache, dizziness and confusion; your child may also have hot, flushed, dry skin.

If you notice symptoms of heatstroke in your child, get him to a cool place and take off his outer clothing, then call for an ambulance. If possible, cover him with a wet sheet. Alternatively, sponge his face and body with tepid water or fan him until medical help arrives.

TEACHING YOUR CHILD ABOUT SAFETY

You can start talking to your child about safety very casually from the age of about 3 or 4 years.

Teach your child his full name and the first couple of lines of his address; some children may even be able to remember their telephone number. You should also discuss what your child might do if you became separated when you are out shopping. Suggest that your child stays where he is, and calls your name loudly a few times. If he can't see you, teach him that he should ask for help from a grown-up with children or a shop worker who is behind the counter of the shop he is in.

Talk to your child about being safe at the playground. For instance, make it a rule that your child should never walk in front of a swing or other moving play equipment, and encourage him to take extra care on high equipment, such as climbing frames. When you go swimming, you could talk to your child about pool safety, reminding him never to run in the pool area in case he slips, and never to dive into water if he doesn't know its depth.

You could also raise his awareness about other safety issues, for instance by pointing out the dangers of leaving toys on the stairs.

Explain what 999 is for and show your child how to dial this number in an emergency.

Ask your child to tell you about any incident at all that makes him feel worried and to let you know if someone he doesn't know tries to talk to him.

DIAGNOSIS CHARTS

CHAPTER THREE

One of the most worrying aspects of being a parent is when your child falls ill, and it can be difficult to know whether you should treat an illness at home or seek medical help. The diagnosis charts in this chapter can help you answer that question. Always consult a doctor if you are concerned about your child's health.

FEVER

A FEVER IS USUALLY A SIGN THAT THE BODY is fighting a bacterial or viral infection. Over-heating may also be the cause. A temperature above 38°C (100°F) signifies a fever. Note other symptoms that may assist your doctor's diagnosis. See also RASH WITH FEVER (*p.186*) and FEVER IN BABIES (*p.58*).

SYMPTOM	POSSIBLE CAUSE
Does your child have a sore throat or is he refusing solid food?	Tonsillitis (*see* Pharyngitis and tonsillitis, *p.223*).
Does your child have a cough, runny nose and unusually noisy breathing?	Croup (*p.224*), asthma (*p.226*) or bronchitis (*p.228*).
Does your child have a cough, runny nose and unusually rapid breathing?	Pneumonia (*p.227*).
Does your child have a cough, runny nose and normal breathing?	A common cold (*p.221*) or influenza (*p.225*). Measles (*p.264*) is also a possibility.
Does your child have a swelling between the ear and the angle of the jaw on one or both sides?	Mumps (*p.268*).
Does your child pass urine more frequently than usual or have a pain or burning sensation when passing urine?	Urinary tract infection (*p.275*).
Does your child vomit with or without diarrhoea?	Gastroenteritis (*p.254*).
Does your child have earache or pull at either ear, or wake up screaming at night?	Inflammation of the middle ear (*p.240*).
Has your child been outside in the sun or in a hot room for several hours?	Your child may have become over-heated.
Does your child seem unwell with a stiff neck, headache, abnormal drowsiness or unusual irritability?	Meningitis (*p.294*).

COOLING DOWN *Moisten a sponge with lukewarm water and place it on your child's forehead. Let the water evaporate to help cool the skin.*

ACTION NEEDED

If he is no better after 24 hours, consult your doctor.
Self-help Bringing down a temperature (*right*) and Relieving a sore throat (*p.198*).

Call your doctor.
Self-help Ease breathing in an asthma attack (*p.195*).

Urgent! Call your doctor at once!
Self-help Bringing down a temperature (*right*).

If she is no better in 48 hours, if symptoms worsen, or if other symptoms develop, consult your doctor.
Self-help Bringing down a temperature (*right*) and Relieving a cough (*p.197*).

See your doctor to confirm diagnosis.
Self-help Bringing down a temperature (*right*).

Get medical advice within 24 hours.
Self-help Bringing down a temperature (*right*).

Get medical advice within 24 hours.
Self-help Giving extra fluids (*p.172*).

Get medical advice within 24 hours.
Self-help Bringing down a temperature (*right*) and Relieving earache (*p.205*).

If self-help measures don't lower the temperature within an hour (*right*), call your doctor at once.

Emergency! Call an ambulance!

Bringing down a temperature

If your child has a temperature, try not to worry. A rise in temperature is part of the body's normal reaction to infection. However, lowering the temperature will help your child feel better. A child whose temperature is allowed to rise and rise will become very uncomfortable and may eventually have a fit – called a febrile convulsion. The following measures are simple things you can do to bring down and control your child's temperature:

• Monitor his temperature with a thermometer (*p.328*). Try a digital thermometer (*below*), a temperature strip or an aural thermometer, which measures the body's temperature through the ear canal.

• Firstly, give him the appropriate dose of liquid paracetamol or paracetamol by suppository if he is vomiting. It can be alternated with ibuprofen, which is licensed for children over 6 months.

• Remove excess clothing from his body – down to underwear or nappy if necessary.

• Remove any sheets or blankets if his illness confines him to bed.

• Make sure the room is ventilated and cool – about 15°C (60°F) – but not draughty.

• Sponge your child's skin and head with lukewarm water (*above left*). Alternatively, place him in a lukewarm bath or shower. Allowing the water to evaporate from his skin, rather than patting him dry with a towel, will help to cool him.

• Make sure he drinks plenty of fluids – give small amounts regularly as he will vomit easily.

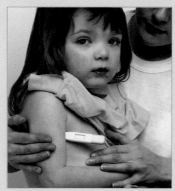

DIGITAL THERMOMETER
Place the digital thermometer in the child's armpit and gently hold the arm in place. After one to two minutes, remove the thermometer and simply read the digital display.

DIARRHOEA

WHEN A CHILD PASSES FREQUENT runny stools, infection is usually the cause. Diarrhoea usually lasts for a few days at most. Make sure your child drinks plenty of fluid while it persists. If the diarrhoea recurs or continues for more than a week, check with your doctor. See also DIARRHOEA IN BABIES (*p.62*).

SYMPTOM	POSSIBLE CAUSE	ACTION NEEDED
If the diarrhoea began within the last 3 days, is there abdominal pain, fever or vomiting?	Gastroenteritis (*p.254*).	Call your doctor. **Self-help** Giving extra fluids (*below*).
Did the diarrhoea start just before an exciting or stressful event or period of time?	A response to excitement or emotional stress. The diarrhoea is likely to clear up quickly.	If the diarrhoea persists or is distressing to your child, consult your doctor.
Has your child had constipatation and diarrhoea at the same time?	Overflow soiling as a result of chronic constipation (*p.255*).	Consult your doctor.
Have you been giving your child any medicine?	A side effect of the medicine she is taking.	Ask your doctor or pharmacist if the medicine may be the cause and if you should stop giving it.
Do your child's faeces contain recognizable morsels of food?	Toddler diarrhoea (*p.255*) if she is under 3.	Consult your doctor.
Are your child's faeces uniformly runny?	Probably a reaction to food (*p.252*) or giardiasis (*p.262*).	Consult your doctor. **Self-help** Giving extra fluids (*below*).

DANGER SIGNS

Phone your doctor at once if your child has any of the following symptoms:

• Abdominal pain for 3 hours
• Vomiting for 12 hours (6 hours in babies)
• Refusing to drink for 6 hours
• Sunken eyes or abnormal drowsiness
• Passing no urine for over 6 hours in a day.

SELF-HELP

Giving extra fluids

The best way to give fluids is an oral rehydrating solution, such as Dioralyte or Rehidrat. Or mix 2 level teaspoons of sugar in 200 ml (7 fl.oz) of cooled, boiled water. Diluted 50:50, unsweetened fruit juice will do. Avoid milk for the first day. Depending on age, give 1–1.5 litres (35–53 fl.oz). Offer fluids every 2 to 3 hours while the diarrhoea lasts. If your child is vomiting, give small sips every hour.

LOSS OF APPETITE

A CHILD MAY LOSE OR GAIN HIS APPETITE depending on how much energy he needs and whether he is in a period of growth. Provided he shows no other symptoms and his growth is normal for his age, you need not worry about any loss of appetite. For children under 1 year, see p.61.

SYMPTOM	POSSIBLE CAUSE	ACTION NEEDED
If your child lost his appetite less than a week ago, does he have a fever, sore throat or rash?	Go to FEVER (*p.170*), SORE THROAT (*p.198*) or SPOTS AND RASHES (*p.184*).	Consult your doctor.
Has your child lost his appetite less than a week ago but has no other symptoms?	Snacking between meals or exercising less than usual. As long as your child seems well, there is no cause for concern.	If he feels ill, get medical advice within 24 hours. **Self-help** Healthy eating and Stimulating appetite (*below*).
Is your child failing to gain weight normally?	Failure to thrive.	See your doctor.
Does your child have swollen glands in the neck?	Glandular fever (*p.270*).	See your doctor.
Does your child have pale faeces and dark urine?	Viral hepatitis (*p.261*).	See your doctor.
Does your child pass urine more frequently or wet the bed (after being dry at night)?	Urinary tract infection (*p.275*).	Get medical advice within 24 hours.

SELF-HELP

Stimulating appetite

A child who is reluctant to eat or who has lost his appetite may need encouraging. Try the following tips:

• If the loss of appetite is caused by illness, do not force your child to eat. A sick child may only want liquids; ice cream and yoghurt will soothe a painful throat and provide some nutrients.

• If your child is very young, make eating fun by preparing pizza faces or playing an eating game.

• Do not expect your child to eat as much as you do at mealtimes; five or six smaller meals or snacks each day may suit a child's immature digestive system and active metabolism.

• Tempt a fussy eater with small portions of various foods.

VOMITING

Vomiting that recurs is often due to an infection of the digestive tract, although an infection elsewhere in the body may also be responsible. A single episode of vomiting is not likely to be serious, however – it's probably due to overeating or excitement. See also VOMITING IN BABIES (*p.60*).

SYMPTOM	POSSIBLE CAUSE
Is your child's vomit greenish-yellow?	Intestinal obstruction (*p.256*).
Does your child have diarrhoea?	Gastroenteritis (*p.254*).
Has your child had continuous abdominal pain for 6 hours?	Appendicitis (*p.253*).
Does your child have pale faeces and dark urine?	Hepatitis (*p.261*).
Is your child abnormally drowsy after recently suffering a blow to the head?	Head injury (*p.291*).
Is your child abnormally drowsy with a headache, stiff neck or flat spots that do not disappear when pressed?	Meningitis (*p.294*).
Does your child have two or more of the following: fever, pain on passing urine, abdominal pain or bedwetting?	Urinary tract infection (*p.275*).
Did your child vomit after a bout of coughing?	Whooping cough (*p.269*).
Did your child vomit before or after an exciting or stressful event?	Children often vomit in reaction to an exciting event or to stress.
Did your child vomit during a journey?	Travel sickness.

Call your doctor at once if your child has any of the following symptoms:

- Vomiting for 12 hours
- Abnormal drowsiness
- Refusing to drink for 6 hours
- Sunken eyes or dry tongue
- Passing no urine for over 6 hours in a day.

Call an ambulance at once if your child has any of the following symptoms:

- Greenish-yellow vomit
- Abdominal pain for 6 hours
- Flat, pink or purple spots that do not disappear when pressed.

ACTION NEEDED

Emergency! Call an ambulance! While you wait, don't give your child anything to eat or drink.

Get medical advice within 24 hours.
Self-help Giving extra fluids (p.172).

Emergency! Call an ambulance! While waiting, do not give your child anything to eat or drink.

Get medical advice within 24 hours.

Emergency! Call an ambulance! While waiting, do not give your child anything to eat or drink.

Emergency! Call an ambulance!

Get medical advice within 24 hours.
Self-help Bringing down a temperature (p.170).

Get medical advice within 24 hours.
Self-help Dealing with vomiting (right) and Relieving a cough (p.197).

If the vomiting persists, consult your doctor.

Give your child a travel sickness remedy, such as a homeopathic remedy (p.321). In a car, try to travel when there is little traffic and open the windows to improve ventilation.

SELF-HELP

Dealing with vomiting

Try taking the following steps to bring relief to a child who is vomiting:

- Support the child's head while she is vomiting. Once she has stopped, sponge her forehead and face. Give her a sip of water so she can rinse out the taste of vomit from her mouth.

- Give your child plenty of reassurance because the experience may upset or frighten her.

- Encourage your child to drink small amounts of either water or rehydrating solution (30 ml/1 fl.oz) every hour. These drinks will help her to replace the fluids which she has lost during vomiting (see Giving extra fluids, p.172).

- Let her lie down and rest for a while. Place a bowl beside her bed in case the vomiting recurs.

SICK BOWL Place a bowl beside your child's bed so she doesn't have to worry about getting to the toilet.

HEADACHE

ANY ACUTE INFECTION THAT TRIGGERS a fever may also bring on a headache. Headaches may occur on their own or, more seriously, with various other symptoms. Consult your doctor if a headache is severe, persistent or recurrent, or if your child is having a particular type of headache for the first time.

SYMPTOM	POSSIBLE CAUSE
If your child seems generally well, might he be anxious about something?	Tension headaches (*see* Recurrent headaches, *p.291*) may be caused by anxiety.
Does your child occasionally suffer from headaches?	An occasional headache is rarely cause for concern.
If your child frequently suffers from headaches, does he get them every day?	Frequent headaches (*see* Recurrent headaches, *p.291*), particularly those occurring at night or early in the morning, may be due to a build-up of pressure.
Does your child get headaches after reading or after using a computer or watching television?	Eyesight problems (*see* Refractive errors, *p.245*) can sometimes cause headaches.
Are the headaches accompanied or preceded by abdominal pain, nausea or vomiting, flashing lights or other visual disturbances?	Migraine (*see* Recurrent headaches, *p.291*).
Has your child recently had a blow to the head?	Concussion (*see* Head injury, *p.291*).
Has your child recently had a cold?	Sinusitis (*p.221*).
Has your child recently had a fever or been vomiting?	Go to FEVER (*p.170*) or VOMITING (*p.174*).
Does your child feel extremely unwell, with two or more of these symptoms – drowsiness, stiff neck, fever, vomiting, refusal to drink, and flat red spots that do not fade under pressure?	Meningitis (*p.294*).

COLD COMPRESS *Fold a flannel or a small towel and dip it in cold water. Wring it out and place it on your child's forehead. Hold the compress there for two or three minutes and then repeat several times. Or you can apply alternate hot and cold compresses to the nape of the neck.*

ACTION NEEDED

If such headaches occur regularly and cause distress, consult your doctor.
Self-help Relieving a headache (*right*).

Self-help Relieving a headache (*right*).

Consult your doctor.

Consult your doctor or optician.

For a first attack, if severe or prolonged, or for frequent attacks, consult your doctor.

Urgent! Call your doctor at once or take him to the nearest accident and emergency department.

Consult your doctor.

Emergency! Call an ambulance!

Relieving a headache

You can treat most of your child's headaches simply and effectively at home. However, some types of headache are serious enough for you to consult your doctor at once. These include headaches that last for more than four hours; headaches that occur when your child seems very unwell; headaches that accompany the development of other symptoms; or headaches that worry you. The following self-help measures might help to relieve the pain of headaches:

• Give your child liquid paracetamol, usually as a syrup. Do not exceed the recommended dose.

• Encourage your child lie down in a cool, dark, peaceful room with his eyes closed. Falling asleep may relieve the headache.

• Hunger can sometimes cause a headache. If your child feels hungry, give him a drink of milk or an easily digestible snack, such as a plain biscuit.

• Dehydration is a common cause of headache. Ask your child if he is thirsty or offer him a drink of water. Children who are in pain can vomit easily, so encourage him to sip the drink. Avoid drinks such as cola as they contain caffeine, which can cause a headache.

• A high-fibre snack – for example, a banana or a wholegrain biscuit such as a flapjack – will raise the level of sugar in the bloodstream slowly. Encourage your child to eat one at the first signs of a headache. If your child suffers from headaches at school he could carry a "snack pack" with him.

• Teach him to breathe properly and to concentrate on relaxing the muscles in his shoulders and neck. If you suspect the headache is related to tension, consider giving him a relaxing massage. Gently working the muscles in his scalp, face, neck and shoulders can work wonders. Alternatively, consider taking him to an osteopath, a chiropractor or to someone qualified to give acupressure (*p.325*).

• If you suspect a food intolerance is causing your child to have headaches, keep a diary of what food he eats and consider an appointment with a nutritionist. If you think your child is sensitive to a particular food, remove it from his diet. Foods that can lead some people to suffer from headaches include sugary and carbohydrate-rich foods such as white bread. Dried fruits, chocolate, tea and hard cheeses can also bring on headaches.

TOOTHACHE

IF YOUR CHILD IS SUFFERING FROM TOOTHACHE, the chances are that one of her teeth is decaying. Take her to see your dentist as soon as you can if pain is affecting her teeth or gums, although you could try self-help measures in the meantime. While natural toothache remedies may help to ease your child's discomfort, toothache is always a sign of a problem that needs the attention of a dentist.

SYMPTOM	POSSIBLE CAUSE
Does your child have continuous intense pain with or without fever?	Your child may be suffering from a dental abscess (*p.250*).
Does your child have bouts of severe throbbing pain or sharp pain lasting minutes and triggered by hot or cold food or drinks?	Your child may have a deep caries (*see* Tooth decay, *p.248*), a deep filling or a tooth fracture which may have caused inflammation of the nerve tissue.
Does your child have continuous, dull pain in several upper back teeth?	The wisdom teeth may be starting to emerge.
Does your child have tender gums just behind the second molars?	Your child may have sinusitis (*p.221*). This is an inflammation of the lining of the sinuses (air-filled cavities in the bones that surround the nose), which can cause pain in the upper back teeth.
If your child had a filling recently, is she experiencing on and off, unpredictable pain?	Your child may have a filling that is uneven or higher than the level of the tooth's biting surface which may cause pain when she bites down on it.
If your child has had a filling recently, does she experience pain only when she is biting or chewing on it?	A tooth that has been filled very recently is often slightly sensitive, particularly to cold temperatures. Sensitivity is especially likely if the child has had a deep filling.
Does your child have painful, red and swollen gums while cutting new teeth?	Teething (*p.56*).

EASING TOOTHACHE If your child holds a well-wrapped hot water bottle against the affected side of her face, she may ease her toothache.

ACTION NEEDED

Urgent! Call your dentist at once! Meanwhile, try the self-help suggestions (*right*).

Get dental help within 24 hours. Try the self-help suggestions while you wait (*right*).

Consult your dentist.

Consult your doctor.

Consult your dentist. Until the child can see the dentist, give soft and liquid foods and ask her to chew on the other side of her mouth.

If sensitivity to heat develops, or if the pain intensifies or lasts for more than a few seconds, make an appointment with the dentist.

Give your baby a hard object, such as a teething ring, to chew on. Over-the-counter gels, drops and powders may also relieve the pain.
Self-help Relieving toothache (*right*) and Natural toothache remedies (*right*).

SELF-HELP

Relieving toothache

The following measures may help to relieve the pain of your child's toothache:

- Give your child an appropriate dose of liquid paracetamol if she is over 3 months old. Do not apply the syrup directly to the tooth as a chemical burn may develop after prolonged contact with the gums.

- A young child may feel better if she is propped up against several pillows.

- A well-covered hot-water bottle, held against the affected side of the face, may help to relieve the pain of a toothache.

- Encourage your child to rinse her mouth with warm salt water.

Natural toothache remedies

The following natural remedies may help to relieve your child's toothache:

Peppermint oil
Dilute a drop of peppermint oil in a teaspoon of olive oil. Soak a bud of cotton wool in the mixture and apply it to the painful area.

Clove oil
Dilute a drop of clove oil in a teaspoon of olive oil. Soak a bud of cotton wool in the mixture and apply it to the painful area.

Lavender oil
Dilute a drop of lavender oil in a teaspoon of olive oil. Dip your fingertip into the mixture and then rub it into the skin covering the jaw to ease the pain.

Steam inhalation
If your child's toothache is the result of sinusitis, try a steam inhalation. Carefully pour hot, but not boiling, water into a heatproof bowl. Add a few drops of lavender oil or tea tree oil to the water. Cover the bowl and her head with a towel. Ask her to inhale the steam through the nose for a few minutes, taking care not to burn herself. Don't leave her unsupervised. Repeat as often as needed.

Homeopathy
Homeopathic remedies (*p.321*) can relieve certain kinds of toothache. Consult a homeopath for a diagnosis.

FEELING UNWELL

I F YOUR CHILD FEELS UNWELL take his temperature and then look for a rash.
Call your doctor at once if your child is abnormally unresponsive or
drowsy, has a temperature of 38°C (100°F) or more, has been vomiting for
12 hours, is breathing fast or noisily, or refuses to drink for 6 hours.

SYMPTOM	POSSIBLE CAUSE	ACTION NEEDED
Does your child have a fever – a temperature of 38°C (100°F) or above – and a rash?	Go to RASH WITH FEVER (p.186).	
Does your child have a fever without a rash?	If he is under a year, go to FEVER IN BABIES (p.58). If not, go to FEVER (p.170).	
Does your child have a rash?	Go to SPOTS AND RASHES (p.184)	
Does your child have a pain in his abdomen?	Go to ABDOMINAL PAIN (p.208)	
Does your child have diarrhoea and vomiting?	Gastroenteritis (p.254).	Get medical advice within 24 hours. **Self-help** Preventing dehydration in babies (p.63) or Giving extra fluids (p.172).
Is your child refusing to eat and drink?	An infectious childhood disease, particularly if the child is listless, irritable or is suffering from other symptoms.	If your child feels no better after 24 hours or develops other symptoms, consult your doctor.
Is your child refusing to eat?	Go to SORE THROAT (p.198).	
Has your child had contact with anyone with an infectious disease in the past 3 weeks?	An infectious childhood disease, as it incubates, might be the cause.	If your child feels no better after 24 hours, or develops other symptoms, consult your doctor.
Might your child be worried or anxious about something?	Problems at school can make a child feel unwell (see Anxiety and fears, pp.131–132).	If the feeling lasts more than a day or if your child regularly refuses to go to school, consult your doctor.

ITCHINESS

ITCHINESS MAY BE DUE TO VARIOUS CAUSES, ranging from allergies to infestation by parasites, and may affect all your child's body or just one part. Severe itchiness can be distressing and scratching can lead to infection, so consult your doctor about the underlying condition without delay.

SYMPTOM	POSSIBLE CAUSE	ACTION NEEDED
Does your child have a rash of itchy spots or patches of inflamed skin?	Go to SPOTS AND RASHES (*p.184*) or RASH WITH FEVER (*p.186*).	
Is your child itchy between the toes, or on the soles of her feet?	Athlete's foot (*see* FOOT PROBLEMS, *p.192*).	If the rash does not clear up within 2 weeks or if it affects your child's toenails, consult your doctor or pharmacist. **Self-help** Apply an antifungal powder, cream or spray to every part of the rash.
Is your child itchy in the anal area?	Threadworms (*p.262*).	Consult your doctor.
Is your child itchy on the scalp?	Go to HAIR AND SCALP PROBLEMS (*p.182*).	
Is your daughter itchy in the genital area?	Go to GENITAL PROBLEMS IN GIRLS (*p.215*).	
If a large area of the body is itchy, has your child been wearing either wool or some kind of synthetic material next to the skin?	Sensitive skin.	Use a washing powder made for people with delicate or sensitive skin. Ensure cotton is worn next to the skin.
Are there thin, grey lines on your child's fingerwebs, wrists, palms or soles?	Scabies (*p.232*).	Consult your doctor.

HAIR & SCALP PROBLEMS

Hair and scalp problems in children are fairly common but are unlikely to be a cause for concern. Any problem with a child's scalp is likely to be due to an infection, a skin condition or a parasite. Actual hair loss is probably caused by constant pulling on the hair or tying the hair back tightly.

SYMPTOM	POSSIBLE CAUSE
Does your child have bald patches where the exposed skin looks normal?	A form of localized baldness, which often may have no apparent cause.
Does your child have bald patches where the exposed skin looks scaly and inflamed?	Ringworm (*p.236*).
Does your child have either a flaky scalp or an itchy scalp that gets better for a few days after a thorough shampoo?	Dandruff (*see* Seborrhoeic dermatitis, *p.230*).
Does your child have an itchy scalp that doesn't improve after a thorough shampoo?	Head lice (*right and p.236*).
Is your child's hair becoming thin, even though he is under 1 year old?	As the baby hair falls out, your infant's hair will become noticeably thinner until the new, stronger hair grows in. This process is normal and is not a cause for concern.
Is your child's hair becoming thin after a recent illness?	General thinning of the hair could be a result of a recent illness. The hair will probably return to its normal thickness over the next few months.
Is your child's hair becoming thin at the same time he is taking medicine?	The thinning of your child's hair could be a side effect of the medicine that he is taking.
Does your child habitually pull or twist his hair?	Habitual hair pulling may indicate an underlying psychological problem.
Is your child suffering from temporary hair loss?	Damage to the hair roots, caused by excessive pulling of the hair or wearing hair in a tight pony tail or plaits.

REMOVING HEAD LICE Special shampoos and treatments for eradicating head lice are available over the counter. Some are more effective than others. The best way to remove head lice is to wash your child's hair in shampoo and conditioners, and painstakingly comb the hair with a fine-toothed comb to remove the lice and the eggs.

ACTION NEEDED

Consult your doctor.

Consult your doctor.

Self-help Wash your child's hair with an anti-dandruff shampoo. If the symptoms do not improve within 2 weeks, consult your doctor.

Self-help Wash your child's hair with an over-the-counter anti-lice shampoo. If your child is under 2 years old or has an allergy, consult your doctor before starting any treatment.

Self-help Cover your baby's head to protect it from the sun and to keep it warm in cold weather.

If you are worried, consult your doctor.

Ask your doctor or pharmacist if the medicine may be causing your child's symptoms and whether you should stop giving it.

If your child is losing a lot of hair or if he has other behavioural problems, consult your doctor.

Encourage your child to change his hairstyle or have a hair cut.

Treating dandruff and head lice

Dandruff
As an alternative to anti-dandruff shampoos, mix a drop of tea tree oil in a teaspoon of olive oil and massage into the scalp. Shampoo normally and brush the scales away.

Head lice
If your child catches head lice, keep him home from school and wash and comb his hair to prevent the lice from spreading. Daily combing with a fine-toothed comb from your pharmacist is the most effective way to break the life cycle of the louse. Use a "conditioner" treatment for regular checks – thoroughly soak the hair with conditioner and carefully comb it through with the fine-toothed comb (*above left*). Add a drop of tea tree oil to the conditioner to help you prevent re-infection.

Natural hair care

Try the following tips to improve the health of your child's hair naturally:

- Encourage your child to eat a healthy diet, including at least five portions of fruit and vegetables a day and oily fish twice a week. Any nutritional deficiency can exacerbate hair and scalp problems so find him a multivitamin and multimineral supplement. If he won't eat oily fish, buy high-strength cod liver oil and add it to dishes containing cod or tuna.

- Encourage your child to wear a hat when he is outside in the sun.

- Massage your child's scalp regularly to stimulate blood flow and relieve stress and tension.

NATURAL SHAMPOO Wash your child's hair regularly with a mild natural shampoo, gently towel dry and apply a conditioner. Avoid harsh chemicals such as the chlorine used in swimming pools and don't use the hairdryer set on the highest heat because of the damage it causes.

SPOTS & RASHES

INFECTIONS AND ALLERGIC REACTIONS ARE RESPONSIBLE for most spots and rashes. If your child shows no other signs of being unwell, the spots or rashes are probably not serious. But if her skin is very itchy or sore, or if she is showing signs of distress, call your doctor.

SYMPTOM	POSSIBLE CAUSE
If there's no itchiness, are there groups of lumps, each with a central depression?	Molluscum contagiosum (*p.235*), a mild viral infection that causes pimples on the skin.
Are there pus-filled areas or golden crusts, often on the face?	Impetigo (*p.235*).
Are there one or more firm, rough lumps?	Warts (*p.231*).
Is there a painful, red lump, possibly with a yellow top?	A boil (*right and p.233*).
Are there tiny, red, itchy spots or fluid-filled blisters?	Prickly heat, caused by unevaporated sweat.
Is the rash itchy, red, scaly or blister-like in patches mainly on the face and around the joints?	Atopic eczema (*p.234*).
Are the patches on the scalp, trunk or limbs?	Ringworm (*p.236*).
Is the rash made up of small inflamed spots in one area?	Insect bites, possibly from mosquitoes or from cat or dog fleas.
Does the itchiness extend to skin that does not have the rash?	Scabies (*p.232*).
Is the rash slightly raised, bright red, blotchy patches?	Urticaria (*p.232*).
Does your child have the same rash as above and a swollen face or mouth at the same time?	Anaphylactic shock (*p.189*).
Are there small, oval, pink spots arranged in lines along the ribs?	Pityriasis rosea (*p.232*).
Are you giving your child any medicine?	An allergic reaction to certain medicines.

Call an ambulance at once if your child develops any of the following symptoms:

- Swelling of face or mouth
- Noisy or difficult breathing
- Difficulty swallowing
- Abnormal drowsiness.

ACTION NEEDED

Consult your doctor to confirm the cause.

Get medical advice within 24 hours.

If the warts are troublesome, consult your doctor.

If it is painful or if more form, consult your doctor.
Self-help Treating a boil (*right*).

Apply cool compresses and avoid soap.

If your child's rash is very itchy, extensive, or weeping, consult your doctor.

Consult your doctor.

Apply cool compresses, calamine lotion or antihistamine cream to relieve the itching.

Consult your doctor.

If the rash doesn't disappear within 4 hours, or if your child has repeated attacks, consult your doctor.

Emergency! Call an ambulance!

Consult your doctor.
Self-help Relieving itchiness (*p.66*).

Urgent! Ask your doctor/pharmacist if the medicine could be the cause and if you should stop giving it.

Treating a boil

A boil develops when a hair follicle becomes infected. After two or three days it will form a white or yellow head and will then either burst or heal on its own. Don't squeeze the boil and don't let your child scratch it. Boils often occur on the face or at pressure points where something rubs against the child's skin.

TACKLING A BOIL Wipe the boil with cotton wool dipped in a salt solution (made from a teaspoon of salt in a cup of warm water) or an antiseptic solution such as surgical spirit. Cover with a plaster.

Lick eczema

Too much licking of the lips or sucking of a thumb can cause a rash around the mouth. The saliva these habits produce is irritating, making the lips turn dry and chapped while the skin around them becomes inflamed and scaly. Over-the-counter corticosteroid cream can help to contain it, but the best way to deal with lick eczema is to moisturize your child's lips with a lip salve and protect the skin with petroleum jelly.

As soon as the habit stops, the eczema heals. Don't make a big issue out of the habit as children usually grow out of it before too long. Just try to discourage it as soon as your child starts.

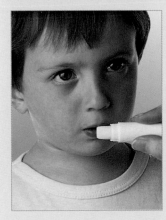

MOISTURIZING THE LIPS You can't really stop a child from excessively sucking their thumb or licking their lips, but you can cover their lips with a moisturizer in a lip salve. This will help to reduce the irritating effects of the saliva.

RASH WITH FEVER

AN INFECTIOUS DISEASE IS THE USUAL CAUSE of a rash combined with a fever (a temperature of 38°C/100°F or over). Viruses are the culprits behind many of these infectious diseases and the body generally deals with them without the need for special medical treatment. Despite this, you should always consult your doctor for a diagnosis if your child has a rash with a fever.

SYMPTOM	POSSIBLE CAUSE
Is your child's rash made up of flat spots that do not disappear when pressed?	Blood infection with meningococcus, a bacterium that causes meningitis (p.294).
If your child's rash is raised and blotchy, or made up of fine spots that turn white when pressed, was it preceded by a runny nose, a cough or red eyes?	Measles (p.264) or, rarely, Kawasaki disease.
Was the rash preceded by a sore throat or vomiting?	Scarlet fever (p.267).
Did the rash appear after your child took some medicine?	Drug allergy.
Is your child's rash made up of itchy spots that blister and dry into scabs?	Chickenpox (p.265).
If the rash is made up of flat pink spots that start on the face or trunk, was your child's temperature 38°C (100°F) or above in the 3 or 4 days prior to the rash?	Roseola infantum (p.267).
Was your child's temperature 38°C (100°F) or below in the 3 or 4 days prior to the rash?	Rubella (p.264).
Is your child's rash bright red and confined to the cheeks?	Erythema infectiosum (p.266).

Call your doctor at once if your child has any of the following symptoms during, or after apparent recovery from, any of the common childhood infectious diseases:

- Abnormal drowsiness or floppiness
- Seizures
- Temperature of 40°C (104°F) or above
- Abnormally fast breathing
- Noisy or difficult breathing
- Severe headache
- Refusing to drink for over 6 hours.

ACTION NEEDED

Emergency! Call an ambulance!

Get medical advice within 24 hours.
Self-help Bringing down a temperature (*p.59 and p.171*).

Get medical advice within 24 hours.
Self-help Bringing down a temperature (*p.59 and p.171*) and Relieving a sore throat (*p.198*).

Urgent! Call your doctor/pharmacist at once to find out whether the medicine may be causing the symptoms and whether you should stop giving it.

If the spots become infected, consult your doctor.
Self-help Bringing down a temperature (*p.59 and p.171*).

If you are concerned about your child's condition, consult your doctor.
Self-help Bringing down a temperature (*p.59 and p.171*).

Consult your doctor but don't take her to the surgery to avoid contact with pregnant women.
Self-help Bringing down a temperature (*p.59 and p.171*).

If you are concerned, or if your child has sickle-cell anaemia (*p.313*), consult your doctor.
Self-help Bringing down a temperature (*p.59 and p.171*).

SELF-HELP

Rashes of some common childhood diseases

The six photographs below will help you to identify the rashes associated with some common infectious diseases in childhood (*see also* Infectious diseases, *pp.263–272*). It is important to remember, however, that a rash may differ in its appearance depending on how severely a child is affected by the disease and on the complexion or colour of the child's skin. Consequently, a firm diagnosis of a rash should always be made by a doctor. However, if you think your child's rash resembles the meningitis rash, call an ambulance.

MENINGITIS
Appearing on the trunk of the body, the spotty meningitis rash does not fade when pressed with a glass.

SCARLET FEVER
The tiny red spots of scarlet fever spread from behind the ears all over the body and last for about a week.

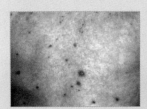

CHICKENPOX
Chickenpox spots appear after two or three weeks' incubation and are larger than most and contain fluid.

RUBELLA
The pink rubella spots start to appear behind the ears and spread to the forehead, chest and limbs.

MEASLES
The scattered pink spots of measles start at the hairline and spread down the body to the legs.

ROSEOLA INFANTUM
The tiny, distinct, pink spots of the roseola infantum rash usually develop on the head and trunk of the body.

LUMPS & SWELLINGS

A LUMP OR SWELLING WHICH APPEARS on, or just below, the surface of a child's skin may be due to a variety of causes. Lymph glands may swell in the fight against an infection in a nearby part of the body. Injuries, bites and stings are other causes. If your child has a persistent or painful lump or swelling, consult your doctor.

SYMPTOM	POSSIBLE CAUSE
Does your child have a painful red lump?	A boil (*p.185 and p.233*) or abscess.
Does your child have a slightly raised, bright red lump?	Your child may have been stung by an insect such as a bee or wasp.
Does your child have a soft lump in the groin or navel area?	Inguinal or umbilical hernia (*see* Hernia, *p.260*).
Does your child have a tender swelling near an infected cut or graze?	The swelling is probably a nearby lymph gland, which has swollen as it helps to fight the infection.
Does your child have a large tender lump on the head after a blow to the head?	Head injury (*p.291*).
Is the lump or swelling on the back of your child's neck?	Atopic eczema (*p.234*) or a viral infection, such as rubella (*p.264*), causing lymph node enlargement.
Is the lump or swelling on the side of your child's neck, and followed by a sore throat and a reluctance to eat and drink?	Tonsillitis (*see* Pharyngitis and tonsillitis, *p.223*), causing lymph node enlargement.
Is the lump or swelling on the side of your child's neck, and followed by earache?	Inflammation of the middle ear (*p.240*), causing lymph node enlargement.
Is the lump or swelling between the ear and jaw?	Mumps (*p.268*).
Is the lump or swelling in the neck, armpit and/or groin?	Glandular fever (*p.270*), causing lymph node enlargement.
Is the swelling in your son's scrotum or penis?	Go to GENITAL PROBLEMS IN BOYS (*p.214*).
Is your child's ankle swollen?	Strain or sprain (*p.281*).

SELF-HELP

Removing a sting

Stings from a bee, wasp or other insect are usually more painful than dangerous. The body's natural response is a mild swelling that is red and sore. If you can see the sting, brush or scrape it off sideways with a credit card, the blunt edge of a knife or your fingernail. Apply a cold compress to the affected area for at least 10 minutes to reduce the swelling and pain.

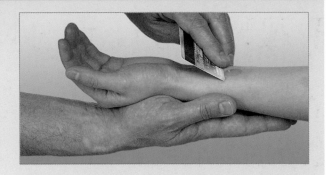

ACTION NEEDED

If a lump is very painful or if more than one lump forms, consult your doctor.

If your child has had an allergic reaction to a sting in the past, or shows symptoms of anaphylactic shock (*right*), get her to a hospital immediately.

Get medical advice within 24 hours.

If your child's swelling or pain persists for more than a week, consult your doctor.

Call your doctor. Take your child to hospital at once if headache, vomiting and drowsiness develop.

Consult your doctor.

If your child feels no better after 24 hours, consult your doctor.
Self-help Relieving a sore throat (*p.198*).

Get medical advice within 24 hours.
Self-help Relieving earache (*p.205*).

Consult your doctor.

Consult your doctor.

If pain is severe or there is no improvement after 24 hours, consult your doctor.

SELF-HELP

Anaphylactic shock

Sometimes, the sting of an insect – or a marine creature such as a jellyfish – produces a severe allergic reaction. The face and neck suddenly swell, the airways constrict and breathing becomes very difficult. The body goes into anaphylactic shock, which requires urgent treatment. It can also occur after a child eats something, such as a peanut, to which she is especially sensitive. If your child goes into anaphylactic shock, take the following action:

• Call an ambulance immediately!

• Support your child in the way that makes it easiest for her to breathe. Reassure her while you wait for help.

• If she loses consciousness, check her condition. If she's breathing place her in the recovery position. If not, give her rescue breaths (*see ABC, pp.330–332*).

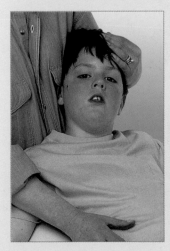

HELP WITH BREATHING *The most important help you can give in anaphylactic shock is to ensure the child keeps breathing. Loosen the child's clothing at the neck and the waist so breathing is made easier. Support the child in a semi-sitting position and provide reassurance.*

PAINFUL LIMBS

MINOR FALLS OR INJURIES CAUSE MANY CHILDREN to experience pain in an arm or a leg but such pain rarely requires medical attention. A child needs urgent treatment if he fractures a bone or dislocates a joint. If you are worried about an unexplained or persistent pain, consult your doctor.

SYMPTOM	POSSIBLE CAUSE	ACTION NEEDED
If your child fell or was injured recently, is movement painful or restricted, or does one of his limbs seem misshapen?	A broken bone or a dislocated joint (*see* Fractures and dislocations, *p.283*).	**Emergency!** Call an ambulance if the injury affects the leg or elbow. If an arm or shoulder is affected, immobilize the injury, then take your child to the hospital. **Self-help** Broken bones (*p.338*).
Is your child's limb swollen?	Bruised or strained muscles or sprained ligaments (*see* Strains and sprains, *p.281*).	If there's no improvement within 24 hours, consult your doctor. **Self-help** Treat the strain or sprain (*p.339*).
Is the pain centred around one or more joints or is it confined to the feet?	Go to PAINFUL JOINTS (*p.191*) or FOOT PROBLEMS (*p.192*).	
Does your child have a fever, with a headache, cough or a sore throat?	Influenza (*p.225*).	If there's no improvement within 48 hours, if breathing difficulties develop, or a rash appears, phone your doctor at once. **Self-help** Bringing down a temperature (*p.59 and p.171*).
Does your child have a fever, with a red or tender area over a bone?	Bone infection (*see* Bone and joint infection, *p.288*).	**Urgent!** Call your doctor at once!
Has your child been experiencing bouts of pain in the lower leg that persist for a few minutes?	Cramp (*p.282*).	**Self-help** Gently massage or stretch the affected leg.
Is your child experiencing none of the above symptoms yet still has a painful limb?	Bruised or strained muscles or sprained ligaments, possibly caused by an unnoticed injury (*see* Strains and sprains, *p.281*).	If your child is in severe pain, is reluctant to use the affected limb, or does not improve within 24 hours, consult your doctor.

PAINFUL JOINTS

Serious disorders of a joint are extremely rare in children. If there is any pain it is usually due to a minor sprain or strain of a muscle or ligament around a joint. If your child suffers from a persistent pain in a joint, or if there are any other symptoms, such as a fever, consult your doctor.

SYMPTOM	POSSIBLE CAUSE	ACTION NEEDED
If your child fell or was injured recently, is there restricted or painful movement in a joint, or is the joint misshapen?	A dislocated joint or a break in a bone near a joint (*see* Fractures and dislocations, *p.283*).	**Emergency!** Call an ambulance if the leg or elbow is affected. If an arm, finger, or shoulder is affected take your child to hospital. **Self-help** Broken bones (*p.338*).
Is your child's joint swollen?	Strained muscles or sprained ligaments near the joint (*see* Strains and sprains, *p.281*).	If the pain or swelling is severe or does not improve within 24 hours, call your doctor.
Is the joint red, hot or swollen, and does your child have a fever or seem unwell?	Infection of a joint (*see* Bone and joint infection, *p.288*). A short-lived arthritis or juvenile chronic arthritis (*p.288*) if more than one joint is involved.	**Urgent!** Call your doctor at once!
Does your child have a limp or a painful hip?	Congenital hip dislocation (*p.286*) in a child just learning to walk. Perthes' disease (*p.286*) or slipped femoral epiphysis in an older child. Bone or joint infection (*p.288*) or irritable hip (*p.285*) in a child of any age. See also Limping (*p.281*).	Get medical advice within 24 hours.
Does your child have a painful knee?	A minor strain or sprain (*p.281*). Bone or joint infection (*p.288*) is possible. If a knee is affected, it may be chondromalacia patellae or Osgood-Schlatter disease. See also Limping (*p.281*).	If the pain is severe, is no better after 24 hours, or recurs, consult your doctor. **Self-help** Treat the strain or sprain (*p.339*).
If more than one joint is involved, does your child have a purplish rash on her limbs?	Henoch-Schönlein purpura (*p.307*).	**Urgent!** Call your doctor at once!

FOOT PROBLEMS

THE MOST COMMON FOOT PROBLEMS in childhood are caused by falls, conditions affecting the skin of one or both feet and ill-fitting footwear. Few of these foot problems are serious. However, if your child suffers from a very painful or swollen foot, or if he finds walking difficult, consult your doctor.

SYMPTOM	POSSIBLE CAUSE
If your child's foot is painful after a recent fall or injury, can he walk on the affected foot?	A bone in your child's foot, toe, or ankle may have been fractured (*see* Fractures and dislocations, *p.283*).
Is walking painful but possible?	Bruised or strained muscles or strained ligaments (*see* Strains and sprains, *p.281*).
If a recent fall or injury is not the cause, does your child feel pain only when wearing shoes?	Your child's shoes may not fit properly, or the lining may be worn.
If your child feels pain only when weight is put on the foot, is there a flattened lump on the sole?	Verruca (*p.193 and* Warts, *p.231*).
Is there an itchy, peeling rash?	Athlete's foot (*p.193*).
If a recent fall or injury is not the cause, and your child feels pain all the time, is there a redness or swelling on his foot or toes?	Infection from a cut or a foreign body, such as a thorn or a splinter, may cause redness or swelling.
If your child is 3 years or older, do his feet appear to be flat?	Flat feet (*see* Minor skeletal problems, *p.284*).
If your child is younger than 3 years, do his feet appear to be flat?	Undeveloped muscles and ligaments in the soles of the feet, which are not a cause for concern at this age (*see* Minor skeletal problems, *p.284*).
If your child's feet appear to have bent or curly toes, are his socks and shoes too small?	Shoes or socks that are too small may cause your child's toes to curl.

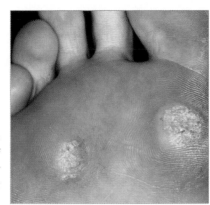

REMOVING A VERRUCA
Scrape the skin of the verruca and cover it with a salicylic plaster every day.

ACTION NEEDED

Take your child to the nearest hospital accident and emergency department. If you are unable to move your child, call an ambulance.

If the pain or swelling is severe, consult your doctor. **Self-help** Treat the strain or sprain (*p.339*).

Replace your child's shoes as soon as they become tight or worn with new shoes that are long and wide enough. Try to buy from shops where the assistants are trained to fit children's shoes.

Self-help Treating verrucas (*right*).

Self-help Apply an antifungal powder, cream, or spray to the rash. Ensure your child's feet are dried properly after bathing. If the rash doesn't clear up within 2 weeks, or if your child's toenails are affected, consult your doctor.

Get medical advice within 24 hours.
Self-help Remove a foreign body with sterilized tweezers. Cover with a clean, sterile bandage and then elevate and support the foot to reduce swelling.

If your child's feet are painful or you are worried about them, consult your doctor.

If you feel your child's feet are not developing properly, consult your doctor.

Replace your child's shoes and socks as soon as they become tight.

Treating verrucas

Verrucas are hard, calloused warts on the soles of the feet. They are caused by a virus and are squashed flat by the weight of the body. Veruccas can be painful – but usually the painful phase is short-lived. Don't pick or scratch a verruca because it may spread.

• Verrucas are highly infectious and are often caught from walking barefoot in communal changing rooms, so encourage your child to wear flip-flops or sandals at a gym or swimming pool.

• Use a pumice stone to remove as much of the skin as possible and cover with a fresh salicylic acid plaster every day until the verruca disappears.

• Your pharmacist can advise you on over-the-counter topical applications including herbal aloe vera gel.

• Echinacea (*p.322*) builds up the immune system and can be applied directly or taken by mouth.

• Stubborn, painful verrucas may need treatment from a chiropodist.

Treating athlete's foot

Athlete's foot is a fungal infection that thrives in the warm, moist conditions between the toes.

• Keep your child's feet clean and dry – use a hairdryer set on low if necessary. Use cotton socks and change them daily. Air your child's shoes after use.

• Sprinkle antifungal powder or spread antifungal cream between your child's toes twice a day.

• Tea tree oil is a powerful natural antifungal.

• Calendula relieves inflammation and soothes the skin, thus promoting healing.

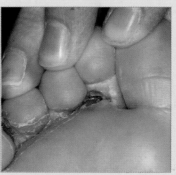

ATHLETE'S FOOT POWDER *Keep your child's feet clean and dry and sprinkle antifungal powder in his socks and shoes and between his toes.*

BREATHING PROBLEMS

BREATHING PROBLEMS ARE OFTEN SERIOUS IN CHILDREN. Children may have difficulty inhaling or their breathing may be noisy or fast. Many children with a minor respiratory infection will wheeze a little. Breathing problems accompanied by danger signs (*right*) require urgent attention.

SYMPTOM	POSSIBLE CAUSE
If your child's breathing problems started suddenly a few minutes ago, could she be choking on a small object?	Inhalation of a foreign body.
Is your child showing one or more of the danger signs (*above right*), having once had an asthma attack in the past or while being treated for asthma now?	Severe asthma (*p.226*) attack.
Is your child showing one or more of the danger signs (*above right*) even when asthma does not seem to be involved?	Bronchiolitis (*p.228*), pneumonia (*p.227*), severe croup (*p.224*) or asthma (*p.226*).
Does your child suffer from repeated episodes of wheezing, shortness of breath or coughing during the night?	Asthma (*p.226*).
Has your child's breathing been crowing and noisy since birth?	Congenital laryngeal stridor, a harmless condition that your child will outgrow.
Has your child's breathing been crowing and noisy since birth, but has recently become faster and accompanied by a fever and a cough?	Pneumonia (*p.227*) or bronchiolitis (*p.228*).
Has your child's breathing recently become faster and accompanied by a fever and a cough?	Pneumonia (*p.227*) or bronchiolitis (*p.228*).
Does your child have a hoarse voice, noisy breathing and a barking cough?	Croup (*p.224*).

If your child's breathing problems are accompanied by any of the following symptoms, you should call an ambulance at once:

- Blue-tinged lips or tongue
- Abnormal drowsiness
- Inability to talk or produce sounds normally.

ACTION NEEDED

Emergency! Call an ambulance!
Self-help Choking (*p.333*).

Emergency! Call an ambulance!
Self-help Administer asthma medications as prescribed. See also Ease breathing during an asthma attack (*right*) and Giving rescue breaths (*pp.331–332*).

Emergency! Call an ambulance!
Self-help Giving rescue breaths (*pp.331–332*).

If your child seems very unwell or if breathing difficulties develop, call your doctor at once.
Self-help Ease breathing during an asthma attack (*right*).

See your health visitor. If there is no improvement by the age of 3 months, consult your doctor.

Urgent! Call your doctor at once!
Self-help Ease breathing during an asthma attack (*right*) and Checking breathing rates (*above right*).

Urgent! Call your doctor at once!
Self-help Ease breathing during an asthma attack (*right*) and Checking breathing rates (*above right*).

Urgent! Call your doctor at once!

Checking breathing rates

A child with an unusually rapid breathing rate may need medical attention. To check your child's rate, make sure she is resting and then count his breaths over a minute. As a child grows, the rate decreases. For a baby under two months the breathing rate is less than 60. For a baby between 2 and 11 months, it is less than 50. For a child between 1 and 5 years, the rate is less than 40. For a child over 5 years, it is less than 30.

Natural relief

Relaxation techniques
Techniques such as yoga will help your child to relax and breathe calmly from the diaphragm. This will help her develop a sense of control when she has difficulties.

Better posture
Adopting a better posture can help your child relax her chest and improve breathing, so preventing difficulties from arising.

Remedies
Finding the right remedy depends on its cause. See herbal medicine (*p.322*) and homeopathy (*p.321*).

Ease breathing during an asthma attack

If your child is having difficulty breathing during an asthma attack, try the following:

- Help your child to sit up (*below*).

- Give any prescribed medicine straight away.

- Keep people away to avoid further worry.

BREATHING POSITION
Help your child to adopt a good position to help her breathe. Encourage her to sit up and lean against a table or the back of a chair, using her arms and elbows as support.

COUGHING

IN OLDER CHILDREN, coughing is usually due to a minor respiratory infection, such as a cold. In very young babies, coughing is uncommon and may be a sign of a serious lung infection. Be alert to a sudden cough in any child who is otherwise well because their airway may be obstructed.

SYMPTOM	POSSIBLE CAUSE
Is your child under a year old?	A common cold (*p.221*) or, rarely, bronchiolitis (*p.228*) or pneumonia (*p.227*).
Does your child have a fever and does he cough at any time?	A common cold (*p.221*) or influenza (*p.225*).
Does your child have a fever, a cough and a rash – or has he recently been exposed to measles?	Measles (*p.264*).
Does your child cough mainly at night, whether or not he has a fever?	Whooping cough (*p.269*) or asthma (*p.226*).
If your child coughs, does the cough come in bouts ending in a whoop, and is there vomiting?	Whooping cough (*p.269*) or other infections.
If your child been coughing for less than 24 hours, was there a sudden onset?	Inhalation of a foreign body.
Has your child been coughing for less than 24 hours, with a stuffy or runny nose?	A common cold (*p.221*).
If your child has been coughing for 24 hours or more, is his nose persistently runny?	An allergy or a recurrent cold (*see* Common cold, *p.221*).
If your child has been coughing for 24 hours or more, is his nose persistently runny, does he get frequent ear infections and is his voice nasal?	Enlarged adenoids (*p.222*).
If your child has been coughing for 24 hours or more and doesn't have a runny nose, has he had pertussis or a viral infection recently?	Cough persisting after whooping cough (*p.269*) or a viral infection.

Call an ambulance at once if your child:

- Has blue-tinged lips or tongue
- Is abnormallly drowsy
- Can't talk or produce sounds normally.

Call your doctor at once if:

- The areas between your child's ribs appear sunken when he breathes in.

ACTION NEEDED

If your child is unwell or if breathing difficulties develop, call your doctor at once.
Self-help Relieving a cough (*right*).

If breathing difficulties develop, call your doctor. If a rash appears, get medical advice within 24 hours.
Self-help Relieving a cough (*right*) and Bringing down a temperature (*p.59 and p.171*).

Get medical advice within 24 hours.
Self-help Bringing down a temperature (*p.59 and p.171*).

Get medical advice within 24 hours.
Self-help Relieving a cough (*right*).

Get medical advice within 24 hours.
Self-help Relieving a cough (*right*).

Urgent! Call your doctor at once!
Self-help Choking (*p.333*).

If your child is distressed, consult your doctor.
Self-help Relieving a cough (*right*).

If your child seems generally unwell or is upset by the cough, consult your doctor.
Self-help Relieving a cough (*right*).

Consult your doctor.
Self-help If the ear infections are causing pain, see Relieving earache (*p.205*).

If your child is distressed or feels unwell, or if the cough persists for more than three months, consult your doctor.
Self-help Relieving a cough (*right*).

SELF-HELP

Relieving a cough

You may be able to help relieve your child's cough with the following:

- Let the child drink soothing liquids, such as warm water mixed with honey. But do not give honey to children under one year of age because it may cause food poisoning. Give plenty of other warm or cool drinks. Ask your pharmacist about over-the-counter cough linctus preparations for children.

- Hang a wet towel in front of a radiator to moisten the air. Steam is a good home remedy for croup.

- Avoid excessive heating of your child's room as this will dry out the air and increase coughing.

RELIEVING A COUGHING ATTACK Sit the young child on your lap, leaning him slightly forwards. Pat his back gently to loosen any phlegm.

Natural cough remedies

Herbal remedies
A few drops of echinacea in warm water will help to boost your child's immune system. A tea made from elderberry will help your child fight the viruses that are responsible for many different coughs. A hot tea made from thyme, marshmallow or hyssop will help to bring up mucus from the lungs.

Aromatherapy
Eucalyptus and peppermint essential oils may help to soothe coughs. Put a few drops of either oil in a bowl of hot water and cover the child's head and bowl with a towel (take care not to burn his face). Ask him to breathe in the steam for a few minutes. Do not leave him alone.

SORE THROAT

Mᴵᴺᴼᴿ ᵛᴵᴿᴬᴸ ᴵᴺᶠᴱᶜᵀᴵᴼᴺˢ ᶜᴬᵁˢᴱ many of the sore throats that affect children. They usually clear up quickly without medical treatment. A very young child who is reluctant to eat or drink may have a sore throat. On occasion, a sore throat may be a symptom of a bacterial infection that requires antibiotics.

SYMPTOM	POSSIBLE CAUSE	ACTION NEEDED
Does your child have a fever, vomiting, a rash and a bright red tongue and throat?	Scarlet fever (*p.267*).	Call a doctor within 24 hours. **Self-help** Bringing down a temperature (*p.59 and p.171*).
Does your child have a fever and either feels pain on swallowing or refuses to eat solids?	Tonsillitis (*see* Pharyngitis and tonsillitis, *p.223*).	If your child is no better after 24 hours, consult your doctor. **Self-help** Bringing down a temperature (*p.59 and p.171*).
Is your child sneezing with a runny nose and a cough?	A common cold (*p.221*) or allergic rhinitis (*p.224*).	If symptoms last for more than a week, consult your doctor. **Self-help** Relieving a cough (*p.197*).
Does your child have no other symptoms except the sore throat?	Inflammation of the throat caused by a minor infection or irritation.	If her throat is still sore after 48 hours, consult your doctor.

SELF-HELP

Relieving a sore throat

The following tips may help to relieve a sore throat:

• Let your child have as many cold, non-acidic drinks such as milk as she wants. A straw makes drinking easier. Also, let her eat ice cream and jelly.

• Give liquid paracetamol regularly but don't exceed the recommended dose.

• If she's over 8, let her gargle with a diluted antiseptic.

• Throat lozenges are good if your child is old enough to suck rather than chew them.

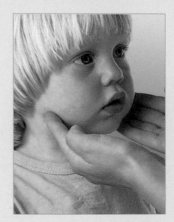

CHECKING THE GLANDS
Your child may complain of a difficulty in swallowing as well as a sore throat. Ask your child to sit still while you run your fingertips below the jaw, from the ears to the chin, to feel the size of the glands. If they feel like large peas, they are swollen.

DROWSINESS

A MINOR ILLNESS, A LACK OF SLEEP or a serious disease, such as meningitis, can cause drowsiness. Call an ambulance at once if your child is unconscious for three minutes; is breathing irregularly, slowly, or quickly; is unresponsive or difficult to wake from sleep; or has blood or fluid leaking from the nose or ears.

SYMPTOM	POSSIBLE CAUSE	ACTION NEEDED
Has your child had a recent blow to the head?	Head injury (p.291).	**Emergency!** Call an ambulance! While waiting, do not give your child anything to eat or drink.
Has your child swallowed something poisonous?	Swallowed poisons may lead to a loss of consciousness.	**Emergency!** Call an ambulance!
Does your child have a fever?	A high fever, resulting from any infection, may cause delirium, particularly if the temperature exceeds 39°C (102°F).	**Urgent!** Call your doctor at once! **Self-help** Bringing down a temperature (p.59 and p.171).
Does your child have diarrhoea with or without vomiting?	Dehydration resulting from gastroenteritis (p.254).	**Urgent!** Call your doctor at once! **Self-help** Preventing dehydration in babies (p.63) or Giving extra fluids (p.172).
Does your child have a stiff neck, headache, vomiting, or flat spots that remain when pressed?	Meningitis (p.294).	**Emergency!** Call an ambulance!
Is your child very thirsty and passing lots of urine; or has he recently lost weight and been uncharacteristically tired?	Diabetes mellitus (p.309).	**Urgent!** Call your doctor at once!
Does your child have red eyes, no appetite, mood swings, withdrawal or aggression?	Substance abuse (pp.160–161).	Consult your doctor.
Have you been giving your child any medicine?	Certain medicines, such as antihistamines, can cause confusion or have a sedative effect on some children.	Ask your doctor/pharmacist if the medicine may be causing the symptoms and whether you should stop giving it.

DIZZINESS

THE SPINNING SENSATION OF DIZZINESS may be accompanied by a feeling of lightheadedness or an attack of faintness. In fainting, a fall in blood pressure causes a brief loss of consciousness. The loss of consciousness during a seizure or fit is due to abnormal electrical activity in the brain.

SYMPTOM	POSSIBLE CAUSE
If your child is feeling dizzy, is she 5 years or older, or under 5 without a fever?	A seizure (*see* Epilepsy, *p.293*).
Has your child fallen to the ground unconscious, either with no other symptoms or looking pale and sweaty?	Your child's unconsciousness is probably a fainting attack. Fainting is due to a fall in blood pressure, possibly caused by emotional stress, anxiety, not eating for some time or being in an overcrowded or stuffy atmosphere for too long.
Your child falls to the ground unconscious – did her face or limbs twitch and did she pass urine or bite her tongue?	Epilepsy (*p.293*).
Does your child feel her surroundings are going round and round?	Labyrinthitis (*p.242*).
Does your child seems unaware of surroundings for a few moments?	An absence seizure (*see* Epilepsy, *p.293*).
If your child is being treated for diabetes mellitus, does she feel faint or unsteady?	Extremely low blood sugar level caused by diabetes mellitus (*p.309*) may cause your child to lose consciousness and, in some cases, to have a seizure.
If she is not being treated for diabetes mellitus, is she under 5 with a fever?	Febrile convulsions (*p.292*).
Does your child feel faint or unsteady?	Low blood sugar level (hypoglycaemia), caused by diabetes mellitus (*p.309*). Low blood pressure due to postural hypotension.

Call an ambulance at once if your child has lost consciousness and any of the following occur:

- Consciousness is not regained within 3 minutes
- Breathing becomes slower
- Breathing is irregular or noisy.

ACTION NEEDED

Call your doctor if the dizziness lasts for 10 minutes or more. Consult your doctor if it was briefer than this and it happens again.

If your child faints regularly, see your doctor.
Self-help Dealing with faintness and fainting (*right*).

Urgent! Call your doctor at once! do not try to open her mouth.

Consult your doctor.

Consult your doctor.
Self-help Sit your child down quietly until she is fully recovered.

Emergency! Call an ambulance if she is fitting! If diabetes has already been diagnosed, give her a glucagon injection while you are waiting.
Self-help As soon as she feels faint, give her glucose tablets.

Urgent! Call your doctor at once!
Self-help Bringing down a temperature (*p.59 and p.171*).

If your child often feels faint, consult your doctor.
Self-help As soon as your child feels faint, give glucose tablets or a glucose or sugary drink. See Dealing with faintness and fainting (*right*).

SELF-HELP

Dealing with faintness and fainting

If your child feels faint, lay her down with her legs propped up on cushions, and carry out the following:

- Loosen any clothing that is tight-fitting and provide fresh air.
- Give calm reassurance.
- Offer a sugary drink or small snack to raise the sugar level in her blood. Do not offer food or drink if she is not fully conscious.
- If she loses consciousness, monitor her condition (*pp.330–332*). If she is breathing, place her in the recovery position (*p.330*). Call an ambulance if she doesn't regain consciousness within 3 minutes.

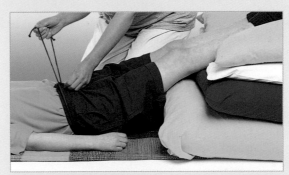

A FAINTING CHILD Prop the legs up on cushions to increase the blood supply to the brain, and loosen any tight-fitting clothing.

Coping with a seizure

Children between 6 months and 5 years are susceptible to febrile seizures when their temperature rises abruptly at the start of a fever. This may appear serious but usually it is not. A child in a seizure may sweat, with a hot forehead and eyes squinting, rolling or fixed. The fists may clench, as the back arches and the body stiffens. Help your child while you wait for the doctor to arrive:

- Lay her down and arrange soft towels and pillows around her to prevent injury.
- Undress her and expose her to fresh, cool air.
- When she's cool the seizures will cease. Put her in the recovery position (*p.330*), covered in a light blanket.

EYE PROBLEMS

OST EYE PROBLEMS, SUCH AS ITCHINESS, redness, watering and discharge, are caused by infections or irritation and are rarely serious. If you cannot use self-help measures to help a child who has an eye injury or a foreign object in the eye, go to your doctor or the nearest accident and emergency department.

SYMPTOM	POSSIBLE CAUSE	ACTION NEEDED
Does your child have any obvious damage to an eye?	Eye injury.	**Emergency!** Take your child to the nearest hospital accident and emergency department.
Can you see a foreign body, such as a speck of dirt, in your child's eye?	A foreign body often causes redness and watering.	If you cannot remove the foreign body or if your child is in pain, call your doctor at once. **Self-help** Removing a foreign body from the eye (*p.341*).
Does your child have a red lump on an eyelid?	Stye (*p.243*).	If the eye becomes painful and red, and if the stye does not heal within a week, or if it recurs, see your doctor.
Are your child's eyes producing tears even when he is not crying?	Blocked tear duct if your child is under a year old.	Consult your doctor.
Has the white of an eye turned red?	Eye irritation may be caused by chemicals, fumes, or viral or allergic conjunctivitis (*p.244*). Iritis (*p.244*), a more serious condition, is also possible.	**Urgent!** Call your doctor at once if your child is in pain. If there is no pain but redness continues for more than 24 hours, consult your doctor. **Self-help** Removing a foreign body from the eye (*p.341*).
Is the red eye accompanied by a sticky discharge?	Severe conjunctivitis (*p.244*).	Get medical advice within 24 hours.
Does your child have red, itchy eyelids?	Blepharitis (*p.243*) or conjunctivitis (*p.244*).	Consult your doctor.
Does your child have itchy eyes?	Allergy, such as hay fever (*see* Allergic rhinitis, *p.224*).	Consult your doctor/pharmacist.

VISION PROBLEMS

Defects in a child's vision are usually picked up in the eye tests routinely conducted at school. However, if you or your child's teacher notice that your child is having difficulty seeing, or has some other kind of vision problem, you need to get it looked at straight away.

SYMPTOM	POSSIBLE CAUSE	ACTION NEEDED
Does your child have double or blurred vision and no other symptoms?	A refractive error (*p.245*) or a squint (*p.245*).	Consult your doctor or optician.
Does the double/blurred vision follow a recent head injury?	Bleeding inside the skull (*see* Head injury, *p.291*).	**Emergency!** Call an ambulance!
Is the double or blurred vision associated with headaches?	Migraine (*see* Recurrent headaches, *p.291*).	If this is the first attack, phone your doctor. If the attacks are frequent, consult your doctor.
Has your child lost all or part of her vision?	Injury to the eye or part of the brain is possible.	**Emergency!** Take your child to the nearest hospital!
Does your child have difficulty seeing near or distant objects?	A refractive error (*p.245*).	Consult your optician.
Do your child's eyes often seem out of alignment?	Squint (*p.245*).	If your child is over 4 months old, consult your doctor.
Does she regularly see flashing lights or floating spots, with a severe headache afterwards?	Migraine (*see* Recurrent headaches, *p.291*).	If this is the first attack, call your doctor. If the attacks are frequent, go to see your doctor.
Is one or both of your child's eyes red or painful?	Iritis (*p.244*).	**Urgent!** Call your doctor at once!
Is your child taking any medicine?	Some drugs may cause blurred vision.	Ask your doctor/pharmacist if the medicine may be the cause and if you should stop giving it.
Might your child have taken someone else's medicine?	Drugs, such as antidepressants, may cause blurred vision.	**Urgent!** Call your doctor at once!

EAR PROBLEMS

EAR PROBLEMS SUCH AS EARACHE are usually caused by an infection. Middle ear infections are common in young children because the Eustachian tubes connecting their ears with their nose and throat are short and easily blocked by mucus, which predisposes to infection. Disorders that affect a child's external ear canal cause such symptoms as itchiness or discharge.

SYMPTOM	POSSIBLE CAUSE
If your child's earache is not severe, might there be something in his ear?	A foreign body, such as an insect or bead, in the ear.
If there is a discharge from the ear, does gently tugging on the earlobe make the pain worse?	Atopic eczema (p.234) or inflammation of the outer ear (p.240).
Does your child have an itchy ear?	Atopic eczema (p.234) or inflammation of the outer ear (p.240).
Did the pain in your child's ear start during or soon after a journey by air?	Barotrauma (p.242).
Is there is a discharge from the ear but no reaction of tugging the earlobe?	Inflammation of the middle ear (p.240).
Does your child have an earache without any other symptom or with hearing problems?	Inflammation of the middle ear (p.240).
If the earache is severe, does your child have a fever, a cold or feel generally unwell?	Inflammation of the middle ear (p.240).
Can you see a red lump inside your child's ear?	A boil (p.233) in the outer ear canal.
If the earache is severe, does your child seem well with no red lump inside his ear?	Inflammation of the outer ear (p.240).

ASSESSMENT

Hearing problems

Hearing defects are often first noticed by the child's parents. In babies, the first sign of deafness is a failure to respond to sounds. In older children, the onset of hearing problems may cause school work to deteriorate. The following are instances when your child may experience hearing problems. In each case, consult your doctor.

• Sneezing or a recent cold may cause the tubes connecting the ears and throat to become blocked. See Common cold (*p.221*) and Allergic rhinitis (*p.224*).

• Hearing problems can start during or shortly after a journey by air, because of barotrauma (*p.242*).

• Hearing problems that either accompany or follow earache may be due to middle ear inflammation (*p.240*). If they follow earache they may also be due to glue ear (*p.241*).

• If the problem is unconnected to any other symptom then earwax is probably blocking the external ear canal.

• Rarely, infectious diseases such as mumps, measles and meningitis may a long-term effect on hearing.

ACTION NEEDED

Get medical advice within 24 hours.
Self-help if you can see the foreign body in his ear and it is not stuck, try to remove it (*see* Foreign objects in the ear, *p.241*). If in doubt, seek medical advice. An insect may be floated out by pouring tepid water into his ear (*see* Foreign objects in the ear, *p.241*).

Get medical advice within 24 hours.
Self-help Relieving earache (*right*).

Get medical advice within 24 hours.
Self-help Relieving earache (*right*).

If the ache persists, consult your doctor.
Self-help Relieving earache (*right*).

Get medical advice within 24 hours.
Self-help Relieving earache (*right*).

Get medical advice within 24 hours.
Self-help Relieving earache (*right*).

Get medical advice within 24 hours.
Self-help Relieving earache (*right*) and Bringing down a temperature (*p.59 and p.171*).

Get medical advice within 24 hours.
Self-help Relieving earache (*right*).

Get medical advice within 24 hours.
Self-help Relieving earache (*right*).

SELF-HELP

Relieving earache

You may be able to reduce the pain of your child's earache with the following:

• Give him liquid paracetamol but do not exceed the recommended dose.

• Wrap a hot-water bottle in a towel for the child to hold against his ear. For a baby, use a warmed soft cloth.

• Lie your child down, or sit him up and prop up his head with pillows. It is possible that lying flat may make his earache worse.

• Do not put ear drops or oil into his ear.

Recurrent earaches

If your child suffers from earaches that regularly recur, try the following:

• Make sure his immune system is functioning well (*see p.163*).

• Make sure he eats a healthy diet and that foods to which he is sensitive are excluded. Food sensitivities can cause excessive production of catarrh making him more susceptible to ear pain and infection.

• Consider taking him to a "hands-on therapist" – for example, an osteopath or chiropractor (*p.323*).

• Carefully dry his ears after swimming with a hairdryer set on a low heat.

• Get his hearing checked regularly.

MOUTH PROBLEMS

THE TONGUE, GUMS, LIPS AND INSIDE LINING of the mouth are rarely afflicted by serious problems. A sore mouth may be upsetting for a child, largely because it hurts to eat and drink. An infant with mouth pain is probably teething – chewing on a hard or cold object can often bring relief.

SYMPTOM	POSSIBLE CAUSE
Does your child have tiny blisters on or around the lips?	Cold sores (*p.231*).
Does your child have redness around his mouth or cracks at the corners of her lips?	Lick eczema (*p.185*).
Does your child have straw-coloured crusts on or around the lips?	Impetigo (*p.235*).
Does your child have soreness affecting the tongue only?	Irritation of the tongue caused by a rough tooth.
Does your child have painful, red and swollen gums?	Gingivitis (*p.249*).
Does your child have painful discoloured areas inside the mouth or on the tongue?	Mouth ulcers (*p.247*).
Does your child feel unwell or have a fever at the same time as having painful, discoloured areas with light yellow spots inside the mouth or on the tongue?	Gingivostomatitis (*p.247*).
Does your child have painful areas with light yellow spots inside the mouth or on the tongue, as well as spots on the hands and feet?	Hand, foot and mouth disease (*p.266*).
Does your child's mouth or tongue have painful areas with a creamy-yellow discoloration that is easily scraped off?	Oral thrush (*p.248*).

Relieving a sore mouth

Relieve your child's discomfort with the following:

- Rinse the mouth hourly with ¼ teaspoon bicarbonate of soda dissolved in 100 ml (3.5 fl.oz) of warm water.

- Give the recommended dose of paracetamol.

- Try soft foods, such as soup and ice cream, while the soreness lasts. Avoid acidic drinks, such as fruit juices.

TREATING MOUTH ULCERS
Some mouth ulcers look like white "curds". Wrap a clean handkerchief around your index finger and wipe away the curds. Rinse the mouth out with solution of bicarbonate of soda.

If the blisters are severe, last for over 2 weeks, or are embarrassing your child, consult your doctor.
Self-help Apply an over-the-counter cream or gel to the sores several times daily until they disappear.

Self-help Apply petroleum jelly to the affected area every few hours. Use a lip salve to moisturize and protect the lips themselves.

Get medical advice within 24 hours.

See your dentist.

Consult your dentist.
Self-help Your child should continue to brush her teeth with care. An antibacterial mouthwash can relieve inflammation. See Keeping your child's teeth healthy (Tooth decay, *p.248*).

If the ulcers fail to heal in 10 days, see your doctor.
Self-help Relieving a sore mouth (*above*).

Consult your doctor.
Self-help Relieving a sore mouth (*above*) and Bringing down a temperature (*p.59 and p.171*).

Consult your doctor.
Self-help Relieving a sore mouth (*above*).

Consult your doctor.

Combating cold sores

Small blisters on and around the lips may appear during an infection, after exposure to a cold wind or the sun, or as a result of stress. These cold sores are caused by the herpes simplex virus and have no cure. You can relieve your child's discomfort and keep the sores under control.

- A cold drink may soothe the discomfort.

- An over-the-counter cream containing the antiviral drug acyclovir may help, especially if you apply it as soon as your child feels the tingling sensation that precedes the sores.

- Calendula cream is a homeopathic remedy that can help heal the skin of a broken cold sore.

Treating gingivitis

Children with red, swollen and tender gums are probably not brushing their teeth properly – and when they do, the gums bleed. The best way to treat this gingivitis is to regularly brush both teeth and gums to remove the bacterial plaque that has accumulated. An antibacterial mouthwash will help relieve any tenderness.

BRUSHING THE TEETH
Encourage her to brush her teeth and gums with a soft toothbrush and a little toothpaste twice a day after breakfast and before bed. Supervise her until she is 6 or 7 years old.

ABDOMINAL PAIN

ABDOMINAL PAIN IS NOT UNUSUAL in children and some children suffer pains that regularly recur. Rarely is the cause serious and the pain soon goes away without any medical or self-help treatment. Occasionally, however, the pain may indicate an underlying disorder that requires prompt medical attention.

SYMPTOM	POSSIBLE CAUSE
Does your child have a painful swelling in the groin or scrotum?	Strangulated inguinal hernia (*see* Hernia, *p.260*) or testicular torsion (*see* Penis and testicle disorders, *p.277*).
Is your child's pain aggravated when the abdomen is gently pressed?	Appendicitis (*p.253*).
Has your child been in continuous pain for 6 hours?	Appendicitis (*p.253*).
Is your child vomiting and has he been in continuous pain for 3 hours?	Appendicitis (*p.253*).
Is your child's vomit greenish-yellow?	Intestinal obstruction (*p.256*).
Does defecation or vomiting relieve the pain, or is there diarrhoea with or without vomiting?	Gastroenteritis (*p.254*).
Is there red material in your baby's faeces?	Intussusception (*see* Intestinal obstruction, *p.256*).
Does your child have a sore throat, cough or runny nose?	An upper respiratory tract infection, such as a common cold (*p.221*), causing lymph node swelling in the abdomen.
Does your child have two or more of the following: fever, pain on passing urine, bedwetting (after being dry at night)?	Urinary tract infection (*p.275*).
Does your child often have recurrent bouts of abdominal pain without seeming unwell?	Anxiety (see *pp.131–132*) or food intolerance (*see* Reactions to food, *p.252*) may be the explanation, but often there is no obvious cause.

Call an ambulance at once if your child has any of the following symptoms:

- Abdominal pain for 6 hours
- Pain or swelling in the groin or testicles
- Greenish-yellow vomit
- Red material in faeces.

ACTION NEEDED

Emergency! Call an ambulance! While waiting, do not give your child anything to eat or drink.

If the pain continues for more than 3 hours, call your doctor at once.
Self-help Relieving abdominal pain (*right*).

Urgent! Call your doctor at once! While waiting, do not give your child anything to eat or drink.

Urgent! Call your doctor at once!
Self-help Relieving abdominal pain (*right*).

Emergency! Call an ambulance! While waiting, do not give your child anything to eat or drink.

Get medical advice within 24 hours.
Self-help Preventing dehydration in babies (*p.63*).

Emergency! Call an ambulance! While waiting, do not give your child anything to eat or drink.

If your child is distressed by his or symptoms, consult your doctor.
Self-help Relieving a cough (*p.197*), Relieving a sore throat (*p.198*), Relieving abdominal pain (*right*).

Get medical advice within 24 hours.
Self-help If your child has a fever, see Bringing down a temperature (*p.59 and p.171*).

Consult your doctor.
Self-help Calm your child's anxiety. If you think food intolerance is the problem try to establish, and avoid, the triggers. See Relieving abdominal pain (*right*).

SELF-HELP

Relieving abdominal pain

The following tips may help you to relieve your child's abdominal pain:

- Fill a hot-water bottle with warm water and wrap it in a towel. Let your child hold it against his abdomen. Encourage him to lie down on a bed or sofa, or to sit in a chair.
- While your child is suffering from abdominal pain, do not give him anything to eat, and only give plain water to drink.
- If you think appendicitis or another serious disorder is a possibility, your child might require surgery. So do not give him anything to eat or drink until you have spoken to your doctor.

Relieving anxiety

Talk with your child about the pain in his abdomen and see if you can establish whether it is linked to any worries he may have.

- Children sometimes complain of pain when they are anxious – discussing their worries may ease the pain.
- If the pain is recurrent, and you suspect it is related to anxiety, consider taking him for a relaxing massage (*p.325*). Alternatively, you could take him to see a hands-on therapist, such as an osteopath or a chiropractic (*p.323*).
- Consider visiting an experienced homeopath who may recommend taking your child's constitutional remedy (*p.321*).

FEELING FOR ABDOMINAL PAIN *Press down firmly but not abruptly with the tips of your fingers to try to locate the pain.*

CONSTIPATION

CHILDREN CAN PASS FAECES in an erratic way. They may defecate four times a day or only once every four days; anything in between is normal. Changes in diet, a minor illness or emotional stress may affect defecation in the short term. If the faeces are hard, or painful to pass, your child is constipated.

SYMPTOM	POSSIBLE CAUSE
If your child has passed faeces in the last 24 hours, was the process painful and was there any blood?	Anal fissure (*see* Constipation, *p.255*).
If your child has passed faeces in the last 24 hours, were they hard and pellet-like?	Your child's diet may not contain enough fibre or sufficient fluid.
Does your child have abdominal pain?	Go to ABDOMINAL PAIN (*p.212*).
If your child usually opens her bowels daily, has she had a fever or been vomiting before becoming constipated?	Loss of fluid as a result of fever or vomiting can disrupt bowel movements, which will return to normal once your child has recovered.
Does your child usually open her bowels less than once every 4 days?	Constipation (*p.255*).
Is your child learning toilet training now or has she recently started?	Children who are nervous about toilet training may resist the urge to open their bowels.
If your child is constipated but has yet to start her toilet training or was trained a while ago, have you changed her diet recently?	Your child's diet may not contain enough fibre or sufficient fluid.

A REGULAR BOWEL HABIT
Encourage, but don't force,
your child to sit on the potty
or toilet at the same time
each day. The knees should
be above the hips.

ACTION NEEDED

Consult your doctor.
Self-help Preventing constipation (*right*).

Self-help Preventing constipation (*right*).

Self-help Encourage your child to drink plenty of fluids. See Bringing down a temperature (*p.59 and p.171*), Preventing dehydration in babies (*p.63*) or Giving extra fluids (*p.172*).

Consult your doctor.
Self-help Preventing constipation (*right*).

If your child does not pass any faeces at all for longer than about 4 days, consult your doctor.
Self-help Perhaps you are anxious about how your child's toilet training is progressing and are making her nervous. Adopt a more relaxed attitude towards your child's toilet training.

Self-help Preventing constipation (*right*).

Preventing constipation

The following tips may help you to relieve or prevent your child's constipation:

• Look at your child's diet to see if the meals she is eating contain a varied and nutritious mixture of foods. If necessary, increase the amount of fruit, vegetables, and other fibre-rich foods, such as wholegrain cereals and bread, beans, carrots, bananas and dried apricots. Balance her diet with energy-giving foods such as pasta, eggs and cheese.

• As well as boosting her fibre intake you will need to increase the amount of fluids that your child drinks. Encourage her to drink fresh fruit juice diluted half-and-half with sparkling water. Reduce milk, which can cause constipation, by cutting out milk drinks, but continue to use milk for cereal and cooking.

• Regular exercise is vital for a healthy digestive system. Encourage your child to run around every day.

• Encourage your child to sit on the potty or toilet at the same time every day. This is the best way to establish a regular bowel habit. Make sure that her knees are higher than her hips and encourage her to rock back and forth. Don't force your child to sit on the potty or toilet and don't worry if nothing happens. Above all, don't make it a source of tension.

• Never give your child a laxative unless specifically recommended or prescribed by your doctor. However, natural laxatives, such as prunes or syrup of figs, may help to relieve occasional constipation.

FIBRE-RICH FOODS
Encourage your
child to eat at
least one fibre-
rich food, such as
wholemeal bread
and salad or fruit,
at every meal.

ABNORMAL FAECES

A CHANGE IN DIET IS ALMOST ALWAYS RESPONSIBLE when a child's faeces smell or look different. Changes in colour, smell, consistency and content do not usually last for more than a few days and are of no concern. If you notice any other symptoms, or if the abnormal faeces persist, take your child to see a doctor.

SYMPTOM	POSSIBLE CAUSE	ACTION NEEDED
If your baby's faeces are green and possibly runny, is he both breast- and bottlefed?	Some types of cow's milk formula may result in green faeces. If the faeces are also runny, your baby may have gastroenteritis (p.254).	See a doctor within 24 hours if you suspect gastroenteritis. **Self-help** Preventing dehydration in babies (p.83). Try a new milk formula.
If his faeces are green and runny, is he breastfed only?	Green, runny faeces are normal in breastfed babies.	If he seems unwell or has other symptoms, consult your doctor.
Is your child, whatever his age, taking any medicines?	Many medicines can affect the appearance of faeces.	Ask your doctor/pharmacist if the medicine may be the cause and if you should stop giving it.
If your child is one year old or more with very pale faeces, has he just recovered from a bout of diarrhoea or vomiting?	Gastroenteritis (p.254) may sometimes cause faeces to be pale for several days.	If your child seems unwell or if the faeces do not return to their normal colour in a few days, consult your doctor.
If your child's faeces are pale, is his urine dark and are his skin and whites of the eye yellowish?	Hepatitis (p.261), which may cause jaundice.	Get medical advice within 24 hours.
Are your child's faeces very pale, floating and foul-smelling?	Malabsorption (p.258), often caused by underlying disorders, such as reaction to food (p.252).	Consult your doctor.
Is there blood on your child's faeces?	Gastroenteritis (p.254), anal fissure (p.257) or inflammatory bowel disease (p.259).	Get medical advice within 24 hours.
Are your child's faeces runny?	Go to DIARRHOEA (p.62 and p.172).	
If your child is under a year old, are his faeces red and jelly-like?	Intussusception (see Intestinal obstruction, p.256).	**Emergency!** Call an ambulance! While waiting, do not give your child anything to eat or drink.

URINARY PROBLEMS

Problems with urinating may be due to a minor infection or, more rarely, to a serious disorder, such as diabetes mellitus. If your child urinates more on some days than others, or if the urine colour changes, this does not necessarily indicate a problem. But if she feels pain when urinating, consult your doctor.

SYMPTOM	POSSIBLE CAUSE	ACTION NEEDED
Does your child pass urine frequently and feel generally unwell or have a fever?	Urinary tract infection (*p.275*).	Call your doctor within 24 hours. **Self-help** Bringing down a temperature (*p.59 and p.171*).
If your child passes urine frequently, has she been taking medicines recently?	Some drugs may cause frequent passing of urine.	Ask your doctor/pharmacist if the medicine may be the cause and if you should stop giving it.
Is your child experiencing school difficulties, a family upheaval, or a change of routine?	Anxiety (*pp.131–132*) or stress may result in your child going to the toilet more often than usual.	If the problem does not clear up within a few days, call your doctor.
Does your child feel pain when she passes urine?	Urinary tract infection (*p.275*).	Call your doctor within 24 hours.
Is the colour of your child's urine pink, red or smoky?	Glomerulonephritis (*p.276*) or urinary tract infection (*p.275*).	**Urgent!** Call your doctor at once!
Is the colour of your child's urine dark brown and clear, and her faeces pale?	Hepatitis (*p.261*).	Call your doctor within 24 hours.
Is the colour of your child's urine dark yellow or orange, or dark brown and clear, while her faeces are normal?	Low fluid intake, vomiting, fever or diarrhoea concentrates the urine and so darkens it.	Give your child plenty to drink and the urine should soon return to normal. If your child has had a fever or diarrhoea, or has been vomiting, give extra fluid (*p.172*).
Is the colour of your child's urine green or blue?	Artificial colouring in food, drink, or medicine.	The colouring will soon pass out of your child's system naturally.
Does your child urinate often and in increased amounts, while also losing weight or being abnormally tired?	Diabetes mellitus (*p.309*).	Call your doctor within 24 hours.

GENITAL PROBLEMS IN BOYS

BOYS OF ANY AGE CAN BE AFFECTED BY A PAIN or swelling in the penis or scrotum. They may also experience pain on urination or a discharge from the penis. Physical injuries to the genitals are most likely in boys of school age. If your son is suffering a severe or persistent genital pain, take him to see your doctor.

SYMPTOM	POSSIBLE CAUSE	ACTION NEEDED
Does your son have a painless swelling in the groin or scrotum?	Inguinal hernia (*see* Hernia, *p.260*) or hydrocele (*see* Penis and testicle disorders, *p.277*).	Get medical advice within 24 hours.
If your son has a painful swelling in the groin or scrotum, has he had a recent injury to his genitals?	Pain that does not subside following an injury may indicate damage to the testicles.	**Urgent!** Call your doctor at once!
If your son has a painful swelling in the groin or scrotum, has he had mumps in the past 2 weeks?	Orchitis (see Penis and testicle disorders, *p.277*).	Get medical advice within 24 hours.
Does your son have a painful swelling in his groin or scrotum that is not the result of either an injury or a case of mumps?	Testicular torsion (*see* Penis and testicle disorders, *p.277*) or strangulated inguinal hernia (*see* Hernia, *p.260*).	**Emergency!** Call an ambulance! While waiting, do not give your son anything to eat or drink.
Does your son have a pain or burning sensation on passing urine?	Urinary tract infection (*p.275*).	Get medical advice within 24 hours.
Does your son have a swelling of the tip of his penis or a discharge from his foreskin?	Balanitis (*see* Penis and testicle disorders, *p.260*).	Get medical advice within 24 hours.
Does your son have a greyish-yellow discharge from his penis?	A foreign body in your son's urethra.	Consult your doctor.

GENITAL PROBLEMS IN GIRLS

ITCHING AND INFLAMMATION are the most common genital symptoms in girls.
These may be painful or may cause an abnormal vaginal discharge. The
symptoms may be due to a fungal or bacterial infection. In some girls, scented
soaps, bubble baths or deodorants may cause the problem

SYMPTOM	POSSIBLE CAUSE	ACTION NEEDED
If your daughter's genital area is itchy or sore, does she have a greyish-yellow or greenish discharge from her vagina?	Infection of the vagina (*below and* Vulvovaginitis, *p.279*).	Get medical advice within 24 hours.
If your daughter's genital area is itchy or sore, does she have a thick white vaginal discharge?	Vaginal thrush (*below and* Vulvovaginitis, *p.279*).	Get medical advice within 24 hours.
Is your daughter's genital area itchy or sore but without a discharge?	Poor hygiene, vulvovaginitis (*see below and p.279*) or threadworms (*p.262*).	Consult your doctor. **Self-help** Change her underwear daily, wash her vaginal area carefully and avoid irritants.
If your daughter is over 10 years old, does she have a thin, white vaginal discharge?	Increased production of sex hormones at puberty.	If irritation accompanies the discharge, see your doctor.

SELF-HELP

Relieving vulvovaginitis

If the itching persists or if she has a discharge, take
her to your doctor as she may have vaginal thrush or
a bacterial infection (*see also* Vulvovaginitis, *p.279*).

• A probiotic cream containing acidophilus can be
applied directly to the vagina to relieve the itching
and inflammation caused by a fungal infection such as

Candida albicans, commonly known as thrush. Probiotics
are particularly useful when the infection is linked with
use of antibiotics.

• If your daughter is susceptible to fungal infections, such
as candida, then encourage her to drink herbal echinacea
to enhance her immune system. See also Can I boost my
child's immune system? (*p.163*).

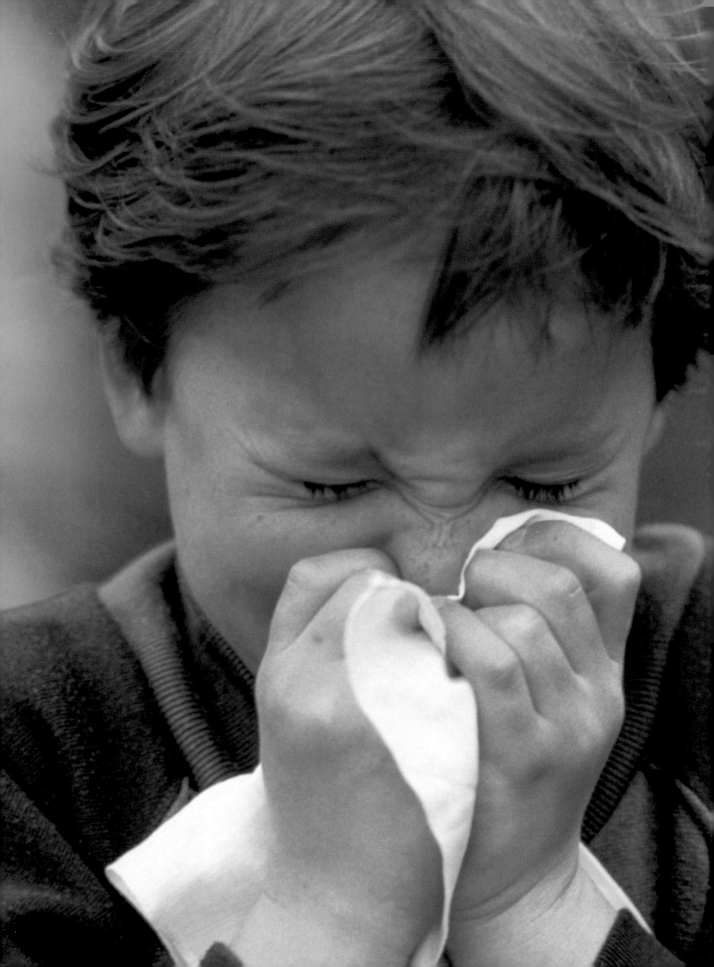

DISEASES
& DISORDERS

CHAPTER FOUR

Even with the best prevention in the world, you can expect your child to fall ill at some point during childhood. This chapter provides a quick but authoritative reference to the diseases and disorders that commonly affect children, with information on symptoms and self-help measures.

VISITING THE DOCTOR
OR THE HOSPITAL

WHEN YOUR CHILD IS ILL, try to get actively involved with the people who
know how to help him. Being a passive bystander who simply worries
too much doesn't do anybody any good, least of all your child. Getting the best
from your doctor means putting your child's interests first. Preparing your child
for a stay in hospital could be the first step towards restoring him to full health.

"we've seen lots of doctors with our daughter and found that being friendly gets the relationship off to the best start"

GETTING THE BEST
FROM YOUR DOCTOR

Before you register with a GP, do
some research to find out the local
doctors' particular areas of interest –
you may prefer someone with an
interest in children. Each surgery
should have a practice leaflet that
outlines any areas of interest along
with opening times and out-of-hours
arrangements. Ask the receptionist,
local pharmacist or neighbours as
to who's good with children.

When you have found a doctor,
think about getting the most from
your appointments. The average
appointment time with a GP is
between 5 and 8 minutes, so if there
is something you'd like to know, be
direct. Doctors often take their cues
from patients, so if you seem vague,
your doctor may assume you are not
ready to hear something.

Make a checklist of facts to take
with you, such as when the problem
started, if symptoms have got better
and whether your child's eating
patterns or behaviour have changed.
Write down what you'd like to ask.

If you can, take a partner, relative
or friend along with you to your
child's appointment – having
another person to discuss it with
afterwards may help you remember
what's been said more clearly.

Get to the surgery in plenty of
time and take things for your child
to do while you wait. During the
consultation, make notes of key
points and ask your doctor to
explain any medical jargon. That
way you will have a clear idea of
what's wrong.

If you don't like the treatment
your doctor is proposing, ask about
alternatives. Bear in mind that if
you are unhappy with your doctor's
diagnosis or advice, you can always
seek a second opinion.

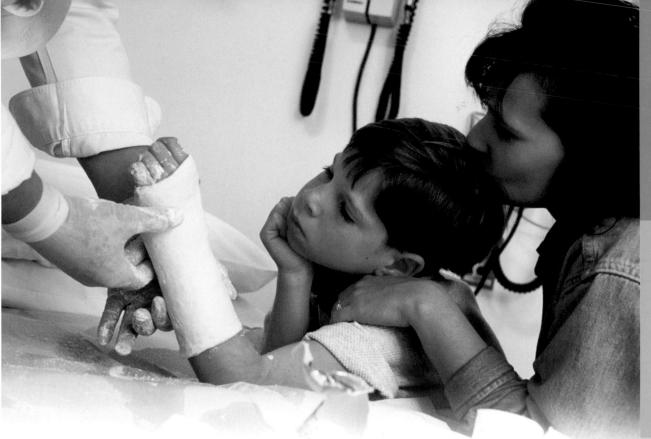

If medication is prescribed, get the full instructions on when and how to administer it and ask about any possible side effects. For further information, talk to the pharmacist when you collect the prescription.

If, after the appointment, you remember something you wanted to ask, either wait until next time or write your doctor a note or send an email, rather than phoning the surgery. Your doctor can then reply at a convenient time.

PREPARING YOUR CHILD FOR HOSPITAL

Studies have shown that children who are prepared before a hospital visit tend to be less anxious, cope more effectively with medical problems, need less medication and adapt more quickly to being back at home than children who have not known what to expect.

If your child has a medical test or operation coming up, you can plan for it. Pre-school children in particular benefit from preparation

because they are more likely to have misconceptions about the cause of their illness. Some might assume it's because they've been naughty.

Think about how you present the subject. Children are very influenced by the reactions of their parents and if you have negative feelings about hospitals, your child may pick this up and feel worried. It's often better to spread information out over a couple of days rather than give it all at once so your child can absorb it. Also, consider timing – the younger your child, the less time you should leave between talking about the visit and the visit happening.

Find out as much as you can. Most hospitals have welcome booklets and many run pre-admission tours that give you and your child the chance to look around, ask questions and meet staff. Children are often most concerned about an anaesthetic and waking up afterwards. If your child is worried about this, ask to meet an anaesthetist and visit the anaesthetic room during your tour.

Be open and honest with your child as you describe, in terms he will understand, what will happen. Props may help younger children. Talk it through with a favourite teddy or invest in a toy doctor's bag so your child can see a stethoscope or blood pressure cuff. There are lots of good books for different age groups on preparing for hospital, so it's worth a trip to a bookshop or library.

Emergency situations are more difficult. Every day in the UK, 6,500 children are taken to accident and emergency departments. Stay with your child to give him reassurance and comfort. As you meet members of the medical team, find out what will happen next so you can give your child a running commentary in terms he will understand.

When you get home, encourage your child to "play out" the situation, perhaps with a toy in the role of patient. Drawing and painting may help a child to express feelings. With an older child, discuss the visit and see if you can detect any concerns.

RESPIRATORY PROBLEMS

Viral infections, such as colds, are the most common cause of respiratory problems in children.

YOUNG CHILDREN ARE PARTICULARLY LIKELY to catch colds and other disorders because they have not had time to build up their immune systems. Allergic disorders, such as asthma and allergic rhinitis (hay fever), are the other main respiratory problems affecting children and asthma is becoming increasingly common. The best protection against respiratory problems is prevention: a good diet, plenty of exercise and fresh air will boost your child's immune system and help her to resist infection.

ANATOMY OF THE RESPIRATORY SYSTEM

▶ *HOW THE RESPIRATORY SYSTEM WORKS*

The respiratory system is made up of the lungs, air passages such as the nose and windpipe, and breathing muscles, including the diaphragm. The airways branch many times into small bronchioles that end in tiny air sacs where the blood collects oxygen in exchange for carbon dioxide and water.

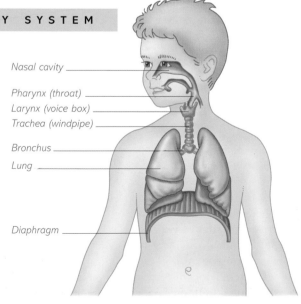

Nasal cavity

Pharynx (throat)

Larynx (voice box)

Trachea (windpipe)

Bronchus

Lung

Diaphragm

COMMON COLD

A viral infection of the nose and throat, the common cold is one of the most frequent illnesses in children. Most have at least six colds a year, more when they start playgroup or nursery. Some otherwise healthy children may have as many as 10 colds a year.

Causes

The common cold can be caused by a range of different viruses. Immunity as a result of infection with one strain does not protect children against another, so that they may get one cold followed by a different one.

School children are particularly likely to catch colds because they are exposed to a wide variety of viruses to which they have not yet built up immunity. Cold viruses are spread in droplets that are sneezed or coughed out and then inhaled by others. The viruses may also be spread through direct contact with an infected person or object.

Medical treatment

Take your child to see the doctor if her cough has not improved after 5 days, if she has other symptoms for longer than 10 days or new symptoms develop.

Take your baby to see a doctor within 24 hours if she refuses feeds, suffers from a fever over 39°C (102°F) or is very unwell. A baby under 2 months should be seen within a few hours if she has any of these symptoms.

How to help your child

Most colds will clear up on their own within a week. In the meantime, the following tips may help you to make your child more comfortable.

Keep her room warm (but not too hot) and increase the moisture in the atmosphere with a vaporizer or a wet towel on a chair near a radiator. Give your child plenty of liquids to drink. A baby with a cold should be given small feeds at more frequent intervals than usual. Giving liquid paracetamol, at an appropriate dose for your child's age and weight, may relieve a sore throat and any accompanying aches.

SYMPTOMS

Symptoms start 1–3 days after infection.
- Tickly or scratchy feeling in the throat.
- Runny nose.
- Sneezing.
- Blocked nose, which may make feeding difficult for a baby.
- Cough and sore throat.
- Watery eyes.
- Aching body.
- Possibly a fever.

Possible complications

Colds can spread down into the bronchi and bronchioles of the lungs, causing bronchiolitis (*see p.228*), bronchitis (*see p.228*) or pneumonia (*see p.227*). These illnesses may be complicated by another, secondary infection caused by bacteria.

The viral infection may also spread up the Eustachian tubes and affect the ears, causing inflammation of the middle ear (*see p.240*), or the sinuses, causing sinusitis (*see below*). In those children who suffer from asthma (*see p.226*), a cold may be enough to trigger an attack.

SINUSITIS

This condition is an inflammation of the lining of the sinuses (air-filled cavities in the bones that surround the nose). The first indication of sinusitis may be symptoms of a common cold, such as a runny nose and coughing, that persist for longer than usual.

Causes

Sinusitis is most often caused by bacterial infection following a cold when mucus produced in the sinuses traps bacteria.

Cilia, the tiny hair-like structures that project from the lining of the sinuses, normally move the mucus along until it drains through narrow passages into the nose and throat. However, if a viral infection such as a cold causes inflammation of the tissues, these passages may become blocked. Mucus then collects in the sinuses, blocking them and allowing bacteria to multiply.

SYMPTOMS

- Runny nose and a persistent nasal discharge.
- Feeling of fullness, or an ache or pain in the cheeks and sometimes the forehead.
- Cough.
- Headache.
- Possible severe pain in the upper back teeth.
- Loss of the sense of smell.
- Sometimes, fever.

STEAM INHALATION One way to relieve the congestion is to make a towel tent over your child's head. Ask your child to inhale the steam from a bowl of hot water.

Medical treatment

Take your child to the doctor within 24 hours of the symptoms appearing. The doctor will examine her and, if sinusitis seems likely, may prescribe antibiotics and/or decongestants. With treatment, the symptoms of sinusitis usually clear up within 7 days.

How to help your child

If the sinusitis is painful for your child, give her paracetamol, according to the recommended dose for her age and size. Encourage her to drink plenty of fluids. A steam inhalation can relieve a blocked nose rapidly. The best way is to use a towel tent. Make sure she does not scald her face: place the bowl on a table, put the towel over her head and tell her not to lean too close to the water. Do not leave her unsupervised. Get her to inhale three times a day. A drop of eucalyptus oil in the hot water may help.

Alternatively, take your child into the bathroom, turn on the hot taps to humidify the air and encourage her to inhale. Keeping the air in the house moist and walking in the open air may also help her.

ENLARGED ADENOIDS

The adenoids are made of lymphatic tissue which is rich in the white blood cells that help fight infection. In some children, they become enlarged following repeated infections and may hamper breathing or obstruct drainage of the middle ears.

Medical treatment

A child with mild symptoms does not usually need any treatment because the adenoids shrink naturally with age. But if your child has severe snoring or speech problems, or often has ear infections, do take her to the doctor.

The doctor may refer your child to an ear, nose and throat specialist, who may assess the size of the adenoids from an X-ray of the area. Surgical removal of the adenoids may be recommended. The operation, called an adenoidectomy, is performed in hospital under a general anaesthetic. A child whose adenoids have been removed will breathe more easily through her nose and will stop snoring at night.

How to help your child

To relieve a dry mouth caused by persistent breathing through the mouth, moisten the air in your child's room with a vaporizer or a wet towel on a chair near a radiator. Encourage your child to sleep on either her side or front to make snoring less likely.

Outlook

In children whose adenoids have not been surgically removed, the symptoms usually start to improve around the age of 7 – this is when the adenoids begin to shrink naturally. By the time your child has reached adolescence, the adenoids will probably have disappeared completely.

LOCATION OF ADENOIDS
The adenoids are pads of lymphatic tissue located at the back of the nasal cavity, beside the entrance to the Eustachian tubes and above the tonsils.

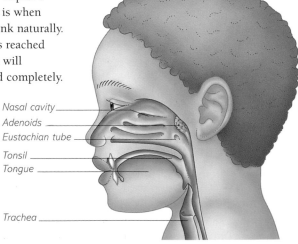

Nasal cavity
Adenoids
Eustachian tube
Tonsil
Tongue
Trachea

PHARYNGITIS AND TONSILLITIS

Often part of a common cold, pharyngitis is an inflammation of the throat and is the most common cause of a sore throat. Tonsillitis (inflammation of the tonsils) often occurs with pharyngitis in children aged up to 8 years.

Causes
Both conditions may be caused by either viruses or streptococcal or other bacteria. Pharyngitis and tonsillitis have similar symptoms, although those of tonsillitis are usually more severe.

Medical treatment
If symptoms persist for more than 24 hours or get worse, phone a doctor. The doctor will examine your child and, if a bacterial infection is likely, may prescribe antibiotics. To confirm the diagnosis, a throat swab may be sent for analysis. The rare cases of quinsy, an abscess on the tonsils, may need surgical drainage in hospital.

How to help your child
Give her liquid paracetamol and plenty of fluids. She is infectious for about 3 days after a sore throat starts.

Outlook
Occasionally, surgical removal of the tonsils is recommended for children who have more than three attacks of tonsillitis a year due to confirmed streptococcal infections.

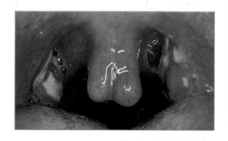

SWOLLEN TONSILS *In tonsillitis, the tonsils are swollen, fiery red and sometimes flecked with yellow or white pus. Rarely, they get so enlarged they block the airway.*

EPIGLOTTITIS

Epiglottitis is inflammation of the epiglottis, the flap of cartilage at the entrance of the trachea that closes when a child swallows. It mainly affects children aged between 2 and 6 years. It can be fatal, but immunization has lowered its incidence dramatically.

Causes
Epiglottitis is caused by the bacterium *Haemophilus influenzae*, which makes the epiglottis swell so much that the passage of air is obstructed.

Immediate action
If your child has difficulty swallowing and breathing, there is a risk her airway may be completely obstructed so call an ambulance immediately or take her to a hospital accident and emergency department. Don't try to look down your child's throat to see

if something is blocking it, because she may start to cry. Crying will increase the production of secretions, which may totally block the narrowed airway.

Medical treatment
After examination, your child will be given antibiotics intravenously. In some cases, an anaesthetic may be needed so a tube can be inserted through the nose and into the trachea. Children who are treated promptly make a complete recovery, usually within a week.

CROUP

Croup is an inflammation and narrowing of the main airway to the lungs, usually caused by a viral infection. It is most common in children aged between 6 months and 3 years. Although it is a mild illness, it can cause severe breathing difficulties needing emergency treatment. Croup starts like a cold with a runny nose and sneezing. Other symptoms develop a day or two later.

SYMPTOMS

- Noisy breathing.
- Persistent, barking cough.
- Hoarse voice.
- Breathing difficult or abnormally fast.
- Bluish tongue; sometimes the skin is also bluish.

Croup tends to come on in the early morning and lasts for a few hours.

Immediate action
If your child is suffering from an attack of croup, with an alarming cough that may be accompanied by wheezing and shortness of breath, phone your doctor immediately.

If your child's symptoms get any worse, or if more severe symptoms develop, particularly a bluish tongue and lips, either call an ambulance or immediately take your child to the nearest accident and emergency department, whichever is quicker.

Medical treatment
After checking how bad the attack is and considering other causes for the symptoms, the doctor may treat mild croup with steroids, either as tablets or to be self-administered through an inhaler. Self-help measures (*see below*) may relieve the symptoms.

Children with a severe attack of croup are usually admitted to hospital. They may be given oxygen and medicated inhalations to ease breathing. If the airways are severely obstructed, a tube may be inserted through the nose or mouth into the trachea. A child with severe croup usually takes a few days to recover.

How to help your child
While you wait for the doctor to arrive, give your child the appropriate dose of liquid paracetamol together with frequent warm drinks. You can also keep the air in her room moist.

To ease an acute attack, take her into the bathroom and turn on the hot taps to humidify the air rapidly.

Outlook
Most children do not suffer from a second attack of croup. However, some appear to be susceptible to the illness. For example, those with asthma (*see p.226*) in particular may be prone to further attacks, and for these children, doctors may recommend treatment with drugs for preventing asthma. Doctors may also prescribe corticosteroids, which can be inhaled at the first signs of an attack of croup.

ALLERGIC RHINITIS

This is an inflammation of the lining of the nose due to an allergic reaction. There are two forms: the seasonal variety, known as hay fever, affecting people in the spring and summer months, while the perennial variety troubles sufferers throughout the year. Allergic rhinitis often runs in families and is most common in children with other allergies. Symptoms of both forms are similar.

SYMPTOMS

- Itchy eyes, nose and throat.
- Blocked, runny nose.
- Sneezing.
- Red, sore, watery eyes.
- Occasionally, dry skin.

Causes
Allergic rhinitis develops when a child inhales an allergen (a substance that causes an allergic reaction) and her immune system produces antibodies and white blood cells as if the allergen were a bacterium or virus. The most common allergens are the pollen of grasses, trees and weeds. Perennial allergic rhinitis is most often caused by house-dust mites, animal dander (flakes of dead skin) or mould spores.

Medical treatment
Take your child to the doctor if she has severe or persistent symptoms that are not improved by self-help measures. The doctor may prescribe a nasal spray containing either a corticosteroid drug

or sodium cromoglicate to alleviate the symptoms. In many children, the rhinitis becomes less severe as they grow older and eventually disappears.

How to help your child
If you know what causes the problem, try to reduce or eliminate exposure to it. A child who has hay fever should stay indoors as much as possible during the pollen season. Keep the windows closed, especially on hot, dry, breezy days, when pollen counts may be high.

If your child is allergic to animal dander, keep animals away from her.

If house-dust mites are causing the problem, keep house dust to a minimum. Dust all surfaces with a damp cloth and treat carpets with insecticide to kill the mites. Enclose your child's mattress in a plastic cover and avoid feather-filled bedding.

If your child has an allergy to mould spores, make sure her bedroom is well ventilated and free of mould and dust. Oral antihistamines that are available over the counter may help if your child's hay fever is severe or if she cannot avoid going outside. Antihistamines have little or no effect on perennial allergic rhinitis.

ALLERGIC RHINITIS *The delicate membranes of the eyes seem to suffer most in an attack of allergic rhinitis. The eyes become red, sore and watery.*

INFLUENZA

A viral infection of the upper respiratory tract, influenza (flu) can affect children of all ages. The influenza virus is spread by coughing and sneezing, and by direct contact. There are small outbreaks of influenza every year.

Medical treatment
If your child has developed flu and is under 2 years of age or at a high risk of complications, phone your doctor at once. Also call a doctor immediately if any of the following symptoms develop: a temperature above 39°C (102°F); abnormally fast breathing; drowsiness; or an unwillingness to eat.

If there is a secondary bacterial infection, the doctor may prescribe antibiotics. If the symptoms are severe, or if your child is at high risk of complications – for example, because of a chronic disorder – she may be admitted to hospital.

How to help your child
A child usually feels worse during the first 2 to 5 days of the illness. In most cases, influenza clears up completely within about 10 days. Keep her in bed in a warm, well-ventilated and

humidified room until her temperature returns to normal. For the aches and fever, give her liquid paracetamol according to her age and size and encourage her to drink plenty of warm fluids.

Possible complications
The flu virus may spread down to the lungs, causing pneumonia (*see p.227*) or bronchitis (*see p.228*). These are often complicated by secondary bacterial infection. This infection may also affect the sinuses (*see Sinusitis, p.221*) or ears (*see Inflammation of the middle ear, p.240*).

Disorders that put children at high risk include chronic heart, lung, or kidney disease; diabetes mellitus (*see p.309*); cystic fibrosis (*see p.295*); or a depressed immune system. Febrile convulsions (*see p.292*) are a possible complication in babies.

SYMPTOMS

Symptoms usually develop 1–3 days after infection, and may come on rapidly.
- Fever, usually above 39°C (102°F).
- Dry cough.
- Muscular ache.
- Stuffy nose.
- Tiredness and weakness.
- Headache.
- Usually, a sore throat.

PREVENTION

The influenza virus has the ability to change its structure. This means that, even though a child has had a bout of influenza, there are always new strains to which she is not immune.

Children with a chronic disorder, such as lung disease, or any defect of the immune system may be recommended to have an annual vaccination against influenza.

Boosting your child's immune system with a diet rich in fruit and vegetables could help her fight the influenza virus.

ASTHMA

A condition that causes frequent episodes of wheezing and breathlessness, asthma is the most common chronic lung disease among children and is on the increase. Most children who develop asthma have had their first attack by the age of 4 or 5. Untreated, asthma may slow a child's growth and is potentially fatal. In young children, the first sign is often a recurring cough, especially with a cold or after exercise. Sometimes, the first sign of asthma is coughing that occurs only at night.

Causes

Many asthmatic children have other allergic conditions, such as allergic rhinitis (*see p.224*) or atopic eczema (*see p.234*). There may be a family history of asthma and other allergic disorders. Individual attacks are usually triggered by a viral infection or by an allergen, such as house-dust mites or, more rarely, by a particular food. Exercising, especially in cold air, may bring on an attack. In some children, attacks may also be triggered or made worse by anxiety.

Asthma symptoms are caused by narrowing of the airways in the lungs – the trachea, bronchi and bronchioles. This occurs because the walls of these airways become inflamed and swollen, the muscles in the walls contract and more mucus is produced.

Medical treatment

If you think your child has asthma, take her to the doctor within 24 hours. If her symptoms are severe, call an ambulance at once or take your child to the nearest hospital accident and emergency department. The doctor will ask about any possible exposure to allergens and if there are factors that could be causing your child anxiety, such as problems at home or difficulties at school.

To check the severity of your child's condition, the doctor will use a peak-flow meter, which measures the capacity to exhale air. A chest X-ray may be carried out to check for any associated infection.

If your child's asthma is mild, the doctor will prescribe a bronchodilator drug – this is a drug that dilates, or widens, the bronchi and bronchioles. The bronchodilator is inhaled to ease breathing during asthma attacks.

If the asthma is more severe, the doctor may also prescribe sodium cromoglicate and/or a corticosteroid. These drugs have to be inhaled regularly to help prevent attacks. Some children require oral corticosteroids or regular treatment with an inhaled, long-acting bronchodilator drug.

Older children may take inhaled drugs with an inhaler (*see far left*). Younger children may use a spacer (*see left*) to inhale the drug. Infants can use a nebulizer, which has a pump that disperses the drug as a fine mist into a face mask.

How to help your child

For a child of 6 or over, the doctor may suggest using a peak-flow meter to monitor the asthma and to warn

TAKING INHALED DRUGS Children over about 8 years old can use an inhaler to breathe in the drugs that can help to relieve their shortness of breath. The idea is to press the spray just as the child begins to inhale.

SPACER A spacer makes it easier for younger children to inhale the drug, which is usually delivered as a spray. The spacer holds the drug before it is inhaled. Always supervise a child who is using a spacer.

you of an impending attack. Keep an asthma diary to chart the symptoms and the peak-flow meter readings from day to day. This record will help the doctor to adapt your child's treatment as the asthma changes, develops or subsides.

Always keep a bronchodilator (either an inhaler or spacer) handy in case of an attack. If your child has a severe attack of asthma, and the normal inhaler does not work, she should take a repeat dose. If that also fails to ease the condition, you need to phone your doctor at once or take your child to a hospital accident and emergency department.

Outlook

At least half the children who develop asthma before they reach the age of 5 will stop having attacks by the time they reach adulthood. However, if your child still suffers from asthma at the age of 14, there is a strong chance that it will persist into adulthood.

PNEUMONIA

Pneumonia is an inflammation of the lungs, usually caused by a viral or bacterial infection. It is most often a complication of an upper respiratory tract infection, such as a common cold, or of an infectious disease, such as chickenpox. Children with cystic fibrosis (*see p.315*) are particularly prone to pneumonia. Pneumonia may start with symptoms of a common cold, such as sneezing and a runny nose.

Immediate action

Phone a doctor at once if your child is breathing fast while resting in bed; if a cough and fever last for more than a few days; or if your child seems far more ill than usual with an ordinary cold. Call an ambulance if your child is drowsy, refuses to eat or drink, or has blue lips and tongue.

Medical treatment

The doctor will listen to your child's chest through a stethoscope and may send a throat swab or blood sample for tests to identify the cause of infection. She may prescribe antibiotics.

Pneumonia can usually be treated at home, but if your child's condition is severe, she may be admitted to hospital. A chest X-ray will confirm the diagnosis and antibiotics will be given. Your child may receive oxygen;

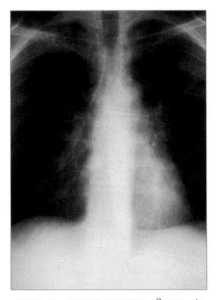

CHEST X-RAY SHOWING PNEUMONIA *Pneumonia causes some of the air sacs in the lungs to fill with fluid. The affected part of the lung shows as a dark shadow.*

rarely, mechanical ventilation will be required. Your child should be able to go home after about 4 days. A cough may continue for about 2 weeks after your child has otherwise recovered. Pneumonia should not result in any permanent damage to the lungs.

How to help your child

Make sure she has plenty of warm fluids to drink. Liquid paracetamol will reduce her fever and relieve a headache. Most children recover within a week. After discharge from hospital, your child should not take vigorous exercise for about a week. Going outside will not harm your child, provided that the weather is not damp or very cold.

BRONCHITIS

Bronchitis is an inflammation of the bronchi (the main airways to the lungs). The condition is usually a complication of a viral infection such as a common cold or influenza, but is sometimes caused by a bacterial infection.

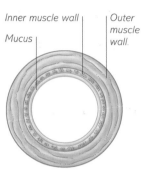

Inner muscle wall

Mucus

Outer muscle wall.

Inflamed wall

Excess mucus

NORMAL BRONCHUS

AFFECTED BY BRONCHITIS

THE EFFECTS ON THE AIRWAYS
In bronchitis, the walls of the bronchi become inflamed, and the glands that line the walls produce excess mucus (see cross-sections, left). The central air channel is narrowed, making breathing difficult.

▢ SYMPTOMS

- Runny nose.
- Persistent cough. Usually dry at first, but may later produce yellowish-green phlegm if there is a bacterial infection.
- Wheezing and shortness of breath.
- Sometimes, a fever.

How to help your child

Keep your child's room moist. Steam inhalations may help to decongest her airways. Give warm drinks to relieve the cough and liquid paracetamol to reduce a fever. Most children recover fully within a week. If she does not improve after 24 hours, phone your doctor – but phone her at once if breathing becomes abnormally fast or the fever rises above 39°C (102°F). Call an ambulance if your child is drowsy or refuses to drink.

Medical treatment

Your child will be examined to see if she has a more serious condition, such as pneumonia or bronchiolitis. The doctor may prescribe antibiotics if a bacterial infection is suspected and a bronchodilator drug may be needed to relieve the wheezing. Children who have recurrent bouts are likely to grow out of the condition by 5 years of age.

BRONCHIOLITIS

This viral infection inflames the bronchioles, usually occurs in epidemics during winter and mainly affects children under 1. It can be more severe in babies born prematurely. It may start like a common cold with other symptoms developing 2–3 days later.

▢ SYMPTOMS

- Dry, rasping cough.
- Wheezing and/or rapid, difficult breathing. In some infants, long pauses (more than 10 seconds) occur between each breath.
- Reluctance to feed.
- Bluish lips and tongue.
- Abnormal drowsiness.

Immediate action

If your child is under 1 year and is coughing and/or wheezing, phone a doctor at once. Call an ambulance if breathing is difficult, if the lips and tongue are blue or if your child becomes drowsy.

Medical treatment

For mild bronchiolitis, the doctor may prescribe a bronchodilator drug and advise you to look after your child at home. Give your child plenty of fluids and small frequent meals. Liquid paracetamol can help to bring down the fever. Thick mucus in the lungs may be loosened by slapping your child's back. Mild bronchiolitis usually improves within about a week.

A child who needs to be treated in hospital may be given oxygen through nasal tubes. She may be fed by means of a tube inserted through the nose or, sometimes, intravenously. In severe cases of bronchiolitis, mechanical ventilation may be required. The child will be allowed to go home when she is able to feed normally again, usually within 7 days. The cough, however, may persist for up to 6 weeks.

Outlook

There is no permanent damage to the lungs. For the next few years, however, many children tend to suffer from wheezing when they have a cold.

SKIN DISORDERS

Children have sensitive skin from the moment they are born, so skin problems are common.

TINY YELLOW-WHITE SPOTS OFTEN APPEAR on the faces of newborn children and young babies, but they soon vanish. In the first couple of days, many newborn babies develop a red blotchy rash, called erythema toxicum, on the face, chest and back. This, too, soon goes away. For the next few years, until their skin becomes less sensitive, children are prone to skin disorders. For example, a skin reaction may be caused by an illness such as measles or by irritation from detergents or other substances. Infections (*see also* Infectious Diseases, *pp.263–272*) and allergies can also cause skin reactions. Most of the skin problems that affect children aren't too serious and usually clear up rapidly. This section may help you to find out what is causing the disorder – the diagnosis charts between pages 180 and 187 could also help you. If you are in any doubt, check with your doctor.

SEBORRHOEIC DERMATITIS

This common inflammation of the skin may affect the body, face and/or the scalp. Its cause is unknown but it may initially appear in the first few months of life. The symptoms vary in severity over a number of months, but generally clear up by the age of about 2.

Medical treatment
Check with your doctor if the rash is extensive or looks infected; if the scalp is inflamed; if other symptoms develop; or if the condition fails to improve in a few weeks. He may prescribe a very mild corticosteroid cream or ointment.

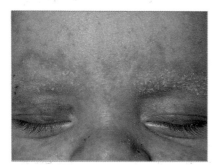

RASH ON A BABY'S FACE *Seborrhoeic dermatitis can affect the skin on any part of the head, including the scalp, as in cradle cap, and even the eyelids.*

How to help your child
As soon as the symptoms appear, clean the affected areas of your child's skin with an emulsifying ointment, not soap. Then apply a mild corticosteroid cream. Try to keep your child from scratching the affected skin as this can lead to a bacterial infection, such as impetigo (*see p.235*), causing the rash to become raw and weepy.

Cradle cap often disappears on its own within a few weeks or months. You can remove unsightly scales by gently massaging baby oil or olive oil into your baby's scalp and leaving it overnight. Next day, comb your baby's hair to dislodge the softened scales and then wash them away.

Over-the-counter shampoos that contain salicylic acid can treat cradle cap. Regular use of a special shampoo or combing your baby's hair daily may

SYMPTOMS

Infants
- A scaly, blotchy rash, usually in the skin creases of the nappy area but also sometimes on other areas of the body.
- Sometimes slight itchiness.
- Thick yellowish scales on the scalp (cradle cap) and sometimes scaly areas on the forehead, behind the ears and in the eyebrows.

Puberty
- A scaly, blotchy rash occurs on the face, behind the ears, on the neck, chest and back, and in the armpits and groin.
- Sometimes itchiness.
- Dandruff, if the scalp is affected. White flakes of dead skin can be seen in the hair, usually near the scalp.

stop the scaly patches from forming. Use over-the-counter anti-dandruff shampoos to control dandruff.

Some children with seborrhoeic dermatitis may develop eczema. The condition may also recur after puberty.

CONTACT DERMATITIS

This dermatitis is an inflammation of the skin caused by contact with irritating substances such as nickel in jewellery, rubber, fabric dyes, plasters, plants, bubble baths, detergents, medicinal creams and cosmetics. It is rare in children under about 12 years.

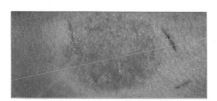

CONTACT DERMATITIS *The symptoms may take several days to appear after contact; how long they persist depends on the irritant.*

Medical treatment
A rash caused by something such as jewellery may be confined to one part of the body. Products such as bubble bath or scented soap may make the rash more widespread.

If you know the cause, remove it or encourage your child to avoid contact with it. Apply a corticosteroid

SYMPTOMS

- An inflamed, scaly rash.
- Intense itchiness.
- Sometimes, blistering and weeping (often caused by contact with plants).

cream or calamine lotion to the rash to help relieve the symptoms. If you cannot identify the cause, see your doctor. He may arrange for some patch tests – small amounts of a range of suspected irritants are applied to your child's skin to see if there's a reaction.

COLD SORES

Cold sores are small blisters that develop singly or in clusters on and around a child's lips. Smaller and more regular in shape than impetigo sores, they are brought on by an acute infection, anxiety or emotional stress, or exposure to either the sun or cold winds.

Causes
Cold sores are caused by a strain of the herpes simplex virus. After the first infection, which may go unnoticed, the virus lies dormant in nerve cells until it is reactivated.

How to help your child
The blisters burst within a few days to form a crust and heal on their own within 2 weeks. Few children need treatment, but if the sores cause discomfort, a cold drink or an iced lolly may bring relief.

If your child gets cold sores often, or if they are severe and upsetting, try a cream containing the antiviral drug acyclovir. This over-the-counter cream reduces the severity and duration of

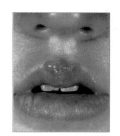

COLD SORE CLUSTER *Cold sores often appear in clusters on or around the lips. The blisters are clear at first; they turn cloudy and form crusts.*

an attack. It is most effective if applied as soon as your child feels the initial tingling sensation around the mouth, before any blisters have appeared. As an alternative, applying aloe vera gel to the affected area may help to ease any discomfort.

If you can identify the trigger factor, you may be able to prevent the sores. For example, if they tend

SYMPTOMS

- A tingling feeling around the mouth, which starts 4–12 hours before any blisters appear.
- Small blisters, which may be itchy or sore and surrounded by a slightly inflamed area.

to develop after exposure to the sun, apply a sunscreen or sunblock to your child's lips before he goes outside.

To reduce the chance of spreading the virus, both to other people and to other parts of your child's body, explain that he should not touch the blisters or suck his fingers, and he should wash his hands frequently.

Outlook
With no cure for cold sores, your child will probably have recurrences throughout life, but outbreaks usually become less frequent with time.

WARTS

Warts are harmless growths on the skin, usually on the hands and feet, caused by a virus. They are contagious, but some people are more susceptible than others. Most disappear naturally within a few months, while some last for years if they are not treated.

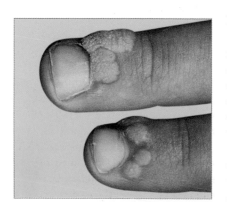

COMMON WART *These hard, rough growths on the surface of the skin are usually frozen off by a dermatologist.*

Medical treatment
Consult your doctor if home treatment is unsuccessful or if a wart on the face or mouth causes your child either discomfort or embarrassment. The doctor may refer your child to a dermatologist, who could remove the warts by freezing, a technique known

TYPES

There are several types of wart, any of which may occur singly or in clusters. The ones that most often affect children are:
- Common warts. These are firm, raised growths, usually with a hard, rough surface. They generally occur on the hands, feet, knees and face.
- Plane warts. These smooth growths are level with the skin or slightly raised. They occur on the hands or face and may cause slight itchiness.
- Plantar warts (verrucas). These hard, horny warts occur on the sole of the foot. They appear flat and are often painful because the child's weight has pushed them into the skin.

as cryotherapy. Plantar warts, or veruccas (*see p.193*), may be scraped off in a technique known as curettage.

How to help your child

Encourage your child not to touch the warts because picking or scratching them may cause them to spread to another part of his body. If you do want to do something about them, you can treat warts on the hands and feet at home. Never attempt to remove a wart on your child's mouth or face.

The simplest way of treating a common or plane wart is to cover the wart with a salicylic acid plaster, which should be changed every day.

If the wart does not respond to this treatment within about 3 weeks, try wart paint, which is available over the counter, and follow the instructions carefully. You will need to protect the normal skin around the wart by covering it with petroleum jelly before you apply the paint.

If your child has a plantar wart, rub the the surface with a pumice stone to remove as much of the overlying skin as possible. Cut a piece of salicylic acid plaster to the exact size of the wart and tape it in place. Replace the plaster every day until the wart disappears, which may take up to 3 months.

Ask your pharmacist about over-the-counter complementary remedies you can apply, including aloe vera gel and tea tree oil, which has powerful antiseptic qualities. Echinacea (*see p.322*) can be applied directly to the wart or taken by mouth to boost the immune system.

Outlook

Eventually, most warts will disappear on their own without any treatment. However, they do sometimes recur for no apparent reason, even after you have treated them. Such tenacious warts may need several treatments to banish them entirely.

SCABIES

Scabies is caused by infestation of the skin by parasitic mites. Anyone can catch scabies – it has nothing to do with a lack of personal hygiene. Both extremely itchy and very contagious, scabies is passed from person to person by close bodily contact, and, to a lesser extent, through the sharing of infected sheets and duvets, clothes and towels.

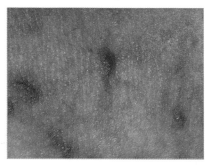

SCABIES MITE BURROW *Thin, grey lines on the skin are the burrows made by female mites. Burrows may be obscured by sores and scabs caused by scratching.*

Causes

Scabies is caused by the mite *Sarcoptes scabiei*, also known as the itch mite. The female mites burrow into the skin to lay their eggs. This causes the intense itching. The eggs hatch in 3 or 4 days and reach adulthood in about two weeks, when they mate again on the skin and the cycle begins once more. The symptoms of scabies may take up to 6 weeks to appear.

Medical treatment

If your child is scratching intensely or shows any other signs of scabies, take him to your doctor within 24 hours. Scabies will not clear up without treatment and scratching may cause impetigo (*see p.235*). The doctor will prescribe a lotion containing benzyl benzoate that kills scabies mites. After a bath and at least once a day, apply this lotion to all areas of your child's

SYMPTOMS
• Intense itchiness, especially at night. • Thin, grey lines (the mites' burrows) between the fingers, on the wrists, in the armpits, between the buttocks or around the genitals. In infants, the palms and soles may be affected. • Sores, blisters and scabs, resulting from scratching. • Inflamed lumps on the body.

body except for the head and neck. Wash it off after 24 hours. Repeat for three or more days. Treat all members of your household at the same time, even if they have no obvious signs. After treatment, wash and iron all clothing and bed linen.

The mites will usually die within 3 days of treatment, but the itching may continue for up to 2 weeks. The doctor may prescribe an ointment to relieve the itchiness. Tell anyone you and your child have been in contact with, so that they can be examined, and treated if necessary.

BOILS

A painful, pus-filled swelling in the skin, a boil develops when bacteria that are carried in the nose infect a hair follicle. Most burst, releasing their pus, although occasionally pus drains away into the surrounding area. Boils generally clear up in two weeks.

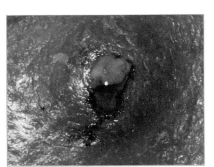

APPEARANCE OF A BOIL *The lump covered by white flakes of dead skin is a boil. Pus has escaped from the boil to form a greenish scab at its centre. The surrounding skin is red because the infection has spread.*

Medical treatment
Take your child to see the doctor if a boil lasts longer than 2 weeks or is very large or painful. The doctor may prescribe oral antibiotics to clear up the infection and may make a small cut in the boil to release pus.

If your child keeps getting boils, the doctor may prescribe an antibiotic cream for you to apply inside your child's nose. The doctor may also suggest that your child washes with antiseptic soap and that you add a few drops of an antiseptic to your child's bath water.

SYMPTOMS
- A small, red lump that becomes larger as it fills with pus.
- Pain and tenderness around the boil.
- A white or yellow "head" of pus at the centre of the boil.

How to help your child
To help a boil burst more quickly, buy an over-the-counter paste containing magnesium sulphate, apply it to the boil and cover with a plaster. When the boil does burst, carefully wipe away the pus with cotton wool soaked in an antiseptic solution and cover the affected skin with an adhesive plaster. Don't poke or squeeze the boil to make it burst or you may spread the infection. (*See* Treating a boil, *p.185*.)

URTICARIA

An intensely itchy, raised rash, urticaria is also known as nettle rash or hives. There are two forms: acute urticaria, which lasts between 30 minutes and several days, and chronic urticaria, which may persist for up to several months. Both may recur.

SYMPTOMS
- Smooth, raised white or yellow lumps surrounded by an inflamed area of skin.
- Extreme itchiness.

Causes
In many cases, the cause is not known. Sometimes urticaria may be due to an allergic reaction, possibly to a food (such as fish), an insect sting, a drug (such as penicillin) or a plant. The rash may affect a small area or it may be widespread.

Very rarely, urticaria is part of anaphylactic shock (*see p.189*). Call an ambulance or take your child to the hospital accident and emergency department at once if he has swelling of the face or mouth; noisy or difficult breathing; difficulty swallowing; and abnormal drowsiness.

Medical treatment
If your child often has attacks of urticaria, try to identify the cause so you can help your child avoid it, if at all possible. An over-the-counter oral antihistamine may relieve the symptoms during an attack – continue this treatment for several weeks after the rash disappears.

If antihistamines do not help, take your child to your doctor, who may prescribe an oral corticosteroid and/or send him to a dermatologist for tests to establish the cause. As your child gets older, attacks of urticaria will probably get less frequent.

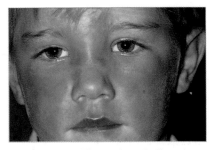

URTICARIAL RASH *The patches of affected skin in urticaria vary in size and shape. The patches are raised, pale, and have red edges, which distinguish them from the surrounding normal skin.*

ATOPIC ECZEMA

About 1 child in 20 develops atopic eczema. The itchy rash usually appears for the first time before a child is 18 months old, and may come and go over a number of years. The cause is unknown, but most affected children have a close relative with eczema or an allergic disorder, such as asthma or hay fever. Intolerance to certain foods may also be responsible.

Medical treatment

If your child has not had the rash before take him to a doctor within 24 hours. If your child has already been diagnosed with atopic eczema, and the rash does not respond to treatment or gets worse, call your doctor in case the rash is infected.

Your doctor may prescribe a mild corticosteroid cream or ointment to reduce the inflammation and itchiness during flare-ups. It is particularly important to use corticosteroid creams as directed and stop when the skin has recovered. If a slight inflammation warns you that a flare-up may be on the way, apply the prescribed cream to affected areas to prevent the rash from developing. If the itchiness is keeping your child awake at night, he may be given an antihistamine. Emollient

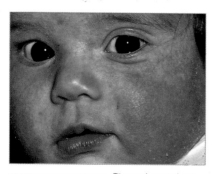

APPEARANCE OF ECZEMA *The rash seen here has the typical appearance of atopic eczema in children under the age of 4 years: the skin is inflamed and may be mildly weepy. The cheeks are one of the prime sites for the rash to develop.*

creams to moisten the skin and alternatives to soap may also be prescribed. If the eczema is severe or widespread, the doctor may suggest your child stops eating certain foods.

How to help your child

Use creams or ointments as directed by your doctor and try the following tips to keep your child's skin from becoming too dry.

When you bathe your child, use a mild cleanser such as aqueous cream or baby soap. Add a bath oil that is specially formulated for eczema, but do not use scented bubble bath.

Keep your child's skin soft and well moisturized by regularly applying an emollient, such as aqueous cream or emulsifying ointment, particularly to warm, wet skin after a bath. Use the emollient several times a day on the affected areas.

In some children, eczema is worse in cold weather, while in others hot weather prompts a flare-up. Wearing cotton clothing next to the skin will help to reduce irritation.

Keep your child away from anyone who has cold sores. Don't give him peanuts, or let him use creams or bath oils containing peanut (arachis) oil.

Possible complications

If your child scratches the rash, the skin may become infected, resulting in weeping blisters. Your doctor may then prescribe an oral antibiotic, or a cream or ointment containing a corticosteroid and an antibiotic or antiseptic.

Eczema herpeticum is a rare, but more serious, complication. It can develop if a child with eczema is infected by the herpes simplex virus (*see* Cold sores, *p.231*). This disorder causes a widespread rash of blisters and open sores, sometimes with a high fever of 40–41°C (104–106°F). The lymph nodes may be enlarged. Your child may have to go to hospital and may be given the antiviral drug acyclovir intravenously.

Outlook

In young children, the rash often disappears before they reach 4 years and may never come back. In other children, the rash may reappear (or appear for the first time) between the ages of 4 and 10 years. As your child grows older, the rash will probably be less extensive and disappear by adolescence. However, up to 50 per cent of children who are affected by atopic eczema develop other allergic conditions, such as asthma.

☐ **SYMPTOMS**

Children under 4 years
- Itchy, inflamed skin, which may be mildly weepy.
- Worst on scalp, cheeks, forearms, fronts of the legs and trunk, although the rash may appear anywhere on the child's body.

Children aged 4–10 years
- Itchy, dry and scaly patches, as well as cracked skin.
- Worst on face, neck, insides of the elbows, wrists, backs of the knees and ankles.
- Skin in affected areas may become thickened over time.

MOLLUSCUM CONTAGIOSUM

This mild viral infection, which causes small, shiny pimples on the skin, is common in children between 2 and 5 years of age. It is easily spread, either by direct contact or indirectly – for example, by touching infected clothing or towels.

MOLLUSCUM CONTAGIOSUM PIMPLES *The pimples usually appear on a child's skin in groups, although they may occur singly.*

Medical treatment
The characteristic appearance of the spots can be confirmed by your doctor. The condition will disappear without treatment and usually leaves no scars, but this can take from a few weeks to a year. Most children have about 25 pimples. Open pimples let the virus spread to other parts of the body.

If your child is receiving treatment that affects his immune system – for example, for leukaemia – the spots can be more widespread and last longer. If your child has lowered immunity

SYMPTOMS

The pimples appear 2–7 weeks after infection, usually on the trunk, face, hands, and (rarely) on the palms or soles. The pimples are:
• Dome-shaped with a central dimple.
• Pearly white or flesh-coloured.

or has many disfiguring spots on a visible area, such as the face, your doctor may refer him to a dermatologist to remove the spots.

After applying an anaesthetic cream to the area, the dermatologist may pierce the pimples with an instrument dipped in podophyllin paint. Alternatively, he may remove the pimples by scraping or by freezing.

IMPETIGO

A highly contagious bacterial skin infection, impetigo mainly affects young children, especially babies. It may appear anywhere on the body, but is most common around the mouth and nose area in children, and the nappy area in babies.

Causes
Bacteria enter and infect the skin when it is broken by a cut, an insect bite or a skin condition such as atopic eczema (*see opposite*) or scabies (*see p.232*).

Medical treatment
Take your child to the doctor within 24 hours if you suspect impetigo. The doctor may prescribe an antibiotic ointment to be put on the sores several times a day, and an oral antibiotic if the infection is widespread

How to help your child
Before applying the ointment, gently dab the crusts with gauze soaked in salt solution and then dry the area to remove them. With treatment, impetigo usually gets better within about 5 days.

Tell your child not touch the sores to stop the infection from spreading. Keep his bedding, flannel and towels separate, and keep him away from other children until the infection has cleared up. Encourage him to shower or bathe daily. Keep his nails short and clean so that infection is less likely to be introduced through scratching. If your child has a cold or a runny nose, apply a little petroleum jelly to the nose and upper lip to stop constant wiping from breaking the skin.

SYMPTOMS

• First, the skin reddens and crops of small blisters appear.
• The blisters then burst, leaving raw, moist sores that gradually enlarge.
• Straw-coloured crusts form as the surface of the sores dries.

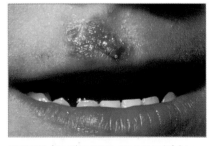

IMPETIGO *Impetigo sores are not painful, although they may be slightly itchy. Without treatment, the condition may last for weeks, or even months.*

HEAD LICE

Small, flat, wingless insects, head lice live on the scalp and suck blood. Head lice are nothing to do with poor hygiene – the insects actually prefer clean hair and skin. School children catch these insects easily through direct contact or by sharing hats or combs.

Checking for head lice

If you think your child has lice, check his hair. The eggs (nits) are more easily seen than the small and almost transparent adults. After the insects

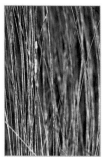

HEAD LICE AND EGGS *The tiny, white ovals are louse eggs. They are firmly attached to the hair shafts. Several head lice are also visible clinging to hairs.*

hatch, the empty nit shells can be seen as small white bumps near the bases of the hairs. If you wet your child's hair and comb it with a fine-toothed comb over a white piece of paper, you may see the lice crawling. If your child does have head lice, check the rest of the family and tell his school.

How to help your child

You can treat your child's head lice at home without a doctor's advice, but if he is less than 2 years old or suffers from allergies or asthma, talk to a doctor before using lice preparations.

To eradicate the head lice, wash his hair with a special shampoo or lotion available from pharmacists (*see p.183*). Some can be applied once; others must be applied repeatedly over several days.

SYMPTOMS

• Intense itchiness on the scalp.
• Tiny red spots (bites) on the scalp.
• Small white bumps near the base of the hairs.

All family members and contacts must be treated at the same time (even if they have no symptoms) to get rid of the lice completely and to prevent your child becoming reinfested. Wash all combs and brushes in boiling water in order to kill any lice or eggs that might be attached to them.

Preventing head lice

To reduce your child's chances of catching lice, discourage him from sharing hats, combs and brushes with family members or school friends. If there is an outbreak at your child's school, use an over-the-counter head lice repellent to prevent your child from becoming infested.

RINGWORM

Ringworm is a fungal infection that affects the scalp or the skin of the body or face. Children can catch it directly from other people, from an animal or from soil. They can also catch it indirectly from hats, combs, clothing or household items, such as carpets.

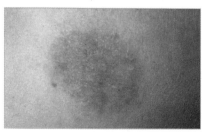

RINGWORM *The fungi can infect any part of the body but they particularly thrive in the damp and warm areas.*

Medical treatment

Take your child to the doctor if you think he has ringworm. For infections on the body or face, the doctor may recommend an antifungal lotion or cream. If the infection on your child's body or face is very widespread, or if his scalp is affected, your doctor may prescribe an antifungal medicine.

To help prevent your child from catching ringworm, keep him away

SYMPTOMS

On the body or face
• Oval or circular, flaky patches with raised, mildly inflamed borders.
• Itchiness.

On the scalp
• Flakes resembling severe dandruff.
• Hair loss.
• Sometimes an inflamed, pus-filled area (a kerion) may develop.
• Usually, itchiness.

from infected people or animals, and discourage the sharing of personal items, such as combs.

ACNE

Acne causes inflamed spots on the face and other parts of the body. It is most common in adolescents and tends to appear at the onset of puberty. The condition often runs in families and is usually more common and severe in boys than in girls.

Causes

At puberty, the skin produces more oily sebum. Acne spots develop when excess sebum and, sometimes, dead skin cells form a plug that blocks a hair follicle. Trapped bacteria multiply, causing the skin around the follicle to become inflamed. Oily substances on the skin, such as cosmetics or hair oil, may make the problem worse.

How to help your child

Your child should not pick, squeeze or scrub the spots in order to prevent the bacteria from spreading. Encourage him to wash his face twice daily with soap and water, and then apply an over-the-counter cream or lotion to the affected areas. These preparations are available in different strengths – your child should try the mildest first and follow the instructions precisely.

If this treatment does not improve the acne after 2–3 months, take him to your doctor, who may prescribe oral antibiotics. Each course will last for between 3 and 6 months. If antibiotics do not help, the doctor may prescribe a retinoid drug, but this may cause side effects, such as dryness of the lips, eyes and nose.

Research suggests that sufferers lack zinc. Healthy sources of zinc are shellfish, nuts, lean meat and skinless chicken. Exposure to sunlight may also help to clear up acne.

SYMPTOMS

- Pimples (small, raised red spots).
- Blackheads (tiny black spots).
- Whiteheads (tender, inflamed lumps with a white centre).
- Cysts (fluid-filled swellings).
- Purplish marks left by healed spots, which gradually fade.

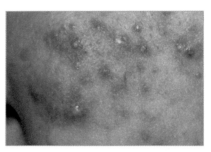

ACNE AFFECTING THE FACE *These spots are typical of acne. The slightly indented purplish marks on the skin are the result of spots that have healed.*

PITYRIASIS ROSEA

A rash of flat, scaly spots, pityriasis rosea generally affects the trunk, arms and legs and is most common in adolescents. Although no specific virus has been isolated, it is believed to be caused by a viral infection.

PITYRIASIS ROSEA *The rash first appears on the trunk, running along the lines of the ribs. It may then spread up towards the neck and down along the arms and legs.*

Medical treatment

Although it is not a serious rash and usually gets better without treatment, take your child to the doctor within a few days to make sure he does not have a more serious skin disease. A corticosteroid cream may soothe the itchiness, but if it is severe, the doctor may prescribe an oral antihistamine.

Pityriasis rosea generally takes between 3 and 8 weeks to clear up. Once your child has had the rash, he is unlikely to develop it again.

SYMPTOMS

- An initial spot (the herald patch) is oval or round, flat and scaly.
- Flat, oval, copper-coloured or dark-pink spots, which appear 3–10 days after the herald patch. After a week, each spot develops a scaly margin.
- Occasionally, itchiness.

How to help your child

The rash usually fades below the elbows and knees and seldom appears on the face. Whenever possible, keep his skin cool and moisturize the areas of skin affected by the rash. You may find that sunlight helps to clear up the rash more rapidly.

PSORIASIS

This chronic skin condition rarely affects children under the age of 10. The rash does not usually itch, but it can be uncomfortable and the look of it may upset your child. It tends to vary in severity and often gets worse during illness or emotional stress.

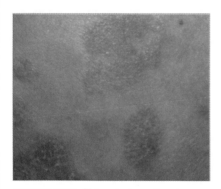

PSORIASIS RASH *The rash shown here is characteristic of psoriasis. The affected area of skin is a sharply defined red patch which is raised and covered by silvery-white scales of dead skin. A large patch such as this may appear on areas of a child's body, such as the elbows or knees.*

Medical treatment

Psoriasis cannot be cured and is likely to recur, but individual attacks can be controlled with prompt treatment. If the rash is severe, widespread or upsetting your child, consult your the doctor, who may refer him to a dermatologist for assessment.

For psoriasis limited to a few small areas, such as the scalp, knees or elbows, the dermatologist may prescribe a cream or ointment containing coal tar, salicylic acid or a corticosteroid. For more widespread psoriasis, an ointment containing dithranol may be prescribed.

Other psoriasis treatments, such as bathing in water containing a coal tar

SYMPTOMS

- Patches of thickened, red skin covered with silvery scales and usually on the elbows, knees or scalp.
- Numerous small, red, slightly scaly patches scattered over the trunk and face.
- Pitted and thickened nails.
- Pain or discomfort if cracks appear in the affected skin.

preparation and moderate exposure to ultraviolet light, may also be helpful.

How to help your child

If your child has mild psoriasis, you may be able to control the condition by keeping the skin well moisturized with an emollient cream. Exposing affected areas to the sun sometimes helps clear up the rash, but do not let your child get sunburned.

PITYRIASIS VERSICOLOR

An overgrowth of a yeast normally present on the skin, possibly triggered by exposure to sunlight or a hot, humid environment, causes the discoloured patches of this skin condition. It is rare in children before they reach puberty.

Medical treatment

Take your child to the doctor if he shows the symptoms of pityriasis versicolor. Although it is not harmful or contagious, the condition may persist indefinitely if not treated.

The doctor will prescribe an antifungal cream or lotion which should be applied once a day to the affected areas. This treatment reduces the yeast to its normal levels in about a week, but should be continued for at least 3 weeks in order to reduce the

chances of the condition recurring. Encourage your child to expose the affected areas of his skin to the air as much as possible since this can also help to discourage regrowth of the yeast. However, it may be some weeks or even months before the skin looks normal again.

SYMPTOMS

- On pale skin, patches are usually darker than surrounding skin; on dark skin, they are usually lighter.
- Slight flakiness.
- Well-defined borders.
- Sometimes, mild itchiness.

PITYRIASIS VERSICOLOR *Areas of dark or tanned skin that are affected by pityriasis versicolor appear as round, flat, pale patches with clearly defined borders.*

EAR & EYE DISORDERS

Most children pick up ear and eye infections as easily as catching the common cold.

EAR AND EYE INFECTIONS are caused by either viruses or bacteria and are common in young children. By the time they reach the age of 7 or 8, most children have become immune to the more common viruses, and infections become less troublesome. Ear and eye infections can cause severe illness and symptoms should never be ignored. Persistent ear infections may lead to hearing difficulties, which can delay speech and learning. Vision problems need to be identified and treated promptly so a child's sight can develop normally.

ANATOMY OF THE EYE AND EAR

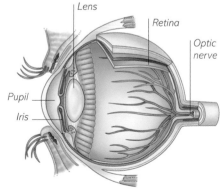

Lens

Retina

Optic nerve

Pupil

Iris

▲ **HOW THE EYE WORKS**
Sight is the most complex sense. Light rays enter through the pupil and register on the retina, where they are converted to nerve impulses that are sent to the brain.

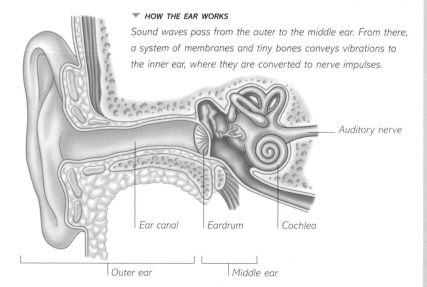

▼ **HOW THE EAR WORKS**
Sound waves pass from the outer to the middle ear. From there, a system of membranes and tiny bones conveys vibrations to the inner ear, where they are converted to nerve impulses.

Auditory nerve

Ear canal

Eardrum

Cochlea

Outer ear

Middle ear

INFLAMMATION OF THE OUTER EAR

This can be caused by bacteria and by seborrhoeic dermatitis and atopic eczema. Infection is more likely if the ear canal is exposed to water for too long, or if it is scratched or irritated by a foreign body or by long-standing wax blockage.

SYMPTOMS

- Itchiness, usually followed by pain.
- Discharge from the canal, which may be thick and white or yellowish.
- Partial deafness, if wax or a discharge is blocking the canal.
- Weeping, crusting blisters.
- Tenderness when the outer, fleshy part of the ear is touched or moved.

Medical treatment

Take your child to your doctor within 24 hours if she has earache, a discharge from the outer ear canal or difficulty hearing. The doctor will probably look into her ear with an auriscope. If there is a discharge of pus, a sample may be sent for tests. If the doctor finds a foreign body or a plug of wax, she may try to

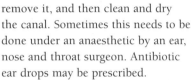

AN INFECTED EAR CANAL
If there is a discharge from the ear canal, do not be tempted to wipe it away. Leave it so that the doctor can send a sample for tests to determine the cause.

remove it, and then clean and dry the canal. Sometimes this needs to be done under an anaesthetic by an ear, nose and throat surgeon. Antibiotic ear drops may be prescribed.

If either seborrhoeic dermatitis or atopic eczema is the cause, the doctor may prescribe corticosteroid ear drops to relieve any itching and tenderness. With treatment, inflammation of the outer ear usually clears up within 7–10 days.

How to help your child

Paracetamol may relieve the pain and a hot-water bottle (filled with warm, not hot, water) or a warm cloth held against your child's ear may also bring some relief.

If your child has been prescribed drops, ask her to lie down with the affected ear uppermost. Hold her head still while you give the drops and for a minute afterwards.

Do not let her swim or get the ear wet until the inflammation has cleared up. Cover the ear with a shower cap during a bath or shower and sponge her hair clean instead of washing it.

INFLAMMATION OF THE MIDDLE EAR

Also called otitis media, this is often a painful complication of an upper respiratory tract infection, such as a common cold, or a throat infection, such as pharyngitis and tonsillitis. It is a common cause of earache in children up to 8 years old.

SYMPTOMS

- Earache.
- Fever and vomiting.
- Waking at night, crying.
- Tugging at or rubbing one ear.
- Partial deafness and irritability.
- A discharge from the ear.

Causes

The middle ear is connected to the back of the throat by the Eustachian tube. In young children this tube is narrow and easily blocked.

When a viral or bacterial infection spreads to the Eustachian tube, the sensitive tissues that line the middle ear become inflamed and produce fluid, and sometimes pus. These secretions are unable to drain away because the tube is blocked by the

inflammation or by enlarged adenoids (*see p.222*). The secretions continue to accumulate, causing pain as they press against the eardrum, which may subsequently split.

Medical treatment

If you think your child has a middle ear inflammation, take her to your doctor within 24 hours. If your child is very young or the pain is severe, phone the doctor at once. The doctor

will examine the affected ear with an auriscope to try to find the cause of the problem.

If there is a discharge from the ear, the doctor will take a sample and send it for tests to identify the infection. The doctor may prescribe a course of antibiotics, which should get rid of the infection and consequently bring down your child's temperature and relieve the pain.

If your child's earache and fever show no sign of improving after about three days, the doctor may prescribe a different type of antibiotic for your child, but antibiotics will only be effective if the infection is caused by a bacterium not a virus.

The fluid sometimes remains in the middle ear for as long as three months after the infection, which may mean that your child continues to be partially deaf.

How to help your child

Give your child liquid paracetamol to combat the inflammation and ease the pain while you wait to see the doctor.

A hot-water bottle wrapped in a towel may also be soothing – fill the bottle with warm, not hot, water. Encourage your child to rest with the affected side of her head turned downwards in order to allow any discharge to drain out. If the eardrum has split it should heal within about a week.

Your doctor or health visitor will probably give your child a hearing test approximately three months after the attack. If your child's hearing is still impaired, glue ear may be the cause (*see below*).

Outlook

As your child grows, the Eustachian tube in each of her ears will widen so that fluid will be able to drain out more easily. As a result, her middle

EASING EARACHE *Lying flat may make the earache worse. Prop your child up with pillows while she rests the painful ear on a hot-water bottle.*

ears gradually become less vulnerable to infection. Your child is unlikely to have attacks of otitis media after she is about 8 years of age.

GLUE EAR

This condition develops when the middle ear becomes filled with a thick, glue-like mucus. The child's hearing is usually affected because sounds cannot be transmitted to the organs of the inner ear. Some children are more prone to the condition than others.

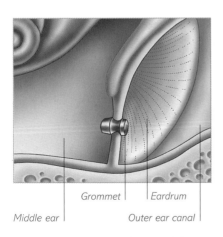

EARDRUM GROMMET *A small tube called a grommet is inserted into the eardrum to let air circulate and dry out the middle ear. The grommet falls out two months to two years later and the eardrum heals.*

Middle ear
Grommet
Eardrum
Outer ear canal

Causes

When the middle ear produces excess mucus, the mucus starts to accumulate, particularly if the Eustachian tube is blocked. If inflammation of the middle ear (*see opposite*) is untreated or is not treated adequately, glue ear may develop.

Medical treatment

Take your child to the doctor if you think she has glue ear. After checking your child's ears with an auriscope, she may decide to send her to an ear, nose and throat specialist, who will test her hearing and may also measure the movements of the eardrum.

If the test results are abnormal, they will be repeated three months later. If the ear has not improved,

SYMPTOMS

- Child may complain of partial deafness and hearing may be worse at some times than others.
- Child may seem inattentive and slow at speaking and/or learning. Pain is seldom a symptom of glue ear, so your child may be affected for some time before the condition is detected.

the specialist may take fluid from the middle ear under general anaesthetic. In some cases, a small cut is made in the eardrum and a tiny plastic tube called a grommet is put in (*see left*). This helps to dry out the middle ear.

Outlook

As your child grows, the Eustachian tube gets bigger and fluid drains much more efficiently from the middle ear. Glue ear is less common in children over about 8 years old.

LABYRINTHITIS

The inner ear, called the labyrinth, contains fluid-filled chambers that are concerned with balance and hearing. Labyrinthitis, or inflammation of the labyrinth, can be a complication of a viral infection and causes dizziness and nausea.

Causes

This is a rare but extremely distressing condition that results from either a virus or bacterium that causes a throat infection, such as pharyngitis or tonsillitis. The viruses or bacteria reach the inner ear via the Eustachian tube. An infection of the fluid inside the sensitive inner ear causes bouts of labyrinthitis in which children lose their balance and become unsteady on their feet. They may also feel nauseous as if they were seasick.

Medical treatment

If you are worried about your child's unsteadiness and think she might be suffering from labyrinthitis, take her to your doctor within 24 hours of the symptoms developing.

The doctor will examine your child and will ask about any recent infectious illnesses. She may prescribe bed rest for about a week as well as a special type of antihistamine syrup to relieve the vomiting and dizziness. No other treatment is required.

SYMPTOMS

The symptoms of labyrinthitis occur in bouts lasting between 5 and 15 minutes. There may be several bouts a day.
- Vertigo, making your child feel that everything is spinning round and round uncontrollably.
- Unsteadiness and falling down. She may need to lean on something to steady herself.
- Nausea and vomiting.

Outlook

Labyrinthitis usually clears up within 1–3 weeks, but it can last for several months. Although frightening, it does not lead to any permanent disability.

BAROTRAUMA

This is a temporary blockage of the Eustachian tube (the passage that connects the middle ear and the throat), in which one or both of a child's eardrums bulges in. It is usually caused by abrupt changes in atmospheric pressure.

THE VALSALVA MANOEUVRE *When the aircraft begins its descent, encourage your child to pinch her nose while keeping her mouth closed, and blow down her nose until her ears go "pop".*

Causes

Air travel is the usual cause of barotrauma. Air flow through the Eustachian tube normally keeps the air pressure inside and outside the middle ear the same. When an aircraft climbs, the air pressure in the cabin falls, and so does the pressure inside the middle ear. When the aircraft descends, pressure outside the middle ear increases, causing the Eustachian tube to shut and pushing the eardrum inwards. An upper respiratory tract infection, such as a common cold (*see* p.221), hay fever (*see* Allergic rhinitis, p.224) or an ear infection (*see* Inflammation of the middle ear, p.240) makes barotrauma more likely.

SYMPTOMS

- Pain as the eardrum bulges in.
- Partial hearing loss.
- Ringing in the ears.
The symptoms of barotrauma usually disappear within 3–5 hours and do not cause any lasting damage.

How to help your child

When an aircraft is coming down to land, sucking on a sweet, swallowing, chewing gum or using the Valsalva manoeuvre (*see left*) will all open the Eustachian tube, allowing air to flow into the middle ear. If there is pain, liquid paracetamol may relieve it. In babies, barotrauma may be prevented by bottlefeeding or breastfeeding during the aircraft's descent. These measures are particularly important for a child suffering from a cold, hay fever or ear infection.

BLEPHARITIS

Blepharitis is an inflammation of the eyelid edges and is often associated with dandruff. It is common in children who suffer from seborrhoeic dermatitis and can also be caused by viral or bacterial infections.

Causes

There are two kinds of blepharitis – infectious and seborrhoeic. The first is caused by bacteria or, more rarely, a virus, and may be accompanied by conjunctivitis (*see p.244*). The second is usually caused by an accumulation of dandruff in the eyelashes. Blepharitis may sometimes be caused by an allergy to eye make-up, such as mascara.

Medical treatment

Take your child to a doctor if you think her eyelids are affected with blepharitis. The doctor will show you how to wipe off any crusting scales from the eyelid margins using cotton wool moistened with warm water. The doctor will take a swab from the eyelids if she suspects infectious blepharitis and send it for tests. If confirmed, the doctor may prescribe an antibiotic ointment or cream, which you can apply at home after you have removed all the scales.

Infectious blepharitis usually clears up within 2 weeks, but doctors usually recommend applying the ointment or cream for a further 2 weeks or more to prevent a recurrence.

Seborrhoeic blepharitis tends to be persistent. Once you have removed the scales of dandruff, tackle the cause of the dandruff – or at least keep it under control to help prevent flare-ups.

▣ SYMPTOMS

- Burning, redness and itching of the edges of the eyelid.
- Scales at the roots of the lashes. The scales in the seborrhoeic form of blepharitis are yellow and greasy.
- Sometimes, eyelashes that grow in the wrong direction or fall out.

INFECTIOUS BLEPHARITIS *The eyelids are red, swollen and crusted with scales. The white of the eye is red, indicating that conjunctivitis is also present.*

STYES

A stye is a pus-filled swelling that forms at the base of an eyelash. Styes are common in children, especially if they are run down. Like other eyelid disorders such as blepharitis, they can be uncomfortable and painful but are not serious.

Causes

When an oil-producing (sebaceous) gland beside an eyelash is blocked and inflamed, a painless swelling develops. If it becomes infected, a stye forms around the bottom of the eyelash. A stye may develop as a complication of blepharitis (*see above*).

Medical treatment

If your child develops styes regularly, take her to the doctor, who may give her an antibiotic ointment. Applying the ointment to a stye three or four times every day can prevent it from recurring. A stye usually gets better in a few days.

How to help your child

Don't try to squeeze the stye to get rid of the pus. To relieve the discomfort, get your child to press a warm cloth to the infected area for about 20 minutes every hour. This also helps the pus to discharge, which hastens healing. To avoid spreading the infection, make sure your child neither touches her stye nor shares a towel or flannel.

▣ SYMPTOMS

- A yellow head of pus on the eyelid around the base of an eyelash.
- Swollen and inflamed eyelid skin surrounding the head of pus.
- Pain or tenderness to the touch.

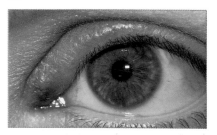

A STYE ON AN EYELID *A stye develops on an eyelid when a blocked sebaceous gland at the base of an eyelash becomes infected, inflamed and painful.*

CONJUNCTIVITIS

This is an inflammation of the thin, transparent membrane (conjunctiva) that covers the whites of the eyes and lines the eyelids. One or both eyes may be affected. Conjunctivitis may also be a symptom of hay fever.

Causes
The usual cause of conjunctivitis in older children is viral infection. In a newborn baby it may be the result of infection by bacteria in the birth canal. In rare cases, infection is transmitted by a mother with gonorrhoea, genital herpes or a chlamydial infection. With prompt treatment, a baby infected during delivery should recover fully.

Medical treatment
Conjunctivitis in a baby will probably be treated in hospital soon after birth. But if symptoms do develop later, see your doctor at once. Although viral conjunctivitis in older children is not serious, take your child to the doctor to rule out the possibility of a serious disorder. Viral conjunctivitis is contagious but usually clears up without treatment within a week.

For bacterial infections the doctor will prescribe an antibiotic ointment or eye drops that usually clear up the problem in a week. Severe infections may need antibiotics given orally or intravenously; they may take 6 weeks to get better. Anti-inflammatory eye drops may relieve the discomfort of allergic conjunctivitis.

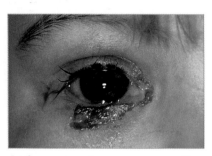

APPEARANCE OF BACTERIAL CONJUNCTIVITIS The whites of the eyes are bloodshot and the eyelashes are gummy with yellow pus. Pus has also collected in the corners of the eyes.

How to help your child
Soak cotton wool in cooled, boiled water and squeeze it out. Gently dab the sticky pus from the eyelashes as often as necessary. To prevent the spread of infection, thoroughly wash your hands after touching the infected eyes, and do not let your child share washcloths or towels with others.

IRITIS

This is an inflammation of the iris and the muscular ring that surrounds it. It may affect one or both eyes. Serious attacks are rare in childhood, but children with juvenile chronic arthritis may suffer from a persistent or recurrent form of iritis.

Medical treatment
Phone a doctor at once if you think your child may be suffering from iritis. To reduce the inflammation the doctor may prescribe either eye drops or an ointment containing a corticosteroid.

If it is treated promptly, iritis often clears up within 1–2 weeks, without any long-term ill effects or worries about the child's vision. However, if the iritis is left untreated, or if it is persistent or keeps recurring, then a child's vision can be at risk of permanent damage.

How to help your child
Holding a pad of cotton wool dipped in cooled, boiled water to the affected eye may help to relieve the symptoms. Make sure that you boil the water first.

SQUINT

A squint, or strabismus, is an abnormality in the direction of the gaze of one eye. Most young babies squint occasionally up to the age of 2–4 months, but a squint after the age of 4 months or a persistent squint at any age is abnormal.

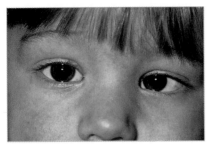

CONVERGENT SQUINT *This child's left eye has a convergent squint. The right eye looks ahead, while the left eye is focused inwards.*

causes the eyes to adjust for near focus too strongly, forcing one eye inwards.

A squint may be due to unequal refraction, which causes the two eyes to produce conflicting images. The weaker eye is poorly controlled and its image is suppressed. To prevent the double vision produced by a squint, the brain ignores the image from the weaker eye; because the eye is not used, its vision may eventually become permanently impaired.

Causes

A baby may develop a squint because the mechanism that coordinates the eyes is not fully developed. In older children a squint may be due to severe longsightedness (*see below*), which

Medical treatment

If your child develops a squint after the age of 4 months or has a persistent squint, consult your doctor. It is important to deal with this as soon as possible while her vision is developing.

□ SYMPTOMS

- An eye that turns too far in or out (convergent or divergent squint), or up or down (vertical squint), when a child looks directly at an object.
- Poor vision in the affected eye.
- Double or blurred vision, which the child may try to remedy by closing or covering the affected eye.

The doctor may send your child to an ophthalmologist who will evaluate her vision and may prescribe glasses if she has a refractive error (*see below*).

Treatment may also involve covering the normal eye with a patch, forcing your child to use the affected eye. In some cases, the position of the deviating eye may be corrected by an operation followed by eye exercises. If treatment is provided within a few weeks of the squint appearing, a child's vision should develop normally.

REFRACTIVE ERRORS

Shortsightedness, longsightedness and astigmatism are focusing problems that cause blurred vision and tend to be inherited. Astigmatism and longsightedness are often present from birth. Shortsightedness starts to develop a few years before adolescence.

Medical treatment

If you think that your child has a focusing problem, take her to your doctor, who will probably refer her to an ophthalmologist or an optician. Her sharpness of vision will be tested and she may be examined with retinoscopy. This technique involves observing the movement of a light shone into the eye and reflected from the retina at the back of the eye. The measurements obtained from the retinoscopy will

help the ophthalmologist or optician to determine whether your child needs glasses and, if so, which kind.

Outlook

In most cases, refractive errors do not become any worse once body growth is complete. But because the focusing power of the lens decreases with age, longsightedness that did not produce any symptoms in a child may become apparent during middle age.

□ SYMPTOMS

If your child is shortsighted or has an astigmatism, she will probably be unaware that anything is wrong. You may notice when your child:

- Sits too close to the television.
- Has problems with school work, or appears to be uninterested, because she cannot see what is going on at the front of the classroom.
- Complains that objects at a distance appear blurred.

If your child is severely longsighted, she may:

- Develop a squint (*see above*).
- Complain that nearby objects appear to be blurred.

MOUTH PROBLEMS

The teeth, gums, tongue and lining of the mouth are prone to damage and infection.

MOST OF THE BODY is protected by tough skin, but the mouth is not and so it is more vulnerable: the tongue and lining of the mouth are damaged easily by chewing coarse food or abrasive objects, and are exposed to a wide variety of potentially damaging infections as well as excessively hot food and drink. A child's first (primary) teeth are replaced by permanent (secondary) teeth, which begin to emerge around the age of 6 years. Both sets must be looked after carefully to avoid tooth decay and gum problems, such as gingivitis and gingivostomatitis.

ANATOMY OF THE TEETH AND TONGUE

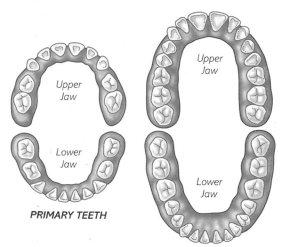

PRIMARY TEETH

SECONDARY TEETH

◀ **DEVELOPMENT OF THE TEETH** *At birth, the primary teeth are already developing in the jaws. The first of these erupt by about 6 months. By the age of 3 years, the entire set of 20 primary ("milk") teeth has come through. Meanwhile, the secondary set of 32 teeth is developing in the jaws and will appear between the ages of 6 and 16 years. As these teeth erupt, the primary teeth are displaced and consequently fall out. The third molars (wisdom teeth) usually break through at 16 or older, although sometimes they never appear.*

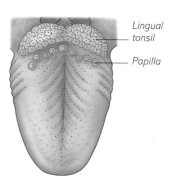

Lingual tonsil

Papilla

▲ **UPPER SURFACE OF THE TONGUE** *Taste buds are located mainly within the papillae on the surface of the tongue. Different types of these papillae, arranged over the surface of the tongue, can detect the four main tastes – sweet, salty, bitter and sour.*

MOUTH ULCERS

Ulcers are open sores on the lining of the mouth or the margins of the tongue. They usually develop for no obvious reason and tend to recur. Ulcers may make the mouth very painful, but they are not serious and usually heal on their own. Children who get repeated ulcers usually grow out of the problem. They may also be due to minor injury or, rarely, to an underlying disorder.

Medical treatment

If your child is in pain, or if the ulcers fail to heal within 10 days, or appear often, take him to your doctor. If an ulcer returns to the same place, a sharp tooth may be the cause.

For recurrent ulcers, the doctor may prescribe hydrocortisone lozenges that can be placed in the mouth, in

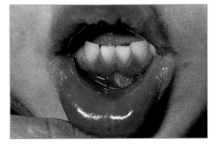

A MOUTH ULCER *This ulcer at the base of the gums has a grey, hollowed-out centre, with a raised, paler rim. The area around the ulcer is inflamed.*

contact with the ulcer, and allowed to dissolve slowly. They work best if they are used as soon as your child has the first signs of soreness in the mouth.

If several ulcers appear but your child has never had ulcers before, they may be due to the first attack of oral herpes simplex (*see* Gingivostomatitis, *below*). Oral acyclovir may shorten the course of the illness if your child starts taking the drug within 36 hours of the appearance of the ulcers.

If the doctor thinks the ulcers are caused by an underlying disease, your child might need to have some tests to find out if anything else is wrong.

How to help your child

Most ulcers heal without treatment within 4–10 days. Ulcers less than 2 mm (¹⁄₁₂ in) in diameter heal quickly; larger ulcers may take longer. Rinsing your child's mouth with a solution of

bicarbonate of soda – mix ¼ teaspoon of bicarbonate of soda in 100 ml (3.5 fl.oz) of warm water – may help to relieve pain or tenderness. An over-the-counter anaesthetic ointment or gel can soothe ulcers and liquid paracetamol relieves the pain.

Acidic, spicy, hot or salty food or drinks may irritate the ulcers. If chewing is very painful, give him soft foods or liquidize his meals. Drinking through a straw prevents liquid from bathing the ulcers.

Echinacea (*see p.322*) can boost a child's immune system. A low daily dose may help to prevent mouth ulcers.

GINGIVOSTOMATITIS

Gingivostomatitis is most common in children between the ages of 6 months and 4 years and causes very painful ulcers to appear in the mouth. It results from a first infection by the herpes simplex virus, which also causes cold sores.

Medical treatment

Take your child to the doctor within 24 hours if you think he may have gingivostomatitis. The doctor may suggest a course of the antiviral drug

acyclovir. A child who is very ill or has been refusing fluids may be admitted to hospital so that acyclovir and rehydrating fluids can be given to him intravenously.

ORAL THRUSH

This yeast infection is most common in babies under 12 months. It is caused when the yeast *Candida albicans*, which lives naturally in the mouth, grows quickly after the oral bacteria that keep it in control are upset by something such as a course of antibiotics.

Medical treatment

If you think your baby may have oral thrush, check with your doctor within a few days. The doctor will examine him and may take scrapings from the inside lining of his mouth for analysis.

You may be given antifungal gel or drops to apply to the inside of his mouth. He may also develop thrush in the nappy area and this will need to be treated at the same time. To help prevent reinfection, make sure you are extra careful when sterilizing feeding bottles and teats. For those mothers who are breastfeeding, the doctor may prescribe an antifungal cream to treat the nipples.

ORAL THRUSH Raised, white spots appear in the mouth and on the gums and soft palate. They form a foam-like coating, which cannot be wiped away, on the tongue.

SYMPTOMS

- A sore mouth, making your baby reluctant to feed.
- Creamy-yellow or white spots on the tongue and the lining of the mouth.

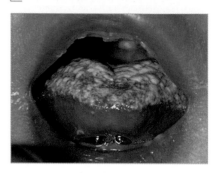

TOOTH DECAY

Tooth decay was once the most common childhood disease, but has greatly decreased, mainly because of fluoride in toothpastes. However, tooth decay continues to occur in some children, perhaps due to over-consumption of sugary foods and drinks.

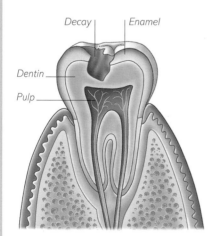

TOOTH DECAY A cavity forms when acids produced by the bacterial breakdown of food erode the tooth's hard outer surface of enamel. The softer layer of dentin beneath is exposed, and as it too is eroded, the cavity gradually enlarges.

Labels on diagram: Decay | Enamel | Dentin | Pulp

Causes

Tooth decay is caused by the bacteria that live in plaque, a sticky coating of saliva and food debris that forms on the surface of the teeth. The bacteria use components of food and drinks (mainly sugars) for energy and, in breaking them down, produce acids. These acids, which are held in close contact with the teeth by plaque, cause calcium and phosphate to be lost from the tooth's enamel (demineralization).

If this continues unchecked, the enamel and eventually the dentin beneath is destroyed. If the problem is left untreated at this stage, the pulp at the centre of the tooth may become infected, resulting in permanent damage to the nerves and blood vessels that it contains.

SYMPTOMS

Early tooth decay does not usually cause any symptoms. The main symptoms of established decay are:

- Sensitivity of the tooth to hot, cold and/or sweet foods or liquids.
- In very advanced decay, the tooth may be brown, have visible pits or holes in the enamel surface and may also be very painful.

Dental treatment

Take your child to a dentist regularly so tooth decay can be detected at an early stage. If symptoms of tooth decay develop between regular check-ups, make an appointment for your child to see your dentist within a few days.

At your child's routine dental examination, the dentist will look at the teeth for signs of tooth decay. X-rays may also be taken to detect areas of decay that are hidden in the crevices of the teeth's biting surfaces.

If the dentist finds signs of early decay, he may simply clean the teeth and scrape them to remove the plaque. This treatment allows the surface of the teeth to come into contact with saliva, which has a natural ability to remineralize tooth enamel. A fluoride gel may also be applied.

To deal with more advanced tooth decay, the dentist may drill the tooth to remove the decayed portion and then insert a filling. If the nerve of the tooth has been irreversibly damaged or destroyed by bacterial infection, it may need to be removed – this may involve your child having an anaesthetic. The entire tooth may need to be taken out if the decay is very advanced.

How to help your child

One of the most important steps you can take is to limit the amount of sweet food and drink that your child consumes. Do not let him indulge in sweet things too often. Discourage him from having sugary snacks and drinks between meals.

Make sure he keeps acidic food and drinks, including fruit juice and all fizzy drinks (both diet and regular), to a minimum. Ideally, your child should have fruit and fizzy drinks only with a meal. Fruit juice should be diluted to half strength with water and preferably drunk through a straw – the same is true of fizzy drinks.

Do not give a baby sweetened drinks in a bottle because the liquid will bathe the teeth and lead to rapid decay. Ask your dentist whether your water supply is fluoridated and if fluoride treatment would be advisable for your child.

Teach your child to brush his teeth twice a day with a fluoride toothpaste – the best times are either following meals or after breakfast and especially last thing at night. You should brush your child's teeth for him or supervise him closely until he reaches the age of 7 years. Before then, children do not have the dexterity to brush their own teeth properly. You could, perhaps, start him off by getting him to brush his teeth himself and then "finish them off" for him.

If brushing his teeth after a meal is inconvenient, it is a good idea for him to chew sugar-free gum. This will stimulate the flow of saliva, which, in turn, neutralizes acid.

Starting at the age of about 2–3 years, your child should regularly visit a dentist for a check-up, usually once every 6 months.

PREVENTION

- Keep your child's diet as low in sugar as you can.
- Teach your child the principles of good oral hygiene.
- Take your child to the dentist regularly.
- Make sure your child eats plenty of the minerals required for forming tooth enamel. They include calcium (found in milk), fluoride (added to most toothpastes), phosphorus (found in meat, fish and eggs) and magnesium (found in spinach, bananas and wholemeal bread). Vitamin A plays a role in the growth of teeth and bones – the betacarotene found in apricots, carrots and dark leafy vegetables is turned into vitamin A by the body.

GINGIVITIS

This inflammation of the gums may develop if a child does not clean his teeth and gums thoroughly. It is caused by the irritant effect of bacteria in plaque, a sticky layer of food debris and saliva that collects on and around the teeth, and at the gum margins.

SYMPTOMS

- Red, swollen and tender gums.
- Gums bleed easily when they are brushed.

How to help your child

Take your child to the dentist within a couple of days if you think he has gingivitis. For mild gingivitis, the dentist may simply encourage your child to look after his teeth properly (see above for advice on oral hygiene). If the gingivitis is more advanced, the dentist may also recommend that your child rinses his mouth with an antibacterial mouthwash to relieve inflammation and tenderness.

When the gums are less tender, the dentist may scale (scrape) the teeth to remove plaque and calculus (hardened plaque). Although gingivitis is a minor problem that can be treated, if it is not checked, it may go on to cause more serious infection, and teeth may be lost as a result.

Outlook

If you and your child look after his teeth properly and regularly, his gums should get better in a few months. Good oral hygiene, combined with regular visits to the dentist for check-ups and scaling, will help to prevent your child from suffering from gingivitis again.

DENTAL ABSCESS

A collection of pus around the root of a tooth, a dental abscess develops when the pulp at the tooth's sensitive core is invaded and destroyed by bacteria. Bacteria enter the pulp cavity if the tooth has been badly damaged or has become severely decayed.

Dental treatment
You should take your child to see a dentist within a few hours of any of the symptoms appearing. The dentist will usually prescribe antibiotics and then wait until the infection settles down before trying to save the tooth. He will drill into the tooth to release the pus and relieve the pressure. The dead and dying pulp is removed, and the resulting cavity is washed, dried and filled – a procedure known as root canal treatment. The dentist may extract the tooth if it is severely affected or if it is a primary ("milk") tooth. A course of antibiotics may be prescribed to clear up any remaining infection.

Following root canal treatment, a tooth usually functions as well as a healthy tooth. If a tooth has been removed, the other teeth often move into the space.

How to help your child
To relieve the pain of the abscess while waiting to see the dentist, give your child liquid paracetamol according to his age and size. A well-wrapped hot-water bottle (use warm, not boiling water) held against the affected side of the face may also provide relief.

Protect your child from abscesses in future by teaching him the basics of good oral hygiene (*see* Tooth decay, p.248), encouraging sensible eating habits (such as avoiding sweet foods and drinks), and taking him to the dentist every 6 months.

> ### ◼ SYMPTOMS
>
> - A persistent and throbbing toothache.
> - Severe pain in the tooth when biting or chewing on it, or when consuming hot foods or liquids.
> - Tenderness, redness and swelling of the gum around the affected tooth.
> - Occasionally, a discharge of foul-tasting pus through an opening in the gum, after which the pain tends to subside.
> - Looseness of the affected tooth.
>
> *If the infection spreads into surrounding tissue, the face and lymph glands in the neck may swell. Eventually, the child might develop symptoms of general infection, such as fever and headache.*

MALOCCLUSION

Malocclusion is a poor fit between the upper and lower teeth when they bite together. Treatment is needed only if the teeth are so crooked or out of position that they look ugly or are difficult to clean, so increasing the risk of tooth decay or gum problems.

Causes
The most common cause is the overcrowding of teeth, a problem suffered by two out of three 12-year-old children. The condition is usually inherited and appears as the child's jaws and teeth develop. It may also occur when primary ("milk") teeth are lost early, because of either decay or injury. When teeth are lost early, the remaining teeth move into the gaps, so that there is insufficient room for the permanent teeth. Overcrowded teeth may grow to be crooked, overlapping

or too prominent. A less common, inherited cause of malocclusion is misalignment of the jaws so that the upper or lower set of teeth is too far forwards or too far back.

Dental treatment
Orthodontic treatment is usually carried out at 11–13 years of age. If the teeth are overcrowded, some may have to be taken out and your child may have to wear a brace. Braces may be fixed or removable. They exert pressure on the teeth to move them

into the right position. In another type of treatment, dentists use a device called a bioblock, which the child bites into, to guide the growth of the jaws. Orthodontic treatment may take up to 2 years to complete. Misalignment of the jaws may be corrected by surgery.

How to help your child
Take your child to the dentist at regular intervals so that the growth of his teeth and jaws can be carefully monitored. If you are at all worried about your child's teeth, or if your child is concerned about his appearance, ask your dentist for advice. He may recommend that you wait to see if the malocclusion corrects itself as the jaws grow, or he may refer your child to an orthodontist.

DIGESTIVE DISORDERS

Mild stomach and intestinal problems are particularly common in babies and young children.

INFECTIONS OF THE DIGESTIVE SYSTEM that result in diarrhoea and/or vomiting are especially frequent in children. At an early age, they put all kinds of things in their mouths and can pick up germs easily with their unhygienic eating habits. Although diarrhoea and vomiting may be troublesome for parent and child, they are rarely persistent enough to be a serious threat to health. Increasingly, children are developing reactions to food such as cow's milk protein or fish, nuts and eggs, but most children grow out of them in time. Some of the less common digestive disorders may cause chronic illness that can affect growth if not treated.

ANATOMY OF THE DIGESTIVE SYSTEM

▶ **DIGESTIVE SYSTEM**

The digestive tract consists of a long tube that extends from the mouth to the anus. As food passes along this tube, it is broken down into minute molecules that can be absorbed into the bloodstream. Associated organs secrete chemicals to assist the digestive process.

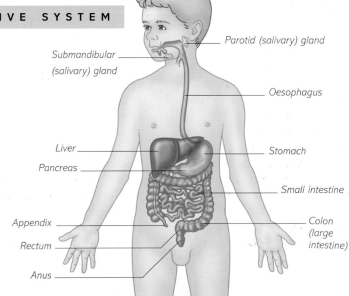

Parotid (salivary) gland

Submandibular (salivary) gland

Oesophagus

Liver

Pancreas

Stomach

Small intestine

Appendix

Colon (large intestine)

Rectum

Anus

REACTIONS TO FOOD

Some children have adverse reactions to certain foods, such as cow's milk protein, lactose, sucrose, fish, eggs and nuts. A food allergy is a reaction to a specific food due to an inappropriate response by the body's immune system. Food intolerance or sensitivity produces similar symptoms for a different reason. A child who has adverse food reactions should see a doctor.

COW'S MILK PROTEIN ALLERGY

Cow's milk protein is the most common cause of an adverse reaction to food. The cause of the allergy is unknown, but the problem usually begins during the first year of life, between a week and several months after starting to drink cow's milk formula. It usually disappears by the time the child reaches 3 years.

Medical treatment

If you suspect your child has an allergy to cow's milk protein, take her to see your doctor. Provided the initial reaction was mild, your doctor will recommend that you exclude all products containing cow's milk from your child's diet for 2 weeks. If the symptoms disappear, your child will be given a small, trial amount of cow's milk. If symptoms come back, the diagnosis is confirmed.

If the initial symptoms were more severe, the reintroduction of the cow's milk should be carried out under the supervision of a paediatrician.

How to help your child

A dietitian will advise you on a new diet for your child, one that is free of products containing cow's milk. Children under 1 year will require a milk substitute. The cow's milk trial will be repeated every 3 months, until your child no longer has an adverse reaction to the protein. The amount of milk given can then be increased gradually. The dietitian will make sure that your child is receiving enough calcium for growth.

LACTOSE & SUCROSE INTOLERANCE

Children can be intolerant to two sugars: lactose, which is found in milk, or sucrose, which is found in many fruits. These same children may also be intolerant to other foods.

The intolerances are due to a deficiency of the enzyme responsible for breaking down lactose or sucrose in the small intestine. Both types of intolerance are usually temporary and may develop as a complication of an infection (see Gastroenteritis, p.254) or another intestinal disorder, such as coeliac disease (see p.256). Some children with an allergy to cow's milk protein are also intolerant to lactose.

Permanent lactose intolerance of genetic origin is common in people of African or Asian descent. Children up to the age of 2 or 3 years tolerate an unlimited amount of milk, but when they grow older they suffer from diarrhoea after drinking only a small amount. Permanent sucrose intolerance may also occur occasionally as an inherited disorder.

Medical treatment

Your doctor will confirm the diagnosis by giving your child a test dose of lactose or sucrose in water and then examining the faeces to see whether an excessive amount of the sugar has not been absorbed.

If a child is intolerant to lactose, a dietitian can design a lactose-free diet. Milk should not be included but your child may be able to tolerate fermented milk products such as yoghurt. A sucrose intolerance needs to be treated with a sucrose-free diet.

SPECIFIC FOOD ALLERGIES

Foods other than milk to which children commonly have allergies are fish, eggs and nuts. The reason why an allergy to a specific food occurs is not known. In many children, no specific cause is found for the symptoms. However, the problem often clears up during the course of a "few foods" diet. In others, exclusion of between one and three foods eliminates the symptoms. Most children outgrow reactions to food.

□ **SYMPTOMS**

Cow's milk protein allergy *causes symptoms that include:*
- Diarrhoea.
- Vomiting.
- Rarely, anaphylactic shock (see p.189).

Lactose and sucrose intolerance *causes these symptoms within 6 hours of drinking milk or eating foods that contain lactose or sucrose:*
- Diarrhoea and abdominal pain.
- Vomiting.

Special food allergies *cause symptoms that include:*
- Rashes, including urticaria (see p.233).
- Swelling of the lips and mouth.
- Diarrhoea and abdominal pain.
- Vomiting.

Medical treatment

If you suspect your child has an allergy to a food, consult your doctor. The doctor will examine your child and may carry out tests to exclude other causes. Your child may be put on a milk-free diet to rule out allergy to cow's milk protein or intolerance to lactose. If your child continues to have symptoms, one of two methods may be tried to find out whether she has an adverse reaction to a specific food.

One method involves comparing your child's symptoms when the suspected food is included or excluded from her diet. In another method, your child is given a "few foods" diet, consisting of specific foods known to be unlikely to induce symptoms. Within a couple of weeks of following this diet, the symptoms usually stop. Then one new food is given every 3 days until symptoms occur or the diet has returned to normal.

ALLERGY FOODS

Children are most often allergic to the following foods, although they may be able to tolerate a food when it is cooked but not when it is raw:
- Fish and shellfish
- Eggs
- Nuts, especially peanuts
- Gluten in wheat
- Chocolate
- Soya products.

APPENDICITIS

A small, worm-shaped tube that branches off the start of the large intestine, the appendix has no known function. It can become infected and inflamed, causing appendicitis. This cause of abdominal pain requires surgery.

SYMPTOMS

- Dull pain in the lower abdomen (see illustration, left). Any pressure on the painful area, movement or deep breathing increases the pain, and a child with appendicitis often lies still.
- Nausea, which may or may not be accompanied by vomiting.
- Fever.
- Constipation or diarrhoea.

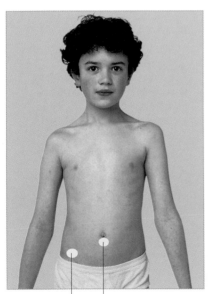

Usual first site of pain
Usual site of pain after a few hours

THE SITE OF PAIN *Pain usually begins around the navel, gradually becomes more severe and migrates to the lower right-hand side of the abdomen. In some children, the pain is in the lower right abdomen from the beginning.*

Immediate action

If the abdominal pain is so severe it makes your child cry out, or if the pain continues for 3 hours, call your doctor at once. Call an ambulance or take your child to a hospital accident and emergency department if the pain has continued for more than 6 hours.

If appendicitis is not treated promptly, the appendix may burst, or perforate. Pain becomes continuous and pus enters the abdominal cavity, causing widespread infection and leading to a potentially fatal condition called peritonitis.

Medical treatment

If appendicitis is suspected, your child will be admitted to hospital. If it is confirmed then her appendix will be removed as soon as possible. She will be given painkillers for about 24 hours after the operation. If the appendix was not perforated, she may go home after 3–4 days. If it was perforated, she will be given antibiotics and will

remain in hospital until the infection has cleared up, which may take about 7 days. After leaving hospital your child will be able to eat normally, but she should avoid sports and strenuous physical activities for about a month.

How to help your child

If your child complains of abdominal pain, it is difficult to know at first how serious it is and how to help. A hot-water bottle wrapped in a towel and held against the site of the pain may be soothing. Try not to give her paracetamol or other painkillers because they may make the diagnosis more difficult for the doctor. The child should not eat or drink anything in case an operation is necessary.

GASTROENTERITIS

Most children have attacks of gastroenteritis (inflammation of the stomach and intestines), causing diarrhoea and/or vomiting. The most common reason is a virus transmitted through the air or by contact with infected faeces. Bacteria in food or drinks may also cause gastroenteritis. Most attacks are mild but severe attacks may be serious, especially in infants, who can become very dehydrated.

Medical treatment

If a bout of gastroenteritis has not improved after 24 hours, call a doctor, even if the symptoms are mild. If your child is under 2 months old and you suspect she might have gastroenteritis, phone a doctor at once. You should also contact a doctor straight away if your infant or child has any symptoms of dehydration (*see* Danger signs, *p.63 and p.172*).

After examination, the doctor will decide whether your child needs to go to hospital or can be treated at home. If the latter, your doctor will explain what to do and how to look after her.

If your child has to go to hospital, she may be given blood tests to determine the severity of dehydration. She may be given rehydrating solution intravenously, and may not be allowed to eat or drink for 24 hours. After this, oral rehydrating solution will be given, followed by the gradual reintroduction of ordinary food.

How to help your child

Give your child plenty of water and clear fluids to prevent dehydration. Buy over-the-counter oral rehydrating solutions from a pharmacist. Give your child bland foods, such as bananas and white rice, and avoid citrus fruits, milk and high-fibre foods for a few days. Be fastidious about hygiene after she has been to the lavatory or when changing nappies. Make sure she washes her hands with warm water and soap.

If your breastfed baby suffers from gastroenteritis (which is very unusual because breastfeeding generally protects against gastroenteritis), give the oral rehydrating solution first and then breastfeed. Provided that the symptoms subside, you may gradually reduce the amount of solution over a period of about 5 days – see the instructions below.

Treatment for bottlefed babies

- **Day 1** Give your baby no milk for the first 24 hours. Instead, give her the oral rehydrating solution at regular intervals throughout the day.
- **Day 2** At each feed time, give your baby a mixture of 2 parts rehydrating solution and 2 parts milk formula.
- **Day 3** Your baby should have recovered completely and be able to return to her normal feeding routine.

Treatment for weaned infants

For a weaned infant, follow the instructions for bottlefed babies above, but do not give any solids on Day 1. From Day 2 to Day 4, give the infant a gradually increasing amount of rice and puréed vegetables and fruit, followed by a light diet. Your child should be able to eat normally again by Day 5.

Treatment for older children

- **Day 1** Instead of milk, give your child rehydrating solution.
- **Day 2** Add rice, vegetables and

unsweetened fruit purée to her diet.
- **Day 3** Add chicken and/or soups to her diet and reintroduce milk.
- **Day 4** Add bread, biscuits, eggs, meat and/or fish to her diet.
- **Day 5** By now, your child should have recovered completely and be able to eat normally.

TODDLER DIARRHOEA

Toddler diarrhoea affects children between the ages of 1 and 3 years. A child who is otherwise healthy passes watery faeces that often contain recognizable pieces of food, such as raisins, carrots, peas or beans.

Medical treatment

Toddler diarrhoea is not serious, but it is a good idea to take your child to a doctor to make sure the condition is not the result of an infection or another disorder. The doctor will check whether your child's growth is normal by measuring her height and weight. Toddler diarrhoea does not affect your child's growth, so failure to grow normally may suggest another disorder. As a precaution, the doctor may send a sample of a stool for laboratory analysis.

SYMPTOMS

- Passes watery faeces with pieces of food in them.
- Child is generally well, but may have a constant nappy rash.

How to help your child

Mash or liquidize the foods she finds hard to chew or digest. She will grow out of the problem by the age of 3 years and without any lasting effects.

CONSTIPATION

A child who passes hard, dry faeces infrequently may be constipated. Just passing stools infrequently does not necessarily mean your child is constipated – the normal frequency for passing stools may vary from 4 times a day to once every 4 days.

Causes

Temporary constipation may be due to dehydration brought on by an illness involving vomiting and fever. From 1–2 years of age, changes in a child's diet may cause constipation. In older children, a lack of fibre-rich foods may be the reason. Chronic constipation may arise if an anal fissure (*see right*) develops after passing hard stools. It can also arise if a child deliberately withholds faeces during toilet training or because she has emotional problems.

Medical treatment

Consult a doctor if constipation lasts for more than a week, if there is pain on defecation or if you suspect chronic constipation. She will ask about your child's diet and recent illnesses. Dietary advice may solve the problem.

For chronic constipation, you will be given a prescription for stool softeners and stimulant laxatives, as well as dietary advice and a suggestion that your child sits on the lavatory at the same time each day to restore a regular bowel habit. After about 2 months, when a regular habit has been re-established, the drug dose will be reduced. The softened faeces produced by laxatives allow an anal fissure to heal, usually within 6 weeks.

If no solution works, the doctor may refer your child to a paediatrician, or a child psychiatrist to investigate emotional causes.

How to help your child

Give your child plenty of fluids to alleviate and prevent constipation. If your child is over 6 months, give more fibre in vegetables, fruit and wholegrain cereals. If constipation is a problem, do not give more than 500 ml (1 pint) of milk a day. School children can drink skimmed or semi-skimmed milk.

SYMPTOMS

- Infrequent defecation.
- Pain when passing stools.
- Hard, dry faeces.

Chronic constipation *symptoms are:*
- Liquid faeces trickling from the anus, which may soil the underwear.
- Pain on trying to pass stools.
- Loss of appetite.
- Blood on the faeces.

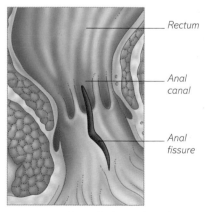

Rectum

Anal canal

Anal fissure

ANAL FISSURE *A tear in the anal canal may occur if a child strains to pass large, hard stools. It makes defecating painful and the child may withhold faeces deliberately.*

COELIAC DISEASE

Rare but serious, this disease is caused by sensitivity of the small intestine to the protein gluten, which is found in wheat, barley, rye and oats. As a result, food is not absorbed properly, a condition known as malabsorption.

Medical treatment

If your child has any of the symptoms, take her to the doctor, who will check her weight and may do blood tests for anaemia and antibodies. If they indicate coeliac disease, you may have to take her to hospital for a biopsy of the small intestine. If this shows changes in the intestinal lining (*see left*), the diagnosis is confirmed.

How to help your child

A child with coeliac disease must follow a gluten-free diet. Many specially produced substitute foods are available, including gluten-free bread, biscuits, flour and pasta. Other foods, such as dairy products, eggs, meat, fish, vegetables, fruit, rice and corn, can be eaten as normal. Check that everyone concerned with the care of your child knows that she can eat only certain foods.

As your child grows up and becomes increasingly independent, make sure she knows the importance of keeping to the diet. Children vary in how they react to renewed exposure to gluten, and you will soon learn how much gluten is likely to cause an adverse reaction and how severe the reaction might be.

Outlook

The symptoms of coeliac disease will clear up within a few weeks of your child starting a gluten-free diet, and she should begin to put on weight. Your child will remain in good health and will grow as expected, but she will have to keep to a gluten-free diet throughout her life.

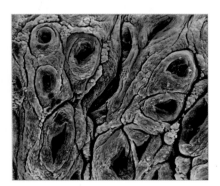

INTESTINAL DAMAGE In coeliac disease, the tiny finger-like projections, or villi, in the lining of the small intestine become flattened, preventing proper absorption of nutrients.

SYMPTOMS

Symptoms develop gradually a few months after a baby starts on solids. Generally caused by foods containing wheat, such as bread, breakfast cereals, and biscuits, they include:

- Weight loss or failure to gain weight.
- Very pale, floating faeces that have an unpleasant smell.
- Pale skin, breathlessness, and lack of energy due to anaemia.

INTESTINAL OBSTRUCTION

This is a partial or complete blockage of either the small or large intestine. The passage of food is obstructed, causing cramping abdominal pain. Treatment is usually needed and complete obstruction of the intestine may be fatal if left untreated.

Causes

In children under 2, the condition is usually caused by a disorder known as intussusception, in which the intestine folds in on itself (*see illustration on opposite page*). Occasionally, it may be caused by a strangulated hernia (*see p.260*) or an inherited abnormality of the intestine.

In children of any age, intestinal obstruction may be caused by Crohn's disease (*see Inflammatory bowel disease, p.259*) and volvulus, or twisting, of the intestine.

There is a chance that the blocked part of the intestine may rupture, leading to peritonitis (inflammation of the lining of the abdominal cavity).

SYMPTOMS

- Intermittent attacks of severe pain in the abdomen.
- Vomiting, which may produce greenish-yellow fluid and occur at increasingly frequent intervals.
- Wind and failure to pass faeces. In partial obstruction, passing wind and defecating usually bring temporary relief from pain.
- Bloodstained, jelly-like mucus on the faeces, in cases of intussusception.
- Fever and swelling of the abdomen, if treatment is delayed.

Alternatively, the blocked part may die and become gangrenous, which is potentially fatal. Dehydration is another serious complication that may develop as a result of the frequent vomiting attacks that are symptomatic of the condition (*see p.63 and p.172 for signs of dehydration*).

Medical treatment

Call an ambulance, or take your child to the nearest accident and emergency department, if you think that she might have an intestinal obstruction. Your child will be examined and fluids may be given intravenously to prevent dehydration from developing. To confirm the diagnosis and to find out the cause of the obstruction, she will be X-rayed.

If intussusception is suspected, a special X-ray examination involving the use of an air or barium enema may be carried out. The child may be given a laxative to clear her bowels. The enema is placed in the anal passage and then, a short time later, an X-ray is taken. The procedure is completed in about half an hour, during which time the child may experience muscle spasms. The pressure exerted by the enema often forces the displaced intestinal tissue back into the right position.

If the enema does not correct the problem, an operation is carried out. Other types of intestinal obstruction require surgery, which sometimes involves removing the obstructed part of the intestine.

Outlook

Your child should grow and develop normally once the obstruction has been treated and cleared, or if only a short section of bowel has been surgically removed. However, if the intestinal obstruction was due to an underlying condition (such as Crohn's disease), the blockage may recur unless the disorder that caused it is being effectively treated.

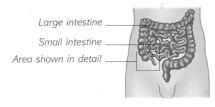

Large intestine
Small intestine
Area shown in detail

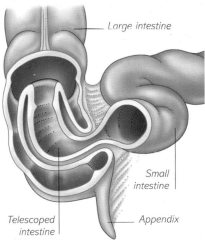

Large intestine

Small intestine

Telescoped intestine

Appendix

INTUSSUSCEPTION *A condition in which part of the intestine telescopes in on itself, intussusception tends to occur in the area where the large and small intestines meet.*

IRRITABLE BOWEL SYNDROME

Irritable bowel syndrome, also known as IBS, is a disorder of the walls of the large intestine. It causes recurrent bouts of abdominal pain which may be accompanied by diarrhoea or constipation – sometimes both.

Causes

In irritable bowel syndrome, the muscles in the walls of the large intestine behave abnormally, leading to problems with digestion. The cause is not clear but it may be due, in some cases, to an abnormally low or high amount of stomach acid or to problems with the enzymes involved in digestion. Stress and anxiety appear to trigger and aggravate the symptoms, perhaps by interfering with the digestive process. Intolerance of, or sensitivity to, certain foods, especially wheat, corn, cow's milk protein, nuts and eggs, can cause abdominal cramps with some muscle spasms.

Irritable bowel syndrome is not common in children, but it is a condition that often persists and symptoms may recur periodically throughout life.

Medical treatment

Take your child to see a doctor if you think she might be suffering from

SYMPTOMS

- Abdominal pain that is relieved by a bowel movement or passing wind.
- Persistent sense of fullness and distension of the bowel.
- Wind and diarrhoea or constipation, or bouts of diarrhoea alternating with periods of constipation.
- Nausea, headache and general lack of energy.

irritable bowel syndrome. A diagnosis is usually made on the basis of the symptoms combined with a physical examination. Sometimes, your child may need an investigation in hospital to exclude another disorder, such as giardiasis (*see p.262*), reactions to food (*see p.252*) or inflammatory bowel disease (*see p.259*).

How to help your child

Certain foods may be making your child's symptoms worse, so it is a good idea to keep a diary of her diet so that you can quickly identify and avoid the problem foods.

Stress and emotional upsets can sometimes increase the severity of the symptoms. Try to identify situations that make your child feel anxious, and if they cannot be avoided, give her extra care and support.

Make sure your child eats plenty of fresh and dried fruit, green leafy vegetables and oat bran. These are all good sources of water-soluble and easily digested fibre. Encourage her to drink plenty of water and to take regular exercise to help with digestion and the progression of food through the large intestine.

Giving your child a high-fibre diet is helpful in many cases of irritable bowel syndrome, especially if the main symptom is constipation.

Sometimes an attack of irritable bowel syndrome is triggered by a bout of gastroenteritis or by an overgrowth of the bacteria that normally inhabit the bowel. Giving probiotics can help restore the optimum balance of bacteria. Probiotics are cultures of the "friendly" bacteria, such as *Acidophilus lactobacillus*, that normally live in the intestine – the idea is that they help to digest food and prevent the unchecked growth of harmful bacteria.

Herbal remedies for IBS include peppermint capsules or teas, as well as chamomile, valerian, rosemary and lemon balm. Homeopathic treatments such as Arg Nit or Nux vomica may be helpful, but generally you will need to take your child to a homeopath for treatment (*see p.321*).

Relaxation and correct breathing for older children can help manage stress and reduce anxiety. IBS sufferers may have more difficulty adjusting to life and experience more stress. Hands-on therapies such as osteopathy and craniosacral therapy may also be worth considering (*see p.323*).

MALABSORPTION

Malabsorption is the result of the small intestine's failure to absorb adequate nutrients, such as vitamins, minerals, fats and amino acids, from food. The problem is always associated with an underlying condition.

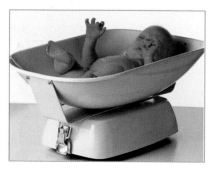

CHECKING WEIGHT *Malabsorption is one possible reason for a child failing to put on weight normally.*

Causes

Malabsorption is sometimes caused by damage to the lining of the small intestine, which interferes with the intestine's ability to absorb nutrients from food. Malabsorption may also be due to a deficiency of the enzymes involved in digestion, which prevents the breakdown of food into units small enough to be absorbed.

Malabsorption is always associated with an underlying disorder, such as Crohn's disease (*see* Inflammatory bowel disease, *p.259*), cystic fibrosis (*see p.315*), coeliac disease (*see p.256*), or adverse reactions to foods such as cow's milk protein or lactose sugar (*see p.252*).

Medical treatment

Take your child to see your doctor if she shows any of the symptoms of malabsorption. Her weight will be checked and compared to what is normal for her age. She will probably be referred to a specialist who will

> ### SYMPTOMS
>
> - Very pale, floating faeces with an unpleasant smell. The faeces contain undigested fat.
> - Diarrhoea.
> - Loss of weight or a failure to put on weight.
> - Listlessness.
>
> *In severe cases, malabsorption results in deficiencies of vitamins and minerals, such as calcium. These deficiencies may, in turn, lead to malnutrition and anaemia (see p.305).*

give her tests to find the underlying cause of the problem. The doctor may also refer you to a dietitian to assess whether your child's diet is adequate for her needs. The underlying cause is treated and your child's diet modified or supplemented, usually ensuring that she grows and gains weight normally. Your child may, however, need to stay on a special diet for life.

INFLAMMATORY BOWEL DISEASE

Crohn's disease and ulcerative colitis both produce chronic inflammation of the intestine. They are rare in children under the age of 7 but more common in adolescents. Although the causes are unknown, genetic factors play a part.

CROHN'S DISEASE

Once a rare condition, Crohn's disease is becoming more common. It may cause inflammation of any part of the digestive tract, but generally affects only the last section of the small intestine (the ileum). As a result of chronic inflammation, the intestinal wall becomes extremely thick, and deep and penetrating ulcers may form.

Crohn's disease reduces the small intestine's ability to absorb nutrients from food (*see* Malabsorption, *opposite*). Thickening of the intestinal wall may also narrow the inside of the intestine to such an extent that the bowel becomes obstructed (*see* Intestinal obstruction, *p.256*). Complications in other parts of the body may include arthritis and inflammation of the eye.

Medical treatment

Take your child to the doctor if any of the symptoms persist for more than a few days. Crohn's disease is less likely to be the cause of the symptoms than some other disorder, such as intestinal infection. If your doctor does suspect Crohn's disease, your child may need to undergo hospital tests, such as a barium X-ray and endoscopic examinations of the intestines, to look for evidence of the disease.

If Crohn's disease is diagnosed, your child may be given anti-inflammatory drugs. Alternatively, she may be given a liquid diet containing proteins that have been broken down into smaller components, making absorption easier. In severe cases, and if your child is badly malnourished,

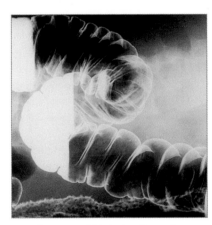

CROHN'S DISEASE *This barium X-ray shows narrowing of the last part of the small intestine due to Crohn's disease.*

she may be given drugs and nutrients intravenously. Blood transfusion may also be needed. If the condition does not improve with medical treatment, or if complications occur, the damaged parts of the intestine may need to be removed surgically.

Outlook

Crohn's disease is a long-term condition and some children continue to suffer from flare-ups of the disease for many years. The symptoms may recur at intervals of a few months or a few years. For other children, Crohn's disease may subside after only one or two flare-ups.

ULCERATIVE COLITIS

This condition causes the colon and rectum to become both inflamed and ulcerated. The first attack of ulcerative colitis is often the worst, and then the symptoms may come and go over a

Crohn's disease *symptoms often develop gradually and include:*
- Diarrhoea. Occasionally, the faeces contain blood, pus or mucus if the colon is affected.
- Spasms of abdominal pain.
- Fever.
- Nausea.
- Poor growth and/or delayed puberty.
- Loss of weight and reduced appetite.
- Sometimes, ulceration of the anus.

Ulcerative colitis *symptoms often include:*
- Bloody diarrhoea.
- Abdominal pain and tenderness.
- A feeling of fullness in the bowel.
- Fever.
- Nausea.
- Loss of appetite.
- Poor growth.
- Weight loss.

long period of time. Bloody diarrhoea is the main symptom; repeated blood loss may cause anaemia (*see p.305*).

Medical treatment

If your child has bloody diarrhoea and abdominal pain, take her to see your doctor within 24 hours. Bacterial infection is the most common cause of these symptoms; but, if your doctor suspects ulcerative colitis, your child may need to have tests similar to those for Crohn's disease.

If ulcerative colitis is confirmed, your child may have to take anti-inflammatory drugs indefinitely. If drugs do not control the symptoms, or if the colon is badly damaged, the affected part may be removed surgically. If a large part is removed, your child may be left with an ileostomy (an opening through the abdominal wall for passage of faeces).

PYLORIC STENOSIS

An uncommon condition that affects babies aged under 2 months, pyloric stenosis is the narrowing of the outlet (pylorus) from the stomach into the small intestine. If it is severely narrowed, only a small amount of food enters the intestine; the rest is vomited.

Medical treatment

Phone your doctor at once if your baby shows any symptoms of pyloric stenosis, or if any signs indicate that she may be dehydrated (*see* Danger signs, *p.63 and p.172*). Until you can see the doctor, feed your child small amounts frequently, so not too much undigested food is in her stomach.

The doctor will examine your baby's abdomen while the baby is feeding, to feel for a swelling in the area of the pylorus. If pyloric stenosis seems likely, your child will be admitted to hospital where she will have another physical examination and an ultrasound examination to confirm the diagnosis.

Intravenous fluids are given if your baby is dehydrated. The obstruction is relieved by a minor surgical operation to widen the pylorus. Your baby can probably leave hospital the next day. After the operation, the amount of your baby's feeds should be gradually increased until feeding is normal again (usually within 48–72 hours).

Outlook

Once pyloric stenosis has been treated, the condition will not recur and there are no permanent ill effects.

▣ SYMPTOMS

The main symptoms of pyloric stenosis usually appear between 2 and 6 weeks after birth:

- Persistent projectile vomiting. This is vomiting that is produced forcefully, and is projected from her mouth — it often reaches some distance from the baby.
- Vomit usually contains milk curds but no bile.
- Dehydration caused by persistent vomiting.
- Constant hunger: the baby often accepts another feed immediately after vomiting.
- Infrequent bowel movements.
- Weight loss and listlessness if the symptoms have been present for more than a few days.
- Baby described as "worried-looking".

HERNIA

A hernia is the protrusion of a part of the intestine through the abdominal wall. Umbilical and inguinal hernias are the most common types in children. In an umbilical hernia, the intestine bulges through the muscle wall at or above the navel (umbilicus).

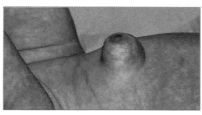

UMBILICAL HERNIA *Usually, an umbilical hernia is at the navel (umbilicus). Sometimes, it appears just above the navel.*

UMBILICAL HERNIA

This type of hernia is the result of a gap in the muscles of the abdominal wall and usually develops a few weeks after birth. It is more common in black babies. In most cases, the hernia disappears without treatment before a child reaches 2 years of age. However, it may persist up to the age of 5 years.

Medical treatment

Check with your doctor if the hernia is particularly large or if it has not disappeared by the time the child has reached the age of 5 years. Your child may need a minor operation to replace the intestine in the abdominal cavity and stitch together the gap in the muscles of the abdominal wall.

▣ SYMPTOMS

Umbilical hernia:
- A soft swelling, usually at the navel.
- Often not present in the morning but may reappear during the day.
- May increase in size if the child cries or tenses the abdominal muscles.
- Not painful.

Inguinal hernia:
- A soft swelling just above the groin crease or in the scrotum.
- Often not present in the morning but may reappear during the day.
- May increase in size if the child cries.

Hernias above a child's navel more often require surgery. An umbilical hernia is unlikely to recur after it has been treated.

INGUINAL HERNIA

Inguinal hernias are most common in boys under the age of 1 year. They occur when the inguinal canal, which normally closes once the testicle has descended shortly after birth, remains open. It forms a space through which a loop of intestine can pass, either into the groin or the scrotum.

Medical treatment

If you detect a swelling in your son's groin or scrotum which you think might be an inguinal hernia, contact your doctor. If the diagnosis is confirmed, your child will need an operation to correct the problem, as an inguinal hernia will not disappear without treatment.

If the hernia is painful or tender, your child may need to be admitted to hospital immediately for emergency surgery. The operation will replace and reposition the intestine in the abdominal cavity and will close the inguinal canal with stitches. An inguinal hernia is unlikely to recur once your child has had the operation.

Possible complications

A strangulated hernia develops when a loop of intestine becomes trapped in the canal, reducing or cutting off its blood supply. The swelling in the groin or scrotum will become hard, tender or painful, and discoloured, and your child may vomit.

If the swelling in the groin or scrotum is painless, take your child to a doctor within 24 hours. If it is painful or tender, call an ambulance or take your child to the nearest accident and emergency department.

HEPATITIS

Hepatitis, or inflammation of the liver, is most commonly caused by viruses. Children are most often affected by the virus that causes hepatitis A. The hepatitis B virus can cause some cases among newborn babies if their mothers are carriers.

Causes

The hepatitis A virus is usually caught by swallowing water or food that has been contaminated with infected faeces. Hepatitis A rarely causes permanent damage to the liver and, after the first attack, your child should be immune to further attacks of the disease. Immunization against the hepatitis A virus may be recommended if you and your family are planning to visit one of a number of countries where the disease is most prevalent.

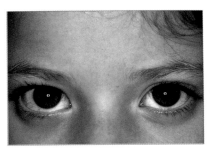

JAUNDICE   In hepatitis, a build-up in the blood of the waste product bilirubin may cause jaundice, a yellowing of the whites of the eyes and skin.

SYMPTOMS

In pre-school children, most hepatitis A infections are mild and do not produce any symptoms. Older children usually do have symptoms, but these are rarely severe, and may include:
- Flu-like symptoms of fever, headache, and weakness.
- Poor appetite.
- Nausea and vomiting.
- Tender upper right abdomen (where the liver is located).

About a week after the other symptoms have appeared, your child may develop jaundice (see photograph, left), often accompanied by dark urine and pale faeces and, sometimes, by diarrhoea. Jaundice may last for up to 2 weeks.

Medical treatment

Make an appointment to see a doctor within 24 hours if your child has any symptoms of hepatitis. Hepatitis A cannot be treated with drugs, but the doctor will advise you on how to care for your child at home. Rarely, an attack may be serious enough for your child to be admitted to hospital, where doctors can keep a close eye on her. The doctor may recommend that all family members should be immunized against hepatitis to prevent the spread of the disease. A child with hepatitis A is infectious for 2 weeks before, and for 1 week after, the onset of jaundice.

How to help your child

Let your child stay in bed if she wishes. While she is vomiting or her appetite is poor, give her small amounts of rehydrating fluid (*see p.63 and p.172*) mixed with fruit juice hourly during the day. As the jaundice decreases, your child's appetite should improve and she can start to eat normally.

Prevent the spread of the hepatitis A virus between members of your family by washing your hands extra carefully and by boiling food utensils. Your child should feel well enough to go back to school from 2–6 weeks after the onset of symptoms.

GIARDIASIS

Giardiasis is an infection of the small intestine caused by the parasite *Giardia lamblia*. Once a problem only in tropical areas, giardiasis now also occurs in temperate countries, where it affects mainly pre-school children.

THE CAUSE OF GIARDIASIS *The parasite* Giardia lamblia *clings to folds in the lining of the intestine. It absorbs nutrients from the fluid in the intestine.*

Medical treatment

Children can catch giardiasis by swallowing food or water that has been contaminated with the parasite, which is a protozoa that interferes with absorption of fat from the small intestine. Most cases of giardiasis are mild and clear up without treatment within 2 weeks. However, if your child has been suffering from diarrhoea for more than 2 weeks, or from severe diarrhoea for over 48 hours, take her to see the doctor, who will want to take samples of her faeces and send them for microscopic examination. If the tests discover the single-celled parasite *Giardia lamblia*, your child will be prescribed a week-long course of an antiparasitic drug.

How to help your child

Make sure that your child drinks plenty of fluids to replace those she has been losing through diarrhoea and to prevent her suffering from dehydration. Be very scrupulous about handwashing after going to the toilet and before preparing food. These precautions will help to prevent the disease from spreading to other members of your family.

THREADWORMS

The most common parasitic worms in temperate countries, these worms live in the intestines and resemble tiny white pieces of thread. Children who suck objects or eat food contaminated with worms' eggs are mostly affected.

Causes

The least harmful of parasitic worms, threadworms (*Enterobius vermicularis*) live in large numbers in the lower bowel. Females emerge from the rectum at night to lay as many as 10,000 eggs around the anus. This causes a child intense irritation.

Medical treatment

If you think your child may have threadworms, take her to your doctor, who may ask you to collect some eggs for microscopic examination (*see* illustration). The whole family will need to be treated with one of three antiparasitic drugs – two are taken in a single dose, the third is taken daily for a week. One course should cure your child, but to prevent reinfection, the family may be treated again in 2 weeks.

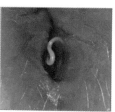

WORMS' EGGS *Collect the eggs for microscopic examination by pressing a piece of sticky tape to your child's anal area. You should do this in the morning before your child bathes or uses the toilet.*

INFECTIOUS DISEASES

Most childhood infections are not serious, but a few can be dangerous and need careful handling.

CHILDREN ARE GENERALLY MORE SUSCEPTIBLE to the various infectious diseases than adults. This is because a child's immune system takes time to build up resistance to the bacteria, viruses, fungi and parasites that are commonly found in the environment – in the air we breathe, the water we drink and the food we eat. The body's defences against infectious diseases range from the antiseptic solution that washes the eyes to the sophisticated white blood cells that hunt down and kill invading germs. Antibiotics can usually cure bacterial infections rapidly and completely, while routine immunization has meant that the main serious viral infections, such as measles, mumps and rubella, are less common than they used to be.

MEASLES

Measles is a highly infectious childhood disease, but widespread immunization has now made it uncommon in the UK and other developed countries. A viral infection that is not usually serious, measles causes fever and a rash.

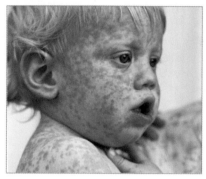

MEASLES RASH *At first, the rash is made up of separate spots, which then merge to give the skin a blotchy look.*

Medical treatment

If you think your child has measles, consult your doctor within 24 hours to confirm the illness. Call the doctor at once if he develops any of the following: earache, abnormally rapid breathing, drowsiness, seizures, severe headache or vomiting.

How to help your child

Let your child stay in bed or be up and around, as he wants. He may feel very unwell. Give him paracetamol to reduce a fever and make sure he drinks plenty of fluids. He will be infectious for 2 days before the rash appears and then for another 5 days. Try to keep him away from other people but any brothers and sisters will probably have been infected already. Most children recover completely from measles within about 10 days of the first signs. A single attack of measles should give lifelong immunity to the disease.

Possible complications

Complications are rare, but some children can develop infection of the middle ear (*see p.240*) or pneumonia (*see p.227*), in which case your doctor will prescribe antibiotics. Serious

complications may develop, especially in children who have chronic heart or lung disease or whose immune system is weak. About 1 child in 1,000 with measles may develop encephalitis, a serious illness caused by the infection reaching the brain or by an abnormal immune response to the measles virus.

☐ SYMPTOMS

Incubation period: 10–14 days.
• Fever.
• Red, watering eyes.
• Runny nose.
• Dry cough.
These symptoms are followed by:
• Tiny white spots with a red base (Koplik's spots) may appear on the insides of the cheeks a couple of days after the first symptoms.
• A flat, blotchy, red rash appears (*see p.187*) 3–4 days after the start of the illness, first on the face and behind the ears, then over the whole body. The rash begins to fade after a few days, the fever drops and your child should start to feel better. In most cases, the rash is gone within a week.

RUBELLA

Often called German measles, rubella is a mild viral infection that is now rare as most children are immunized against it. It may cause a rash and swelling of the lymph nodes but, in about 25 per cent of cases, there is no rash and your child may barely notice it.

Medical treatment

Call your doctor if you think your child may have rubella but do not take him to the surgery because of the risk of infecting pregnant women. Rubella is only serious if a woman contracts it early in pregnancy when it can cause damage to the developing baby.

Call your doctor at once if your child shows any of the following symptoms: a rash of flat, dark-red spots that do not fade when they are pressed; severe headache; vomiting; a general lack of energy; or feeling unusually drowsy. All of these may indicate a more serious illness than rubella.

☐ SYMPTOMS

Incubation period: 2–3 weeks.
• Mild fever.
• Swollen lymph nodes at the back of the neck and behind the ears. Some children may have enlarged lymph nodes in other parts of the body, such as the armpits and groin.
• A non-itchy rash (*see p.187*) may develop after 2–3 days but usually disappears within about 3 days.
• Some children may complain of pains in their joints.

There is no specific medical treatment for rubella, but the doctor will examine your child closely and may confirm the diagnosis by taking a blood sample for laboratory testing.

How to help your child
Give him paracetamol to bring his fever down and encourage him to drink plenty of fluids. Keep him away from pregnant women and warn anyone who might be pregnant. Rubella is infectious from 1 week before the rash appears until about

4 days after the rash disappears. Children usually feel much better within about 10 days of the first symptoms appearing. Once he has recovered, your child should be immune to the disease for life.

Possible complications
Rare complications are possible and include inflammation of the brain (encephalitis) and thrombocytopenia (see p.307), a disorder in which the number of platelets (clotting agents) in the blood is abnormally low.

RUBELLA RASH *Tiny, flat pink spots appear first on the face and quickly spread to the body, arms and legs. The spots merge as the rash spreads.*

CHICKENPOX

A common childhood infection, chickenpox, also called varicella, usually affects children under 10. It is most common in late winter and spring. It is caused by a virus and its main symptom is an itchy, irritating rash.

Medical treatment
Most children with chickenpox do not need to be seen by a doctor. Call your doctor at once if your young baby contracts chickenpox, or if your child has a reduced immunity or is prone to eczema and has been exposed to chickenpox. Your child should see the doctor if pus is coming from his spots or if the skin around the spots is red.

Call your doctor at once if your child starts coughing or has seizures, rapid breathing, abnormal drowsiness, persistent or recurrent fever, or seems unsteady when walking.

Your doctor may give your child antibiotics to prevent a secondary infection caused by bacteria. Children with eczema may be given an antiviral drug such as oral acyclovir. If your child is at high risk of complications, your doctor may admit him to hospital for a 5-day course of intravenous acyclovir or injections of varicella zoster immune globulin.

How to help your child
Soothe your child's itchy spots with calamine lotion. Over-the-counter oral antihistamines may also help, as does giving your child a bath in warm water containing a handful of bicarbonate of soda. Give paracetamol to reduce a fever and provide plenty of drinks. Keep your child's fingernails trimmed and try to stop him scratching the spots to stop them becoming infected.

Chickenpox is infectious from the day before the rash has appeared until the blisters have formed scabs, so keep your child away from anyone at high risk of complications during this time.

Possible complications
The most common complication is a secondary infection with streptococcal bacteria, caused by scratching the spots. Children with eczema (see p.234) are particularly prone.

Most at risk are children with a deficient immune system (because

SYMPTOMS

Incubation period: 2–3 weeks.
- Mild fever or a headache that starts a few hours before the rash appears.
- A rash, mainly on the body, made up of spots that turn into itchy blisters (see p.187). The blisters dry up in a few days and form scabs. The spots appear in batches and your child will usually have spots at different stages of development at the same time.
- Spots in the mouth can develop into ulcers and make eating uncomfortable.
- Some children with chickenpox may develop a bad cough.

they are taking oral corticosteroids or having chemotherapy, for example) and newborn babies, who can develop chickenpox if the mother contracts it late in pregnancy.

Outlook
Your child should feel better within 7–10 days of the symptoms starting. One attack of chickenpox should give lifelong immunity from this disease, but the virus remains dormant in nerve cells in the body and may cause shingles in adulthood.

ERYTHEMA INFECTIOSUM

Mildly contagious, erythema infectiosum is a viral illness that causes a red rash on both cheeks. Also known as fifth disease, it tends to be most common in the spring among children over the age of 2.

Medical treatment

There is no specific treatment needed for erythema infectiosum, but call your doctor if you are worried about your

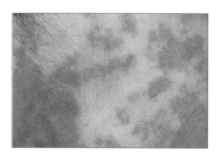

DISTINCTIVE RED CHEEKS This infection is also called "slapped cheek" disease because of the bright red rash on the cheeks.

child or if he has a blood disorder which can lead to complications. Do not take your child to the doctor's surgery because of the risk of infecting others. Your child may have a blood test to check the diagnosis.

How to help your child

Give your child paracetamol to bring the fever down and encourage him to drink plenty of fluids. He is unlikely to be infectious after the rash appears but, just in case, it is best to keep your child away from anyone who might be pregnant. If a pregnant woman contracts the disease she may suffer a miscarriage. The rash may recur over

a period of several weeks or months. Once your child has recovered from erythema infectiosum he is unlikely to get it again.

■ SYMPTOMS

Incubation period: 4–14 days.
- Bright red cheeks, as if they have been "slapped".
- A pale area around the mouth.
- Fever.
- A rash that appears 1–4 days after the redness on the cheeks and lasts for 7–10 days. The rash usually appears on the arms and legs and sometimes on the body. Blotchy or with a lacy pattern, especially on the limbs, the rash can vary according to the temperature. It may, for example, seem worse after a warm bath or after spending time out in the sun.
- Joint pain – but this is rare.

HAND, FOOT AND MOUTH DISEASE

Common in children up to the age of 4 years, hand, foot and mouth disease usually occurs in epidemics during the summer and early autumn. It is a mild viral infection which causes blisters to appear in the mouth and on the hands and feet.

How to help your child

There is no specific treatment for hand, foot and mouth disease. All you can really do is ease the symptoms. For

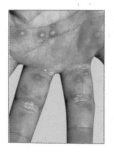

BLISTERS ON THE FINGERS In hand, foot and mouth disease, blisters commonly appear on the fingers, the backs of the hands or on the top surfaces of the feet.

example, if your child is suffering from painful mouth ulcers, give him liquid paracetamol in the appropriate dose. You may find that salt-water rinses help to soothe the pain (*see p.207*).

Make sure your child drinks plenty of fluids each day – water or milk are best. Do not let him drink fruit juices, because these are acidic and so may make the pain in his mouth worse. If your child is reluctant to eat solid food then do not force him.

The blisters on your child's hands and feet will usually clear up within

■ SYMPTOMS

Incubation period: 3–5 days.
- Mild fever.
- Blisters on the inside of the mouth, which may develop into sore, shallow ulcers.
- Child has lost appetite and does not want to eat.
- Blisters on the hands and feet, which usually appear 1 or 2 days after those in the mouth. The blisters are not usually itchy or painful.

about 3 or 4 days, and the fever should have disappeared by then, too. However, the ulcers in the mouth may last for as long as 4 weeks. Once your child has had a single attack of the disease he should be immune for life.

ROSEOLA INFANTUM

Most children will have caught roseola infantum by the time they are 2 years old. This viral infection causes a high fever, which comes on suddenly and lasts for about 4 days, followed by a rash of tiny pink spots.

Medical treatment

There is no specific treatment for roseola, but phone your doctor at once if your child has a temperature of 39°C

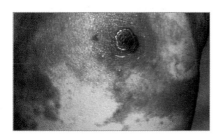

ROSEOLA RASH *In the second phase of roseola, a rash of tiny pink spots appears and lasts for about 4 days.*

(102°F) or above, if he has a febrile convulsion (*see p.292*) or is drowsy or irritable. While waiting for the doctor to arrive, try sponging your child with lukewarm water to bring down the fever or give him an appropriate dose of liquid paracetamol.

The doctor may want to do blood or urine tests to confirm the diagnosis and check for bacterial infections – meningitis, for example, produces similar symptoms. Recovery is quick. Your child should feel completely better by the time the rash has gone. Complications are rare in otherwise healthy children, but a child with a

suppressed immune system could develop hepatitis (*see p.261*) or pneumonia (*see p.227*).

SYMPTOMS

Incubation period: 5–15 days.
* A fever of 39–40°C (102–104°F), although your child may otherwise seem well.
* Sometimes, one or more febrile convulsions (*see p.292*).
* Some children also suffer from mild diarrhoea, a cough, enlarged lymph nodes in the neck and earache.

About 4 days after the start of the fever, the illness enters its second phase:
* Child's temperature suddenly goes back to normal.
* A rash of tiny pink spots appears (*see p.187*), usually on the head and trunk, and lasts for about 4 days.

SCARLET FEVER

Scarlet fever is caused by streptococcal bacteria. Once common among children, it has become rare in developed countries since the introduction of antibiotics. The most obvious feature of the illness is the scarlet rash.

Medical treatment

Call your doctor within 24 hours of the symptoms appearing. Your doctor will confirm your child has scarlet fever by looking at his symptoms and doing a throat swab culture. He will usually prescribe a 10-day course of antibiotics. Phone your doctor at once if your child's urine is red, pink or smoky, or if your child has a fever that lasts for 5 days.

How to help your child

Liquid paracetamol will help to reduce the fever and ease any pain. Make sure

that your child finishes the course of medication, and keep him away from other children until he has done so. Your child should feel better within about a week of the illness starting. If he is not his usual self by then, check with your doctor just in case – rheumatic fever is a possibility. Your child will be immune for life after one attack of scarlet fever.

Thanks to antibiotic treatment complications of scarlet fever are rare, but do include rheumatic fever, which can lead to permanent heart damage and glomerulonephritis (*see p.276*).

SYMPTOMS

Incubation period: 2–4 days.
* Vomiting.
* Fever.
* Sore throat and headache.
* Rash which appears within 12 hours of the first symptoms developing (*see p.187*). It affects the neck and chest first, then spreads rapidly. It is most dense on the neck and in the armpits and groin. It does not affect the face. The rash lasts for up to 6 days and the skin then peels.
* Cheeks are flushed and there is a pale area around the mouth.
* In the early stages the tongue has a thick white coating with projecting red spots. The coating peels by the fourth day, leaving a bright red "strawberry tongue", still with the spots.

MUMPS

A mild viral infection, mumps causes a fever and a swelling of one or both of the salivary (parotid) glands. These are in front of and below the ears, inside the angle of the jaw. Mumps was much more common among children until routine immunization began.

Medical treatment

If you think your child has mumps, phone your doctor to confirm the diagnosis. Phone immediately if your child has a severe headache (with or without vomiting) or has pain in the abdomen. A child suffering from a severe headache will be admitted to hospital for tests to rule out encephalitis or bacterial meningitis.

How to help your child

Swollen glands may be painful but some paracetamol will make your child more comfortable and reduce the fever. Give him plenty of fluids to drink but avoid fruit juices: they stimulate the flow of saliva so may make pain in the glands worse.

Children generally feel much better in about 10 days. Problems affecting the testicles and pancreas do not usually have long-term ill effects and infertility as a result of inflamed testicles is rare. Your child is usually immune to mumps after one attack.

Possible complications

Occasionally, adolescent boys with mumps develop inflamed testicles, a condition called orchitis (*see* Penis and testicle disorders, *p.277*). This starts about a week after the mumps.

Very rarely, serious disorders such as pancreatitis (inflammation of the pancreas), encephalitis and meningitis may develop, either before or after the salivary glands have become swollen.

SYMPTOMS

Incubation period: 14–24 days.
- Fever.
- Tenderness and swelling of one or both sides of the face, giving your child a puffy, hamster-like appearance. This usually comes on 1 or 2 days after the fever starts and may last 4–8 days.
- Pain in the jaw, ear and abdomen.
- Swelling of other glands.

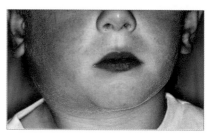

SWOLLEN GLANDS *The most obvious feature of mumps is the swelling of the salivary glands, just below the ears. The swollen glands may be painful.*

TETANUS

A serious illness affecting the central nervous system, tetanus is now rare in developed countries where children are immunized against it. Bacterial spores enter the body through a deep wound, particularly one contaminated by garden soil or animal manure.

Causes

Tetanus is caused by a poison produced by a bacterium called *Clostridium tetani*. Paradoxically, these bacteria inhabit the intestines of both humans and animals without ill effects. Because of this, clostridium bacteria can be found wherever faeces contaminate the soil.

When a wound contains infected dirt, the bacteria can spread into the bloodstream and breed. The bacterial

toxin causes the voluntary muscles of the body to contract violently and painfully – first the jaws, then the face and neck. When the toxin causes the back muscles to contract, the body may suddenly arch backwards.

Immediate action

Tetanus is a medical emergency. If you think your child is showing any of the symptoms of tetanus, call your doctor immediately or take your child to the

SYMPTOMS

Incubation period: 3–21 days.
- Cannot open the mouth because of contractions in the muscles of the jaw. This gives the condition its alternative name of lockjaw.
- The child finds it hard to swallow.
- Muscles in the face contract, making the child look as though he has a fixed smile. This is known as *risus sardonicus*.
- Spasms of muscles in the neck, back, abdomen and limbs. These spasms can be agonizingly painful and may happen over a period of 10–14 days. The spasms may make it difficult for the child to breathe.

nearest accident and emergency department for urgent treatment.

Medical treatment
If your child has cut himself and you think the wound may have been infected with contaminated soil, take him to your doctor at once. If he suspects tetanus your child will need to go into hospital. If the infection is mild – there is only stiffness around the site of infection and convulsions, if any, are weak – he may need only sedative drugs and a light diet.

More severe cases of tetanus need more urgent treatment. At first, an endotracheal tube will be inserted into the windpipe, or a tracheostomy into his trachea, to help your child breathe; muscle relaxants and sedative drugs will be administered to relieve the muscle contractions and spasms; and mechanical ventilation will keep his breathing going.

Outlook
Tetanus can still be fatal, but with prompt hospital treatment most children will recover completely. Many will feel better within 3 weeks but children who have suffered a severe attacks may take longer.

☐ PREVENTION

Your child will usually be immunized against tetanus when a baby. If he does suffer a deep wound, do not wait to see if any symptoms develop. Take him at once to the nearest accident and emergency department, even if he has been immunized against tetanus. To prevent the disease developing, the doctor may operate on the wound to clear away all the foreign bodies and dead tissue. Your child may be given further injections of the tetanus vaccine.

WHOOPING COUGH

Also known as pertussis, this bacterial infection is most dangerous in babies under 6 months. Many children in developed countries are immunized against it, so it is rare. The characteristic symptom is a cough, sometimes followed by a whoop.

Medical treatment
Call your doctor within 24 hours if your baby is under 6 months and has a cough, or if your child vomits from coughing or has a cough that lasts more than a week. Phone at once if your child's tongue or lips turn blue during a coughing attack or if he has a seizure.

Your doctor may take a sample from your child's throat and send it for laboratory testing so the diagnosis can be confirmed. Antibiotics can help children recover more quickly, but are effective only if they are given in the early stages. If your child turns blue or has had a seizure he may be taken into hospital, especially if he is under 6 months old.

If you have other children they will be given a 10-day course of antibiotics to lessen the severity of the infection if they do get it.

How to help your child
Give your child plenty of fluids to drink and soft, but not crumbly, food to eat. When he has a coughing attack it may help if you slap him gently on the back.

If necessary, your doctor will show you how to help clear lung secretions with simple physiotherapy techniques. Your child may need someone with him at night. Try to get other adults to take turns with you to prevent you becoming exhausted.

Outlook
Your child may continue to cough for several months. If a child is generally ill, or the cough has not improved after 6 weeks, a chest X-ray may need to be arranged. However, permanent lung damage is rare. In some children, the cough may come back if they catch a viral infection in the following year.

☐ SYMPTOMS

Incubation period: about 7 days.
- Short, dry cough, often occurring only at night.
- Runny nose.
- Slight fever.
- Sore, pink and runny eyes as in conjunctivitis.

The next stage of the illness may last between 8–12 weeks with the following symptoms:
- Bouts of 10–20 short, dry coughs that may happen during the day and at night.
- Long attacks of coughing followed by a sharp indrawing of breath, which may produce a "crowing" or "whooping" sound – babies may not "whoop".
- Vomiting brought on by the persistent coughing.
- Pauses in breathing – i.e. for more than 10 seconds.
- Seizures.

Very occasionally, an air passage may become blocked by mucus, causing either part of a lung to collapse or pneumonia to develop.

GLANDULAR FEVER

Glandular fever is caused by the Epstein-Barr virus, which attacks the white blood cells that fight infection in the body. Also known as infectious mononucleosis, the disease may be difficult to diagnose because of its similarities to other illnesses. It is most common in adolescents and young adults but can infect people of any age, including young children.

Medical treatment

If you think your child may have glandular fever, take him to the doctor as soon as possible. A specific blood test, called a Paul-Bunnell test, is the best way to confirm the diagnosis. The test looks for antibodies to the virus and for an increased number of monocytes, the white blood cells that give glandular fever its medical name.

A positive test also rules out other possible infections with similar symptoms. Glandular fever shares the same kind of muscular pains as influenza (*see p.225*) and a similar sore throat and infected tonsils as tonsillitis (*see p.223*). Occasionally, the illness starts with a rash that is similar to rubella (*see p.264*).

The doctor will not be able to offer any treatment. As the infection is caused by a virus, antibiotics do not help and may even bring on a rash that affects the whole body. He will probably advise bed rest until the fever settles down.

How to help your child

You and your child will have to accept that the disease needs to run its course. However, you may be able to help alleviate some of the symptoms. Make sure he has plenty of cool drinks and does not get overtired. Giving him paracetamol will help to reduce a high fever. He may want to stay in bed or he may be happier pottering around the house.

The infection is easily spread – one of its common names is the "kissing disease" because it can be spread by mouth-to-mouth contact – so he should avoid very close contact with other children.

There are various measures you can take to boost your child's immune system so that he is better able to fight the virus. Encourage him to eat a healthy diet that includes at least 5 portions of fruit and vegetables a day, and oily fish twice a week.

Any nutritional deficiency can make his tiredness worse, so give him a multivitamin and mineral supplement. If he will not eat oily fish, buy high-strength cod liver oil and add it to cod or tuna.

Various nutritional and herbal supplements may help to restore a healthy immune system by boosting the body's ability to heal itself. The herbal immunity enhancer echinacea (*see p.322*) can be taken continuously or rotated with other antiviral herbal treatments. Homeopathic remedies (*see p.321*) can be taken alongside herbal therapy. Visit a homeopath to get advice about your child's constitutional remedy – giving it at high strength may boost his ability for self-healing.

Possible complications

The most common complication of glandular fever is hepatitis (*see p.261*). More rarely, other complications may include pneumonia (*see p.227*) and rupture of the spleen. Problems of the nervous system, blood circulation and breathing may also develop.

Outlook

Most children will be able go back to school after a couple of weeks but some may need to rest for longer. Once back at school your child should still avoid energetic sports for a few weeks so that he does not get too tired. A few children develop chronic fatigue syndrome (*see p.296*).

☐ SYMPTOMS

Incubation period: about 10 days.
- Swollen lymph nodes, or "glands", in the neck just under the middle of the jaw, and/or in the armpits or groin.
- High fever of about 39–40°C (102–104°F).
- The fever may last only a few days or for several weeks.
- Extremely sore throat.
- Tiredness and lethargy.
- Weight loss and lack of appetite.
- Headache.
- Spleen may become enlarged.
- May be muscle pain.
- Perhaps a rash.
- Tender, painful abdomen.

☐ RELAXATION

Encourage your child to try some relaxation techniques such as yoga and abdominal breathing. Keep the sessions short, regular and as child-friendly as you can. Therapeutic massage or other touch therapies such as aromatherapy (*see p.325*) are also useful for reducing any stress and tension your child may be experiencing, and for helping to restore a feeling of wellbeing.

MALARIA

A serious health problem in tropical and subtropical areas, malaria is increasing elsewhere as more and more people travel to regions where the disease is prevalent. Malaria is caused by parasites that enter the blood after a bite by an infected mosquito.

Causes

Malaria is caused by a protozoa called *Plasmodium*, which is transmitted from one person to the next by mosquitoes that feed on blood. From the liver, the parasite periodically invades the red blood cells when the symptoms of the disease develop and take hold.

Medical treatment

Call your doctor at once if your child has any symptoms of malaria. He will be taken to hospital where his blood will be tested for the parasites. If the tests are positive he will be treated with antimalarial drugs.

Take your child to the nearest hospital at once if he has any of the following: seizures, drowsiness or yellowing or extreme paleness of the skin. If there are complications, he may need treatment in an intensive care unit. If he is treated quickly he

PROTECTION

If you plan to visit a region where malaria is common, you and your family will need to take antimalarial drugs for several days before you depart and for the duration of your stay. Ask your doctor about which to take as different drugs are recommended for travel in different countries. Try to avoid mosquito bites by wearing protective clothing, applying anti-mosquito lotions and sleeping under mosquito nets.

SYMPTOMS

Symptoms of malaria usually develop 6–30 days after infection. But sometimes they may appear as much as a year later if the child has taken antimalarial drugs which have been only partly effective. The main symptoms are:
• High fever alternating with shivering.
• Headache.

Other symptoms include:
• Nausea and vomiting.
• Pain in the abdomen and back.
• Joint pain.

Falciparum malaria can result in very serious complications affecting the kidneys, liver, brain and blood.

may be better in only a few days or up to 2 weeks, depending on the severity of the attack. The more severe form, falciparum malaria, may be life-threatening if complications affect the brain or the kidneys.

TYPHOID FEVER

Typhoid fever, also known as enteric fever, is caused by bacteria that infect the digestive tract. Children usually catch the disease by consuming food or water contaminated with bacteria from the faeces of an infected person.

Causes

Typhoid fever is caused by a bacterium called *Salmonella typhi*. A similar but less virulent illness, paratyphoid fever is caused by the bacterium *Salmonella paratyphi*. Once inside the digestive tract, bacteria enter the bloodstream, causing a fever and other symptoms of blood poisoning. Typhoid is common wherever sanitation is poor and where flies carry the bacteria from human faeces to supplies of food and water.

Medical treatment

Call your doctor within 24 hours of the appearance of possible typhoid symptoms. If the doctor suspects that your child might have typhoid fever, he will probably be taken into hospital where the diagnosis can be confirmed by testing his urine or faeces, or by carrying out a blood test. He will be treated with antibiotics, which may be given intravenously if his symptoms are severe.

SYMPTOMS

Incubation period: 7–14 days.
• Fever that rises to 39–40°C (102–104°F) and stays at that level without daily fluctuations for up to 4 weeks.
• Headache.
• Lack of energy.
• Pain in the abdomen.
• Constipation or diarrhoea.
• Rash of raised pink spots on the abdomen and chest which develops during the second week of illness and lasts for about a day.
• Intestinal bleeding/perforation or other complications may develop by the third week if illness is not treated.

A child will usually start to feel better several days after the start of treatment and be completely recovered within 2 or 3 weeks.

Possible complications
With prompt treatment, complications such as internal bleeding, pneumonia (*see p.227*), meningitis (*see p.294*) and cholecystitis are rare.

Protection
The typhoid vaccine will give several years' protection against the disease although, for some countries, you may need a booster before travelling.

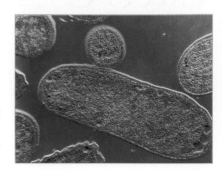

SALMONELLA TYPHI *BACTERIA These bacteria are responsible for typhoid fever. They invade the wall of the small intestine before entering the bloodstream.*

HIV INFECTION AND AIDS

Most of the children affected by HIV (human immunodeficiency virus) contract the virus from their mother before or during birth. Treating the mother during pregnancy reduces the risk of passing on the virus. HIV infection produces few symptoms but it damages the immune system, leading to AIDS (acquired immune deficiency syndrome) so that illnesses, such as pneumonia, can develop.

Causes
HIV infection is transmitted through blood-to-blood contact or via blood products, as in blood transfusion. The HIV virus particles attach themselves to the surface of white blood cells, destroying them and thus reducing the efficiency of the immune system.

The condition gradually debilitates the body, eventually leading to full-blown AIDS when the immune system is so weak that potentially fatal illness such as pneumonia (*see p.227*) and tuberculosis develop unhindered.

Nearly all cases of HIV in children are due to transmission from their HIV-positive mothers, during either pregnancy or birth. This is called perinatal transmission.

Medical treatment
Children who are infected with HIV or who have developed AIDS require careful medical supervision. If the doctor suspects that a baby has HIV,

both parents are given counselling. With the parents' consent, the baby is given a blood test. If HIV antibodies are present, the baby has been exposed to the virus. This is not the same thing as infection. Although the mother's HIV antibodies may remain in the baby's blood for a year or more, a different test called HIV PCR can positively confirm or exclude the presence of the virus in the first 4 months of life.

The doctor may prescribe drugs, such as zidovudine, in combination to attack the virus and to slow down the development and progress of the disease. Regular injections of gamma globulin and antibacterial drugs can also help the child, by preventing or fighting opportunistic infections, such as pneumonia.

How to help your child
If you are an HIV-positive mother, you are advised not to breastfeed your

□ **SYMPTOMS**

Most infants infected before or around the time of birth will have symptoms before they are 2 years old. But some may not develop symptoms until they are more than 5 years old, and a few cases have been diagnosed as late as 12 years. Some of the many possible symptoms in children are:

- *Failure to thrive.*
- *Recurrent diarrhoea.*
- *Enlarged lymph nodes in the neck, armpits and groin.*
- *Frequent infections, particularly of the ear and sinuses, and often with fever.*
- *Attacks of pneumonia.*
- *Delay in normal development.*

child because of the small risk of transmitting the virus in your milk. If you were treated while pregnant and also avoid breastfeeding, the chances of passing on the infection are less than 5 per cent. If your child has HIV infection or AIDS, you will be given advice on how to manage the illness.

Outlook
An increasing number of HIV-infected children are surviving into adulthood. But the progressive nature of the infection means that nearly all infected people eventually succumb to it.

UROGENITAL PROBLEMS

Urinary tract infections cover a range of disorders, from bedwetting to glomerulonephritis.

Most urinary tract infections, such as cystitis and urethritis, clear up quickly with treatment. However, all urinary infections and any other disorders affecting the kidneys, the bladder or the genitals need medical attention to check for any structural defect that may have been present from birth. Most serious kidney disorders, such as glomerulonephritis, are now treatable, including the most common childhood kidney cancer, Wilms' tumour.

ANATOMY OF THE UROGENITAL SYSTEM

▶ **GIRL'S UROGENITAL SYSTEM**
A girl's urinary system – kidneys, ureters and bladder – filters waste products, surplus water and excess salts from the blood. The genital system, made up of two ovaries, the uterus, and various ducts, produces hormones and, from puberty, one or more eggs every month.

▶ **BOY'S UROGENITAL SYSTEM**
A boy's urinary system also has kidneys, ureters and bladder. Urine and, after puberty, semen pass out of the body through the urethra and penis. The testicles produce hormones that are responsible for the male characteristics that appear at puberty.

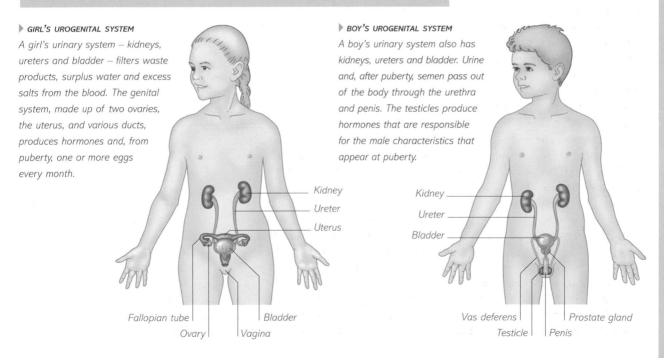

Kidney
Ureter
Uterus
Fallopian tube
Ovary
Bladder
Vagina

Kidney
Ureter
Bladder
Vas deferens
Testicle
Prostate gland
Penis

BED WETTING

Children vary greatly in the age they become dry at night, but few can control their bladders before the age of about 3 and bed wetting, or enuresis, is common. Reliable control day and night may be gained any time between the ages of 3 and 5. There is usually no need to worry unless your child continues to wet the bed after the age of 5 or starts again after being dry.

HELPFUL TIPS

- Constipation may put pressure on the bladder so try to help your child have regular bowel movements.
- Look carefully at your child's diet. Think about the foods that may cause bladder irritation. Keep a food diary and if you identify foods that may be causing the problem, eliminate them from her diet.
- Encourage your child to avoid drinks, such as chocolate and cola products, that contain caffeine.
- If your child has experienced an emotional upset, such as moving house or changing school, or if she feels insecure after the birth of a baby brother or sister, take more time with her, give her a relaxing massage or practise some calming yoga together.
- Homeopathic remedies such as Equisetum or Causticum can help (*see p.321*).

STAR CHART *Sticking a star on a chart after each dry night is a satisfying way for your child to mark progress. The chart also allows family members to see how well the child is doing and to give praise for good results.*

Causes of bed wetting

Bed wetting usually happens because the parts of the nervous system that control the bladder are not yet mature. It may also develop if a child has a urinary tract infection (*see p.275*) or is anxious (*see* Anxiety and fears, *pp.131–132*). Rarely, a congenital defect of the urinary tract or diabetes mellitus (*see p.309*) is the cause.

Medical treatment

Consult your doctor if you are worried about your child wetting the bed, especially if she is 5 years old or over, or if the problem starts again after your child has been dry at night for a prolonged period, usually between 6 and 12 months.

The doctor will examine your child and will test a urine sample for infection or diabetes (*see p.309*). If a physical cause for the bed wetting is found, treatment will be given; for example, antibiotics may be prescribed to treat a urinary tract infection. If no physical reason is found, follow the advice given here (*see also* Toilet training, *p.74*).

How to help your child

A child may be less likely to wet the bed if she gets into the habit of passing urine at regular times during the day and just before going to sleep. Never punish your child if she does have a bed-wetting accident or you will increase her anxiety and make the problem worse. Always praise your child for dry nights.

A chart on which your child can stick a star after each dry night may help her motivation (*see left*). Some children become completely dry after using a star chart for a few weeks without having any other treatment. But if your child becomes discouraged because the chart reflects poor results, stop using it.

If methods involving praise and encouragement are unsuccessful, try an enuresis alarm (available from your doctor or local clinic). This device has a detector, which is placed under the bottom sheet and activates a buzzer if urine is passed. The alarm wakes the child, who stops the urine stream and gets up to go to the toilet. The amount of urine passed before the child wakes becomes less and less. After a few months, most children wake up before the alarm starts or sleep through the night without wetting the bed. Remove the alarm when your child has been dry at night for 6 weeks, but use it again if the bed wetting returns.

Outlook

Most children stop wetting the bed without medical treatment. However, some benefit from using medication called DDAVP, which is a spray made from a naturally occurring hormone that has the effect of concentrating the urine. Those who are treated often improve within a few months. The older a child is, however, the longer it may take for the condition to improve.

URINARY TRACT INFECTIONS

In general, girls suffer from more infections of the urinary tract than boys, but newborn male babies are more susceptible to infections than female babies. An infection may affect the urethra (causing urethritis), the bladder (causing cystitis) and/or the kidneys (causing pyelonephritis). Prompt treatment prevents scarring of the kidneys, which is most likely to affect children under 5. Scarring of the kidneys from recurrent infections may lead to high blood pressure or kidney failure in adult life.

Causes
The most common cause of urinary tract infections comes from bacteria which enter the urethra from the rectum. Bacteria may also spread to the urinary tract via the bloodstream. The reason girls are more prone to urinary infections than boys is because their urethras are shorter.

Children who have urinary reflux are especially vulnerable to infection. In this congenital condition, when the bladder empties, some urine passes backwards towards the kidneys. A tendency to reflux usually disappears without treatment by 9 years of age.

Children who have congenital malformations of the urinary tract,

suffer from chronic constipation (*see p.255*), or have kidneys scarred from a previous infection, are also more susceptible to infection

Medical treatment
Your child should be seen by a doctor within 24 hours if she shows signs of having a urinary tract infection. The doctor will probably collect a urine sample from your child or ask you to do so. A baby suffering from urinary infection symptoms may have to go to hospital to have urine withdrawn from the bladder via a hollow needle passed through the skin. The urine is tested to rule out an underlying disorder and to confirm that infection is the cause of the symptoms.

If an infection of the urinary tract is confirmed, the doctor may prescribe oral antibiotics which may be given for up to a week. A seriously ill child may need to be treated in hospital with intravenous antibiotics. A day or two after treatment for infection has ceased, your child's urine will be tested again and if there is still some infection, she may be given another course of antibiotics.

In some circumstances, further investigations may need to be carried out to see if your child's kidneys have been scarred or if there is a structural abnormality of the urinary tract. Special tests for urinary reflux may

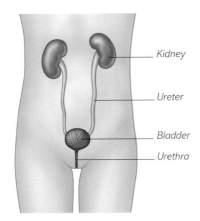

SITES OF INFECTION *Infections of the urinary tract may affect only the urethra, but more commonly spread upwards to affect the bladder or the kidneys.*

Kidney

Ureter

Bladder

Urethra

☐ **SYMPTOMS**

In children under 2 years of age, the symptoms include:
• Fever.
• Diarrhoea.
• Vomiting.
• Lack of energy or irritability.

In older children, symptoms are usually more specific, and may include:
• Burning sensation on passing urine.
• Passing urine increasingly often.
• Pain affecting the lower back or one side of the abdomen.
• Bed wetting after being dry at night.
• Urine that is red, pink or smoky in colour, due to the presence of blood.
• Fever.

be performed in some children. Because children with these conditions are often prone to recurrent infections, they may be prescribed antibiotics for several years, as a preventive measure.

How to help your child
Give your child plenty of fluids to drink. A high fluid intake dilutes the urine, easing the pain and discomfort when passing urine and helps to get rid of bacteria. It may also help to boost her immune system, improve her general health and stimulate her resistance to infection.

To prevent further infections, encourage your child to pass urine at least every 4 hours (or before each meal) and before going to bed. After your child uses the toilet, show her how to wipe her bottom from front to back to prevent bacteria spreading from her rectum to her urethra. Encourage her to bath or shower regularly, without irritants, such as scented soaps or bubble bath. Constipation should always be treated.

GLOMERULONEPHRITIS

This is an inflammation of the glomeruli, the filtering units in the kidneys. The inflamed glomeruli produce less urine and let blood and protein into the urine. It usually affects both kidneys and may follow an infection by streptococcal bacteria or by viruses.

BLOOD IN URINE
The presence of blood gives urine an abnormal appearance. It looks darker and cloudier than normal clear, pale-yellow urine.

Medical treatment
Phone your doctor at once if you think your child has glomerulonephritis. She will probably need to go to hospital, where her urine will be tested and her intake and output of fluid measured. If the diagnosis is confirmed, she will need to stay in hospital for treatment. To lessen the strain on the kidneys and prevent the accumulation of fluids, your child may be put on a diet that is low in sodium and protein, and her intake of fluids may be restricted. If your child does not want to, she will not need to stay in bed.

If the condition was caused by a bacterial infection, your child may be given antibiotics. If she has high blood pressure, this may need to be treated until it returns to normal.

With treatment, the condition usually clears up within a week. Glomerulonephritis does not usually

SYMPTOMS

In post-infective glomerulonephritis, the symptoms begin about a week after the infection. Whatever the cause, the main symptoms are:

- Urine that is red, pink or smoky in colour, caused by the presence of blood (*see* photograph, *left*).
- Passing a smaller amount of urine than usual.
- Sometimes, a headache.

Fluid may also accumulate in the tissues, leading to swelling, particularly of the face and legs. High blood pressure is a rare complication.

have any lasting effect on a child's kidneys and it does not often happen again. Very rarely, it may be followed by nephrotic syndrome (*see below*).

NEPHROTIC SYNDROME

Nephrotic syndrome is an uncommon disorder, mainly affecting children aged between 1 and 6. A large amount of protein is lost via the kidneys and the reduced levels of protein in the blood leads to oedema (accumulation of excess fluid in the body's tissues).

Medical treatment
Your child should be seen by a doctor within 24 hours if parts of her body are swollen. The doctor will examine her and test her urine for protein. If nephrotic syndrome is suspected, she will need to go to hospital for further tests. If the diagnosis is confirmed, she will receive corticosteroids in hospital.

Within 10 days, as the excess fluid in the body is excreted by the kidneys, there should be an improvement in the oedema, bringing a rapid fall in weight. Your child will probably be kept in hospital until tests show a marked reduction in the amount of protein being lost in the urine.

How to help your child
Once your child is home again from hospital, you may be asked to test a sample of her urine every day, using strips that change colour when protein is present.

If the test shows that protein is present in the urine, phone your doctor for advice. Children who have nephrotic syndrome are susceptible

SYMPTOMS

- Swelling of parts of the body, usually developing gradually over a period of several weeks.
- Reduction in the quantity of urine.
- Weight gain.
- Sometimes, diarrhoea, loss of appetite and unusual tiredness.

to infections and to the formation of blood clots in veins.

Outlook
Most children recover fully with no further problems. For those who have one or more relapses, corticosteroids and/or another medication are prescribed for a year or more.

PENIS AND TESTICLE DISORDERS

A variety of penis problems can affect young boys. These include a tight foreskin, a tight foreskin stuck in the retracted position (paraphimosis), inflammation of the tip of the penis and foreskin (balanitis) and an abnormally placed urethral opening (hypospadias). The most common disorders of the testicle are an abnormal collection of fluid around a testicle (a hydrocele) and an undescended testicle. Adolescent boys are prone to the disorders of testicular torsion and inflammation of the testicles (orchitis).

TIGHT FORESKIN

In the first few years of life, a boy's foreskin cannot usually be pulled back over the tip of his penis. Never try to retract your son's foreskin by force or you may injure the tissues, resulting in bleeding, inflammation and the formation of scar tissue.

In most boys, retraction of the foreskin becomes possible during the second year of life, but in some boys it may not happen until they are about 4 years old. After this age, inability to pull back the foreskin is abnormal.

Causes

A tight foreskin may be due to the strands of tissue that attach it to the penis at birth remaining for a longer time than normal. It may also be due to phimosis, an abnormally narrow opening in the foreskin (*see below*).

Phimosis may be congenital but is sometimes due to scarring caused by recurrent inflammation (*see* Balanitis, *p.278*) or by forceful attempts to retract the foreskin. A boy with phimosis is at increased risk of urinary tract infections (*see p.275*).

Medical treatment

Take your child to a doctor if he is older than 4 years and his foreskin cannot be retracted and/or he is having problems with passing urine. The doctor will examine your son and, if he has phimosis, may recommend circumcision, an operation to remove the foreskin (*see p.278*). If the foreskin is attached to the penis and the diameter of the outlet is normal, the tissues may be separated surgically. Both operations are performed under general anaesthetic.

□ **SYMPTOMS**

Phimosis *may have only one symptom – difficulty in retracting the foreskin. But if your son does have phimosis, the narrowed opening may cause the following symptoms:*
- Ballooning of the foreskin when the child passes urine.
- A narrow stream of urine.

Balanitis *causes symptoms such as:*
- Swelling of the penis and, in uncircumcised boys, the foreskin.
- Pain or itching.
- White discharge from the penis.
- Genital area may be red and moist.

Testicular torsion *causes symptoms such as:*
- Sudden, severe pain in the abdomen.
- Severe pain in the testicle.
- The affected testicle may be noticeably higher than normal in the scrotum.
- Possibly, nausea and vomiting.
- After a few hours, the scrotum may become swollen, red and tender.

Orchitis *causes symptoms such as:*
- Pain in the testicle.
- Sometimes, fever.

□ **PENIS CARE**

- Help your son learn to wash his penis in the bath or shower. Remember that retraction of the foreskin may not be possible until he is about 4 years of age, so gently wash the area without attempting to retract the foreskin by force.
- After washing in warm water, gently pat the skin of the penis dry with a towel. Try not to rub the skin to avoid further chafing.
- Clothe him in cotton pants rather than synthetics.

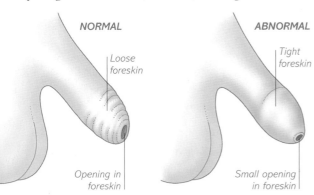

NORMAL

Loose foreskin

Opening in foreskin

ABNORMAL

Tight foreskin

Small opening in foreskin

PHIMOSIS *When there is an abnormally small opening in the foreskin, the foreskin becomes tight and is hard to retract over the glans of the penis. Passing urine may also be difficult.*

PARAPHIMOSIS

This condition is the result of forcibly retracting a foreskin that is affected by phimosis (*see p.277*). It may cause the foreskin to become stuck in the retracted position, causing swelling and pain.

Medical treatment

If your child's retracted foreskin has become stuck, take him to the nearest accident and emergency department at once. He will be anaesthetized or sedated so that the doctor can gently compress the penis and return the foreskin to its normal position.

In some cases, the doctor may need to make an incision in the foreskin to free it. Paraphimosis will probably recur unless circumcision (*see below*) is performed to correct your son's phimosis.

BALANITIS

An inflammation of the foreskin and the head of the penis (glans), balanitis is usually caused by a bacterial or fungal infection. It is often the result of inadequate cleaning of the penis. Phimosis (*see p.277*) tends to make cleaning difficult and so may increase the likelihood of inflammation

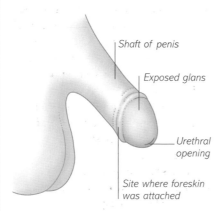

Shaft of penis

Exposed glans

Urethral opening

Site where foreskin was attached

CIRCUMCISION This operation involves removing the foreskin to expose the glans. It may be recommended if the foreskin is tight or a boy suffers from recurrent balanitis.

occurring. Balanitis may also appear as a reaction to chemicals in detergents or soaps, or to irritating materials such as wool.

Medical treatment

If the balanitis does not clear up with self-help treatment (*see below*) within 3 days, take your child to see a doctor. He will probably be given either an antifungal or antibiotic cream or an oral antibiotic. These will usually clear up the infection within a week.

If your son suffers from recurrent attacks of balanitis, the doctor may recommend circumcision (*see below left*). You could also think about boosting his immune system to help him resist infection (*see p.163*).

How to help your child

In most cases, balanitis clears up when hygiene is improved. Make sure your son washes his penis and genital area twice daily. After the inflammation has disappeared, the penis should be washed thoroughly every day to prevent recurrence. If the balanitis is due to irritation by chemicals or material, make sure that your son wears cotton underwear and that his clothes are thoroughly rinsed after washing. He should also avoid using scented soaps.

HYDROCELE

This painless swelling of the scrotum occurs when fluid accumulates in the space around a testicle. Hydroceles are common in newborn babies, and they usually disappear without treatment by the age of 6 months. The sudden appearance of a hydrocele in an older boy may be the result of an injury.

Medical treatment

If a scrotal swelling persists beyond the age of 6 months, or if it makes its first appearance after this age, take

your son to a doctor. In these cases, the hydrocele may be associated with an inguinal hernia (*see Hernia, p.260*), and will need surgical treatment.

A hydrocele that suddenly appears in an older boy should also be assessed by a doctor. It is likely to be caused by an injury and will probably get better without treatment. Tests, including ultrasound scanning, will be done to exclude damage to the testicle.

UNDESCENDED TESTICLE

In some boys one or, less frequently, both testicles fail to descend into the scrotum before birth. All newborn male babies are examined to determine whether the testicles have descended normally. If a testicle has not descended, a further examination is carried out at about 3 months because descent often occurs naturally up to this age.

Medical treatment

If a boy's testicle has still not descended at 3 months of age he will probably need an operation to move the testicle down into the scrotum. This is usually when he is 2 or 3 years old. As long as the operation is carried out at the right time, your child's sexual development and fertility should not be affected. However, there may be a slightly increased risk of testicular cancer developing later in life.

TESTICULAR TORSION

This happens when a child's spermatic cord (the cord from which the testicle is suspended) becomes twisted, cutting off or reducing the blood supply to the testicle. Testicular torsion causes acute pain. If the torsion is not corrected within hours, the affected testicle may be permanently damaged.

Medical treatment

If your son is experiencing a pain in one of his testicles, call an ambulance or take him to the nearest hospital accident and emergency department immediately. An operation can be carried out to untwist the spermatic cord and stitch both the testicles to the scrotum to prevent torsion recurring. A testicle that has been irreversibly damaged will be removed.

Provided treatment is carried out in time, your child's testicle should function normally. If a testicle has been removed, the remaining testicle should allow your son to have a normal sex life when adult.

ORCHITIS

This is an inflammation that affects one or both testicles and is usually a complication of mumps (*see p.268*). However, it can occasionally be caused by a bacterial infection that enters through the penis and spreads along the vas deferens. The affected testicle is red and swollen, and can also be extremely painful.

Medical treatment

If your son has not had mumps within the past 2 weeks, call an ambulance or take him to the nearest accident and emergency department immediately in case he is suffering from testicular torsion (*see p.278*).

Alternatively, if your son has had mumps recently, take him to your doctor within 24 hours. Give him paracetamol to relieve the pain. If there is a bacterial infection, the doctor may prescribe antibiotics. Orchitis is not serious and usually disappears within a week. However, in some cases, the illness may lead to reduced fertility in adult life.

VULVOVAGINITIS

This usually minor inflammation of the vulva and vagina is common in young girls. Common causes include poor hygiene, tight clothing, bubble baths or scented soap. In some girls, there may be no obvious cause for the symptoms; the vulva and vaginal lining are just particularly sensitive and an itch is quickly made worse by scratching.

Causes

As well as the causes given above, bacteria from the rectum may infect the vulva and vagina if your daughter wipes her bottom from back to front after a bowel movement. Less often, a bacterial infection may be due to the presence of a foreign body (such as a crayon or a forgotten tampon) in the vagina. A possible cause in young girls may be an infestation by threadworms (*see p.262*). After puberty, thrush is a common cause.

Medical treatment

If she is very uncomfortable, has a vaginal discharge or experiences pain when she passes urine, your daughter should be seen by a doctor within 24 hours. You should also consult a doctor if other symptoms persist for more than 2 weeks. The doctor will

examine your daughter and, if it is possible that she has an object lodged in her vagina, she will need to go to hospital where the object can be removed under a general anaesthetic.

A vaginal swab may be taken to check for infection. If she does have a bacterial infection, an antibiotic cream or oral antibiotic may be prescribed. An antifungal cream or pessaries (which are inserted into the vagina) may be used to combat thrush.

For persistent irritation when there is no infection, the doctor may prescribe an oestrogen cream, which thickens the skin of the vulva and the vaginal lining.

How to help your child

Vulvovaginitis that is not caused by an infection usually clears up with self-help treatment (*see p.215*).

SYMPTOMS

- Inflammation, soreness and itchiness affecting the genital area.
- Pain on passing urine.
- Greenish or greyish-yellow vaginal discharge, if bacterial infection is the cause. The discharge may be smelly if the infection is caused by a foreign body in the vagina.
- Thick, white vaginal discharge, if thrush is the cause.

Twice a day for a week, your daughter should sit in a bath to wash her genital area, without using scented soaps or bubble baths. After washing, apply a barrier cream such as zinc ointment to her genital area.

Your daughter should wear loose-fitting underwear made of cotton but not synthetics. These should be changed daily.

If possible, encourage her to expose her genital area to the air for a little while each day.

To keep the vulva and vagina free of irritating faecal material, make sure she wipes her bottom from front to back after a bowel movement.

MUSCLE & BONE
DISORDERS
Children are prone to musculoskeletal problems, but their powers of recovery are good.

CHILDREN ARE AT HIGH RISK from problems with their muscles, bones and joints – fractures, sprains and strains, dislocations and cramp are commonplace. This is because they are generally very active yet their bones and joints are immature and still growing. Some disorders, such as Duchenne muscular dystrophy, result from genetic abnormalities or birth defects. Minor musculoskeletal disorders, such as in-toeing and out-toeing, are quite common.

ANATOMY OF THE SKELETON

▶ **HOW THE SKELETON WORKS**

The skeleton is the strong internal framework that provides support for the body. As well as supporting the soft tissues, the skeleton also protects the organs and provides anchorage for muscles. During childhood, the skeleton is continually growing and changing shape. In childhood, most of the long bones contain cartilage. The cartilage in these areas grows and absorbs calcium to develop into bone. Limb, hand and foot bones, the areas in which most growth occurs, are made up of a diaphysis (shaft), which is the main part of the bone, and an epiphysis (growing region) at either one or both ends. During childhood, the epiphyses gradually turn to bone, leaving a cartilage plate where growth continues until adult height and size is reached in late adolescence.

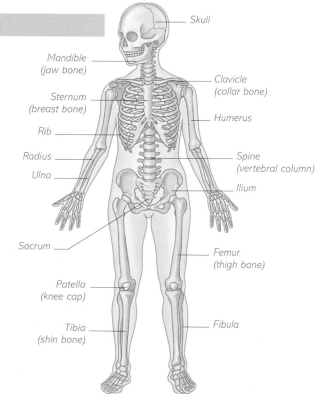

Skull

Mandible (jaw bone)

Clavicle (collar bone)

Sternum (breast bone)

Humerus

Rib

Radius

Spine (vertebral column)

Ulna

Ilium

Sacrum

Femur (thigh bone)

Patella (knee cap)

Tibia (shin bone)

Fibula

LIMPING

A limp is usually caused by a minor injury that will get better on its own. It could, however, be caused by an underlying disorder that requires prompt treatment to prevent permanent disability. Never ignore a limp in a child.

Causes
Pain from disorders involving a joint, muscle or bone around the hip or in the leg or foot may cause a limp. The site of pain can be misleading; an abnormality in the hip may cause pain in the thigh or knee.

The following are some possible causes: irritable hip (see p.285); bone or joint infection (see p.288); Perthes' disease (see p.286); muscle strain (see below); juvenile chronic arthritis (see p.288); verruca (see Warts, p.231); or a sharp object in the sole of the foot.

A child may limp because his legs are unequal lengths. A bone may be short from birth or may fail to grow because of a spinal cord abnormality or cerebral palsy (see p.295), leading to muscle weakness of one side of the body. A limp may be due to apparent shortening of a leg, as a result of congenital hip dislocation (see p.286) that was detected late or of spinal curvature such as scoliosis (see p.287).

Children with a disorder of the muscles and/or the nervous system, such as muscular dystrophy (see p.289) or cerebral palsy (see p.295), may have muscle weakness or a lack of coordination, causing walking problems that resemble a limp. A limp may also develop as part of a behavioural problem in a child with emotional or psychological difficulties.

Medical treatment
Take your child to the doctor if he has a limp with no obvious cause, such as a splinter, or is old enough to walk but refuses to do so. Call a doctor at once if your child also has a fever, rash or hot, swollen joints – these could signal a bone or joint infection that requires immediate medical treatment.

The doctor will examine your child and may carry out X-rays, blood tests and/or scans to help diagnose the cause of the problem. Your child may be referred to a paediatrician or orthopaedic surgeon and may need to go into hospital for further tests or observation. The treatment will depend on the underlying cause.

A limp due to a minor injury will probably get better within a few days. A limp due to most other causes should disappear once the underlying problem has been treated. In a few cases, the underlying cause, such as unequal leg length or muscular weakness, cannot be cured, and walking problems may remain.

STRAINS AND SPRAINS

Strains and sprains are often caused by falls or vigorous physical activity. If a muscle is overstretched and the muscle fibres are damaged, it may result in a strain. A joint is sprained when one or more of its ligaments is overstretched or torn. Unless they are severe, such injuries can usually be treated at home.

Medical treatment
Take your child to the doctor if the pain and swelling are severe just after the injury has occurred – for example, if the child cannot walk on an injured ankle. You should also take your child to the doctor if there are any milder symptoms that have shown no improvement within a few days.

The doctor will examine the injury and may arrange for an X-ray to be taken to rule out the possibility of fractured bones (see p.283).

The injured part may need to be strapped or wrapped in a compression bandage. Your child may also have to use crutches for a leg injury or wear a sling if the arm is affected.

SYMPTOMS
- Pain and tenderness, increasing with movement of the affected area.
- Swelling in the injured spot.
- Muscle spasm (tightness of a muscle produced by involuntary contractions).
- Limping, if a leg is affected.
- Bruising, which may appear a few days after the injury.

For a very severe strain or sprain, non-steroidal anti-inflammatory drugs (NSAIDs) may be prescribed to reduce the pain and the swelling and to speed the healing process. Your child may have to wear a splint or plaster cast.

How to help your child

For the first 48 hours or so after the injury has occurred, you should treat a sprain by means of the four-step process known as RICE – rest, ice, compression and elevation (*see* First aid, *p.339*).

Do not apply heat to the injury for the first 48 hours, but do give your child paracetamol if he needs pain relief. The pain and swelling should begin to ease after 1 or 2 days of rest, and your child may begin to exercise the sprained or strained limb gently. Homeopathic creams such as arnica or rhus tox may also be helpful if taken straight after the injury.

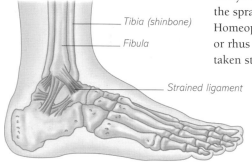

Tibia (shinbone)

Fibula

Strained ligament

SPRAINED ANKLE *The ankle is the most commonly sprained joint. The injury may occur during a fall when the foot is twisted on to its outside edge.*

Outlook

A minor strain or a sprain should heal within 2 weeks. Once the pain has disappeared, your doctor may suggest exercises that will strengthen the affected part or he may refer your child to a physiotherapist. If the affected ligament or muscle is allowed to heal properly and is exercised, it will recover fully and not be permanently weakened.

Preventing strains and sprains

Teach your child to warm up before taking part in any sport or strenuous physical activity. A warm-up routine should include movements that mobilize the joints and warm up the muscles, followed by gentle stretches.

CRAMP

Cramp is when a muscle strongly contracts and cannot relax. The pain is usually sudden and severe, but rarely lasts for more than a few minutes. As well as being painful, the muscle feels hard and tight, and there may be a lump or distortion in the affected area.

Causes

An attack of cramp can be triggered by vigorous exercise, lying or sitting awkwardly or continuously repeating a movement. Cramp can come on suddenly at night during sleep and sometimes while swimming soon after eating a meal.

Cramp is usually due to the inability of a hard-working muscle to remove the lactic acid produced when glucose is turned into energy. The muscle appears to lock and is only relieved when circulation is restored.

Exercise-related cramp may be partly caused by the loss of salt from the body through sweating. Rarely, a recurrent or prolonged attack of cramp may be caused by a lack of calcium in the blood.

How to help your child

As soon as your child feels an attack of cramp he will probably cry out, so help him as quickly as you can. Hold the affected limb – it is most likely to be the calf muscle below the knee – in your hand and gently massage and stretch the tightened muscle to relieve your child's cramp.

If it is the calf muscle, you can show him how to stretch it. Firstly, you need to gently pull the toes of his affected leg towards you. Then push his foot back so that his toes are pointing upwards. Hold each of these two positions for a few minutes. Repeat the exercise until the pain starts to subside.

If there is still some residual pain, fill a hot-water bottle with warm, not

SYMPTOMS

- Cramp frequently affects the calf muscle in the legs.
- Muscle feels hard and tight.
- Lump may appear temporarily.

boiling, water and wrap it in a towel. Hold it to the affected area for a few minutes. Alternatively, you could give your child a hot bath or shower.

Cramp can be a frightening experience, so reassure your child that cramp is common, temporary and not serious. To help relieve the pain, you can give him paracetamol or ibuprofen according to his age and size.

To help prevent cramp, make sure that your child drinks plenty of fluids during exercise, particularly in hot weather. These will help him to preserve the salt in his body. If the cramps continue and there is no obvious cause, ask your doctor to check there is no underlying disorder.

FRACTURES AND DISLOCATIONS

Common causes of fractures and dislocations in children are falls, sports activities and traffic accidents. The bones most often broken are those in the leg and arm and the collar bone. Dislocation can happen when the ligaments that hold the bones of a joint, such as the elbow, are stretched or torn, so that the bones are displaced. When a joint is dislocated, bones may also be fractured.

Immediate action

If you think your child's neck or back may be injured, do not move him. Call an ambulance at once. If you suspect a fracture or dislocation of another part of the body, call an ambulance or take your child to the nearest accident and emergency department immediately. While waiting for an ambulance, support or immobilize the broken limb (see First aid, pp.338–339).

Medical treatment

Once at the hospital, your child will be X-rayed to check whether the affected bone is fractured and/or dislocated, and to identify the site and seriousness of the injury.

Your child may be given a local or a general anaesthetic so that any displaced bones can be manipulated back into the correct position. In some cases, surgery may be needed to reposition the bones and repair any damage to surrounding tissues.

The affected limb may have to be put into a plaster cast or held in a splint to keep the

bones in the correct position as they heal. In severe cases, your child may need traction, or have metal screws, rods, pins or plates inserted to hold his bones in position.

Fractures in children generally heal more quickly than they do in adults. A small bone, such as a finger bone, that does not bear weight may heal in a week or two. Large, weight-bearing bones such as the femur (thigh bone) may take several months. Dislocations, such as the displacement of the curved end of the humerus from its normal position in the socket of the ulna, will usually heal within a week or two.

As soon as it is safe for your child to use the affected part, he will be given physiotherapy to prevent the muscles and joints from stiffening up and becoming weak.

GREENSTICK FRACTURE *Because children's bones are supple, the long bones of the arms and legs tend to bend and to crack on only one side.*

Outlook

As long as the bones involved in a fracture or joint dislocation have been properly repositioned and kept in place while they knit together and heal, your child should make a complete recovery. The stiffness of the associated muscles may take several weeks or even months to disappear entirely. Fractures of a joint may slightly increase the risk of arthritis in later life.

BONE HEALTH

Childhood is the most important time to lay the foundations for healthy bones and joints. A child's diet needs to include essential nutrients – for example, calcium, vitamin D, vitamin K, magnesium and other minerals, such as boron, zinc, manganese and copper.

The recommended daily intake of calcium is 450 milligrams for children up to the age of 6 years, increasing to 550 milligrams a day for children up to the age of 11.

Encourage your child to drink plenty of milk and eat enough cheese, yoghurt,

nuts and pulses to ensure adequate calcium supplies. Fatty fish, such as herring, salmon and tuna, are rich in vitamin D, which is also made by the body when the skin is exposed to ultraviolet B rays in sunlight. Many breakfast cereals and margarines have been fortified with vitamin D.

Regular exercise, such as running, tennis, hockey and walking, helps to build a strong bone mass. If the exercise is weight-bearing then so much the better. Children who exercise regularly are more likely to do so as adults.

MINOR SKELETAL PROBLEMS

When your child begins to stand and then walk, it is a very exciting time. Sometimes, you may find yourself worrying that the positions of his legs and feet are not quite right. Many children walk pigeon-toed or splay-footed (in-toeing or out-toeing), or they may appear to have bowlegs, knock-knees or flat feet. Generally, these problems are caused by the position of the baby in the womb or are a normal variation. Rarely, they may indicate an underlying disorder.

IN-TOEING Inward curving of the front part of the foot (known as hooked forefoot) is a common cause of in-toeing. The web space between the big toe and the second toe is also often increased.

PIGEON TOES AND SPLAY FEET

Inward rotation of the whole leg from the hip is the most common reason for a child to have pigeon toes, known as in-toeing. Other causes are curving of the front part of the foot (*see top right*) and bowlegs (*see below*). By contrast, outward rotation of the whole leg at the hip causes splay feet, or out-toeing.

Medical treatment
Consult your doctor if you are worried about the inward or outward position of your child's legs or feet. Inward-curving feet usually improve without treatment by the age of 3 or 4 years. Otherwise, they can be treated by gentle manipulation of the feet and immobilization in casts. Surgery is rarely needed in this situation. Hip rotation usually corrects itself by the age of 8 years and, again, the need for surgery is rare.

Walking splay-footed almost always corrects itself within a year of the child starting to walk and does not cause problems even if it persists.

BOWLEGS AND KNOCK-KNEES

A slight outward-curving of the leg bones is normal in toddlers. However, in bowlegs, the outward curve is exaggerated and the tibia (shin bone) is rotated inwards. In knock-knees, the legs curve inwards so that the knees seem to be trying to touch each other. Bowlegs usually correct themselves by the age of 3 or 4 years; knock-knees are usually outgrown by the age of 11.

Medical treatment
Check with your doctor if you are concerned about your child's legs. There is probably no problem but, very rarely, a child may need to have an operation to correct a severe or persistent deformity, which can be the result of a disorder of bone growth, such as rickets.

FLAT FEET

If a child has flat feet it means that the soles of his feet rest on the ground, as if the normal arch of the foot does not exist. You can see this in the footprint – instead of the usual line where the instep touches the ground, the foot leaves a broad impression from the heel to the toes. An affected child may feel some pain beneath the ankle and along the instep.

Flat feet are normal in children up to the age of about 2 or 3. Some children may have flat feet for longer than this but they usually do not cause problems. In rare cases, flat feet are caused by an underlying abnormality of the bones or joints that makes the feet painful, stiff and weak.

Medical treatment
If you are worried about whether your child's feet are flat or not, consult your doctor. He will probably check their appearance, mobility and strength. If all these features are normal, the feet are normal and no treatment will be required. If there is an underlying disorder, treatment may include immobilizing the feet in casts and, rarely, surgery.

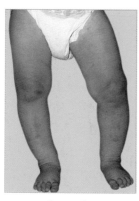

BOWLEGS Outward-curved legs prevent the knees from touching; the shin bone is rotated inwards.

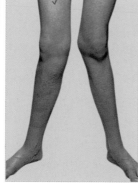

KNOCK-KNEES The legs are curved inwards so that the knees touch and the feet lie apart.

CLUBFOOT

This is a congenital deformity, also known as talipes, in which the foot is twisted out of shape or position. Clubfoot affects three times more male babies than female babies, and in half of all cases, both feet are affected.

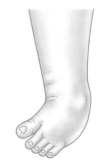

FEATURES OF CLUBFOOT
The heel of the foot is turned inwards and the rest of the foot is bent downwards and inwards. In some cases, the tibia (shin bone) is turned inwards and the leg muscles are underdeveloped.

Causes

Clubfoot is usually detected during a baby's routine examination at birth. There are two main causes. Postural clubfoot is caused in the womb when the position of the baby's foot forces it to be compressed. Unusually large babies are prone to this. Structural clubfoot is caused by an inherited abnormality of the bones in the foot.

The clubfoot may point either upwards or downwards. In a common variety of talipes, the clubfoot points upwards and outwards; in another, it points downwards and inwards. Sometimes the deformity is barely noticeable and the foot seems normal.

Medical treatment

If the mobility in the foot is normal, your child has postural clubfoot and needs no treatment. The problem will usually correct itself within a few weeks of birth.

If the mobility is restricted, your child may have structural clubfoot and will need treatment. In mild cases, this may involve some physiotherapy combined with exercises to stretch the ligaments. Following some instruction, you will be able to perform these on your child at home.

In more severe cases, the foot may need manipulation and then adhesive strapping and splinting to hold the foot in position. If the foot has not straightened by the age of 3–6 months, your child may need to have an operation to straighten it.

After the operation the foot is put in a plaster cast for at least 3 months. In most cases, this is successful. A small number of children may need a series of operations over a 5-year period to improve the function and appearance of the foot, which may never be completely normal.

IRRITABLE HIP

For some unknown reason, irritable hip often develops within about 2 weeks of a mild upper respiratory tract infection, such as a cold. The lining of the hip joint becomes inflamed and fluid accumulates inside the joint, causing symptoms to develop suddenly. Children aged between 2 and 12 years are most susceptible to irritable hip.

SYMPTOMS

- Limping.
- Pain in the hip, groin, thigh or knee.
- There may be a mild fever.

Medical treatment

Take your child to a doctor within 24 hours if he has a pain in the hip, groin, thigh or knee, and/or a limp without an obvious cause.

If the doctor confirms irritable hip to be the diagnosis, you can give your child paracetamol or another painkiller to soothe his discomfort and encourage him to rest in bed until the condition improves, usually between 1 and 7 days. However, if the pain is very severe, your child may need to go to hospital for blood tests to rule out a bacterial infection.

His hip may also be X-rayed and scanned with ultrasound to rule out conditions such as Perthes' disease (*see p.286*) or joint infection (*see p.288*). In some cases, traction may be applied to the hip to relieve both the muscle spasm and the pain.

Outlook

Your child should make a complete recovery, but if he becomes too active too soon after the treatment, the problem may flare up again and he may need to take non-steroidal anti-inflammatory drugs (NSAIDs). If pain recurs in the hip despite the treatment, the problem may be due to Perthes' disease (*see p.286*) or juvenile chronic arthritis (*see p.288*).

PERTHES' DISEASE

This condition affects children, particularly boys, aged between 4 and 8 years. Poor blood supply causes progressive softening, followed by reforming and hardening, of the head of the thigh bone, or femur. Perthes' disease will get better spontaneously within 2–4 years, but a child should have treatment as early as possible in order to prevent the hip joint from becoming deformed.

SYMPTOMS

- Limping.
- Pain in the hip or knee.
- Restricted movement at the hip.

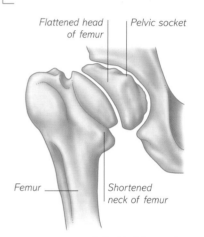

FEMORAL DEFORMITY *If the hip joint continues to bear a child's weight while he has Perthes' disease, the head and neck of the femur may become deformed.*

Flattened head of femur | Pelvic socket

Femur | Shortened neck of femur

Medical treatment

If your child is suffering from a pain in the hip or knee and/or a limp, take him to your doctor within 24 hours. After examining your child, the doctor may send him to hospital for an X-ray of the hip joint to check what is causing the problem.

Treatment depends on the severity of the disease. Less severe cases may be cured by resting in bed for a week or two until the pain subsides, with regular monitoring by X-ray. But if the joint is at risk of becoming deformed, your child may have to wear calipers, splints or a plaster cast. In very severe cases, an operation may be needed to fix the head of the femur more firmly within the pelvic socket.

Outlook

Any deformity of the hip can usually be prevented and the joint will recover and function normally. The sooner Perthes' disease is identified and treated, and the less severe the disease, the more likely it is to be completely cured. In some very severe cases, it is impossible to prevent the joint from becoming deformed and, as a result, there is a risk of arthritis of the hip later in life.

CONGENITAL HIP DISLOCATION

One in every 250 babies is born with a hip dislocation, in which the head of the thigh bone, or femur, lies outside the socket of the pelvis or is unstable and likely to slip out of position. All babies are screened soon after birth and again in check-ups during the first year of life. Congenital hip dislocation runs in families and is more common in girls than in boys.

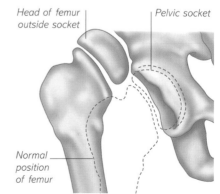

A DISLOCATED HIP *In a newborn child with a dislocated hip, the rounded head of the femur (thigh bone) does not sit in the cup of the pelvic socket as it should do. Instead, it lies above the socket but usually moves into the correct position soon after birth.*

Head of femur outside socket | Pelvic socket

Normal position of femur

Causes

The underlying cause is not known, but one or both of a baby's hips may be dislocated or unstable because the fibrous capsule surrounding the hip joint is weak or because the pelvic socket is abnormally shallow.

Congenital hip dislocation is usually spotted when a doctor checks a baby soon after birth when he manipulates a newborn baby's thighs and hips. If a hip is dislocated, he may feel a jolting or a jerking sensation as the head of the femur moves into the socket of the hip. Some hospitals use ultrasound to confirm the diagnosis.

If the problem is not detected at birth, or during one of the routine check-ups during a child's first year, it may not be discovered until your child begins to walk. At this point, you may notice that he has a limp or that the back of the affected leg has more skin folds below the buttock than the unaffected leg.

Medical treatment

Consult your doctor if you suspect that your child may have a congenital hip dislocation. If your baby's hip abnormality has not corrected itself by about 2 weeks of age, he may need to wear double nappies or a splint to move the head of the femur into the socket and to keep it in position.

The splint is usually worn for 2–4 months and your doctor will give you advice on how to care for your baby during this period. When the splint is eventually removed, the hip joint should be normal.

If your baby's congenital hip dislocation is not discovered until later, the head of the femur may have to be moved into the socket and held in place by traction for several weeks. Following traction, your child may have to wear a splint or plaster cast for several months. If the problem is not discovered until your child starts to walk, he may need to have a series of operations to correct the disorder.

Outlook

The sooner your child receives treatment, the better. If he is treated in early infancy, he should be able to walk normally and is unlikely to suffer any ill effects later in life. However, if treatment is delayed, or if your child has no treatment at all, there may be a risk of a permanent limp and the early onset of arthritis in the affected hip.

SCOLIOSIS

This condition causes an abnormal sideways curvature of the spine. Scoliosis can be due to a structural abnormality of one or more vertebrae or to a local muscle weakness. It is most common in girls, starting around the time of the adolescent growth spurt.

Causes

One reason for scoliosis is that a child's legs are of unequal length so that, as he grows, his pelvis tilts over to one side and the shoulder is raised on the opposite side. This alters the line of the head and shoulders. As the spine tries to bring the line back to the horizontal, it starts to curve.

Scoliosis is rarely noticeable at birth and is usually so mild that it only becomes apparent when a child grows or when his back is X-rayed for an entirely unrelated reason.

In true scoliosis, the vertebrae become narrower on one side of the spine, forcing it to lean to one side and to twist back again higher up towards the neck.

Medical treatment

If you suspect your child seems a little crooked, watch his bare back when he stands up and bends forwards. If you think you can see a curvature, consult your doctor. He may refer your child to an orthopaedic surgeon for monitoring and to check whether the curvature gets worse over time. A mild curvature that is not progressive does not usually need any treatment.

However, in progressive cases, a child may need to be fitted with a plastic body cast or spinal brace to prevent the curvature of the spine from becoming worse. Sometimes, the deformity of scoliosis is severe enough to warrant surgery.

Outlook

If scoliosis is treated promptly, it should not get worse and your child is unlikely to have any long-term ill effects. But left untreated, progressive scoliosis may, in some children, cause severe deformity of the ribcage and spine, leading to breathing difficulties and recurrent chest infections.

☐ SYMPTOMS

- Sideways curve of the spine.
- Pelvis tilts to one side.
- One shoulder is held higher than the other.
- Chest is more prominent on one side than the other.

The curvature of the spine may be accentuated when your child bends forwards to touch his toes with his knees kept straight.

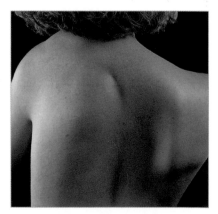

APPEARANCE OF SCOLIOSIS *In scoliosis, the spine curves to one side, usually the right, and one shoulder is higher than the other.*

JUVENILE CHRONIC ARTHRITIS

Chronic arthritis is a long-term inflammation of the joints. Three types can affect children, depending on which joints are affected. Their underlying cause is not known, but genetic factors play a part and they may initially be triggered by a viral infection.

Medical treatment

Take your child to a doctor within 24 hours of the onset of joint pain or stiffness, a limp or a rash with a fever. After examining your child, the doctor will arrange for blood tests in order to make sure the problems are not caused by other disorders.

If four or fewer large joints, such as the knee or shoulder, are affected the child may have pauciarticular arthritis. If small joints, such as those of the hands and feet, are affected, he may have polyarticular arthritis. If the small joints are affected but there are additional symptoms of general illness, the child may be suffering from systemic juvenile arthritis.

Whichever diagnosis is confirmed, your child will need to receive some physiotherapy to maintain his muscle strength and joint mobility. He may need to wear splints at night to prevent joint deformity and during the day to rest the joints.

Your doctor may prescribe aspirin and non-steroidal anti-inflammatory drugs (NSAIDs), such as ibuprofen, to relieve the pain and swelling. If these are ineffective, your child may need corticosteroids.

In very severe cases, surgery may be needed to replace joints that are damaged and painful, or to lengthen muscles that are causing the deformity. Until your child has recovered, his eyes will probably need to be tested regularly for iritis (see p.244).

Outlook

One-third of affected children recover completely, no matter which type it is. Another third have symptoms for many years. Unfortunately, for the final third the condition will continue to grow worse.

☐ SYMPTOMS

- Pain, redness, swelling and stiffness of affected joints.
- Limping, if feet or legs are affected.
- In polyarticular arthritis, a mild fever.

Systemic juvenile arthritis affects the whole body, causing the following symptoms, which may appear several weeks or months before the joints become affected:
- Temperature above 39°C (102°F).
- Swollen glands throughout the body.
- Blotchy, non-itchy rash.

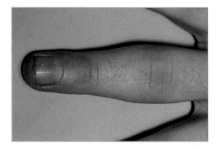

ARTHRITIS AFFECTING THE HANDS *In cases of polyarticular arthritis, the joints of the fingers are red, inflamed and swollen. The neck and jaw may also be affected.*

BONE AND JOINT INFECTION

Bacteria carried through the blood from an infected site, such as a wound or a boil elsewhere in the body, is the most common cause of bone or joint infection. In some cases, the infection spreads directly from nearby tissue.

BONE INFECTION

Without prompt treatment, infection of a bone may become chronic and very difficult to eradicate. It is most common in the long bones of the arms and legs – the humerus and femur, respectively. Children of 3–14 years, especially boys, are most susceptible.

Medical treatment

Phone a doctor at once if you think your child has a bone infection. He will be admitted to hospital for tests, including a blood culture and a bone scan. If confirmed he will be treated with antibiotics; rarely, an infected bone may be surgically removed.

☐ SYMPTOMS

In bone infection the symptoms may be:
- Severe pain in the affected arm or leg.
- Child is unwilling to move the affected limb or let it be touched.
- Fever.
- Swelling and inflammation of the skin over the bone if treatment is delayed.

If the infection is caught early enough, your child should recover completely without any permanent damage.

JOINT INFECTION

In this condition the tissues within a joint are infected with bacteria, causing the joint to become inflamed and fluid to collect within it. If the infection is not identified and treated promptly, the cartilage that covers the surface of the bones inside the joint may be damaged, causing the joint to become stiff and deformed.

Joint infections are most common in children up to the age of 2 years and in adolescents. With prompt treatment, sufferers from joint infection can make a complete recovery.

Medical treatment

If you suspect your child has a joint infection, contact your doctor, who will probably send him to hospital for an ultrasound scan of the joint. To confirm the diagnosis is a bacterial infection, fluid may be removed from the joint with a syringe and sent for microscopic analysis. Your child may also need blood tests to identify the source of the infection.

Your child will be prescribed a course of antibiotics, but an operation may be needed to drain the infected fluid from the affected joint.

SYMPTOMS

In joint infection, the symptoms may be:
- A hot and swollen joint.
- Severe pain in the affected joint.
- Fever.

Once the infection has cleared up completely, your child may need to receive physiotherapy, which will help to keep the joint flexible. As long as the infected joint is identified early enough and treated promptly, your child should make a full recovery.

DUCHENNE MUSCULAR DYSTROPHY

Progressive weakness and the wasting away of muscle are the main features of this congenital disorder. Of the several types, the most common and serious is Duchenne muscular dystrophy, which affects only boys.

SYMPTOMS

- Weakness in the leg muscles, which may cause your child to walk late (over the age of 18 months) and waddle, climb stairs with difficulty, fall easily and roll on to his front, and climb or "hand walk" up his own legs.
- Enlarged calf muscles.
- Inward curvature of the lower spine.

Causes

Duchenne muscular dystrophy is linked to a gene on the X chromosome and affects about 1 in 3,500 boys worldwide. The condition usually appears before 5 years of age.

The gene in question is responsible for producing the protein dystrophin, which is thought to be essential for structural support inside muscle cells. When the gene is defective, the protein is not produced and the muscle cells degenerate and waste away.

A boy born to a woman who is a carrier of Duchenne muscular dystrophy has a 50 per cent chance of developing the disorder. If he has sisters, they would have a 50 per cent chance of becoming carriers.

Medical treatment

Consult your doctor if you think your child might have muscular dystrophy. After examining him, your doctor may send him to a neurologist, who may request tests in hospital in order to confirm the diagnosis.

As yet, there is no substantial treatment or cure for the progressive weakness and wasting of muscles experienced by sufferers of the various muscular dystrophies. Your child will have physiotherapy to prevent contractures, in which the shortened muscles around the joints cause the joints to be positioned abnormally and painfully. The physiotherapy will allow your child to maintain some form of mobility. If you wish you can learn how to help him with these exercises.

Genetic testing

A woman with a family history of Duchenne muscular dystrophy can ask to be tested to find out if she is a carrier. If she is, and she still wants to have a baby, she will be offered genetic counselling to explain the risks of the baby being affected. Tests can also be performed during pregnancy to see if the fetus has been affected with the abnormal gene.

Outlook

The muscle weakness of a child with Duchenne muscular dystrophy increases and gradually spreads to affect more and more of the muscles that control his movements. As a result, it will not be long before he will be unable to perform simple tasks or to walk. He will need a wheelchair, usually by the time he is 8–11 years of age. He may become increasingly vulnerable to chest infections and may not survive past his early 20s.

NERVOUS SYSTEM DISORDERS

Many children with nervous system disorders will be developmentally delayed.

THE BRAIN IS THE CONTROL CENTRE of the nervous system and most of its development is complete by the time a child is about 5 years old. A brain injury or infection before then may have serious long-term consequences, so early recognition and treatment is vital. A few nervous system disorders, such as cerebral palsy, are incurable. Generally, a child's brain recovers from injury or infection better than an adult's.

ANATOMY OF THE NERVOUS SYSTEM

▶ **THE BRAIN AND NERVOUS SYSTEM**
Composed of the brain, spinal cord and many millions of nerve cells, the nervous system is the control centre for all voluntary activities and involuntary bodily functions. Nerves are responsible for the perception of sensations, such as touch, taste, smell, vision and hearing.

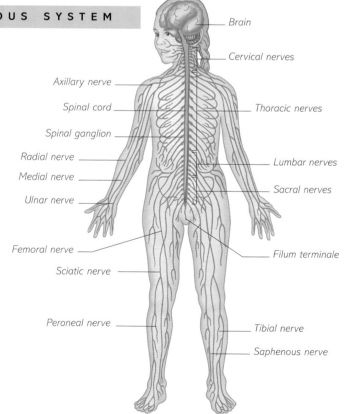

- Brain
- Cervical nerves
- Axillary nerve
- Spinal cord
- Thoracic nerves
- Spinal ganglion
- Radial nerve
- Medial nerve
- Lumbar nerves
- Ulnar nerve
- Sacral nerves
- Femoral nerve
- Filum terminale
- Sciatic nerve
- Peroneal nerve
- Tibial nerve
- Saphenous nerve

HEAD INJURY

Most children suffer some bangs or knocks to the head, and these are rarely serious or have any long-lasting effects. The main risk of a head injury is bleeding inside the skull, which can lead to brain damage, resulting in some physical or mental disability.

Immediate action

If your child falls down and cracks her head – for example, when trying to get out of her cot or while playing on a climbing frame – she may be knocked unconscious. Call an ambulance and check her airway, breathing and

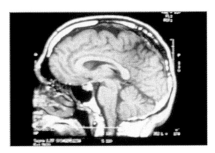

SCAN OF BRAIN *Bleeding inside the skull can cause a blood clot – as shown in this MRI scan – which may cause damage to the brain tissues.*

circulation (*see* First aid, *pp.330–332*) while you wait. If she is confused or abnormally drowsy, vomits persistently, or has fluid or watery blood leaking from her nose or ears, take her to the nearest hospital.

Medical treatment

A doctor will examine her and take any necessary action. A cut on her scalp may need to have stitches. If a fracture is suspected, your child's skull will be X-rayed and scanned (*see left*).

If the scan shows signs of a brain haemorrhage, your child may need an emergency operation to stop the bleeding and remove a blood clot. If your child has a fracture of the skull or a severe concussion, she will be kept in hospital for observation for at least 24 hours after the injury.

SYMPTOMS

Mild head injury *symptoms include:*
- Slight headache.
- Bump or swelling.
- Vomiting.

More serious head injuries *involve:*
- Brief unconsciousness, or concussion
- Confusion.
- Inability to remember what happened just before the injury.
- Dizziness.
- Blurred vision.
- Vomiting.

How to help your child

After hospital treatment a child with a severe head injury needs several weeks' rest. If she had a minor head injury, let her rest for 2–3 days. Watch her for the first 24 hours and take her to the hospital at once if any of the following develop: abnormal drowsiness; slurred or incoherent speech; irritability; vomiting; confusion; or fluid or watery blood leaking from the nose or ears.

RECURRENT HEADACHES

Most children have headaches from time to time but some suffer recurrent ones, which may be severely debilitating and interfere with school work. The two main types are migraine and tension headache. Very rarely, they are caused by a brain disorder.

MIGRAINE

Children who have frequent migraines usually have a family history of the disorder. Emotional stress is the most common trigger, but other triggers may include: foods, such as oranges and other citrus fruits or cheese; hunger; too much sun; and tiredness. Children rarely have more than one or two migraines a month.

Medical treatment

If your child develops the symptoms of a migraine, take her to your doctor, who may suggest that, if possible, you try to identify and eliminate the potential trigger factors.

Anti-emetic medicine may be prescribed to prevent vomiting during the attacks. Drugs to prevent migraine may be prescribed if your child has

---

SYMPTOMS

Migraine *causes some children to see sparkling lights or zigzag lines, as if these were a warning sign of an imminent attack. Other symptoms of migraine follow and may include:*
- Pain, affecting one or both sides of the head.
- Vomiting.
- Dislike of light and noise.
- Lightheadedness or dizziness.
- Tingling, weakness, or numbness of an arm or hand.
- An attack may last from 2 hours to as long as 2 days.

frequent attacks. During a migraine attack, you can give her paracetamol and let her rest in a darkened room to help relieve pain.

Frequent attacks may be followed by long periods when your child experiences no migraines at all. Propranodol may help to reduce the frequency of migraine attacks.

TENSION HEADACHE

Muscular tension in the face and neck – for example, from clenching or grinding the teeth – may cause tension headaches. Emotional stress is the most common trigger.

How to help your child

Give your child paracetamol to relieve the pain and try to identify and reduce any causes of stress. If the headaches continue, see your doctor, who may refer your child to a consultant.

BRAIN DISORDERS

Brain disorders, such as tumours, are extremely rare. If your child shows any of the symptoms or if you suspect your child could have a brain disorder, consult your doctor, who will examine her and may arrange for hospital tests. The treatment and outlook will depend on the nature of the problem.

□ SYMPTOMS

Tension headaches include the following symptoms:
- Pain that can affect any part of the head.
- Sometimes, other signs of tension, such as abdominal pain.

Brain disorders include the following symptoms:
- Headache that wakes a child at night, is present on waking in the morning, or is made worse by coughing.
- Convulsions.
- Changes in behaviour.

FEBRILE CONVULSIONS

These seizures are triggered when a child's body temperature rises abruptly, often during an upper respiratory tract infection, such as a cold. The convulsions may develop at the onset of a feverish illness, or an infection in a part of the body other than the brain.

Immediate action

Phone a doctor at once if your child has a seizure or her temperature rises above 39°C (102°F). If the seizure lasts for over 3 minutes (10 minutes if she has been given diazepam after a previous seizure), call an ambulance.

REDUCING YOUR CHILD'S TEMPERATURE Sponge your child with lukewarm water to reduce a fever. Do not place a child who has had a seizure in a bath; he or she could drown.

Medical treatment

The doctor will check for infections such as meningitis (*see p.294*). She may take a throat swab and blood and urine tests. She may give antibiotics for a bacterial infection. The doctor will explain how to deal with any future attacks and may prescribe diazepam (an anticonvulsant drug) for use at home. The drug can be squirted into the child's rectum during an attack to shorten the duration of convulsions.

How to help your child

Seizures are most common in children between 6 months and 5 years because their brains are immature. Although frightening, they are rarely serious and cause no long-term problems. About a third of children who have had one attack will have a second less than 6 months later. A few children do go on to develop epilepsy (*see p.293*).

□ SYMPTOMS

The first stage of the seizure, which lasts about 30 seconds, involves:
- A loss of consciousness.
- Rigid body.
- Breathing stops for up to half a minute; when it starts again, breathing may be shallow and barely detectable.
- Passing urine and/or faeces.

The second stage of the seizure, which may last less than 5 minutes, involves:
- Child remains unconscious.
- Limbs and/or face twitch.
- Rolling back of the eyes.

At the end of the second stage, the child regains consciousness and may then fall into a deep sleep for an hour or two. She may be confused, sleepy and irritable when she wakes up.

Try to bring down a high temperature to prevent convulsions (*see p.59 and p.171*). Give regular paracetamol and/or ibuprofen. If your child has a convulsion, place her in the recovery position (*see p.330*). Carry on trying to reduce the fever.

EPILEPSY

Around 1 in 200 children has recurrent seizures, or fits, with a condition called epilepsy. A single seizure does not mean a child has epilepsy. Of the different types of epileptic seizure two are most common in children – tonic-clonic and absence seizures.

Causes

Children with epilepsy sometimes have a structural abnormality in the brain, but usually there is no obvious cause. Individual attacks may be brought on by a trigger, such as flashing lights.

During a seizure, there is chaotic and unregulated electrical activity in the brain, which causes an alteration in consciousness and sometimes uncontrollable movements of the limbs and/or head. There are many causes of seizures other than epilepsy (*see opposite*).

Medical treatment

If your child has never had a tonic-clonic seizure before, phone a doctor at once. If she remains unconscious for longer than 10 minutes, whether the attack is her first one or not, call an ambulance or take your child to the nearest accident and emergency department. While you wait for the ambulance, you should check her airway, breathing and circulation (*see* First aid, *pp.330–332*).

If your child has any other type of seizure, arrange to see the doctor and tell your doctor of any subsequent seizures. The doctor will probably ask you to describe your child's behaviour and symptoms before, during and after any seizure.

Tell your doctor, too, what your child was doing just before the seizure as this may help to pinpoint possible triggers. Your child will often need to have an electroencephalogram (EEG) to identify the type of epilepsy and may also have a brain scan to discover whether a structural brain abnormality might be the cause. Blood tests may rule out other possible causes, such as low blood sugar.

Children with epilepsy usually need anticonvulsant drug therapy until 2–4 years have passed since the last seizure. Medication should then be gradually reduced over several months. In very rare cases, when drugs do not control your child's seizures and scans indicate a structural brain abnormality, surgery may be suggested to correct the problem.

How to help your child

If your child is experiencing a tonic-clonic seizure, then place her in the recovery position (*see* First aid, *p.330*) and stay with her until she has fully regained her composure.

If your child has another type of seizure, sit her down quietly, and stay with her until she is fully recovered and alert. Reassure your child calmly and quietly, and do not try to stop the seizure by slapping or shaking her.

Outlook

More than three-quarters of children with tonic-clonic epilepsy who have been free of seizures for 2 years do not have them again. Most children with benign partial epilepsy outgrow the condition and need no medication after puberty. Absence seizures are not so easy to predict and the outlook varies with the individual.

Most children, even those who do not outgrow epilepsy, have no other disability and can go to normal

More than three-quarters of children with epilepsy suffer from tonic-clonic seizures. The second most common are absence seizures. Generally, a child will have only one type of seizure. But some children have more complex forms of epilepsy and may suffer from two or more different types of seizure.

Tonic-clonic seizures *include the following symptoms:*
- Irritability or unusual behaviour for a few minutes before the seizure.
- A rigid spasm, which lasts for up to 30 seconds, during which the child usually falls unconscious to the floor and breathing becomes irregular.
- Jerky movements of the limbs or face that may last from 20 seconds to several hours. The child may bite her tongue and there may be loss of bladder or bowel control.
- After convulsions stop, the child may stay unconscious for a few minutes or, more rarely, for up to 10 minutes.
- When the child regains consciousness, she may have a headache, feel disoriented and confused, and will probably want to sleep.

Absence seizures *include the following symptoms:*
- Child stops normal activities and stares into space, unaware of the surroundings, for 10–15 seconds, but does not fall to the floor.
- Child has no memory of the seizure.

Benign partial epilepsy *is another, less common, seizure. It causes jerking of one side of the face or of one limb. The child may also lose consciousness.*

schools and participate in most sports. Your doctors will advise you on which precautions you or your child should take, and whether there are any activities that should be avoided.

MENINGITIS

Meningitis is an inflammation of the membranes, or meninges, that cover the brain and spinal cord. Bacterial meningitis can be life-threatening, although antibiotics given in the early stages usually lead to a full recovery. Viral meningitis is less serious.

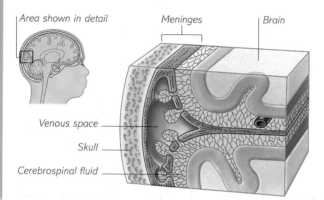

Area shown in detail

Meninges

Brain

Venous space

Skull

Cerebrospinal fluid

THE MENINGES *Three layers of protective membranes, known as the meninges, cover the brain and spinal cord. Meningitis is caused by infection of the meninges by viruses or bacteria.*

Bacterial meningitis

This is most common in children under the age of 5, although it can occur at any age. Also called meningococcal meningitis, it usually appears in isolated cases and is most often caused by *Neisseria meningitidis* and, rarely, by *Haemophilus influenzae*. The neisseria bacteria are normally present in the nose and throat, where they are usually harmless. Why they cause meningitis in some children is not understood.

Viral meningitis

Epidemics of viral meningitis, which is most common in children over the age of 5, may strike in the winter months. The viruses responsible include those that cause influenza, chickenpox, glandular fever and AIDS. No one yet knows why they infect the meninges and cause meningitis.

Immediate action

If your child is abnormally drowsy or develops at least two of the symptoms of meningitis, take her to a doctor at once or to the nearest accident and emergency department.

Your child may be given a lumbar puncture to test for either viral or bacterial meningitis and, in some cases, to identify the organism responsible. Blood samples will also be taken for culture in the laboratory to identify bacteria.

Medical treatment

If bacterial meningitis is suspected, your child will be started on a course of high-dose antibiotics immediately. As soon as the laboratory results are available, the antibiotic treatment will either be continued or changed to target the particular bacterium that has been identified.

Your child may also need to be given intravenous fluids, as well as anticonvulsant drugs if she is having convulsions. Treatment may continue for up to 10 days.

If viral meningitis is confirmed, the antibiotics can be discontinued and only painkillers prescribed. The infection should clear up within 5–14 days, depending on the particular virus involved. Viral meningitis rarely has any after-effects.

Bacterial and viral forms of meningitis are similar in the early stages. But symptoms of bacterial meningitis are usually more severe and tend to develop rapidly, sometimes within a few hours.

Infants may have vague early symptoms, which may include:
- Abnormal drowsiness.
- Fever.
- Vomiting.
- Reluctance to feed.
- Increased crying; restlessness.

Older children may have the above and the following symptoms:
- Severe headache.
- Dislike of bright light and loud noise.
- Rigidity of muscles, particularly the muscles of the neck.

Later symptoms in children of all ages with bacterial meningitis include:
- Increasing drowsiness and, occasionally, loss of consciousness or convulsions.

Some children with meningitis develop:
- A characteristic rash consisting of flat, pink or purple spots that do not fade when they are pressed (see p.187).

Protection

Routine immunization gives protection against *Haemophilus influenzae* and one type of meningococcal meningitis. To help prevent the spread of bacterial meningitis, antibiotics may be given to those in close contact with an affected child, especially the family living in the same household.

Outlook

A few children may have some brain damage, resulting in deafness, seizures or learning difficulties, especially if treatment is delayed. Rarely, the illness may be fatal, even if treated promptly.

ENCEPHALITIS

A rare condition, this inflammation of the brain can be caused by
any viral infection. For unknown reasons, the viruses spread via
the blood to the brain from elsewhere in the body. In newborn
babies, the herpes simplex virus is the most common cause.

Causes
Rarely, encephalitis can develop after
herpes simplex (the cause of cold
sores), measles, rubella or chickenpox.
Encephalitis can vary in severity from
being mild and harmless to a serious
and life-threatening illness.

Most children make a full recovery,
but very rarely, encephalitis can prove
to be fatal. In a few cases, there is
permanent brain damage, which
may cause weakness of an arm and/or
leg, learning difficulties, behavioural
problems or epilepsy (*see p.293*).

Medical treatment
Phone a doctor at once if your child is
abnormally drowsy or if she has a fever
plus any two encephalitis symptoms.
Tests and brain scans will be needed.
In the early stages of the illness, the
tests may show nothing, even if the
disease develops later. A lumbar
puncture will look for bacterial
meningitis (*see opposite*).

If the encephalitis is due to the
herpes simplex virus it will be treated
with the antiviral drug acyclovir.
There are no drugs to treat other

viral infections. Mechanical ventilation
may be needed if your child develops
breathing difficulties.

SYMPTOMS

- Abnormal drowsiness that progressively
  worsens, possibly leading to coma or
  a fever.
- Irritability.
- Vomiting.
- Double vision or an obvious squint.
- Weakness of a limb on one side of
  the body.
- Convulsions.

*In mild cases, symptoms may be barely
noticeable. For example, a child with
chickenpox encephalitis may have only
slight unsteadiness in walking.*

CEREBRAL PALSY

Cerebral palsy is term for an incurable condition that covers
any abnormalities of limb movement and posture resulting from
damage to the brain. Cerebral palsy is particularly common in
babies born prematurely or weighing less than 1.5 kg (3⅓ lb).

Causes
The brain damage can occur in late
pregnancy, at birth, in the newborn
period or in early childhood. Damage
usually happens before birth, but
cerebral palsy may not be recognized
until your child is several months old.

Some children have stiff muscles
in one or more limbs, making normal
movement difficult. This problem may
first appear from the age of 6 months.
Other children may make irregular and
involuntary writhing movements

Many children with cerebral palsy
have learning difficulties, epilepsy
(*see p.293*) and problems with hearing
and eyesight. Speech and language

problems are common due to slow
learning, poor hearing and poor
coordination of the muscles used
in speech. A child may also develop
behavioural or feeding problems.

How to help your child
If you are concerned that your baby is
not developing properly, see a doctor,
who may need the help of various
tests, scans and specialists. Even then,
a precise diagnosis is difficult to make.

Children with mild or moderate
disability can attend normal schools
and expect a near-normal life. Those
who are more severely affected may
need special education.

SYMPTOMS

- Stiffness of the arms and legs on
  being picked up.
- Reluctance to use one hand or arm.
- Feeding difficulties.
- Not sitting by the age of 1 year.
- Delayed motor milestones.

OCCUPATIONAL THERAPY *Puzzles and games
involving fine hand movement can improve
concentration and coordination.*

NEURAL TUBE DEFECTS

The neural tube is the part of an embryo that develops into the brain and spinal cord, and the back of the skull and vertebrae. If it fails to develop properly, a baby may be born with defects in any of these parts. The most common type of defect is spina bifida.

Medical treatment

A child with a mild defect may have no symptoms and need no treatment. More severe defects may need surgery; in hydrocephalus, for example, a tube may be inserted into the brain to drain off fluid. Despite treatment, a child may remain permanently disabled. He will receive physiotherapy and help with learning to live with disability.

PREVENTION

The risks are substantially reduced if a woman takes a small amount of folic acid once a day for a month before she conceives and during the first month of her pregnancy. Early in pregnancy, defects can usually be detected by blood tests and ultrasound scans.

SYMPTOMS

- The spinal cord, the brain or the membranes (meninges) that cover them are exposed, to a greater or lesser degree. This makes these vital nerve tissues vulnerable to damage and infection.
- A dimple or a tuft of hair may be the only indication that a defect is present.
- A large, fluid-filled swelling, covered by a thin membrane or by skin, may indicate a more severe defect.

Symptoms, if there are any, depend on the severity of the neural tube defect and may include:
- Weakness or paralysis of the legs.
- Deformity of the legs.
- Urinary and/or faecal incontinence.
- The skin below the level of the abnormality is insensitive to pain.
- Sometimes, hydrocephalus (water on the brain).
- In some cases, the child may experience learning difficulties.

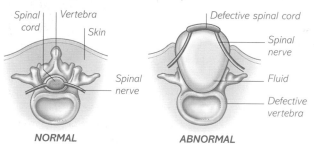

Spinal cord | Vertebra | Skin | Spinal nerve

NORMAL

Defective spinal cord | Spinal nerve | Fluid | Defective vertebra

ABNORMAL

SPINAL SECTION In this severe neural tube defect (right), a fluid-filled sac covered by a thin membrane has developed between a vertebra and the skin.

CHRONIC FATIGUE SYNDROME

The most important symptom of this disorder is severe fatigue that can last for months or even years. Sometimes, it is triggered by a sore throat or another viral illness, such as glandular fever, but not always. Unrecognized depression may be another cause.

Medical treatment

A severe infectious illness will leave a child feeling tired and below par, but if the fatigue lasts for more than a month, see your doctor. He will check for any physical cause for the illness and may arrange for blood tests.

Usually, test results and physical examination are normal, although in a large number of sufferers tests show evidence of a recent or current viral infection. There is no particular

treatment for this disorder, but a regular daily routine with sufficient rest and a healthy diet will help.

How to help your child

If your child has been away from school for a long time, help her to make a gradual return. Ask teachers about anything that might be making your child anxious. Once your child is able to go back to school full time she can be considered to be cured.

SYMPTOMS

- Severe fatigue that prevents the child getting up from bed at the usual time.
- Feeling of weakness in the limbs.
- Pain in the head, the abdomen or the muscles of the limbs.
- Reluctance to eat or to take part in any social activities.
- Exhaustion after any physical or mental exertion.
- Difficulty in concentrating.

But if one or more relapses occur, you may need the help of a paediatrician and/or a child psychiatrist in identifying the cause of the problem.

DYSLEXIA

Between 4 and 10 per cent of children are dyslexic, so in an average class, at least one or two will be affected. Spelling is usually the most obvious difficulty. As well as visual dyslexia, some also experience an auditory form of the condition.

Causes
Dyslexia has a genetic link and may be passed on from either parent, although it seems stronger in the male line. There is often a family history of dyslexia or reading difficulties. A child's language environment also plays a part.

Medical treatment
About half of those affected need help. Children at risk can be identified as young as 3. Usually, non-specialist teachers pick up the problem when a child is learning to read at school at around 6 or 7. Once identified, a child is assessed by a psychologist or specialist teacher to gauge her strengths and weaknesses, and whether she needs extra support. If she does, the next

step is to find a teacher who can help her develop the skills and best strategies she needs for effective learning as well as boosting her morale.

How to help your child
It is easy for a dyslexic child to feel discouraged, so be positive about her achievements, however small, and help her to build on her strengths. Read to her even when she can read herself to help improve her vocabulary, and work with her teachers to ensure she has the best possible support. As she grows, she might find using a computer easier than relying on handwriting.

With the right support and help, she should be able to reach her full academic potential.

> ### ▢ SYMPTOMS
> - Able to recognize individual letters and figures but has trouble getting them in the right order.
> - May have difficulty recognizing different sounds, holding information in her short-term memory and processing language at speed.

A CHILD WITH DYSLEXIA *Recognizing letters is not difficult but using them to spell words can be a particular problem.*

DYSPRAXIA

This developmental coordination disorder affects between 5 and 6 per cent of children, most commonly boys. Broadly speaking, it is a motor learning problem in which a child has difficulty planning and organizing smoothly coordinated movement.

Causes
The exact cause is unknown but it is often linked with premature birth or low birth weight. Children are affected to varying degrees and other family members may have similar problems.

Medical treatment
Dyspraxia often goes unrecognized and children are labelled as being lazy or not trying. Dyspraxia can be associated with educational, social and emotional

problems that continue into adult life. Sometimes, occupational therapy or physiotherapy can help.

How to help your child
She can easily lose self-esteem, so avoid criticism and comparisons with more able children. She needs to take part in activities she is good at and to do as much as she can for herself. Praise her efforts and successes. Before she starts school, explain her difficulties to the

> ### ▢ SYMPTOMS
> - Typically, a child may be late reaching developmental milestones such as sitting, crawling and walking.
> - Later, she may find it difficult to learn activities such as hopping, skipping and pedalling a bike, tying shoelaces or fastening buttons.
> - She may tire easily, seem particularly accident prone and may have a tendency to drop things, which can be frustrating for the child and her family.

teachers. She should improve with age as she learns to deal with specific things she finds hard.

BEHAVIOURAL PROBLEMS

Many children grow out of their behavioural difficulties, but some require professional help.

THE MAJORITY OF CHILDHOOD HABITS are so common that they should be considered normal. Infants often suck their thumbs, bang their heads and hold their breath for an alarming length of time. School children are affected by tics and compulsions, while children of all ages bite their nails or pull or twirl their hair. Most of these habits do little harm and may provide a child with comfort in times of stress and anxiety, or else become an expression of anger, boredom or frustration. However, parents often find it hard to know whether a condition needs attention or not. Children usually grow out of their behavioural problems or their upsetting and odd habits, but some, such as attention deficit hyperactivity disorder (ADHD) and autism, require expert help. Talking to a doctor can help to relieve a parent's anxiety and determine whether treatment is likely to be needed.

ADHD (ATTENTION DEFICIT HYPERACTIVITY DISORDER)

A child who is particularly restless, unable to concentrate and performs poorly at school may have attention deficit hyperactivity disorder. About 4 per cent of primary school children are affected, and are best diagnosed by a child psychiatrist or a paediatrician.

Causes
It is not usually known why children have ADHD, but in certain cases the cause is thought to be either subtle brain damage or psychological stress. In some severe cases there may be an inherited, genetic component. More boys than girls are diagnosed with ADHD. The condition tends to appear between the ages of 3 and 7 years.

Medical treatment
Consult your doctor if you suspect your child's behaviour is abnormal and shows symptoms that might be related to ADHD. The doctor may want him to visit a psychiatrist, psychologist or paediatrician for assessment. Tests, including brain scans, are almost always normal and the diagnosis is made on the child's symptoms and on the observations of the doctor.

Treatment depends on the severity and cause. A clear routine and consistent expectations of behaviour, specialist educational advice and a "few foods" diet may be helpful (see p.253).

Severe ADHD may be treated with psychostimulants, which can calm children and improve concentration while decreasing their aggression and impulsivity. Research shows that 70–80 per cent of children with ADHD respond positively to these drugs.

Outlook
Most children with ADHD improve with treatment as they get older. In a few cases, antisocial behaviour appears later in childhood.

Symptoms of ADHD may go unnoticed until a child goes to school and his restless behaviour can be compared with that of other children.

SYMPTOMS
- Lack of concentration.
- Excessive restlessness.
- Impulsive and excitable behaviour.
- Destructive, disruptive and accident-prone behaviour.
- Irritable and aggressive behaviour.

AVOID THESE

If your child is hyperactive, you may be able to help counteract, or at least alleviate, some of his symptoms by eliminating the following ingredients from his diet:
- Any foods and drinks that contain the additives tartrazine and benzoic acid.
- Caffeine, contained in cola drinks.
- Foods that are high in salicylates, including apples, grapes, apricots, peaches and plums. Salicylates are also found in potato skins, spinach, carrots and broccoli, and in peppermint and liquorice.

AUTISM

Autism affects a child's ability to relate to other people. Usually noticeable before the age of 3, it tends to affect boys more than girls. The cause is unknown, but there are genetic factors. Asperger's syndrome is the mildest form of autism.

Medical treatment
Check with your doctor if your child seems to have difficulty relating to others, if you are worried about his speech or language development, or if he has learning difficulties. If autism is suspected, your child may need to see a psychologist, psychiatrist or paediatrician, who will assess his

condition. There is no cure as such for autism, but your child may be helped by communication and language therapy and by special education.

Most autistic children attend schools for children with learning difficulties, although a few go to mainstream schools where they receive specialist support. Parents can add to

SYMPTOMS
- Child may fail to make eye contact or point to objects in order to draw people's attention to them.
- Repetitive behaviour, such as flapping the hands or moving a toy.
- Delay in developing speech or language skills.
- Apparent indifference to the presence of other people.
- Preference for solitary activities.
- Little interest in creative play.
- Dislike of changes in routine.
- Learning difficulties.

this by teaching their autistic children as many self-help skills as possible.

Outlook
Autistic children who receive speech and language therapy and appropriate educational interventions tend to improve gradually throughout their childhood and adolescence. Some achieve a degree of independence as adults, but almost all remain disabled

to a certain extent and continue to find relating to other people difficult. Children with the milder form of autism known as Asperger's syndrome have normal intelligence and are able to form relationships with people.

ASSESSING CHILDREN WITH SPECIAL NEEDS
Specialists watch a boy playing in order to assess his motor skills and sensory-processing abilities.

DEPRESSION

Depression is usually considered an adult problem, but it affects 1 in 200 children under 12. While feeling fed up is normal from time to time, depression is a persistent feeling of unhappiness that may lift briefly but does not go away.

Causes
There is evidence that depression is linked to chemical changes in the part of the brain that controls mood. These changes prevent the brain from working normally and may cause many of the symptoms.

Depression can be triggered by experiences, such as the death or loss of a loved one, bullying at school, family breakdown or adapting to a chronic illness. It can be related to prolonged stress – for example, if a child feels under pressure to do well at school – or can begin for no apparent reason.

Family history is also important. Studies show that children are more likely to become depressed if a parent or close relative suffers from depression. A child's environment also plays a role. The rate of mental health disturbance among children is twice as high in inner cities as in rural areas.

Depression can be hard to spot. Children often internalize feelings and may appear fine to the outside world. If your child does not want to do things, seems miserable and fed up

and is approaching or going through puberty, it is easy to assume it is just part of growing up.

Medical treatment
For most children, identifying the cause of the problem and working together on coping strategies will help. However, if things do not get better or if depression is causing serious difficulties, your doctor may suggest a referral to your local child mental health service. Individual treatment should start with a psychological approach. Medication can be effective, but this is not a first-line treatment, particularly before adolescence.

How to help your child
Spend time talking together. At first he may seem irritable and push you away. But finding time to do something regularly together every day will help. It could be as simple as washing and drying the dishes together, cooking or walking the dog. Try to find out what is making him feel miserable and explore ways of coping. Make an effort

SYMPTOMS

- Moody, irritable, tearful, easily upset.
- Seems miserable and unhappy a lot of the time.
- Becomes withdrawn and avoids friends and family.
- Self-critical about everything.
- Feels guilty about things.
- Feels persistently hopeless.
- Difficulty concentrating.
- Does not look after appearance.
- Difficulty getting to sleep or waking.
- Tiredness and lack of energy.
- Frequent minor health problems such as headaches or tummy aches.
- Threatens self-harm or suicide.
- Comfort eating or loss of appetite.

to understand how he is feeling. Keep talking about it. If he is having a hard time at school and things do not improve after telling you, he is likely to stop talking about it. It is easy to assume the problem has gone away.

Outlook
Depression can affect a child's whole life, leading to a loss of confidence, problems making decisions, difficulties in getting on with family and friends, an inability to study, work and pass exams, and a difficulty getting up to face the day.

DAMP (DEFICITS IN ATTENTION, MOTOR SKILLS AND PERCEPTION)

In many ways, DAMP is similar to autism (*see p.299*) because the children who are affected can have difficulties in how they relate socially to other people. But DAMP also has similarities with dyspraxia (*see p.297*) because the problems the affected children experience with perception mean that they can struggle with reading and writing.

(*see p.299*) ... (*see p.297*)

SYMPTOMS

- Problems with motor skills and with attention.
- Perceptual problems that children with DAMP experience mean that they can have particular difficulties with reading and writing.
- Lack of confidence and self-esteem.
- Difficulties with forming relationships and relating to people socially.

Medical treatment

The label DAMP originated in Sweden and is not so well known to health and education professionals in the UK. The term autism may be more helpful in unlocking the right resources.

No specific medical treatment exists, but the most important point is to ensure that your child gets the right educational and therapeutic help – help that targets every area with which he is experiencing specific difficulty.

A statutory assessment carried out by the Local Education Authority will not only gauge a child's strengths and weaknesses in the classroom, but will also identify any areas in which a child needs extra support. It would be a good idea to discuss your child's condition with a community paediatrician, who may refer you to a specialist centre.

How to help your child

DAMP can lower a child's confidence and self-esteem so, as well as working together on the things that he finds difficult, it's important to set aside time at home to enjoy and focus on the activities that he does well. For instance, he might enjoy pursuing a particular hobby. It might be helpful for him to have some time at school when he can take part in activities that he finds he can do well and also enjoys – it would be worth discussing this with his teacher. You might find it useful to contact the National Autistic Society (*see p.345*) for further support and information.

(*see p.345*)

Outlook

The good news is that the problems associated with DAMP often get better as children get older.

CONDUCT DISORDERS

All children misbehave every now and then, whether it's being cheeky, disobedient or simply mischievous. But a conduct disorder constitutes a more serious problem. It means persistent disobedience and aggressive and disruptive behaviour to a degree that affects a child's development and interferes with the ability of the child and his family to live a normal life.

SYMPTOMS

- Problems at school.
- Antisocial behaviour that may get worse as a child grows, leading to a hostile and defiant attitude, truancy and a tendency to develop bad habits such as stealing and lying.
- Inability to follow rules – either at school or at home.
- Lack of self-esteem.

Causes

One sign of a child who may have a conduct disorder is that he is experiencing problems at school. Antisocial behaviour can result in a child being rejected by his peers. One study showed that among children aged between 3 and 7 who had been diagnosed with a conduct disorder, more than half had already been asked to leave two or more schools due to their difficult behaviour.

Boys are twice as likely as girls to have a conduct disorder. Half do get better, but half get worse and as they grow these children are at risk of developing a hostile and defiant attitude, ignoring rules, getting into physical fights, being prone to stealing and lying and playing truant from school. They could begin to take risks with their own health and safety – for instance, by taking illegal drugs.

There are a number of factors that could predispose a child to developing a conduct disorder. These include a naturally "difficult" personality, a learning problem such as difficulty with reading or writing, depression (see p.300) and/or a history of being bullied or abused. Children with attention deficit hyperactivity disorder (see p.299) are also more at risk of developing a conduct disorder because of the problems they face in terms of exercising self-control, paying attention and following rules.

Medical treatment

If your child has serious problems for more than three months, in which he makes life difficult both at home and at nursery or school, it would be worth consulting your doctor. He may decide that the best course of action is a referral to your local child and adolescent mental health service.

Treatment often consists of either individual, group or family therapy. A psychotherapist would work with your child to look into what could be causing the problems and suggest practical ways of improving your child's difficult behaviour. This could include helping your child learn how to limit and control his behaviour as well as training in social skills.

Helping your child identify with a suitable role model might be helpful. Support would also involve family work – perhaps including education and information about the condition, help with giving your child's life a firm structure and setting and sticking to a consistent and clear set of rules.

How to help your child

There is a great deal that parents can do for their child at home. Discipline that is fair and consistent, along with praise and rewards for good or improved behaviour will help. Giving your child your attention when he is behaving well will give him a clear message about the sort of behaviour you would like to see.

Talk to your child's teacher and agree a code for his conduct at school, clearly setting out the behaviour you both expect within the context of the school rules. Discuss this with your child and agree with him what will happen if he breaks any of the rules, along with what reward he may receive if he sticks to the agreed code for a set time. It is important that you implement your agreed course of action if he breaks the rules.

It might also be worth talking to the school's educational psychologist to see if any further ideas might help or whether your child could be offered any particular support.

Outlook

If your child's conduct problems are recognized at an early enough stage, and if appropriate and comprehensive treatment and support are given, there is a good chance he will outgrow them. Most children with mild conduct disorders show a marked improvement in a short time if they are given help – perhaps with counselling and practical support offered to their parents.

FAECAL SMEARING

Toddlers are naturally curious and will probably be interested in what they produce when you begin toilet training. However, if an older child tries faecal smearing, it could be a sign of deep distress or an indication of extreme anxiety or abuse.

How to help your child

Although it may be horrifying for parents, it's perfectly normal behaviour for a young child to try handling the contents of his potty. If you discover your toddler experimenting with his potty contents, try to stay as calm as you can. Don't tell him off. Instead, simply explain that he should not be playing with it as it belongs in the potty and must stay where it is until it goes down the toilet.

The more matter of fact you are, the better. If you display horror, shock or anger, your child might be intrigued by your reaction and be tempted to try faecal smearing again. The next time your child uses the potty, keep a close eye on him and immediately afterwards flush the contents down the toilet. He might like to help by pulling the handle. Try offering him an alternative creative activity, such as drawing or painting.

If you experience the problem of faecal smearing with an older child, look for other symptoms of distress or anxiety. Talk very gently to him and try to find out if anything is wrong. It would be best to consult your doctor, who may refer you to the local child and adolescent mental health service, where specialists could help uncover the cause of the problem and advise on the best approach for supporting and helping your child.

BLOOD & CIRCULATORY DISORDERS

The most serious blood disorders, such as leukaemia, were once fatal but now can be cured.

A FULLY FUNCTIONING HEART and blood system are essential for a child's health and vitality. If there is a circulatory disorder, such as Henoch-Schönlein purpura, it is vital for the symptoms to be recognized as early as possible to maximize the chances of a successful cure. The most common serious birth defects affect the heart and, like leukaemia, many of these are now also curable.

ANATOMY OF CIRCULATION

▶ **HOW THE CIRCULATION WORKS**

The heart pumps blood through the arteries, veins and capillaries. Oxygen and nutrients are delivered by the blood to all parts of the body and waste products are removed. Blood is returned to the lungs for reoxygenation and elimination of carbon dioxide.

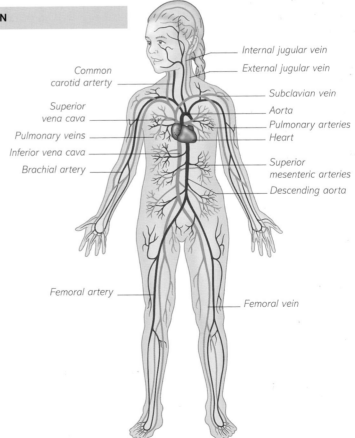

Common carotid artery

Superior vena cava

Pulmonary veins

Inferior vena cava

Brachial artery

Internal jugular vein

External jugular vein

Subclavian vein

Aorta

Pulmonary arteries

Heart

Superior mesenteric arteries

Descending aorta

Femoral artery

Femoral vein

CONGENITAL HEART DISEASE

Congenital heart disease means that a child is born with one or more malformations of the heart. About 1 child in 140 is born with a heart defect. Some children get better without treatment, but others need surgery. The risk of having a child with a heart defect is increased if a woman has poorly controlled diabetes, takes certain drugs during pregnancy, has previously had another child with a heart defect or, in rare cases, has been infected with rubella in early pregnancy.

Types of heart defect

The more common heart defects are:
- Ventricular septal defect: a hole in the septum allows blood to flow from the left to the right ventricle. Oxygenated blood that should go to the body returns to the lungs.
- Patent ductus arteriosus: the blood vessel that acts as a bypass in a baby's circulation before birth fails to close after birth.
- Atrial septal defect: a hole between the atria (upper heart chambers).
- Aortic stenosis: narrowing of the aortic valve.
- Pulmonary stenosis: narrowing of the pulmonary valve.

Rarer defects include:
- Transposition of the great arteries: the position of the aorta and pulmonary artery are reversed.
- Coarctation of the aorta: a narrowing of the aorta.
- Tetralogy of Fallot: a combination of 4 defects – a thickened right ventricle, a ventricular septal defect, pulmonary stenosis and a displaced aorta.

Medical treatment

The problem may be detected when a doctor routinely examines a newborn baby. Sometimes, symptoms of heart disease are not apparent until later in childhood or even until adult life.

Take your child to see a doctor if you suspect she has a congenital heart abnormality. The doctor will refer her to a specialist, who will arrange for a chest X-ray, an electrocardiogram (ECG) and an ultrasound heart scan to reveal what kind of abnormality your child has and how severe it is.

☐ SYMPTOMS

Symptoms vary with the nature and severity of the defect or defects. There are three possible signs of congenital heart disease:

Heart murmur:
- Abnormal heart sounds can be heard when a doctor listens to an affected child's heart through a stethoscope. Most murmurs are not a sign of congenital heart disease but are due to high blood flow. However, they may be due to a narrowed pulmonary or aortic valve, or another form of heart defect.

Feeding problems and loss of weight:
- In some babies with congenital heart disease, the heart is unable to pump efficiently, causing them to feed slowly and to have difficulty finishing feeds.
- Affected babies may also breathe rapidly and sweat, especially after feeding.
- Children with congenital heart disease grow at a slower rate than children who have healthy hearts.

Poor oxygenation of the blood:
- Bluish discoloration of the tongue and lips (cyanosis). Several defects prevent blood circulating effectively through the lungs so the blood going to the body carries less oxygen than it should.
- Breathlessness on exertion.

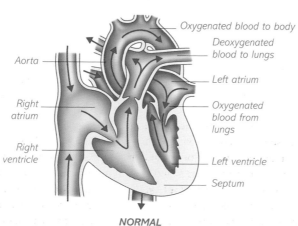

VENTRICULAR SEPTAL DEFECT *A hole in the septum allows blood to flow from left to right ventricle. Oxygenated blood that should flow into the aorta and out to body tissues instead returns to the lungs.*

Aorta

Right atrium

Right ventricle

Oxygenated blood to body

Deoxygenated blood to lungs

Left atrium

Oxygenated blood from lungs

Left ventricle

Septum

NORMAL

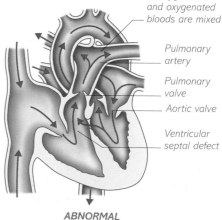

Deoxygenated and oxygenated bloods are mixed

Pulmonary artery

Pulmonary valve

Aortic valve

Ventricular septal defect

ABNORMAL

In many cases, the defects improve on their own. Some may need urgent surgery, but others can wait for surgery until later in childhood. Preventative antibiotics will be prescribed whenever dental treatment is needed or if your child needs surgery to minimize the risk of bacterial endocarditis – an infection of the heart valves.

How to help your child
Unless advised otherwise, encourage your child to lead a completely normal life, with a normal amount of exercise. In rare cases, particularly if your child has a heart abnormality that causes bluish discoloration of the tongue and lips, the doctor may tell you to restrict the amount of exercise she takes.

If you know that your child has congenital heart disease, always check with a doctor if your child develops a fever, lacks energy and has a poor appetite – these symptoms could be signs of bacterial endocarditis.

If your child is prescribed antibiotics to prevent bacterial endocarditis, always make sure she takes the full course. Also make sure that your child always carries a card (obtained from the doctor) stating that she has congenital heart disease.

Outlook
The outlook depends on the type of heart defect and how severe it is. In many children, ventricular septal defects close on their own before the child is 5 years old. Those that do not close are treatable by surgery, as are many other heart abnormalities, such as atrial septal defect, patent ductus arteriosus or narrowing of an aortic or pulmonary valve. Thanks to great advances in surgery, children with heart disease, even those with very severe defects, usually grow up to lead normal lives.

LISTENING TO A CHILD'S HEART *The doctor will use a stethoscope to listen to your child's heart. Abnormal sounds may indicate the presence of a defect.*

CHOLESTEROL AND HEART DISEASE

There is growing evidence that children who are genetically susceptible to heart disease as adults can be helped to reduce the risks if they are encouraged to follow a healthy lifestyle.

Atherosclerosis, which happens when the lining of the arteries "furs up" and thickens because of eating too much cholesterol, may develop over a period of 30 or more years. By encouraging your child to be physically active and eat a healthy diet, you are helping reduce her risk of heart disease when she is older. Lifestyle changes are best applied to the whole family.

Here are 5 tips for a healthy lifestyle:
• Eat plenty (5 portions) of fresh fruit and vegetables every day.
• Restrict the amount of fatty meats and full-fat dairy products in the diet – they are high in saturated fats and raise cholesterol in the blood.
• Encourage regular exercise.
• Prevent smoking in your home and make sure your child understands the risks of smoking.
• Help your child to manage stress and tension. If she tends to be anxious or a worrier, consider taking her to yoga classes or to have a massage.

IRON-DEFICIENCY ANAEMIA

A child with anaemia has insufficient haemoglobin in her red blood cells and so her tissues receive insufficient oxygen. A child with mild anaemia may have no symptoms. Iron-deficiency anaemia is the most common form of anaemia affecting children.

SYMPTOMS
• Pale skin.
• Lack of energy.
• Breathlessness on exertion.

Causes
Red blood cells are manufactured in the marrow of bones such as the femur (thigh bone). They normally circulate in the blood for about 120 days before they become defective and are destroyed. If not enough red blood cells are made,

it is probably because the child lacks a substance, such as iron, which is an essential ingredient of haemoglobin and vital for healthy red blood cell formation. A child may not have enough iron in her diet or she may not be absorbing or using it effectively.

Long-term iron-deficiency anaemia may impair mental development and function. If too many cells are being destroyed, there may be a genetic fault as in sickle-cell anaemia (*see p.313*) and thalassaemia (*see p.314*).

Medical treatment

Take your child to see your doctor if you suspect she has symptoms of anaemia. The doctor will ask about your family history and your child's general health and diet.

If the doctor suspects anaemia, your child's blood will be analysed to determine the number, shape, size and colour of the red blood cells – in iron-deficiency anaemia, for example, they appear smaller and paler than normal. Subsequent tests, such as measuring the level of iron in the blood, may be needed to make a precise diagnosis.

The doctor may give you advice on what sort of foods your child should be eating. She may also need to take iron supplements, usually for about 3 months, to build up her iron stores.

If your child is under 6 months and was premature, she will probably already have been prescribed iron supplements. If not, the doctor may prescribe them at this time. Premature babies often do not have sufficient iron stores to compensate for the low-iron content of a milk-only diet during the first 6 months of life, before they start on solids.

How to help your child

Children are less likely to develop iron-deficiency anaemia as they grow and if they eat a varied diet. Try to make sure that your child's diet contains foods that are rich in iron – dark green leafy vegetables, sardines and meat. The iron in green vegetables is best absorbed by the body when eaten with protein such as meat, eggs or cheese. If your child will not eat iron-rich foods, talk to your doctor about giving her an iron supplement.

If your baby is not eating solids by the age of 6 months, there is a risk that she will develop iron-deficiency anaemia even if she has milk formula enriched with iron. This condition may become apparent between the ages of 12 and 18 months.

LEUKAEMIA

Leukaemia is a form of cancer in which the bone marrow produces many abnormal (leukaemic) white blood cells, and fewer normal white cells, red cells and platelets. The leukaemic cells infiltrate the liver, spleen and lymph glands and undermine the immune system. The most common form of leukaemia in children is acute lymphoblastic leukaemia.

 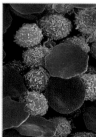

NORMAL   *LEUKAEMIA*

ACUTE LYMPHOBLASTIC LEUKAEMIA Seen under a microscope, blood taken from a person with leukaemia (above right) shows a large number of abnormal white blood cells.

Medical treatment

If you think your child might have leukaemia, consult your doctor, who will examine her and may send her to hospital for blood tests. If the tests cannot exclude leukaemia, he will need a bone marrow biopsy, in which cells are removed from the bone marrow and analysed.

Treatment for acute lymphoblastic leukaemia is divided into two phases. In the first phase, which usually lasts weeks rather than months, your child will be given drugs to destroy the leukaemic cells. This treatment continues until a bone marrow biopsy shows that there are no abnormal cells. At this point, your child is said to be in remission.

The second phase of treatment lasts for 2 years and your child will undergo periods of intensive drug treatment aimed at destroying any

■ SYMPTOMS

- Pale skin.
- Pink or purple flat spots on the skin.
- Easily bruised skin.
- Lack of energy.
- Swollen lymph nodes in the neck, armpits and groin.
- Fever.
- Pain in limb bones and joints.
- Bleeding gums.

leukaemic cells left in the body. Much of this treatment is given on a day-care basis. During this time help your child to lead as normal a life as possible. Keep her away from anyone with a viral infection, particularly chickenpox or measles, because the drugs increase susceptibility to infection.

Outlook

With the medical treatments currently available, there is full recovery in about 70 per cent of children who have been diagnosed as having acute lymphoblastic leukaemia.

HENOCH-SCHÖNLEIN PURPURA

Small blood vessels become fragile and leak blood into the skin to cause a rash. The joints, kidneys and digestive tract are also affected. Most common in children aged between 2 and 10 years, the cause may involve an allergic reaction or bacterial infection.

Medical treatment

Consult your doctor within 24 hours of any symptoms appearing that might indicate your child has Henoch-Schönlein purpura. The doctor may need to send her to hospital for blood tests to rule out other possibilities. Your child's urine will also be tested: the presence of red blood cells and protein in the urine indicates that the kidneys have become inflamed.

If symptoms are mild, no treatment is needed. If your child has severe abdominal pain she may be given corticosteroids, which should bring about rapid improvement. If the kidneys are affected, the doctor may carry out repeat urine and blood tests to ensure the condition is improving.

How to help your child

If your child's symptoms are causing pain or discomfort, try giving her paracetamol. Let her stay in bed if she wants to. Henoch-Schönlein purpura may last a few days or up to a month and symptoms may come and go.

Most children who have the illness make a complete recovery, and there are no long-term ill effects. Any inflammation of the kidneys usually disappears in a few days, but in some children the kidneys remain inflamed for up to 2 years.

*A **TYPICAL RASH** The spots of Henoch-Schönlein purpura may be pink, red or purplish, and either flat or raised. Individual spots vary widely in size.*

SYMPTOMS

- Rash, which is present in all cases, is made up of pink, red or purplish spots that are filled with blood and do not fade when pressed.
- The rash first appears on the buttocks and the backs of the arms and legs, especially around the ankles and elbows, and then spreads to the front parts of the limbs.
- Joint pain and swelling.
- Abdominal pain, often with vomiting and diarrhoea.
- Blood in the faeces.

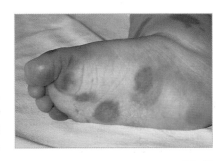

THROMBOCYTOPENIA

Sufferers from this condition have an abnormally low number of platelets in the blood. In children, it generally develops as part of a disorder called idiopathic thrombocytopenic purpura (ITP), which usually follows within 2 weeks of a viral infection.

Medical treatment

Consult your doctor at once if your child has the rash and symptoms of bleeding that might be caused by ITP. The doctor will need to send her to hospital for tests to confirm that she has ITP and not another illness with similar symptoms.

Most children with ITP do not need treatment, but they should avoid strenuous activities until symptoms clear up, usually within a few weeks.

The platelets are essential for blood clotting so if your child has bleeding from the nose or mouth, or has a very low blood platelet count, she will be treated in hospital. She may be given a short course of corticosteroid drugs, platelet transfusions or, sometimes, intravenous gamma-globulin in order to speed recovery and reduce the risk of severe bleeding.

A brain haemorrhage, in which there is bleeding around or within the brain, is a possible complication but is very rare. Most children are free from symptoms within about 2 weeks. In some cases, however, blood platelet levels may take 6 months or more to return to normal.

SYMPTOMS

- A widespread, flat purple rash caused by bleeding into the skin; the rash does not fade when pressed.
- Bruising from only minor pressure.
- Nosebleeds.
- Bleeding in the mouth.
- Blood in the urine as a result of bleeding in the kidneys.

HORMONAL PROBLEMS

A fault in the production of hormones may affect physical and/or mental development.

HORMONES ARE CHEMICAL MESSENGERS that are released directly into the bloodstream by the glands of the endocrine system. They all have different but vital roles to play in the way the body functions. They control growth, the production of energy, biochemical activities such as digestion, and sexual development and function. They also help the body to deal with stress, danger and fatigue.

ANATOMY OF THE ENDOCRINE SYSTEM

▶ *ENDOCRINE SYSTEM*
The glands of the endocrine system are controlled by the pituitary gland at the base of the brain. This master gland controls the release of many of the body's hormones into the bloodstream, which distributes them to all parts of the body. Some glands, such as the testicles and ovaries, are inactive until puberty.

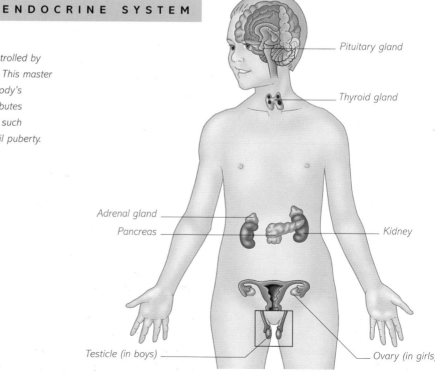

Pituitary gland
Thyroid gland
Adrenal gland
Pancreas
Kidney
Testicle (in boys)
Ovary (in girls)

DIABETES MELLITUS

Insulin is a hormone that enables body cells to use and store the sugar glucose. In childhood diabetes, cells in the pancreas suddenly stop making insulin and the lack of the hormone causes a build-up of glucose in the blood and a disturbance of the body's chemical processes. Unused glucose is excreted in large volumes of urine passed frequently, causing thirst. Children suffering from diabetes mellitus need daily insulin injections, even when they reach adulthood.

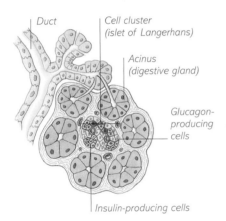

Duct
Cell cluster (islet of Langerhans)
Acinus (digestive gland)
Glucagon-producing cells
Insulin-producing cells

CELLS IN THE PANCREAS *The pancreas has several types of cell. Some secrete insulin to lower the blood glucose level; others secrete glucagon to raise it.*

Immediate action
Phone a doctor at once if you think that your child might have diabetes mellitus. If your child has already been diagnosed with diabetes mellitus, check with the doctor if you ever have any worries about your child's condition. Phone as soon as possible if your child has an infection or an attack of gastroenteritis, because these conditions may make it difficult to control the blood glucose level.

Medical treatment
If symptoms suggest that your child might have diabetes mellitus, your doctor will arrange for his urine and blood to be tested for glucose levels.

If the glucose level is abnormally high, your child may need to go to hospital immediately for further investigations and for insulin treatment to begin. If your child is dehydrated from passing large amounts of urine, intravenous rehydrating fluids may be given as well as insulin. The length of time your child will have to stay in hospital will depend on his age and the severity of his condition.

The long-term control of your child's diabetes mellitus will be carried out under medical supervision. The aim is to provide enough insulin to keep his blood glucose level within the normal range, so that he is able to lead a normal life. To do this he will need to eat regular, balanced meals and to have injections of insulin twice or, sometimes, three times a day.

If your child's blood glucose level falls too low because of too high a dose of insulin, missing a meal or a sudden burst of exercise, he may have a hypoglycaemic attack. Your doctor will explain how to recognize the hypoglycaemia and what to do if your child has an attack. The doctor will prescribe glucagon, which can be injected to stop an attack.

How to help your child
Your doctor will show you how to test for the amount of glucose in your child's blood, and how to record the

In diabetes that has not been treated or that is poorly controlled, there is too much glucose in the blood (hyperglycaemia). Because the cells are not able to use glucose for energy, the body has to use fats and protein as alternative energy sources. This disruption of normal internal processes produces:
- Frequent passing of urine (which sometimes causes bed wetting in children previously dry at night).
- Excessive thirst.
- Tiredness and lack of energy.
- Poor appetite.
- Severe weight loss.

In more severe cases, there may also be:
- Vomiting.
- Abdominal pain.
- Abnormally fast breathing.
- Drowsiness and confusion, which, without treatment, may be followed by loss of consciousness and coma.

results. The measurements obtained from the tests allow the amount of insulin your child is to be given by injection to be adjusted to the correct level. You will also need to learn how to give injections and how to store and dispose of used bottles and syringes.

You can also help your child by making sure he has properly planned meals, with consistent proportions of fats, protein and carbohydrates, served at regular times.

A child aged 5 or over should have a diet of about 30 per cent fats, about 15 per cent protein and the rest carbohydrates. Children younger than 5 years may eat more fats. Your child's diet should also be high in soluble and insoluble fibre. Soluble fibre is found in baked beans and oat-based dishes, such as porridge; foods containing insoluble fibre include wholemeal breads, pasta, and cereals. You do not have to make special meals for a diabetic child and you will be given advice by a dietitian at the hospital. A similar healthy, well-balanced diet will benefit all members of the family.

If your child has a poor appetite for any reason, make sure he gets the same amount of energy in the form of glucose drinks as he would be gaining from a healthy diet. Make sure that you give your child the normal amount of insulin.

Exercise can trigger an attack of hypoglycaemia, so you may have to adjust your child's diet and dosage of insulin if he is taking part in a sports event or strenuous exercise. Ask the doctor who is supervising your child's treatment for advice.

Your child should carry a medical identification card or bracelet that indicates that he has diabetes mellitus and shows the medication that he is taking. Everyone involved in caring for your child, such as teachers, needs to know what to do if he has a hypoglycaemic attack.

As your child gets older, encourage him to take as much responsibility as possible for the control of his own diabetes mellitus. Even quite young children can understand the need to eat regularly and to watch for and treat the symptoms of hypoglycaemia. They can learn to inject themselves and to test and record their own blood glucose levels.

The main signs of hypoglycaemia
• Abdominal pain.
• Sweating.
• Dizziness, and/or confusion.
If your child shows any of these signs,

immediately give him a sweet drink or sweet food, such as chocolate or a biscuit. If your child will not eat or drink, or blood glucose drops so low that he becomes drowsy or loses consciousness, give an injection of glucagon in order to bring the glucose level back to normal.

Outlook
A well-controlled blood glucose level should let your child live a normal life, with a normal amount of exercise. It should also reduce the chance of any complications developing.

The complications that can affect older sufferers, such as problems with the heart, circulation, kidneys, eyes and nervous system, do not usually develop during childhood. Typically, they develop about 10–15 years after the onset of the disease.

DIABETES INSIPIDUS

Diabetes insipidus is due to a deficiency of an entirely different hormone to diabetes mellitus and has nothing to do with glucose, or with energy use. The main symptoms, however, are similar to those of diabetes mellitus.

Causes
In most cases, diabetes insipidus is caused by the failure of the pituitary gland to secrete antidiuretic hormone (ADH). ADH normally acts on the kidneys to cause them to concentrate the urine and so restrict the amount of fluid that is excreted from the body via the bladder.

Failure of the pituitary gland to produce ADH results in the passage of large amounts of urine and excessive thirst. The failure may be due to an injury to the gland or, less commonly, a tumour. In rare cases, the disorder develops because the kidneys fail to respond to normal levels of ADH.

Medical treatment
Call your doctor at once if you notice your child has the symptoms of diabetes insipidus or if he has any of the following signs of dehydration: sunken eyes, abnormal drowsiness or weight loss.

The doctor will take a sample of urine and arrange for it to be analysed. Diabetes insipidus is a possibility if the urine is not adequately concentrated. Your child will probably need to have further tests in hospital to confirm the diagnosis and to find out the cause.

If your child's pituitary gland is not producing ADH in sufficient quantities, he will need to take synthetic ADH. If

SYMPTOMS
• Excessive thirst.
• Frequent passing of large quantities of very pale, weak urine.

Dehydration can occur as a result of the excessive fluid passed as urine.

his kidneys are failing to respond to normal levels of ADH, your child will be treated with a low-sodium diet and, paradoxically, a diuretic drug.

Outlook
A damaged pituitary gland may heal and return to functioning normally, but sometimes the diabetes insipidus continues throughout life. However, treatment will enable the person to live a normal, active life and there are no long-term complications.

HYPOTHYROIDISM

The hormones of the thyroid gland are essential for a child's normal physical and mental development. In hypothyroidism, insufficient hormones are produced, and if the condition is not treated, it may affect a child's growth and learning abilities.

Causes

A child may have hypothyroidism from birth, usually caused by a small thyroid gland. A disease of the thyroid gland or an underactive hypothalamus or pituitary gland (both of which stimulate the thyroid gland to produce thyroid hormones) may also cause the condition. Hypothyroidism tends to run in families and may be associated with autoimmune diseases such as vitiligo, rheumatoid arthritis, diabetes mellitus and pernicious anaemia.

Medical treatment

All babies have their blood tested for hypothyroidism within a week of birth. If your child is shown to have an underactive thyroid gland, he will be given treatment before any symptoms appear.

Take your child to the doctor if you suspect he is suffering from hormone problems. The doctor will probably take a blood sample to measure the levels of hormones. If these tests confirm hypothyroidism, your child will be given tablets of synthetic thyroxine (the main hormone produced by the thyroid gland), which he will then have to take for the rest of his life.

SYMPTOMS

In older children, the symptoms of hypothyroidism include:
- Reduction in the child's growth rate.
- Poor concentration.
- Lack of energy, poor appetite and weight gain.
- Goitre (enlarged thyroid gland).
- Constipation.

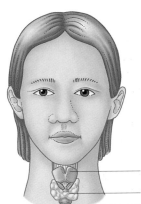

THE THYROID GLAND
This gland is located at the base of the neck in front of the trachea. The gland helps to regulate the body's energy levels and growth.

Thyroid cartilage
Thyroid gland
Trachea

GROWTH HORMONE DEFICIENCY

All children need growth hormone if their bodies are to grow normally. The hormone is produced by the pituitary gland, which is located at the base of the brain. If there is a deficiency of growth hormone, the child will grow slowly.

Causes

Normally, the growth hormone from the pituitary gland stimulates the development of the bones of the skeleton and the production of proteins of which the body's other tissues are composed.

If the pituitary gland has a congenital fault or has a disease such as a tumour, or if a child has a head injury, then the production of growth hormone may be insufficient to stimulate normal development.

Medical treatment

Take your child to your doctor if you are worried about the rate at which he is growing. The doctor will arrange to have his height measured at regular intervals so that his growth can be plotted on a chart.

If the doctor finds that his rate of growth is slower than normal, your child may need to go to hospital for tests, such as X-rays of bones and an analysis of the growth hormone levels in the blood. If growth hormone

SYMPTOMS

- Slow rate of growth.
- Short stature and chubbiness.
- Delayed development of sexual characteristics in older children.

deficiency is diagnosed, he may need to take synthetic growth hormone, which you will need to inject daily until he reaches the end of puberty.

Outlook

Treatment improves a child's growth rate. However, your child may reach the normal adult height expected for your family only if treatment begins by about the age of 6 years.

GENETIC DISORDERS

Medical scientists may be able to replace or even repair faulty genes in the not too distant future.

THE BIOCHEMICAL INFORMATION NEEDED for the normal growth and development of a fetus is carried on around 30,000 pairs of genes packed in 23 pairs of chromosomes. This is the human genome. If any of these genes, or indeed a whole chromosome, is abnormal then a baby may be born either with a defect or a condition that manifests itself later in life. Genetic counselling and analysis allows couples with a family history of one of the roughly 4,000 inherited diseases to assess their chances of having an affected child. Tests during pregnancy are available and may reveal whether a fetus is affected. The Human Genome Project and other discoveries have generated advances, not only in our understanding of DNA, genes and how genes work but also in the technology needed to manipulate them.

SICKLE-CELL ANAEMIA

Sickle-cell anaemia is a serious, inherited blood disease, most common among, although not exclusive to, people of African descent. The red blood cells become distorted into a sickle shape and can block narrow blood vessels. The cells are also destroyed more easily than normal red blood cells, producing anaemia. Children who have sickle-cell anaemia are at increased risk of pneumococcal pneumonia. Occasionally, blood supply is reduced to the kidneys, spleen or brain, causing damage to these organs.

☐ SYMPTOMS

- Lack of energy and breathlessness.
- Episodes of jaundice (yellowness of the skin and whites of the eyes).
- Attacks of severe pain in the bones, chest or abdomen, resulting from blockage of narrow blood vessels, which reduces the oxygen supply to tissues. Dehydration, cold or severe infection makes attacks more likely.

Causes

The red blood cells become distorted because they contain an abnormal type of haemoglobin (the oxygen-carrying pigment) known as haemoglobin S. The sickle cells are more fragile than normal red blood cells. Because of their shape they sometimes block the narrow blood capillaries, causing extreme pain and preventing oxygen from reaching the cells of the body. The blood clots that develop may cause some areas of tissue to die or become infected.

If a child inherits the abnormal gene responsible for producing this haemoglobin S from each parent, the child will develop sickle-cell anaemia. If a child inherits the abnormal gene from one parent and a normal gene from the other, the child will have sickle-cell trait and will be a carrier but otherwise completely healthy. However, carriers can pass on the abnormal gene to their children.

Medical treatment

Babies that are affected by sickle-cell anaemia are usually identified by blood tests at birth. Check with your doctor if you are unsure whether your child might be at risk or if she is showing any of the symptoms of sickle-cell anaemia. The diagnosis can be confirmed by blood tests.

Treatment includes taking folic acid supplements which will reduce the severity of the anaemia. Penicillin given regularly will help to prevent infections, immunization will be given against pneumococcal infection, and painkillers will need to be taken when your child is in pain.

How to help your child

To reduce the likelihood of painful attacks, your child should drink plenty of fluids (to prevent dehydration) and make sure she does not become chilled. Phone a doctor at once if your child has a painful attack accompanied by the following:
- Fever.
- Sudden paleness.
- Persistent vomiting or severe diarrhoea.

☐ PREVENTION

If you know you are at risk of sickle-cell anaemia, you can have a blood test to detect the abnormal gene. If both you and your partner are carrying this gene, ask for genetic counselling before starting a family. Tests can be carried out during early pregnancy to find out whether a fetus has the disease; if the fetus is affected you may consider the option of termination.

- Difficult or fast breathing.
- Abnormal drowsiness or lack of energy.

If your child has severe abdominal pain or tenderness, call an ambulance. She may need to be admitted to hospital for pain relief and treatment of dehydration or any infection.

Outlook

With good medical care, most affected children survive into adulthood. If symptoms are severe, a child with sickle-cell anaemia may be considered for bone marrow transplantation if a suitable donor is found. A successful transplant provides a complete cure.

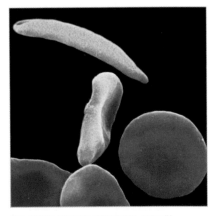

RED BLOOD CELLS IN SICKLE-CELL ANAEMIA
Seen through a microscope, blood taken from a person affected by sickle-cell anaemia shows distorted, sickle-shaped red blood cells.

THALASSAEMIA

This form of anaemia is most common among people of African, Mediterranean or Asian origin. There are two types: thalassaemia minor usually has no symptoms; thalassaemia major causes slow growth and deformity of the skull and other bones if left untreated.

Causes

Thalassaemia is due to an abnormality in the gene responsible for producing haemoglobin. A child who inherits the faulty gene from both parents develops thalassaemia major and cannot make normal haemoglobin. Her red blood cells are small, fragile and rapidly broken up, leading to severe anaemia. A child who inherits the faulty gene from one parent develops thalassaemia minor; her red cells are slightly smaller than normal but she has no symptoms.

Medical treatment

Thalassaemia is diagnosed by blood tests. Thalassaemia minor does not require treatment. Thalassaemia major needs monthly blood transfusions, from the age of a few months. The transfusions may cause damage to internal organs eventually, a problem reduced by regular desferrioxamine infusions. With these treatments, children have a good prospect for normal growth and development, and many survive into middle age.

☐ **SYMPTOMS**

- Pale skin.
- Chronic tiredness.
- Shortness of breath.

☐ **PREVENTION**

The parents or other close relatives of a child with thalassaemia, and any prospective parent with thalassaemia, can have genetic counselling to establish the risk of having an affected child. Prenatal tests are available and parents can choose to have a termination if the fetus is shown to be affected.

FRAGILE X SYNDROME

This inherited chromosomal abnormality affects approximately 1 in 3,600 boys and 1 in 5,000 girls. Its name comes from the fact that sufferers have a fragile spot on the long arm of the X chromosome in every one of their cells. It is a relatively common cause of learning difficulties and also causes a slightly abnormal physical appearance.

Causes

The mutation of a particular gene on the X chromosome can affect the development of the brain, leading to difficulties in learning and behaviour. Fragile X syndrome is the most common cause of congenital learning difficulties. Boys are more severely affected than girls, because the latter have 2 X chromosomes, one of which is normal, and boys have only one.

Medical treatment

A woman without any symptoms is able to carry the defective gene on an X chromosome and pass it on to some of her children. For mothers known to have fragile X syndrome, prenatal diagnosis is possible by DNA analysis of cells taken at amniocentesis.

If you think your child may be exhibiting some symptoms of fragile X syndrome, see your doctor. The disorder may be suspected only after puberty, when the physical features are more apparent. After examining your child, the doctor will assess his learning ability and arrange for chromosome and DNA analysis of a blood sample. If the tests show your

☐ **SYMPTOMS**

- Relatively large head.
- Delay in mental development, which is usually slight in girls and moderate to severe in boys.
- Delayed speech development, which is usually more severe in boys.
- Hyperactivity and attention deficit hyperactivity disorder (*see p.299*).
- Features of autism (*see p.299*).
- Square jaw, long face, large ears and large testicles in boys at puberty.

child has the defective chromosome, you will be referred for genetic counselling to discuss the risks of further children being affected.

There is no specific treatment. If your child is not already receiving help for speech or learning difficulties, the doctor may send her to be assessed by a speech therapist and/or psychologist.

HAEMOPHILIA

This genetic disorder affects about 1 in 10,000 boys. It causes episodes of spontaneous bleeding and is due to deficient activity of factor VIII, a clotting factor in the blood. Girls who carry the faulty gene may pass the disorder to some of their sons.

Causes
In haemophilia, the blood either takes a long time to clot or else it does not clot at all. This is because the boys who develop the disorder are born with a faulty gene that prevents them from producing factor VIII, one of a number of key ingredients in the process of clotting the blood.

Haemophiliacs live in fear of a cut or a scratch because this can start the bleeding that is hard to staunch. However, sufferers are affected in different ways – bleeding may, in fact, start without any apparent cause.

The gene is sex-linked and is found on the X chromosome so that nearly all haemophiliacs are males, while most females in haemophiliac families are carriers. A daughter can be a sufferer if her father has haemophilia and her mother is a carrier.

Medical treatment
If your son shows signs of abnormal bleeding, see your doctor, who will ask about symptoms. If haemophilia seems possible, she will arrange for blood tests to assess the blood's ability to clot. If haemophilia is confirmed, your son's bleeding episodes may be treated with injections of factor VIII, which you will be taught to administer.

Severe bleeding may need hospital admission. If a boy bleeds frequently, parents can give factor VIII by drip as a prevention. The frequency and severity of bleeding varies greatly from boy to boy. Some haemophiliacs suffer from only the occasional episode of minor bleeding. When the condition is more severe, recurrent internal bleeding can cause muscles and joints to swell up and become damaged, even deformed.

□ SYMPTOMS
- Prolonged bleeding after an injury or even a minor surgical operation, such as tooth extraction.
- Painful swelling of muscles and joints as a result of internal bleeding.

Outlook
It is best for children with haemophilia to avoid possible hazards, such as contact sports. Provided an affected child has prompt treatment with factor VIII when bleeding occurs, or has regular infusions, the muscles and joints may not be damaged, and life expectancy should be normal.

□ PREVENTION
Women with a history of haemophilia in their family can be tested to find out if they have the haemophilia gene. If they have, they can receive genetic counselling to assess the risk of having an affected child.

CYSTIC FIBROSIS

Cystic fibrosis is a serious inherited disease affecting about 1 in 2,000 children. For a child to have the disorder, the faulty gene must be inherited from both parents, who are carriers but have no symptoms of the disease.

Causes
A defective gene causes the secretion of sticky mucus that cannot flow freely through the airways and so leads to recurrent chest infections, which can cause progressive lung damage. It also causes deficient secretion of pancreatic enzymes (which help in the digestion of food), leading to an inability to absorb nutrients properly from the intestines (*see* Malabsorption, *p.258*) and diarrhoea.

Medical treatment
Although cystic fibrosis is present from birth, it may not be diagnosed for some months or even years, during which time damage to the lungs may

□ SYMPTOMS
- Failure to grow normally and to gain a normal amount of weight.
- Persistent coughing.
- Chronic diarrhoea, typically with pale, oily, strong-smelling faeces.

have already begun. The screening of newborn children for cystic fibrosis is now being introduced.

If your child has any of the symptoms of cystic fibrosis, take her to a doctor, who will refer her to a paediatrician for tests if cystic fibrosis is considered possible. Your child's sweat will be analysed and she will also have genetic tests.

If the tests confirm cystic fibrosis, your child will need to take pancreatin with meals to help her digest her food properly. A diet that is high in energy and protein is usually recommended, along with vitamin supplements. The doctor will prescribe antibiotics and

recommend regular physiotherapy for treatment of chest infections and to help prevent chronic lung disease.

How to help your child

A physiotherapist will show you how to give chest physiotherapy exercises (*see right*) to help loosen the thick mucus that obstructs the bronchi in your child's lungs. Do these exercises twice a day (more when your child is ill). Call your doctor at the first sign of any illness so your child can be treated quickly. To absorb enough nutrients for normal growth, she needs to eat high-energy snacks.

Outlook

There is no cure for cystic fibrosis, but earlier diagnosis and new methods of treatment mean that most affected

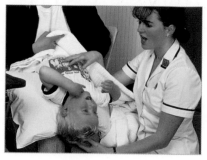

CHEST PHYSIOTHERAPY *A physiotherapist demonstrates the exercises that a parent needs to practise in order to help loosen the thick mucus that accumulates in the lungs of a child who is suffering from cystic fibrosis.*

children survive well into adulthood. A few severely affected children have had a heart-lung transplant, which has improved their quality of life and increased their life expectancy.

PHENYLKETONURIA

This inherited disorder affects about 1 baby in 10,000. Babies are routinely screened for phenylketonuria by a blood test soon after birth. A defect in body chemistry causes a build-up of the amino acid phenylalanine (a constituent of protein) in the blood.

Causes

If it is left untreated, phenylketonuria will cause severe brain damage. This is because the body does not possess the enzyme necessary for breaking down phenylalanine. As a result, this amino acid accumulates and affects the function of the nervous system.

Medical treatment

At birth, affected babies show no signs of any abnormality, but if the condition is not quickly diagnosed, symptoms may soon develop.

A special diet, which must be continued throughout life, is the main treatment for phenylketonuria and should be started in the first weeks

after birth. The main reason for this is that the amino acid phenylalanine, which is present in most protein foods, must be restricted while at the same time making sure the child still eats enough protein for growth. The recommended diet is mainly vegetarian and special food supplements will be prescribed. Affected babies will need to be given special milk substitutes.

Outlook

The majority of children who have been treated for phenylketonuria attend normal schools and have normal intelligence. However, a few do suffer from behavioural problems and experience learning difficulties.

DOWN'S SYNDROME

This is the most common chromosomal abnormality, affecting about 1 in every 700 babies. The risk of giving birth to a Down's syndrome baby increases sharply in women over 37 years old, and a third of all Down's babies are born to women in this age group. The risk is also greater in women who have already had a Down's child. Down's syndrome is usually detected at birth.

Medical treatment

After examining your child for typical features of Down's syndrome, the doctor will arrange for chromosome analysis of blood samples to confirm the diagnosis. Ultrasound examination of the heart may be performed to look for defects; X-rays of the abdomen may be taken if an intestinal defect is suspected. Surgery may be required to correct any defects. Your child will have follow-up care from speech and occupational therapists as well as special educational help.

Possible complications

Many Down's children have a heart defect, and some suffer an intestinal abnormality. Down's children are at greater than average risk of developing an underactive thyroid gland and acute leukaemia (see p.306). They are likely to have unstable neck joints (which may mean restricting some activities). They may also have hearing problems and be susceptible to infections.

Outlook

Many children with Down's syndrome survive into early middle age, but a small proportion die before they reach the age of 5, usually because of severe heart problems. Adults who have Down's syndrome are susceptible to the early development of Alzheimer's disease and atherosclerosis (hardening of the arteries).

Advances in educational methods, however, have meant that more Down's children reach their full potential than in the past, and most are educated at mainstream schools.

SYMPTOMS

- Upward-sloping eyes, which have prominent skin folds at the inner corner of the eyelids.
- Small, round face and full cheeks.
- Large tongue that tends to protrude.
- Flat back to the head.
- Floppy limbs.
- Slow physical development.
- Learning difficulties.
- Short stature.

PREVENTION

All pregnant women should be offered a blood test and an ultrasound check to determine the risk of having a Down's baby.

Women who have an increased risk are offered amniocentesis, in which a sample of amniotic fluid is taken from the womb and analysed for abnormal chromosomes. If the amniocentesis tests show that the fetus has Down's syndrome, the parents of the child can decide whether or not they would like to consider a termination.

MCAD DEFICIENCY

MCAD deficiency is a common inherited disorder, affecting about 1 in 8,000 children. MCAD is an enzyme that is essential for the breakdown of fats. For a child to have this disorder both parents must carry the faulty gene.

Causes

When levels of the enzyme medium-chain acylCoA dehydrogenase (MCAD) are very low, fat cannot be broken down properly, blood sugar falls and the liver starts to dysfunction. The child is well if eating normally. But if she is ill or has to fast she may lose consciousness. Even if her life is saved, there can be long-term neurological damage.

Medical treatment

Fasting should be avoided and during illnesses the child should have regular glucose drinks. If she is vomiting she will need intravenous glucose.

This is a lifelong condition but it can be prevented by avoiding fasting. Newborn screening, allowing detection of the condition before the child is unwell, is being introduced.

COMPLEMENTARY
THERAPIES

COMPLEMENTARY THERAPISTS practise holistic ("whole person") health. This simply means that all aspects of your child's health and wellbeing are taken into consideration, even if his problem seems to be located in one part of his body only. Your doctor, nurse, physiotherapist and other healthcare practitioners may practise holistic health, too.

Are they safe?

Never treat serious injuries and illness without seeing a doctor. *Use your common sense: if your child is ill, take him to the doctor first. Discuss the pros and cons of conventional treatment and stress that you will use it where necessary and/or appropriate. Explain that you are interested in complementary therapies and ask for information and recommendations. These therapies are relatively safe but there can be problems:*

- Using a complementary therapist instead of a doctor may delay appropriate treatment for your child.
- Complementary therapists opposed to conventional medicine may misdiagnose a treatable condition.
- Some herbal treatments can be harmful if used incorrectly. Make sure you see a qualified herbalist.
- Homeopathic and herbal remedies can both cause adverse reactions. If this happens, stop the treatment and check with your doctor.
- "Hands on" therapies use physical manipulation which, in rare cases, can cause structural injury.

COMMONLY ASKED QUESTIONS

A holistic practitioner looks at your child as an individual, with his own personality and temperament and considers a range of treatment options, which may include complementary therapies. The answers to the following five questions will help you to get a clearer understanding of what is involved in complementary therapies and holistic health.

What is complementary health and why is it so popular?

Complementary therapists nearly always use a holistic approach, which many parents find reassuring and helpful. The therapist aims to bring your child to full health by restoring his body's natural balance and maximizing his ability to heal himself. After taking a thorough 'holistic history', listening and talking to your child, the therapist will normally offer carefully monitored treatment.

Complementary therapies are becoming more and more popular as ideas about health are changing. Science is no longer thought to hold all the answers and many parents want to take more responsibility for their children's, as well as their own, health. Parents are concerned about the over-use of medication such as antibiotics and frustrated by doctors' lack of time to listen or to explain, and are interested in pursuing other treatment options.

Can complementary therapies be used alongside conventional medicine?

In general, complementary therapies work well alongside conventional treatments – indeed, this is why they are called complementary. It is important that your doctor and complementary therapist are happy to work alongside each other. Ask the therapist to contact your doctor, so establishing communication between them.

If your child is taking medication prescribed by his doctor, check on any possible interactions this may have with herbal medicines. Your pharmacist will also be able to give you information about this.

Some doctors have additional training in complementary therapies such as homeopathy or osteopathy and many are able to offer advice on complementary health. If, for example, you take your child to the doctor because he is suffering frequent viral infections, the doctor will first check for any serious

FIRST CONSULTATIONS

A typical first consultation with a holistic practitioner may take an hour or more and will include questions about different areas of your child's life, including:

His general health and history of illness

What, if any, medication he is taking

Any allergies or food sensitivities

Any family history of illness

What he eats and his favourite foods

What exercise he takes

Any recent changes in his life, such as a new school or moving house

Anything that has upset him recently – perhaps a grandparent has moved away or a favourite pet has died

Any fears – perhaps Dad may have started working away from home and he's worried he won't come back

His temperament, emotional health and personality, whether he tends to worry, how he copes with criticism or making mistakes

The holistic practitioner will also take into account your particular family values – for example, your cultural group and ethnicity, your religious and spiritual beliefs – as these will affect how you think and feel about your child's symptoms.

disease and may suggest dietary or lifestyle changes. He may also suggest that your child see a medical herbalist who may prescribe the immunity-enhancing herb echinacea (*see p. 322*).

Alternatively, he may recommend relaxation techniques such as short and child-friendly yoga sessions or therapeutic massage or other touch therapies (*see p. 325*) to reduce any stress or tension. Some doctors' surgeries have an osteopath or chiropractor on their staff.

Why are some doctors opposed to complementary therapies?

Treatments given in conventional, or "evidence-based" medicine undergo randomized controlled trials (RCTs), which are used to formulate the guidelines from which doctors work.

Some doctors feel uncomfortable with, or even actively opposed to, complementary medicines where the use of treatments is based largely on observation of whether or not they work. Some doctors believe that the benefits of complementary therapies

are only in the relationship between the therapist and child, and in the time and attention given. In other words, there is a kind of "placebo" effect. These doctors view the treatment itself, such as the specific remedy used, as irrelevant.

The benefits of time, touch and attention, and the environment in which the treatment is given are not easy to analyse within the current framework used for evidence-based medicine. Trials are expensive to run and increasingly reliant on finance from pharmaceutical companies. Healthcare decision-makers want evidence that complementary medicine can deliver safe and cost-effective treatments, and at present this evidence is inadequate.

How do I find a complementary practitioner?

If your doctor cannot help, personal recommendations can be a good way of finding someone, so ask at school or a playgroup about local, reliable and child-friendly practitioners.

Most of the complementary therapists produce leaflets or web sites with their services and prices clearly marked. Always find out how much the treatment will cost you before booking an appointment and make sure you find out how many appointments your child will be expected to attend.

Chiropractors and osteopaths are, at present, the only complementary practitioners who are regulated by law in the UK, but other therapists, such as homeopaths, acupuncturists and medical herbalists, belong to professional regulating bodies and gain reliable qualifications. It can be very confusing trying to come to grips with the various qualifications, so don't be scared to ask – it is important for you to know.

What will happen at a complementary consultation?

Most practitioners will use a holistic approach and will spend an hour on the first consultation and take a detailed holistic history along the lines mentioned on p.319. Think about the questions you may be asked and talk them through with your child beforehand so you are ready with the answers.

You will certainly be asked about your child's diet, so keep a food diary for at least a week beforehand. Ask your child how he is feeling and note any specific symptoms such as tummy cramps or headaches. Many therapists use questionnaires and will often send them in advance of the first appointment.

Take a pen and paper with you to the consultation so you can write notes, or ask your therapist for written information. Make sure you understand what is happening and what treatment your child is being given. Ask for clear instructions on administering herbal or homeopathic remedies. Both you and your child must feel comfortable with the practitioner, so don't be afraid to change if you are not.

Complementary therapies often take longer than conventional drugs to work and lifestyle changes, as well as the therapy, may make your child feel worse before he feels better. Physical healing with touch or with "hands-on" therapies, such as osteopathy and chiropractic, can work quickly but may also need to be repeated.

Ask for a contact telephone number or email address and check that you can get in touch with your child's therapist if you are worried or if you remember an important question or relevant piece of information after you have left.

"...herbal medicine is used to treat headaches, eczema, asthma, mood swings, sleeplessness and hormonal imbalance"

SUITABLE THERAPIES

The following therapies might be suitable for your child.

Homeopathy

Homeopathy is a form of natural medicine that works on the principle of treating "like with like". The idea involves using a substance that can produce symptoms in a healthy child to cure the same symptoms in a sick child. If, for example, your child suffers from summer hay fever caused by grass or flower pollen, he could be treated with a homeopathic remedy called "mixed pollen".

This kind of treatment is known as first aid homeopathy. Most of the commonly used remedies, such as arnica for bruising and chamomilla for a teething baby, are available in high-street chemists. The remedies are prepared in different potencies, which are indicated on the container – use the 12C potency for home use.

Homeopathy is also used to treat more complicated conditions such as migraine headaches, irritable bowel syndrome, recurrent infections, joint aches and pains, tiredness and viral infections such as glandular fever.

Always make sure that you take your child to see the doctor first so that a diagnosis can be made and a conventional treatment given. To use a homeopathic remedy for the above conditions, your child will need an appointment with a homeopath who will take a detailed holistic history (*see p. 319*).

The homeopath will prescribe a remedy for your child which is based on his particular (individual) constitution. This is constitutional homeopathy and is different from home or first aid homeopathy. As your child gradually matures, his constitutional remedy may change so it is important he is reviewed regularly by the homeopath.

HOMEOPATHY

Useful tips for taking first aid homeopathic remedies at home:

Homeopathic remedies are prepared in different potencies – use the 12C potency for first aid or home use.

Touch the remedy as little as possible. Drop it on to or under your child's tongue and allow it to dissolve. Your child should not eat or drink anything or clean his teeth for half an hour before and after taking the remedy. You can crush and dissolve remedies in water – or, for very small babies, granules and instantly dissolving tablets are available.

Take one dose and wait to see what relief it brings.

Repeat the dose (maximum 3 times a day) only if your child's symptoms are unchanged.

Once your child is better, the remedy should be stopped.

If your child is no better – or if the symptoms change – then the choice of remedy needs review.

ECHINACEA

A plant native to the USA, echinacea is popular as a safe and powerful immune-system booster to fight colds, flu and other infections. It acts by stimulating various immune system cells and by boosting your child's own production of a virus-fighting substance called interferon. Echinacea needs to be taken at frequent intervals – as often as every couple of hours during an acute infection. It may be used for prevention of colds if taken at the first hint of illness.

Herbal medicine

Herbal remedies are prepared from the leaves, flowers and other parts of plants. Many conventional medicines such as aspirin are highly purified forms of a particular substance extracted from a plant whilst herbal remedies, such as chamomile and echinacea, are made from whole parts of the plant and so contain different active ingredients. St. John's wort, for example, contains the same substance used in many modern antidepressants – for example, Prozac or Seroxat – but it contains other substances that have powerful immune-boosting properties.

Herbal medicine is used to treat many conditions such as headaches, tummy pains, eczema, asthma, mood swings, sleeplessness and hormonal imbalance. Herbal remedies are available as extracts (tinctures), capsules and teas (infusions).

After taking your child's detailed holistic history and discussing diet and lifestyle changes, the herbalist may prescribe a remedy containing a mixture of carefully selected herbs. If your child is already taking a conventional medication, ask your doctor or pharmacist about possible interactions before letting him take herbal remedies.

If you decide to buy the herbs yourself, make sure that you use a good-quality supplier. Some herbal treatments can be harmful if they are used incorrectly, so it is important to find herbs packaged specifically for children.

Generally, children between 4 and 6 years of age need a quarter of the recommended adult dose. Children between 7 and 12 years of age need half the recommended adult dose.

Provided you have the right dose, it is quite safe to split capsules and sprinkle them over your child's food. You can also add tinctures to sauces or drink. To hide the bitter taste of some herbs, try adding the correct dose to a fruit purée lollipop before freezing or to water in an ice cube mould and add to drinks.

Nutritional therapy

A nutritional therapist will examine the details of your child's diet, looking for causes of poor digestion or poor absorption of food from the intestine. Such causes include nutritional deficiencies, allergies, intolerances or sensitivities to food and environmental factors.

After making a diagnosis, the therapist will recommend changes in diet and prescribe food supplements

"...herbal remedies such as chamomile are made from whole parts of the plant and so contain different active ingredients."

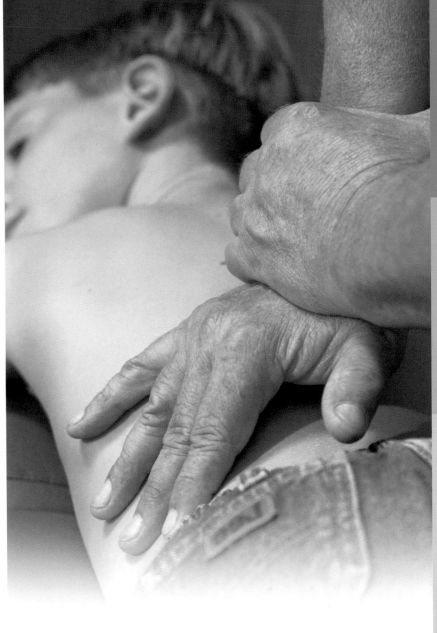

as a treatment. The idea is that good health is directly related to the quality of the food that a child eats, and that an inadequate diet will affect the mood, fitness and wellbeing of your child.

Nutritional therapy is used to treat conditions such as fatigue, chronic fatigue syndrome, irritable bowel syndrome, digestive disorders, arthritis, hormonal imbalance and period problems, asthma, eczema, allergies and food intolerances or sensitivities. It is important to take your child to see his doctor first in order to exclude serious disease.

Nutritional therapy may also be applied by dietitians, naturopaths and clinical ecologists. More unusual diagnostic procedures may be used in iridology, hair testing, kinesiology and vega testing, although random controlled trials of these suggest such tests do not provide reliable data. Hair testing may give an indication of toxic overload of heavy metals such as lead and is the most likely to be offered for your child.

Hypnotherapy

Hypnotherapy is a natural way of making contact with the inner (subconscious) self. The process of hypnosis involves a pleasant state of relaxation, rather like a daydream, which in itself provides a feeling of wellbeing. While your child feels this sense of calm, negative images can be replaced with positive ones through suggestion or visualization.

By visualizing positive and desired outcomes your child will be able to learn both coping strategies and emotional life skills that will give her confidence in his ability to manage his feelings when faced by difficult situations.

Hypnotherapy can be used to treat many conditions including fear and phobias, pain, stress, weight problems, period problems, bed wetting, asthma, allergies and skin problems. A review of 15 controlled trials of hypnosis in children found promising findings for pain, bed wetting and chemotherapy- (cancer treatment) related distress.

Osteopathy and chiropractic

Osteopaths and chiropractors are both skilled practitioners of "hands-on" techniques that diagnose and treat disorders of the spine, joints and muscles.

Chiropractors view the spine as the key support that protects the nervous system and links the brain with the body, whilst osteopaths are most concerned with the body's framework and how well it is functioning. Both chiropractors and osteopaths use manipulation of the spine, which may produce a sudden "popping" feeling as a joint stretches and relaxes. Chiropractors will often take X-rays on site and interpret them for you.

Osteopathy and chiropractic are well known for treating pain in the

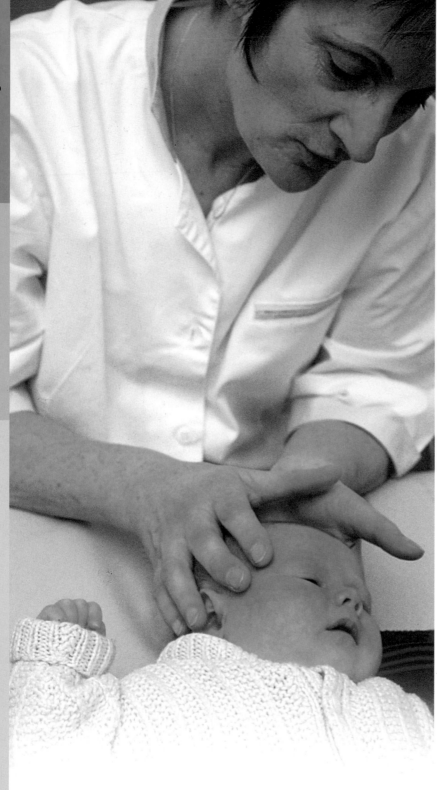

back, neck and joints and may also be good for conditions such as asthma, digestive disorders, glue ear, headaches, vertigo, period pain and hormonal imbalance. Before taking your child to see a chiropractor or an osteopath, make sure his doctor has examined him to exclude any serious disease.

Craniosacral therapy

Osteopaths, chiropractors and craniosacral therapists apply this "hands-on" technique to establish the health of the fluid and membranes (meninges) that protect the brain and spinal cord. Craniosacral therapy is based on the theory that there is both a movement between the bones of the skull and a rhythm that flows 10–15 times each minute from the head (cranium) to the base of the spine (sacrum).

Craniosacral therapy is perhaps best known for its use with newborn babies although, later in life, it may also help to improve general health, relieve chronic pain and clear up common ailments such as headaches. The craniosacral therapist takes a detailed holistic history of the pregnancy and birth and diagnoses mechanical strains that may have affected both mother and baby during the birth.

By placing hands on the head or back or sacrum of your baby, the craniosacral therapist feels a rhythm in his body. Then, by gently guiding and releasing any tension in this cranial rhythm the therapist enables your baby's self-healing mechanisms to correct any imbalance.

Acupressure

This ancient Chinese therapy is based on the belief that the energy of life circulates throughout the body in a number of channels called

"...by placing hands on the head or back or sacrum of your baby, the craniosacral therapist feels a rhythm in his body"

---

meridians. Along each meridian lie a number of influential points (acupoints) which, if massaged, can affect the flow of energy and rebalance the harmony of the body.

The squeezing, pushing and kneading massage – often with the thumb – involved in acupressure may be less daunting than the needles of acupuncture. What's more, you can learn to do it yourself – although you need to press gently when you treat a child. Acupressure may help in the relief of abdominal pain, nasal congestion, diarrhoea and constipation, as well as earache, eye irritation, toothache, nausea, hiccups and travel sickness.

Massage

Therapeutic massage has been used for hundreds of years to treat the aches and pains in muscles and in stiff joints. Massage is also good for improving mobility and for bringing about a feeling of wellbeing.

Massage may help to treat stress-related conditions such as anxiety, sleeplessness and depression, as well as digestive disorders. Relieving stress and tension may enable the immune system to function more effectively in conditions such as glandular fever and chronic fatigue syndrome. Massage could also prove useful in treating constipation.

Aromatherapy

Aromatherapy uses the therapeutic power of essential oils, which are highly aromatic oils extracted from specific plants. The oils can be used in massage, baths and foot baths, and, in certain circumstances, in steam inhalation.

Examples of oils used in massage include mandarin, which works to soothe a restless child and to help with sleeplessness; and rose, which strengthens the stomach during emotional upsets as well as keeping the skin in good condition.

Remember that pure essential oils should be added to a carrier oil before being used directly on the skin. In addition, carrier oils should be chosen carefully where there is any family history of an allergy to nuts or soya.

Add the following to 10 ml of carrier oil, such as almond or grape seed oil: for babies between 3 and 12 months, one drop of pure oil; for 1–5-year-olds, 2 drops of pure oil; for 6–12-year-olds, half the recommended adult dose. Once mixed with a carrier oil, the oils may be added to bath water, dropped on to a flannel in the shower or used as a massage oil.

Reflexology

Reflexologists base their therapy on the theory that specific areas, or reflex points, of the feet and hands correspond to parts of the body. Detailed maps of these areas enable a therapist to be particularly accurate about where the reflex points are.

By applying moving finger or thumb pressure to one or more points, the therapist aims to correct imbalances of energy, encourage self-healing, stimulate the function of an organ and improve circulation. Reflexology may bring relief from various common ailments such as headaches, sinusitis and constipation. Ask your reflexologist to teach you how to use some of the points in your child's hands or ears. You can then treat him anywhere and any time.

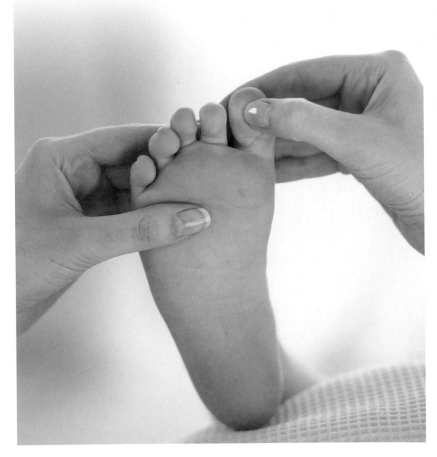

DISEASES & DISORDERS

325

COMPLEMENTARY THERAPIES

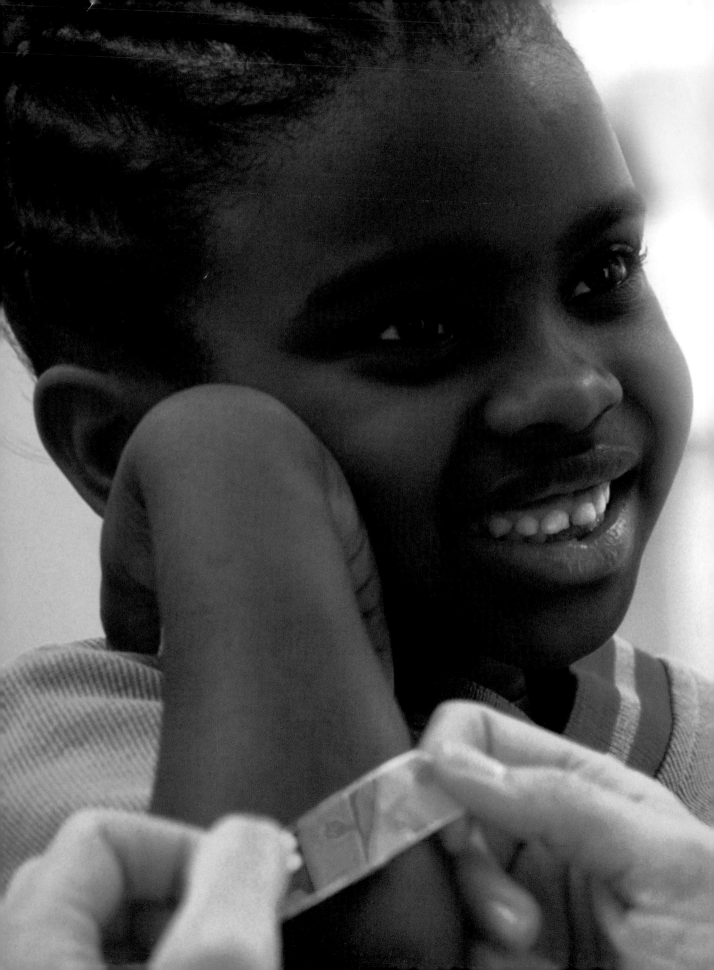

FIRST AID
& NURSING

CHAPTER FIVE

Although many accidents can be prevented, children are naturally adventurous and will sometimes get hurt. This chapter explains basic first aid procedures for children. Bear in mind, though, that there is no substitute for taking a practical first aid course when it comes to being prepared for accidents and emergencies.

NURSING A SICK CHILD

Most illnesses do not require specialist nursing care. However, make sure your child does not become dehydrated, especially if she has diarrhoea or a fever, or has been vomiting. A sick child may not have much of an appetite; small helpings of favourite foods may be tempting but do not force your child to eat.

CHECKING A PULSE

In certain circumstances, it may be useful to check a child's pulse. All you need to learn is where to place your fingertips. Where an artery lies just below the skin, you can feel the pressure of the blood as the heart pumps it around the body. The two easiest places are on the wrist and at the neck. In babies, check the pulse in the upper arm.

Press lighty with your fingertips – not your thumb – until you feel the pulse. Count the beats per minute and try to tell if the pulse is weak or strong, regular or irregular. A pulse that is abnormally fast or slow may be a sign of an illness. In beats per minute, a baby's pulse is about 140, a toddler's pulse is about 120, and the pulse of an older child is about 100. (*See also* Checking breathing rates, *p.195*.)

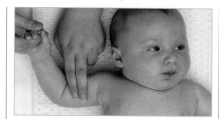

TAKING A BABY'S PULSE
Place the tips of your two forefingers on the inside of the upper arm.

TAKING A CHILD'S PULSE
Place three fingers in a line just below the wrist creases at the base of the thumb.

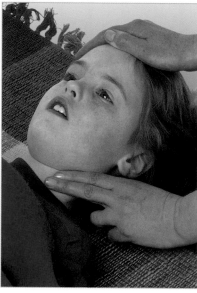

TAKING A NECK PULSE
Place two fingers in the hollow between the windpipe and the large neck muscle.

TAKING A TEMPERATURE

If your child seems to be unwell and you suspect a fever, take his temperature with a thermometer (*see right*) every 2 or 3 hours until it returns to normal. A temperature of 38°C (100°F) or above is a fever.

A child over the age of 7 can hold a digital thermometer under his tongue. For younger children, do not put a digital thermometer in his mouth – place it the armpit or use a temperature strip on the forehead. These will give a reading that is about 0.6°C (1°F) less than true body temperature so this amount should be added to the reading to obtain the accurate body temperature.

USING A DIGITAL THERMOMETER
With your child sitting still, hold the digital thermometer either in her armpit or in her mouth under her tongue. Wait for the thermometer to "bleep" – after about a minute – then remove it and read the temperature from the digital display.

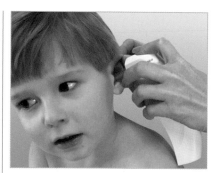

USING AN AURAL THERMOMETER
Place the aural thermometer in your child's ear. Hold the tip gently in position for the recommended time and then remove to read the temperature. The disposable tip should be replaced with a new one after every use.